Researching
the Value
of Project
Management

Researching *the Value* of Project Management

Janice Thomas, PhD
Centre for Innovative Management,
Athabasca University

Mark Mullaly, PMP
Interthink Consulting, Inc.

PMI®
Project Management Institute

ISBN: 978-1-933890-49-4

Published by: Project Management Institute, Inc.
                     14 Campus Boulevard
                     Newtown Square, Pennsylvania 19073-3299 USA.
                     Phone: +610-356-4600
                     Fax: +610-356-4647
                     E-mail: customercare@pmi.org
                     Internet: www.pmi.org

PMI Publications welcomes corrections and comments on its books. Please feel free to send comments on typographical, formatting, or other errors. Simply make a copy of the relevant page of the book, mark the error, and send it to: Book Editor, PMI Publications, 14 Campus Boulevard, Newtown Square, PA 19073-3299 USA.

To inquire about discounts for resale or educational purposes, please contact the PMI Book Service Center.

PMI Book Service Center
P.O. Box 932683, Atlanta, GA 31193-2683 USA
Phone: 1-866-276-4764 (within the U.S. or Canada) or +1-770-280-4129 (globally)
Fax: +1-770-280-4113
E-mail: book.orders@pmi.org

The paper used in this book complies with the Permanent Paper Standard issued by the National Information Standards Organization (Z39.48—1984).

10 9 8 7 6 5 4 3 2 1

Table of Contents

1

Introduction

I nvestments in project management have to compete with investments in all other organizational initiatives. As with any investment, organizations would like to be assured of receiving good value for the investment being made or proposed in project management. To address this concern, executives and proponents of project management need a rigorous, objective, and well-thought-out method of identifying, measuring, and demonstrating value from project management initiatives. This is especially true given today's relentlessly increasing demands for greater corporate accountability, higher productivity, and lower costs. Without the ability to clearly define its value and impacts, project management simply joins the long line of other organizational functions or initiatives (such as total quality management, information systems, training, and human resources) struggling to prove their worth to their organizations.

Although the holy grail of demonstrable project management value is often discussed and even proclaimed in consulting and practitioner literature, the actual value resulting from investments in project management has been hard to define—let alone measure. Few rigorous studies have been undertaken, and those that exist struggle to provide indisputable and strong evidence (see Chapter 2). Even the more rigorous and quantitative efforts suffer from failing to enroll enough organizations to be broadly relevant and statistically credible. Many investigations have been focused on only a limited definition of both value and project management. Paradoxically, the more the concept of *value* is pinned down to a definition, the easier it becomes to identify why it is insufficient. Limiting value to ROI ignores all the intangible benefits of a particular topic of discussion. Equating value to intrinsic or subjective closely held beliefs means that there is no possibility of comparing benefits. Other research that provides insights into the multiplicity of potential benefits that executives, practitioners, and consultants associate with implementing project management make no effort to quantify these values. Where empirical evidence does exist, it is tantalizing but fragmented and incomplete.

In order to provide credible evidence of the value that project management provides to organizations, the Project Management Institute (PMI) requested proposals for research designed to quantify the value of project management in the summer of

2004. The international research community responded with an array of different approaches to answering this question. This monograph documents the three years of fieldwork and cross-disciplinary analysis conducted between May of 2005 and June of 2008 by the team that won this competition.

This winning research proposal was based on our assessment of what it would take for the project to be a success from the perspective of the primary stakeholders. We wished to find unequivocal and compelling evidence of the value organizations recognize when project management is appropriately implemented. Also, our aim was to provide practical guidelines for practitioners, consultants, and executives to measure the value of project management initiatives. Additionally, we sought perception by the academic and practitioner communities of the value, rigor, and appropriateness of the answers to the value statements and practice guidelines. This monograph should enable you to assess how well we have achieved these goals and will be supplemented with practice guidelines in the near future..

For those of you reading a research monograph for the first time, you may find parts of it to be too detailed. A research monograph is not meant to entertain or provide silver bullets or golden nuggets (although you may find some of each throughout these pages, and, in particular, in the conclusions). A research monograph is meant to provide a detailed and documented treatise on a specific topic. It is meant to lay the groundwork for future research on the topic and describe how the research was conducted. It should clearly document the findings of the study along with the academic and practical application of these findings. A good research monograph should explain the research in sufficient detail that subsequent researchers can use, critique and improve on the methods that were used and the assumptions that were made in order to further our understanding of the topic of interest.

This monograph is comprised of 10 chapters with additional appendixes. Each chapter is described below. As much as possible, we have written this monograph so that it is possible to read each chapter without the benefit of earlier chapters. However, to fully understand the work and to be able to effectively evaluate the relevance of the conclusions in your own mind, we encourage you to work through the monograph in its entirety. A thorough read will improve your understanding of the work as a whole and help you evaluate the rigor of the study and evaluate the relevance and value of the findings.

Chapter 1	*Introduction*
	This chapter introduces both the project and this research monograph. The original impetus and history of the project are discussed, along with the objectives that the research team set for themselves in conducting the project. The introduction also outlines the purpose and role of the monograph, and provides guidelines for the reader in maximizing their value in reading this document.

| Chapter 2 | *Literature Review* |

Literature Review

This chapter provides a review of the most significant literature that encompasses both the work that formed the foundation of the initial proposal and the additional articles that were published over the course of the four years of this project. The first section of the literature review seeks to develop an understanding of the organizational literature on "value" quantification and recognition. We conclude this section by reviewing attempts to evaluate the value contributed to an organization by different organizational functions, including project management. Lessons learned from this review helped us to identify key questions that would need to be answered and constructs that would need to be explored to successfully complete this research project. The second section of the literature review documents the conceptual model that we proposed as the foundation for our exploration of value in a project management and organizational context.

The primary findings from this literature review are threefold:
- First, the question of quantifying the value of organizational functions has not been satisfactorily answered in a wide range of different organizational disciplines. Therefore, there is no tried and true method for answering this question.
- Second, the measurement of the value that an organizational function provides to an organization needs to be elaborated to include a wider variety of benefits—many of which will not be quantifiable but can be clearly recognized and documented.
- Finally, the value of any organizational improvement activity must be judged in the context and situation from which it arises and how well the improvement itself fits within the context of the organization, industry, and geography in which it is embedded.

Arising from this review, the following research questions formed the initial focus for this project:
- What are the practices implemented within organizations that represent their approach to project management?
- To what extent are these practices appropriate in managing projects within the context of the organization?
- What is the value that organizations have realized as a result of adopting these practices?

Chapter
3

Methodology And Methods

This chapter describes the methodological approach to this research. It starts with a theoretical view of what a project such as this one needs in order to be successful and how research with such needs may be addressed. Particular attention is paid to defining and describing the mixed-methods approach adopted in this study. It concludes with details of the timeline and an overview of the methods implemented during our inquiry.

Chapter
4

Qualitative Methods

This chapter provides a detailed review of the qualitative methods used in this study. Readers with either a strong qualitative-methods background, or no interest in the mechanics of the qualitative analysis can likely forego reading this chapter but may want to refer back to it for reference if necessary.

Chapter
5

Quantitative Methods

This chapter describes the quantitative methods adopted by this study. It provides details of the methods so that we do not need long methodological discussions when discussing findings. Readers with either a strong quantitative-methods background, or no interest in the mechanics of the quantitative analysis can skip this chapter and refer back to it if necessary.

Chapter
6

Context

The context of the organization defines the underlying environment in which an organization operates, as well as the internal structures and organizational practices that, in turn, influence the project management implementation. To understand context, it was necessary to explore the attributes of organizations that go beyond what is being done in terms of project management. This chapter identifies the demographics of those case studies included within our study, illustrating the broad cross-section of organizations that contributed to the research effort. We also explore the contextual differences associated with these organizations, in order to be able to identify those dimensions of context that are most meaningful in determining appropriate strategies for implementing project management.

| Chapter 7 | **Implementation** |

In order to evaluate the value project management delivers to organizations, we need to know what organizations implement when they claim to implement project management. This chapter defines our understanding of implementation, derived from what has in actual fact been implemented, that organizations refer to as project management. We avoided specifically evaluating the various implementations against any one model, which by the admissions of most model authors are incomplete and not fully representative of the overall domain of project management. We also avoided adopting a strictly maturity-based means of assessment, although a comparative understanding of maturity does emerge from the implementations that are described. Instead, we have endeavored to understand what in actuality has been implemented and the underlying motivations and objectives that led to those implementations. Project management here is defined broadly to include all elements an organization introduces to manage projects and can range from pert charts to portfolio management and governance.

| Chapter 8 | **Value** |

This chapter sets out to explore the types of value project management implementations deliver to the organizations that invest in them. To be able to assess value, it is necessary to understand the dimensions of value that organizations can realize from project management. It is equally important to understand how these dimensions of value are currently evaluated and measured. This chapter endeavors to explore the dimensions of value that can be associated with project management implementations, and the degree to which these different values are in fact being observed in the case-study organizations associated with this research.

Chapter 9	**Drivers of Value**
	This chapter presents the integrated analysis that has been conducted to date within the research study. Each of the previous chapters has presented what was found in the case-study organizations that illustrate context, implementation and value. Each of these components represents a piece of the overall whole that illustrates how organizations deliver project management value. This chapter examines the relationships between these constructs and provides insights into how value is generated and can be destroyed through investments in project management.
Chapter 10	**Conclusions**
	This chapter presents the overall findings of the research study. It draws on the detailed findings of the individual chapters to present an integrated view of the main findings and results of the study. This chapter does not repeat the specific conclusions from each of the earlier chapter findings. Instead, it seeks to provide a high-level survey of the findings and their implications for both future research and practice. In particular, we deal with what we think are the most significant attributes and findings from this study, its limitations and directions for future research. Those looking for a quick overview of the findings might like to start here.
Appendix A	**Case Study Descriptions**
	This chapter provides short case descriptions are provided for 62 of 65 organizations who participated in this study. These descriptions provide a précis of each of the organizational implementations, introducing the organization and its environment and the rationale for implementing project management. The project management implementation is described and provides an overview of what was implemented, how the implementation was conducted, and observations regarding its appropriateness. Finally, the value being realized by the organization as a result of its implementation is identified.
Appendix B	**References**
	This chapter provides a complete list of the references that appear throughout this research monograph.

Appendix C	**Project Team Members**
	This chapter identifies the members of the team that have contributed to the success of this project over the last four years. The work that has been presented here is a result of their efforts, and the success of this project would not have been possible without them.

TABLE 1-1—*Monograph road map*

2

Literature Review[1]

INTRODUCTION

The initial premise for this research project was that before you could hope to understand the value of project management, you would first need to investigate prior research into valuing organizational functions (and project management in particular) and then devise a research strategy incorporating the lessons from this earlier research. Thus we started the project, and this chapter, by conducting a review of prior "value" quests to ensure we learned from their experience and avoided reinventing the wheel. We conclude by describing the initial conceptual model and key constructs that we used to focus our efforts and from which to build a methodological approach.

It should be noted that exploring the question of "value" and the measurement of performance in organizations touches on a huge variety of managerial disciplines, including but not limited to: accounting; decision making; finance; performance measurement; total quality management; managerial information; organizational theory; value creation; resource dependency; investment; strategy; economics; and the list could go on. The coverage of the research and literature reviewed and cited in this chapter is necessarily selective. Literally hundreds of articles and studies bear on the focus areas important to this study and we have compiled several EndNote library databases of articles numbering well over 500 at this point. It is simply not feasible to include all of these articles in this chapter. We have done our best to highlight and cite the literature that was most influential in the development of this research study. In making choices on what to include (and cite) and what to exclude, we have attempted to stay focused on providing a solid introduction to the literature that provided the foundation for our conceptual model.

---

1   Much of the material in this chapter was previously published in conference papers and then in *Project Management Journal*, September 2007, pp. 74-88. It is derived from our original literature review conducted in the summer of 2004. Relevant literature published since this date has been reviewed and the chapter updated as appropriate.

MEASURING ORGANIZATIONAL VALUE

Efforts to determine the value of organizational activities has been a longstanding pursuit in a number of disciplines (see Lepak, Smith, & Taylor, 2007). The conceptual approaches to the value question can be roughly categorized as follows:

- Return on investment approaches,

- Balanced scorecard approaches, and

- Organizational competency approaches.

Each of these approaches to valuing organizational interventions are briefly introduced (assuming these are not new approaches to most business people and management academics). We make reference to the project management literature that has referenced these approaches. We also discuss the criticisms of such approaches.

Return on Investment Approaches (ROI)

Traditional financial measurement systems for supporting decision making and control were largely predicated on economic models of investment. These transaction-based financial measures adequately measured whether value had been created or destroyed in the short term (Ashton, 2005) as long as the data needed for the assessment was available. For our purposes, we include under this heading measures that deal specifically with financial value, such as:

- **Cost-Benefit Ratio   B/C Ratio = Benefits/Costs**
  Cost-benefit ratio is a standard economic tool that has been used for decades, if not centuries, to help make cost-effective decisions in business and society. Derived from the field of economics, cost-benefit methods provide detailed approaches to identifying and estimating the tangible and intangible costs and benefits associated with decision outcomes. However, the economists continue to disagree on which variables to include and how to find valid and reliable estimates of appropriate indicators for these variables. Both Knutson (1999) and Smith and Barker (1999) discussed the use of this approach in a project management context, but neither article is empirical in nature.

- **Return on Investment   ROI = (Benefits-Costs)/ Costs X 100**
  Measuring ROI stems from a time when it was easy to base the value of an enterprise on the value of its financial assets (like revenue, real property or equipment). The assumption is that for every dollar invested, there is a directly correlated financial return attributable to that investment. The need for the calculation of project management's ROI often comes up in

practitioner discussions and literature, however empirical studies are scarce. The few empirical attempts to calculate the ROI of project management focus on one narrow view of project management improvement that is generally referred to as project management maturity.

- **Maturity-Based ROI Metrics**
  Maturity/ROI = [(Predicted Profit Margin – Current Profit Margin) X Annual Project Revenues] / Annualized Project Management Expenditures
  The work of the team of Ibbs, Kwak, and Reginato (Ibbs, 2000; Ibbs & Kwak, 1997; Ibbs & Kwak, 2000; Ibbs & Reginato, 2002; Ibbs, Reginato, et al., 2004; Kwak & Ibbs, 2000; Kwak & Ibbs, 2002; Reginato, 2002) over the last decade focused on recognizing the benefits of investment in project management competency through measures of maturity in an organization's practice of project management. In this way, their work uses both ROI and benchmarking to value the investment in project management. Higher maturity scores are hypothesized to correlate with higher levels of predicted project performance. The corresponding theory was that investment in project management increases an organization's project management maturity standing and this improvement results in enhanced project performance that should translate into cost savings and other benefits.

  Others have contributed to this stream of research (Crawford & Pennypacker, 2001; Pennypacker & Grant, 2003), through survey-based research attempting to associate firm self-report data on maturity measures and project performance. While flawed, many of these approaches provide some interesting insights that deserve further exploration.

One important criticism applied to this approach today is that the complexity of large bureaucracies makes it very difficult to show how investments in the administration of the bureaucracy contribute to the bottom line. Given that management—and the management of projects in particular—is inherently grounded in the bureaucracy of organizations, the demonstration of a return on investment in this regard can be expected to be challenging. Proponents such as Phillips and Philips (2004) stated that the biggest challenges of conducting ROI evaluations relate to ensuring credible, valid results in a reasonable time frame; demonstrating that the results exhibited are appropriately apportioned and attributable to the program or initiative being investigated; and isolating the impacts of the program or initiative from other context-specific and situational factors. The underlying message is that this is not a terribly difficult thing to do. However, practical literature recognizes that "achieving a results-oriented evaluation focus can be time consuming, labor intensive, and sometimes perceived as intrusive" (Burkett, 2005a), and attempts to provide shortcuts and advice on how to conduct this sort of analysis in a cost effective manner. Others question the usefulness of the approach to decision makers based on the time and resources it takes to appropriately conduct this sort of analysis (Kaufman & Watkins, 1996). Thus, the return on investment of ROI interventions is itself being called into question.

Valuation from the industrial perspective in which ROI calculations are grounded is not as useful or relevant in information- and service-based industries, or the so-called knowledge economy, where it is commonplace for a company to be valued as much for its intangibles—its business processes, customer lists, trademarks and patents, knowledge, skills, and business relationships. As Githens (1998) points out, in the project management context these metrics are criticized for their role in preserving the status quo. ROI measures emphasize capital investment and the yield of predictable returns over increases in intellectual capabilities. As one executive put it to us recently, "Calculating an ROI of project management wouldn't be very useful to me. Project management is too many things. Even if I had an ROI, I still wouldn't know what specifically to invest in." Cabanis-Brewin (2000) echoed these criticisms in stating that these methods do not recognize the value of the cultural change and "soft" human factor benefits.

There is no question that bottom-line results are important for all types of organizations, regardless of their profit orientation. All organizations need to pay attention to revenue and costs to remain financially viable. However, not everything that an organization does can be translated into monetary terms. For instance, the link between employee satisfaction and corporate performance is difficult, if not impossible, to establish. However, many organizations believe that keeping employees satisfied is an important corporate goal. Translating employee or customer satisfaction into a monetary value or evaluating outcomes in financial terms is very difficult to calculate in any valid or credible way. In not-for-profit or government organizations, measuring objectives in financial terms is even more problematic; a significant majority of their undertakings are to create a social or public good, which is not readily quantified and does not produce a direct financial return.

Another major criticism of ROI approaches is that in order to calculate ROI, you must have a baseline measurement of useful indicators of pre- and post-cost and benefits. In order to calculate ROI, you need detailed data on both costs and returns. Though many of us would expect that at least the costs of organizational initiatives would be readily available, researchers have found that neither the costs nor benefits of most initiatives are easy for managers to provide. Kaufman and Watkins (1996) explain why:

"However, more often than not, well-intentioned people commit to an intervention and deliver it with quality, enthusiasm, and professionalism but never calibrate the extent to which it delivers useful results. Rarely

are there useful indicators of the costs consequences of our investments.
In addition, without utilizing data that include all the critical variables
of return, we are not able to compare investment with those of other
organizations and thus cannot compare the track records of different
approaches." (p. 89)

They conclude that "For most organizational activities, detailed data either do not exist or are unavailable to compute a realistic return on investment" (p. 97).

In addition, ROI measures beg the question of what is the appropriate comparator to determine if you are obtaining a good return. Cost and return variables tend to vary by organizational context as mentioned previously (see Burney & Matherly (2007) for a review of the variability of performance measures across organizations). Private organizations often have different concerns and considerations than public organizations and government and social sectors will have even more diverse factors to incorporate into ROI calculations. Unless the ROI calculations are completed using the same methods of estimation, there is no way to compare ROIs across organizations in order to evaluate or benchmark the performance of your investment.

Thus in spite of the perceived desire for an ROI calculation for such organizational interventions, most executives often do not have solid data upon which to base such analysis and are often wary of accepting those calculations that are presented.

Balanced Scorecard Approaches

Given the difficulties and constraints of using ROI to measure value in an organizational setting, many researchers have sought to develop more sophisticated measures. While the realization of financial returns in the short run remains critical (especially in situations where shareholder value is paramount), there has been a marked shift towards wanting to measure the intangible value drivers that will prepare an organization for value creation in the future. By the late 1980s and early 1990s, researchers were widely reporting on the limitations of traditional financial measures to assist managers in the emerging "knowledge society" (Beischel & Smith, 1991; Eccles, 1991; Eccles and Pyburn, 1992; Fisher, 1992; Kaplan, 1983, 1984; Keegan, Eiler & Jones, 1989; McNair, Lynch & Cross, 1990; Maskell, 1989; Wisner and Fawcet, 1991). Clearly these researchers recognized the need for internal performance measures that focused on both performance drivers and outcomes and combined both financial and non-financial measures. The search for a balanced performance measurement was on.

By far the most prevalent of these expanded approaches in the North American context is the balanced scorecard approach developed by Kaplan and Norton (1996 a and b). In Europe, the Skandia Business Navigator (see, for example, Bartlett & Mahmood, 1996) was developed at roughly the same time. More recent examples of this balanced approach to performance measurement include the Value Dynamics

Framework (Boulton, Libert, & Samek, 2000), the Value Chain Scorecard (Lev, 2001) and the Value Reporting Disclosure Model (Eccles, Herz, Keegan, & Philips, 2001). All of these models attempt to provide frameworks that will allow organizations to develop a measurement system that will align with—and in turn drive—strategic results. For the purposes of this research, we chose to use the Balanced Scorecard Model as the exemplar of these types of approaches for three reasons. First, it appears to be by far the most well known of these models in most parts of the world (the Skandia model is next-most popular, but appears to be mostly known in Europe). Second, some would argue (Ashton, 2005) that the most recent incarnation of the Balanced Scorecard Model (Kaplan & Norton, 2004) incorporates many of the features of the other models. Third, while there is limited reference to any of these approaches in the project management literature, the Balanced Scorecard has received some attention. Githens (1998) and Cabanis-Berwin (2000) advocated a balanced scorecard approach as a response to the challenges of measuring ROI.

Balanced scorecard (BSC) metrics try to evaluate organizational performance using a variety of financial and non-financial measures including:

- Learning and growth,

- Internal measures,

- Customer perspectives, and

- Financial perspectives (such as ROI).

In particular, this approach attempts to measure the knowledge-based and intangible benefits associated with organizational effectiveness today. Webber, Simsarian, & Torti (2004) gave a thorough review of the application of this approach. BSC metrics have the theoretical advantage of attempting to evaluate all the benefits and costs of each organizational action in the context of the specific organization's strategy. Kaplan and Norton (2004) argued that value is indirect, contextual, bundled, and potential (pp. 29-30), and that the critical causal links between value drivers and financial outcomes are heavily dependent on the strategic context. Organizations realize value from intangible value drivers only by creating the conditions that transform value potential into realized value. Thus, the selection of appropriate metrics is key to the success of this approach. It be could argued that the explosion of project success metrics in the last 10 years (see for example Jugdev and Mueller (2007) for an overview) could be attributed to the popularity of the search for appropriate balanced scorecard metrics. Recent studies reported at the 2008 PMI Research Conference attest to the growing popularity of balanced scorecard concepts in project management research.

In Europe, another model has also been developed based on this approach in combination with total quality management perspectives. This model, developed by the European Foundation for Quality Management (EFQM), seeks also to evaluate organizational performance based on a wider variety of potential measures.

Building from the EFQM model, Westerveld (2003) defined a Project Excellence Model and Bryde (2003) derived a Project Management Performance Assessment model to be used to evaluate the performance and contribution of project management within the organization. Bryde published the results of his survey as an effort to explore the value of project management in a way that built on the structure of the EFQM model. The study intent and constructs are interesting, but the small sample size and weakness of construct validity limits its usefulness.

There are also many criticisms of these BSC approaches. Ittner and Larcker (2003) point out that many people attempting to apply the BSC approach fail to tie the metrics back to corporate strategy – often because commonly available or easy-to-acquire measures substitute for the more difficult but appropriate strategic measures. For example, while Crawford and Pennypacker (2001) advocate use of a "balanced family" of metrics associated with shareholders, employees, and communities, they do not discuss how to select and quantify these metrics or link them to corporate strategy. They appear to be falling into the trap that Ittner and Larcker discuss of failing to link measures to strategy, setting faulty performance targets, and measuring the targets ineffectively. In addition, attempts to quantify intangible benefits fall prey to criticisms of how they are estimated. Crawford and Pennypacker's empirical work using this approach also is compromised by the common issue that organizations do not often collect or maintain the kinds of information necessary to do this kind of evaluation on a comprehensive or consistent basis.

In addition, while many authors show how the BSC approach focuses an organization on improving measurable performance in order to optimize operational efficiency (Bontis, Dragonetti, Jacobsen, & Roos, 1999; Roos, Roos, Dragonetti, & Edvinsson, 1998; Russ, 2001); Voepel, Leibold, Eckhoff, and Davenport (2006) argue that this single-minded focus on a small number of relatively rigid measures results in a "tyranny of measurement" that conflicts with creativity, innovation, and adaptation. Likewise, they argue that the internal focus of the BSC approach encourages organizations to ignore external circumstances, often to their own detriment.

Some academics point out that research in this area faces significant challenges "to isolate the financial performance effects of a particular driver" (Ashton, 2005, p. 65). Some of the financial measures that are recommended in the BSC literature, like earnings per share (Crawford & Pennypacker, 2001), are notoriously difficult to associate with individual organizational initiatives as there are typically too many other activities and initiatives occurring in organizations at the same time to be able to tie share prices to improvements in one specific area. Finally, it is our professional opinion arising from consulting and research conversations with hundreds of executives that executive management often views estimates of the BSC metrics as speculative and debatable rather than representing the concrete definition of value that they are looking for.

Organizational Competency Approaches

Emerging at roughly the same time as the balanced scorecard approach, the competency-based perspective of strategic thought emphasizes the impact that internal organizational competencies or "resources" have in determining the long-term, sustainable competitive advantage of firms. According to this perspective, each firm develops a unique combination of corporate assets and capabilities that allows it to generate income based on the exploitation of these competencies (see, as a starting point, Barney, 1991; Grant, 1991; Peteraf, 1993; Wernerfelt, 1984). Strategic competencies are those that contribute to sustainable competitive advantage for firms. Competencies can reflect the abilities and specific skills that a firm possesses or the cognitive characteristics that allow the organization to deploy these skills in a specific way. The common understanding is that these firm specific assets and competencies are knowledge-related, tacit, difficult to trade, and typically shared among the agents of the firm. Recent resource-based research has placed significant emphasis on evaluating not just the impact of individual resources but also the importance of looking at the way resources, are bundled within a firm and how that creates value (Denrell, Fang, & Winter, 2003; Eisenhardt & Martin, 2000; Lippman & Rumelt, 2003). Thus, the question emerges as to whether or not project management as a universal discipline of practice could be capable of generating long-term competitive advantage to a firm.

Jugdev (Jugdev, 2002; Jugdev & Thomas, 2002; Jugdev, 2004, Jugdev & Mathur, 2006; Jugdev, Mathur, & Fung, 2007) has made the most rigorous attempt to evaluate project management's capacity to generate long-term competitive advantage. Her research looks at the formation and enhancement of project management capabilities through the use of maturity models as frameworks for competency development. Her conceptual arguments assert that maturity models do not in themselves generate advantage, as they are easily copied. Her empirical findings from a small sample exploratory study (2002) suggest that project management may be an enabler rather than a strategic asset. Jugdev and Thomas (2002) do, make a clear case that easily copied competencies, such as project management maturity models, do not yield the long-term strategic advantages that today's organizations are looking for from their investments. In recent survey-based research, Jugdev and her colleagues (2006, 2007) show that while an investment in the tangible assets of project management is important for achieving competitive parity, investment in the intangible elements of project management are more likely to result in delivering a competitive advantage to the organization investing in them.

The following table summarizes the key theoretical contributors to these approaches to understanding and quantifying organizational value, the relevant project management articles, and the criticisms and concerns that have been documented regarding their use.

Theory and Application to Project Management References	Understanding	Main Concerns
Focus: Financial Measures		

COST BENEFIT RATIO:

| Knutson (1999) Smith & Barker (1999) | B/C Ratio = Benefits/ Costs | • Ensuring credible, valid results in a reasonable time frame;
• Demonstrating that the results exhibited are appropriately apportioned and attributable to the program or initiative being investigated; and
• Isolating the impacts of the program or initiative from other context-specific and situational factors.
• Querying the use of ROI to the knowledge economy where intangibles are also valued. |

RETURN ON INVESTMENT:

| Phillips (1998) Phillips & Philips (2004) Ibbs et al. (1997, 2000, 2002, 2004) | Base the value of an enterprise on the value of financial assets (things like revenue, real property or equipment). The assumption is that for every dollar invested, there is a directly correlated financial return attributable to that investment

ROI = (Benefits-Costs)/ Costs X 100 | |

MATURITY-BASED ROI METRICS:

Ibbs (2000) Ibbs & Kwak (2000) Kwak & Ibbs (2000) Ibbs & Reginato (2002) Kwak & Ibbs (2002) Reginato (2002) Crawford & Pennypacker (2001) Pennypacker & Grant (2003) Ibbs, Reginato, et al. (2004)	Uses both ROI and benchmarking to value the investment in project management. Higher maturity scores are hypothesized to correlate with higher levels of predicted project performance. Maturity/ROI = [(Predicted Profit Margin – Current Profit Margin) X Annual Project Revenues] / Annualized Project Management Expenditures	• Have a role in preserving the status quo, emphasizing capital investment and returns over intellectual capital and yielding predictable returns (Githens, 1998). • Do not recognize the value of the cultural change and "soft" human factor benefits. (Cabanis-Brewin, 2000). • Easily copied competencies do not yield the long-term strategic advantages. (Jugdev & Thomas, 2002).

Focus: Knowledge Based, Financial And Intangible Elements		
BALANCED SCORECARD METRICS:		
Kaplan & Norton (2000a and b) Building from the EFQM model: Westerveld's (2003) Project Excellence Model Bryde's (2003) Project Management Performance Assessment Model Webber, Simsarian, & Torti (2004)	Use of customer, learning and growth and other internal measures, as well as ROI, to evaluate all the benefits and costs of each organizational action in the context of the specific organization's strategy. The selection of appropriate metrics is therefore key to the success of Balance Scorecard Approaches	• Organizations do not often routinely collect or maintain this kind of information. • Setting faulty performance targets and measuring the targets ineffectively (Ittner & Larcker, 2003). • Attempts to quantify intangible benefits fall prey to criticisms of how they are estimated. • Many applications fail to tie the metrics back to corporate strategy – often because commonly available or easy to acquire measures substitute for the more difficult but appropriate strategic measures (Ittner & Larcker, 2003). • Estimates of BSC metrics are not hard numbers executives seek; they are thought speculative and debatable. • Some financial measures, for example, earnings per share (Crawford & Pennypacker, 2001), are notoriously difficult to associate with individual organizational initiatives; there are typically too many other activities and initiatives in organizations at the same time to be able to tie share prices to improvements in one specific area vs. another. • Small numbers of relatively rigid measures results in a tyranny of measurement that conflicts with creativity, innovation, and adaptation (Roos et al., 1997; Bontis, Dragonetti et al., 1999; Russ, 2001; Voepel et al., 2006). • The internal organizational focus can be an issue as external circumstances can be overlooked.

RESOURCE-BASED VIEW:		
Wernerfelt (1984); Barney (1991) Grant (1991) Peteraf (1993) Jugdev et al. (2002, 2004, 2006, 2007)	Emphasizes the impact that internal organizational competencies have in determining the long term, sustainable competitive advantage of firms. Each firm develops a unique combination of corporate assets and capabilities that allow it to generate income based on the exploitation of competencies. Competencies can be both abilities and specific skills that a firm possesses or cognitive characteristics to deploy them in a specific way.	• Operationalizing the attributes of interest and synthesizing appropriate measures. • Competencies are knowledge-related, tacit, difficult to trade, and typically shared among the agents of the firm. Thus the question emerges as to whether or not project management could be capable of generating long-term competitive advantage to a firm.

TABLE 2-1—*Review of common measures of value*

The Problematic Quest for Organizational Value

Efforts to determine the value of organizational activities has been a longstanding pursuit in a number of disciplines. Recent examples of articles exploring organizational performance across a number of disciplines include: General (Carmeli, 2004; Guha, Kettinger, & Teng, 1997; Henri, 2004); information systems (Bardhan, Krishnan, et al., 2007; Gordon & Tarafdar, 2007; Kohli, 2003; Kohli & Baron, 2003; Sherer & Baron, 2003; Rau, 2003; Reich, 2007); total quality management (Eriksson et al, 2003; Mele, 2007; Vokurka,Lummus, et al., 2007); human resources (Hesketh, 2006; Kearns, 2005; Lian, 2006; Russ-Eft, 2005; Solovy, 2003). The quest for value continues unabated and unanswered well into the 21st century.

Project management clearly is not the only organizational initiative that has struggled with equivocal results in ROI research. Researchers from as disparate disciplines as information systems (Barua, Lee, & Whinston, 1996; Barua & Mukhopadhyay, 2000; Powell & Dent-Micallef, 1997), human resources (Hesketh & Fleetwood, 2006), total quality management (Erickson et al., 2003; Guler, Guillen and Macpherson, 2002; Montes, Jover & Molina Fernandez, 2003; Powell,

1995, Westphal, Gulati, & Shortell, 1996, 1997), and expert systems (Mottiwalla & Fairfield–Sonn, 1998) blame these unsatisfactory results on the paucity of empirical research, the inability of researchers to generate comprehensive data, the absence of effective means of taking into account contextual factors, and problems in adequately measuring all impacts. Motiwalla and Farfield-Sonn (1998) went so far as to suggest that on the basis of the studies conducted so far, the data and the methods employed did not allow researchers to determine if the lack of performance payoffs for investment in expert systems was due to failure of the systems to deliver value, poor implementations failing to deliver value, or value lagging the measurement time period. While many comprehensive evaluation models have been proposed, the authors suggested that the economic, time, and access constraints associated with these evaluations made a full evaluation practically impossible to conduct (Motiwalla & Fairfield-Sonn, 1998).

In addition, Marcus and Soh (1993) suggested that all component parts of the IT investment process must be taken into account to get a more effective evaluation of IT benefits. These researchers all point to the need for a comprehensive measurement framework considering all dimensions of "white-collar" performance (Tuttle & Romankowski, 1985), including: efficiency, effectiveness, productivity, quality, quality of work life, innovation, and productivity. Additional benefits such as autonomy, control, and satisfaction could also be added to this list. Clearly the researchers were identifying the need for a form of evaluation drawing on Balanced Scorecard or Organizational Competency techniques to better understand the impact of information systems. Zhang (2007), for one, following up on this suggestion, showed that the performance impacts of IS investments "depend on the presence of certain firm-specific resources that complement the IS" (p. 156) such as an appropriate organizational culture and firm-specific knowledge. Again, though, he reports that empirical research into these areas is still scarce.

Ultimately, while it may be tempting to focus directly on the relationship between the entire project management intervention package and global organizational outcomes, cautions applied to TQM research apply equally here.

Hackman and Wageman (1995) say that "It is maddeningly difficult to do such research well, for several reasons:"

- First, there are serious measurement problems associated with even standard indices of firm performance such as market share, profitability or stock price (Brief, 1984; Penning, 1984; Kaplan & Norton, 1992).

- Second . . . Exogenous disturbances can significantly obscure the link between work processes and organizational outcomes.

- Third, temporal issues can obscure intervention-outcome relationships (Whetten & Cameron, 1994).

Taken together, these three difficulties can make it nearly impossible to detect statistically the direct effects of TQM on global measures of organizational outcomes."

Another temptation is to identify the value of different independent activities or initiatives associated with implementing project management—such as training, project management maturity, or the value of any one project—and extrapolate from there. Several recent studies addressed project success factors. These studies include success factors on projects, project management, and the organization (Cooke-Davies, 2002b); the influence of project management offices (PMOs) on reported project performance (Dai, 2002; Dai & Wells, 2004); the impact of project management software acceptance on project success (Bani-Ali & Anbari, 2004); and the association of project risk management practices with reported project success (Voetsch, Cioffi, & Anbari, 2004). Despite their importance, these studies do not result in the measure of the overall value of project management implementation, as the approaches do not hold constant the impact of all other project management or organizational initiatives taking place in the organization at the same time.

The pursuit of value remains an ongoing quest. Recent organization theory reviews of value creation (Lepak, Smith, & Taylor, 2007) recognize that value creation is important and that it is ". . . equally difficult to find agreement among scholars regarding (1) what value creation is, (2) the process by which value is created, and (3) the mechanisms that allow the creator of value to capture the value." (p. 180). However, the complexity and importance of the question of value cannot be escaped. ". . . The subject of value creation is made complex by its subjective nature, multiple levels of analysis, and the theoretical discipline scholars use to study it." (p. 192).

Given the multi-level, complex nature of the value construct, it is unlikely that self-reported survey data, limited case studies, or studies of the value of independent elements of project management will result in rigorous and generalizable insights. To successfully conduct a research project of this magnitude and complexity requires a carefully constructed and rigorously implemented data collection strategy guided by an integrated and coordinated cross-functional, cross-national team (Easterby & Danusia, 1999). Until now, there were no sources of funding willing to sponsor such an undertaking.

The remainder of this chapter describes the conceptual framework devised to broadly and definitively demonstrate in an integrated fashion the value that can accrue to organizations that effectively implement project management. Methodological questions are dealt with in future chapters.

Conceptual Framework

As you can see from the above discussion, valuing organizational initiatives is a difficult activity fraught with challenges. Voelpel, Leibold, Eckhoff, and Davenport (2006) further assert that traditional business performance measures suffer because they are all to some degree rooted in increasingly questionable assumptions of an underlying industrial economy. They suggest that what is missing in these measures is a contextual understanding of the complex web of interrelated factors, relationships, and activities that need to be taken into account in a holistic manner in order to assess an organization's performance in the knowledge economy. Empirical research that has tried to evaluate the quantifiable value of organizational initiatives like project management confirms the difficulty in addressing these challenges. To provide a comprehensive picture of organizational value, researchers suggest that studies of this kind must address three sets of questions (Hackman & Wageman, 1995; Montes et al., 2003) to be successful:

- **First, what has actually been implemented?** Distinguishing between rhetoric and reality of any organizational initiative will be the challenge (Zbaracki, 1998). Empirical demonstration that project management has actually been implemented within an organization, and identification of the component capabilities that define project management in each context in terms of function, purpose, and practices, is important. Looking at both the nature and the quality of the implementation will be important. Going further, the researcher must attempt to tease out which benefits are associated with which portions of a project management implementation. That is, if a project management office (PMO) is implemented without appropriate training (or vice versa) are benefits realized? Exploring the value of either of these separately does not answer the question; it is the interaction of the various elements of the implementation that collectively contribute to the realized value.

- **Second, has this implementation resulted in the improvements in organizational functioning that we would expect?** Here we need to assess process criteria effectiveness; in other words, the degree to which the implementation has delivered efficiencies or improvements in how the underlying processes of project management actually operate and the project results that they deliver. Many would expect effective project management to improve the way projects are managed, leading to more satisfied customers and employees/team members, and reductions in overruns and delays. What evidence exists to support or refute this?

- **Finally, to what degree has this implementation resulted in improvements to bottom-line organizational effectiveness in terms of concrete outcomes?** Management literature makes it clear that it is very difficult to link the success of any organizational intervention directly to bottom-line profit (Eriksson & Hansson, 2003; Kwak & Ibbs, 2000). In these studies, noise caused by the organizational and business context within which the initiative is embedded has been difficult to minimize. To be able to truly demonstrate the business value of a function, therefore, careful attention needs to be paid to this context.

Clearly, empirical evaluation of the value of implementing project management presents significant challenges to researchers, as what must be undertaken to satisfy these three different dimensions of assessment involves very different data, methods, and analytic strategies.

In reviewing the organizational value research in IT, TQM, expert systems, and human resources, it becomes clear that the conceptual model underlying this research must incorporate appropriate measures of what has been implemented in each organization, the process and outcome impacts of this implementation, the fit between what was implemented and the business orientation and environment within which the organization functions, and appropriate measures of the benefits and costs of the project management implementation (extrapolated from Hackman & Wageman, 1995). In preliminary work (Thomas & Mullaly, 2005), we identified the relationships that can occur between the components of project management and the accrued benefit to the stakeholder(s). Different attributes can provide a starting point for the identification and elaboration of the relationships and variables that need to be measured and statistically explored in this research.

Distinguishing between the rhetoric and the actuality of what has been implemented is also essential, as is the assessment of the fit between these initiatives and the organizational and business environment. The choice of what will have been implemented (the project management implementation in the context of any one organization) will be influenced by the business orientation of the organization—its focus, strategic direction, and vision of itself as an entity—and the environment within which the organization operates, which will, in turn, be influenced by its industry, customers, economic context, and the types of projects the organization typically manages.

In understanding the impact of project management *to a specific organization*, there are three direct influences that will govern whether value is actually being realized:

- First, the fit of what has actually been implemented needs to be understood in the context of the business orientation and the environment; in other words, to what degree did the organization "get it right" in establishing a context of project management that is appropriate for them and the types of projects they manage?

- Second, the process impacts of what has been implemented must be assessed and measured; in other words, to what degree does this framework better influence the delivery of projects? Are the processes more efficient, more effective, or more capable of delivering projects more reliably? Has the project management process improvement allowed the organization to improve market focus or differentiate its market services?

- Third, the tangible business outcomes resulting from using what has been implemented must be evaluated; in other words, to what degree do these project management capabilities actually deliver a bottom-line impact in terms of reduced costs, optimized efficiency, or increased revenue? What is the return to the organization for investing in the project management capabilities it has established?

Figure 2-1 reflects the initial conceptual model that we designed to help us understand how project management creates value in today's organizations. This diagram suggests how different attributes can provide a starting point for the elaboration and identification of the relationship and variables that need to be measured and statistically explored in this program of work. Each of the constructs is discussed in the following sections.

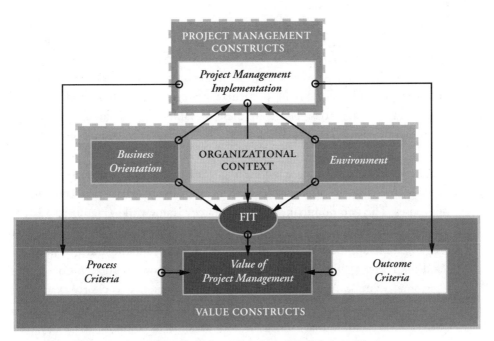

FIGURE 2-1—*Conceptual model developed from Thomas and Mullaly (2005)*

Organizational Context

Bruner (1990) asserted that it is impossible to understand the metrics and reference system of a company without first understanding the situated, contextual interpretations that are embedded within the management practices of the company. The conceptual model we defined first recognizes that there is an external context that influences how the managerial practices are adopted within each organization and ultimately determines the success of any organizational initiative. This is the context within which the initiative is being launched and takes into account organizational, strategic and economic considerations. Although not always readily apparent, these variables are likely to influence the results of the project management initiative in at least three ways. First, if the project management initiative does not "fit" with the organization or its strategic or competitive environment, it is unlikely to deliver desired results (Kimberly & Evanisko, 1981). Second, something else going on in the organization may weaken, jeopardize, or overstate the potential benefits from the project management initiative (Damanpour, 1987, 1996). Finally, we need to account for the lag between the time the project management initiatives are undertaken and the time the benefits occur (Damanpour & Evan, 1984). Without understanding the context, it is impossible to know what other organizational or environmental activities may be influencing resulting value.

In order to understand the organizational context, we need to explore each of the following in some detail:

- **Strategic Context.** The strategic context in which an organization operates can be described by: the number and type of customers, suppliers, and competitors and how they engage with them; the organization's size and position in its market; growth rates; and its particular strategic approach to addressing its organizational activities. Some of these variables can be measured directly (number of customers, size of market), while others need to be assessed based on the researchers' knowledge of the organization (strategic focus, industry).

    In order to differentiate among the strategic focuses of organizations, we needed to select an appropriate strategic framework to use for comparison purposes. The two dominant business strategy frameworks (Hambrick, 2003) are the Miles and Snow (1978) typology, which focuses on different ways that organizations approach their product market domains and the strategy dynamics, and the Porter (1980) typology, which focuses on how an organization creates customer value as compared to its competitors. The first is clearly examining strategy as a function of internal focus, while the second is focusing on external drivers. Many additional strategy frameworks are in common use today (see, for example, Chakravarthy & White, 2002; Treacy & Wiersema, 1995; Walker & Ruekert, 1987). For our purposes, we chose to use the Treacy and Wiersema (1995) model because of its focus on both the content of strategy (similar to

Porter, 1980) and the organizational implications of a particular strategy choice (closely related to the strategy, structure, and fit literature underpinning this study and discussed under the Fit section following). The Treacy and Wiersema (1995) model seems particularly appropriate, given its suggestion that organizations that have taken leadership positions in their industries typically do so by focusing on delivering superior customer value in line with one of three value disciplines—operational excellence, customer intimacy, or product leadership. This model's focus on how organizations deliver value through strategy and the organizational design features that support it seems ideal to further this research. As a result, the strategy of each case-study organization within the research is evaluated based on whether it pursues a strategic focus of operational excellence, customer intimacy, or product leadership (strategic innovation).

- **Economic/Political/Cultural Context.** Common financial measures can be used to assess the economic context that an organization is operating in. Measures such as gross domestic product, gross domestic product per person, current account balance, and the inflation rate give us solid measures to assess economic influences. Taking into account the nature of change in the economic context will require learning from local researchers and accounting for finance literature on the health of relevant economies.

  Similarly, the political structure is also likely to influence the project management implementation. Centralized systems such as that in China have much more influence on motivating change in organizations than do Western political systems. Similarly, political economies that are being supported by aid agencies are much more likely to adopt practices at face value as a term of receiving aid than organizations operating in a more capitalistic environment. Thus, the political structure within which the organizations operate will also need to be documented.

  National culture is also likely to play a significant role in both what is recognized and implemented as project management and what outcomes are valued. Case-study researchers will pay particular attention to how the national culture comes into play in each organization. In addition, measures of national culture such as those of Hofstede (2001) will also be collected to be used in future quantitative analysis. Trompenaars and Hampden-Turner's (1997) theories of the impact of culture on organizations will also likely prove useful in future analysis.

- **Organizational attributes.** In order to understand the organizational context within which project management is being implemented, it is necessary to understand the nature of the organization's work system (structure, systems) and its soft structure (shared valued, style of management, skills, and staff). To do this, we focus on four organizational attributes as follows:

o **Organizational structures** are established to coordinate work. Mintzberg (1979) suggested that the three particularly important constructs to understand with respect to organizational structure are formalization, centralization, and specialization. Formalization is defined as the degrees to which formal rules and procedures govern decisions and working relationships. Centralization examines whether decision-making authority is closely held or delegated. Specialization is the degree to which tasks and activities are divided and the degree to which workers have control over this work. Thus, we collect data to measure these constructs for each organization, particularly around decision-making structures and process orientation. In addition, we look at the ownership structure and organizational structure adopted by the organization (whether functional, weak matrix, strong matrix, or project-driven).

o **Project data** (number, type of projects, duration, performance, etc.) on each organization will provide the foundation for us to understand the project activity of each case study. Each of these organizations is involved in managing projects. Much research in the project management world has examined the need to manage different types of projects differently (Wheelwright & Clark, 1992; Shenhar & Dvir, 1996; Dvir, Lipovetsky, Shenhar, & Tishler, 1998; Crawford, Hobbs, & Turner, 2006). The types of projects an organization engages in should therefore be a primary input to choosing an appropriate project management implementation. Thus, we need to collect data on the numbers and types of projects each case-study organization engages in. Soderlund (2004) identified a typology of different kinds of organizations engaging in project activity. He suggests that there are organizations that do projects for customers (i.e., projects are the product of the organization), organizations that do projects for new product development or research; and organizations that do projects to internally support the primary focus of their organization. Using the project information collected from each organization, we will categorize organizations based on the particular type of projects they engage in, recognizing that there will likely be some organizations that engage in two or even all three types of projects.

o **Organizational culture**, as evidenced by the shared beliefs (about innovation, risk, etc.), management and communication styles, working habits, ethics, power structures, and how they work together all shape the organizational behavior of organizational members. Beliefs about risk, innovation, entrepreneurship, standards, collaboration, and professionalism are all likely to influence the kinds of practices that are deemed to be acceptable, useful or valuable in an organization. Handy (1993) suggests a useful link between organizational structure and culture that suggests the usefulness of collecting this data.

o **People who actually do the work in organizations** provide a large part of the context within which the implementation of project management will be required to function. A clear description of the age, education, attitudes toward project management, professional attitudes, morale, and job satisfaction of the members of the organizations of interest will help us understand the organizational context within which project management is being implemented.

The choice of what will have been implemented (the project management implementation in the context of any one organization) will be influenced by the business orientation of the organization—its focus, strategic direction and vision of itself as an entity—and the environment within which the organization operates. This, in turn, will be influenced by its industry, customers, economic context, and the types of projects the organization typically manages. Clearly, careful study of these contextual variables goes a long way to addressing Voepel et al.'s (2006) criticism of metrics like the BSC that focus solely on the internal performance impacts of organizational initiatives.

Project Management Constructs

Our understanding of the nature of project management, what it entails, and the functions it performs has been expanded from the simplistic tools-and-techniques approach embedded in some popular guidelines and textbooks to a much more complex understanding of the philosophy, culture, and human understanding required to implement effective project management (Winters et al, 2006). The historical foundations of project management are firmly rooted in a "process of planning" (Kerzner, 1994). Many practitioners within the project management field, however, still view the discipline as being comprised solely of planning and control techniques. Project management, in this context, is a mechanistic system that is designed solely to deliver projects on time, on budget, and to scope (Morris, 2001). The implication is that a project is an absolute, concrete, and well-defined construct that needs to be rigorously defined, circumscribed, and controlled. This prevailing view presents the idea of a ". . . project as a physical thing . . . rather than a human system." (Thomas, 2000, p. 28; see also Cicmil, Williams, Thomas, & Hodgson, 2006). The weakness of this perspective is that project management ignores both the underlying needs of the projects that organizations have initiated as well as the ultimate delivery of business value by those projects. Without connecting projects with their underlying business context, ". . . project management is a profession that, in the long term, business and industry are not going to get very excited about" (Morris, 2001, p. 25).

Based on the view that it is concerned solely with single-project delivery, project management operates to:

1. Clearly and unambiguously define tasks (Morris, 1994);

2. Organize project tasks (Morris, 1994); and

3. Evaluate projects in terms of:

    (a) The project's boundary within the parent organization; and

    (b) A way of "monitoring a project's progress against plan" (Ritz, 1990). This monitoring can include the evaluation of goal fulfillment, performance measurement, and the attainment of critical success factors (Cooper & Kleinschmidt, 1987a&b; Lechler, 1997; Pinto & Slevin, 1989).

The understanding of the role of project management in organizations has continued to evolve in terms of meaning and complexity. This more complex understanding of project management is embedded in literature that discusses project management as a legitimization process (Sapolsky, 1972; Lundin & Söderholm, 1995); action generation (Starbuck, 1982; Packendorff, 1995); a way of organizing as opposed to organization (Lundin & Midler, 1998; Packendorff, 1995; Weick, 1979); control versus communication or learning processes (Thomas, 2000; Thomas & Tjaeder, 2000); a self-organizing complex system (Cicmil, 2000; Cooke-Davies, Cicmil, Crawford, & Richardson, 2007). Project management can also be viewed as a communication process, a matter of making sense of the work being undertaken, a process for enterprise-wide strategy delivery. In essence, "[projects are] created out of the expectations, inter-subjective understandings and reproductive actions undertaken by the humans involved in them" (Thomas, 2000, p. 35).

Taking these varying understandings of project management as a starting point, scholars and practitioners alike are starting to rethink what it means to manage projects (Cicmil, Williams, Thomas, & Hodgson, 2006; Winter, Smith, Morris, & Cicmil, 2006). Looking at this work, it becomes clear that what constitutes a project, what it means to manage a project, and the tools and techniques that are used in practice are not only the clearly defined models of project management standards that are referred to above. Both researchers and practitioners are looking for more practical understanding of the actuality of project work, which, in many respects, is coming to be recognized as more complex than allowed for in standards and guidelines that are designed to be generalizable across most projects, most of the time (Thomas & Buckle-Henning, 2007).

Recognizing project management in this more complex, interpretive manner causes us some problems in terms of identifying how we can appropriately measure what organizations are implementing and calling project management in each unique organization. The inherent variation in what organizations call project management collides directly with the needs of this study to be able to articulate what has been implemented within organizations, and what can be collectively recognized as being project management. One possible response to this challenge is the adoption of one of the many project management or organizational project management maturity models that are available in the marketplace (Cooke-Davies & Arzymanow, 2003; Hillson, 2003; Ibbs & Kwak, 2000; Jachimowicz, 2003; Sawaya & Trapanese, 2004; Skulmoski, 2001). The astute reader may, in fact, be wondering why one of these models was not chosen for use in this study—especially as at least two of the project team members own proprietary maturity models and PMI—a major sponsor of the study—had recently launched the Organizational Project Management Maturity Model (OPM3®).

Truthfully, each of these models (where we had access to them) were evaluated as potential instruments for use in this study. What we found was that none of them had the depth and breadth of variables we felt were important to include in order to evaluate all aspects of the project management implementation within an organization. Each of these instruments were created for a specific purpose and to shed light on some aspects of project management or performance, but in doing so also often left others in shadow or, at times, complete darkness. As per Callon's (1990) insights, each set of predetermined metrics serves to identify certain activities and initiatives as essential or detrimental to the advancement and development of an organization or function. In particular, most of the existing instruments focused on the tangible elements of project management, ignoring or under-considering the intangible and innovative capabilities that are necessary to manage projects in a high-uncertainty, high-ambiguity, knowledge-based economy.

In addition, from a practical perspective, each of the instruments underlying these models on their own ran to a large number of questions or items—most of which have never been tested for either their reliability or validity in scientific terms. Given the scope of the data we needed to collect from each organization, we had to trade off the use of an established instrument alongside our other data collection requirements against the willingness of organizational participants to complete the instrument.

The decision was made to develop instruments that, as much as possible, are based on published research. The instruments use items that have been, where possible, tested in previous studies, and specifically focus on data collection. Rather than pursue specific evidence of project management knowledge and practice as defined within any specific instrument, we chose to develop a more detailed understanding of the processes through which practice and knowledge claims are identified. The approach we adopted was one where self-evident "best practices" emerged in organizational practice, in light of Latour's (1987, 1999) work, rather than looking for any particular set of externally identified "best practices."

We also recognized that we needed to do two things in collecting information on project management implementation within organizations. First, we needed to collect information that would allow us to identify what each organization has implemented in the name of project management. To do this we would need to understand:

- The history of project management implementation. In developing project management, as they recognize it in the organization, who did what, when, why, and how? What are the strategic drivers of the project management implementation?

- What organizational infrastructure have they created to support project management in the organization: Some questions here included: What level of infrastructure support do they have? Is there a PMO? What level does it report to? How many project managers are there? What is the budget for project management? What are their human resource policies?

- What project management practices have they implemented with respect to organizational integration, portfolio management, program management, project management, value realization, and resource management?

- What tools do they use: software, guidelines, databases, reference sources?

- What types of people are responsible for managing and working on projects? What human resource policies exist to support projects?

- What training and development do they offer their project management personnel, and what is the quality and intensity of this training?

Second, as previously noted, we needed to distinguish between the rhetoric and the actuality of what has been implemented (Abrahamson, 1991; Zbaracki, 1998). That is, we need to discern whether the policies that have been created are implemented or just sit in binders and are not used. To do this, we need to ask similar questions of different levels in the organization. We need to ask people to tell us what the policy is and what they actually do to manage projects. We need to compare this to the formal documentation of the policies and procedures that we can see in documents. In this way, we elicit both the theories in use and espoused theories (Argyris & Sch n, 1978) of project management for each organization.

Finally, we need to reiterate one key point here. When we refer to the "project management implementation," we are referring to much more than project management in the narrow terms it is often described. We are referring to all the practices, processes, standards, structures, and supports that an organization puts in place to manage projects at the organizational level. In this study, a "project management implementation" is the sum total of governance, portfolio, program, or project management practices, standards, policies, structures, people, and training that organizations invest in to facilitate and control the management of projects in the organization.

Fit

Underlying this conceptual model is the inherent assumption derived from the literature that the value of a project management implementation is a function of what is implemented and how well the implementation *fits* the needs of the organization (derived from the organization and business environment) using it. This research joins a long history of management research exploring fit, alignment, and performance. It also joins a very small set of empirical research in the project management domain that explores the relationship between a project management implementation at the organization level, its relationship to the organizations strategies, and its impact on performance.

Strategic alignment and the concept of fit have been recognized as central themes in the field of strategic management for some time (Venkatraman, 1989; Venkatraman & Camillus, 1984). Porter (1996, p. 73) contends that:

> *Strategic fit among many activities is fundamental not only to competitive advantage but also to the sustainability of that advantage. It is harder for a rival to match an array of interlocked activities than it is merely to imitate a particular sales-force approach, match a process technology, or replicate a set of product features.*

Early organization theorists contended that organization structure had to be aligned with strategy to be effective (Child & Mansfield, 1972). Strategy formulation theorists recognized the importance of fitting or aligning the organization's strategy with both the internal and external context of the firm through an assessment of opportunities and threats (see Andrews, 1971; Ansoff, 1965). Arguably, one of the highest-selling management books of recent decades, *In Search of Excellence* (Peters & Waterman, 1982), focused on the performance achieved by attaining a level of alignment between strategy, structure, and systems and skills, staff, style, and goals. Handy (1993) drew upon an institutionalist perspective to suggest that appropriateness of fit is the distinguishing factor in those organizations that achieve high performance. Where there is appropriateness of fit, "there is an effective match between people, systems, tasks and environment and suitable linkages between those four components." (p. 139). Penning's (1992) work on goodness of fit highlights these relationships as well. More recent work continues to focus on the necessity to align key systems, processes, and decisions within the firm to implement strategy (see, for example, Kaplan, 2005).

The concept of strategic alignment—or strategic fit—has been investigated in many different sub-disciplines of management, including: strategy (Miles & Snow, 1978; Miller, 1996; Porter, 1985); compensation (Balkin & Gomez-Mejia, 1987, 1990; Balkin & Bannister, 1991; Boyd & Salamin, 2001; Montemayor, 1996); human resources management (Purcell, 1999; Truss & Gratton, 1994; Tyson, 1997); and information systems management (Chan & Huff, 1993; Henderson & Venkatraman, 1993; Kearns & Lederer, 2000). More recently the question of aligning project management to strategy has come to project management (Morris & Jamieson, 2005; Sribannaboon, 2006; Sribannaboon & Milosevic, 2006). A two-way influence between business strategy and project management exists that determines the degree of alignment present.

To date, most of the research on alignment noted above has focused on vertical alignment, that is, studying the importance of aligning lower-level decisions with upper-level strategies within different fragments of the organization. Kathuria and Porth (2003) argued that horizontal alignment across functional activities of the organization is also important. Ultimately, decisions within a function should be aligned both vertically with the strategy of the organization, but also horizontally across decision areas at their own level. Unfortunately, the concept of strategic alignment in much of the research has been approached in a fragmentary way.

This review of the strategic alignment and fit literatures supports the assertion that the fit between the project management implementation, the organization's strategy, and the organizational and environmental context will likely play a significant role in determining the value an organization realizes from its project management implementation. Thus, we need some way to be able to assess the fit between the project management implementation and the organizational and business environment. This information is likely to be reflected in analytical results derived by reviewing the statistical relationships among these variables. However, asking for a perceptual response to this question was seen as also providing valuable insights. Answers with respect to the alignment and satisfaction of participants with what has been implemented are also to a certain extent likely to reflect the "fit" of the implementation.

Organizational Value

In most organizations, expenditures on project management do not have direct impacts on revenue or profits. While project management is often "sold" on an efficiency agenda (Thomas, Delisle, Jugdev, & Buckle, 2002), improvements in project management do not always reduce costs and may increase them in the short run (Bridges, 1986). Most project management improvements do not yield tangible revenue and cost impacts but are more usually associated with improving less tangible aspects of the project, often related to meeting stakeholder expectations around cost, timing, quality, and process. This results in a number of different kinds of benefits for organizations including possibly preparing the organization for future activities (Shenhar, Dvir, Levy, & Maltz, 2001). Thus we found it necessary to enrich our understanding of value and what we will be looking for in this project by exploring the multiple meanings and kinds of value that can be at play in any organization at any one time.

We started by looking at what dictionary definitions of value can tell us about the types of value project management might contribute. Originating 700-800 years ago as the understanding that something of value "has worth," the concept of value has evolved to cover a broad range of dimensions and perspectives. Measures of worth extend from the tangible and concrete (such as money, duration, and quantity), to physical characteristics (such as sound, light, and phonetic quality), and to more emotive magnitudes of esteem, desirability, significance, and relative worth. Reviewing the dictionary definitions of value (Dictionary.com – 22 September 2006) shown in the table below, we can easily see the breadth as well as the specificity with which the term value is used.

Value–noun

1.	Relative worth, merit, or importance, such as the value of a college education, or the value of a queen in chess.
2.	Monetary or material worth, as in commerce or trade: This piece of land has greatly increased in value.
3.	Worth of something in terms of the amount of other things for which it can be exchanged.
4.	Equivalent worth or return in money, material, services, etc.: to give value for value received.
5.	Estimated or assigned worth; valuation: a painting with a current value of $500,000.
6.	Denomination, as of a monetary issue or a postage stamp.

7.	Mathematics: (a) Magnitude; quantity; number represented by a figure, symbol, or the like: the value of an angle; the value of x; the value of a sum. (b) A point in the range of a function; a point in the range corresponding to a given point in the domain of a function: The value of 2x where x= 2 is 4.
8.	Import or meaning; force; significance: the value of a word.
9.	Liking or affection; favorable regard
10.	Values in sociology: The ideals, customs, institutions, etc., of a society toward which the people of the group have an affective regard. These values may be positive, as cleanliness, freedom, or education; or negative, as cruelty, crime, or blasphemy.
11.	Ethics: Any object or quality desirable as a means or as an end in itself
12.	Fine Arts: (a) Degree of lightness or darkness in a color (b) The relation of light and shade in a painting, drawing, or the like.
13.	Music: The relative length or duration of a tone signified by a note.
14.	Values in mining: The marketable portions of a body of ore.
15.	Phonetics: (a) Quality (b) The phonetic equivalent of a letter, as the sound of "a" in hat, sang, etc.

Value–verb (used with object)

16.	To calculate or reckon the monetary value of; give a specified material or financial value to; assess; appraise: to value their assets.
17.	To consider with respect to worth, excellence, usefulness, or importance
18.	To regard or esteem highly: He values her friendship.
	Origin: 1275–1325; ME < OF, n. use of fem. ptp. (cf. valuta) of valoir < L valēre to be worth]

TABLE 2-2—*Dictionary definition of value (dictionary.com on 22 September 2006)*

Considering the dictionary definitions for value established in Table 2-2, in the context of project management, a range of understandings from financial, through measures of process, to socio-emotive meanings can be exemplified. Taking a financial perspective, the worth (definitions 4 and 16) that project management brings can be interpreted as ROI or cost-benefits analysis. Extending this to a process viewpoint (definitions 5 and 6), the need for project management is quantified as a reflection of the worth of the project to the organization. From a resource perspective, the organization's gain in the use of good or bad practice and the optimization of resources (definitions 2 and 3) can also be quantified. The project management process itself also has values associated with it as part of its own mechanistic definition (definition 7). Perhaps more challenging but informative definitions arise from the value of project management to an organization being interpreted from a relativist-subjective perspective (definitions 1, 15, and 17) where value is in the "eye of the beholder," depending on the beholders' own experiences and other organizational contexts. This can also extend to cover the political and control interplay between the project and the organization (in definitions 17, 18).

Given this wide variety of ways in which value can be perceived, restricting an assessment of value solely to those measures that are expressed in financial terms would surely limit both our understanding of the benefits derived from implementing project management and the contributions project management makes to the operations of the organization. Thus, we need a model for understanding value that incorporates all aspects of the construct and which can form a full and complete basis for understanding value in the context of project management.

Borrowing a longstanding evaluation framework from human resources development evaluation literature (Kirkpatrick, 1998; Phillips, 1998) and modifying it slightly for our use, we initially elected to study five types of organization value.

- **Level 1 – Satisfaction.** This can be the simplest measure of value. Do the key stakeholders perceive that the project management initiatives provided value? This is measured through perceptions and self-report satisfaction levels, as well as through the use of objective measures (such as repeat customers) wherever possible.

- **Level 2 – Aligned Use of Practices.** This measures the fit between espoused theories and theories in use (Argyris & Schön, 1978). Did the project management implementation result in the desired processes? Do practitioners of project management actually apply the practices as they are described by the organization? Do project team members demonstrate clear and consistent understanding of the expectations placed upon them and on their appropriate responses? This is assessed through a comparison of practices, policies, and procedures with what actually happens on projects.

- **Level 3—Process Outcomes.** What project process improvements have been realized from the project management implementation? How effective is the project management process within the organization? This is evidenced by changes over time in things like numbers of change requests, budget performance, learning from past projects, and reliability of delivery. The work of Crosby (1979) provided some illustration of how the cost of quality provides a possible approach to quantifying value. This work found that well developed quality systems had a cost of quality of as little as two percent, where the costs of quality for a poor or neglected quality system could be as high a 20 percent of overall costs. Extrapolating to the project management domain suggests that the impacts of prevention activities (planning, risk management, training, supplier qualification, and partnering), appraisal and assessment activities (project tracking, control, and communications) and failure-related activities (re-work, claims, loss of future business) will contribute to our understanding of project management value.

- **Level 4 – Business Outcomes.** What business outcomes are related to the process improvements that have been made? Improving project management can result in a number of different business outcomes, depending on the nature of the organization. For organizations that undertake projects for clients, for instance, improving project management practices may improve customer satisfaction and their organization's ability to attract new customers through reputation effects, word-of-mouth, and potential advertising opportunities.

  Research suggests that repeat business arises out of customer satisfaction and that even small increases in customer retention can have a dramatic impact on profits (Reichheld & Sasser, 1990). For organizations that do manufacturing or research projects for product development, improving project delivery speed and reliability can improve an organization's time-to-market performance, which has in turn been shown to significantly improve organization and product performance. Organizations that do projects primarily for internal purposes such as organizational change and information technology projects can benefit from increased ability to achieve strategic goals.

- **Level 5 – Return on Investment.** For every dollar invested in the project management initiative, what return in terms of cost savings, revenue, etc., can be attributed to it? This measure is calculated based on the quantification of the direct business impacts identified in Level 3 and 4 benefits analysis, as compared with the reported expenditures on project management. The reader might at this point ask why we bother with this calculation if ROI has the limitations noted earlier. One of the primary limitations of ROI is that many benefits have to be estimated, and it will, in many cases, be hard to see where the numbers are coming from. This study takes the approach that despite these inadequacies, those measures that we do find will be rigorously documented. So the ROI, to the extent that we are able to derive it, will at least be based on an organizational understanding and measures that can be used for the insights it provides, while still recognizing its inherent limitations and recognizing that this measure will be the most difficult and time-consuming to calculate.

Clearly, understanding the value project management delivers to organizations is not a simple accounting exercise. In conducting the research, we recognized that evidence of all five types of value statements would need to be documented and evaluated. As well, wherever possible, efforts would be made to quantify the value derived by each organization. What may be even more important, however, is the pattern of project management implementations and the types of benefits received by different organization types. We chose to examine the data with a view of deriving relationships between categories of investment in project management and categories of benefits. Where we would be able to identify these patterns, we would also likely be able to identify specific benefits associated with developing specific project management capabilities. This would in turn provide an analysis that would be far more than a simple assessment of the average ROI that results from investing in project management. We should be able to show that investing in a particular form of project management would provide a specific type of benefit in a specific context. This type of result would not simply provide value statements for project management. It should also provide guidance for those making the decision to invest in project management as to where best to spend their money to get the type of result they most desire and require.

CONCLUSIONS

The key findings from this literature review are threefold:

- First, the question of quantifying the value of organizational functions has not been satisfactorily answered in a wide range of different organizational disciplines. Therefore, there is no tried-and-true method for answering this question. A significant challenge will be the availability, reliability, and defensibility of data, particularly to perform the calculations of financial value that would be required to arrive at an ROI measure.

- Second, the definition of the value that an organizational function provides to an organization needs to be elaborated to include a wider variety of benefits, many of which will not be quantifiable but can be clearly recognized and documented.

- Finally, the value of any organizational improvement activity must be judged in the context from which it arises and how well it fits within the context of the organization, industry, and geography that it is embedded.

The quest to evaluate the value that different organizational initiatives provide to the parent organization is considered important both from academic and practical perspectives. Considerable resources have been deployed in the effort to effectively address these questions in a number of management disciplines. Usually, these efforts have failed to achieve the results that any of us would like to see. Our undertaking will have to be carefully planned and managed to recognize the riskiness of the undertaking while ensuring the academic rigor and practical value.

Embedded in the conceptual model are three key constructs that must be understood in order to evaluate the value that an organization is deriving from its investment in project management:

- First and foremost, given that project management is clearly not the same thing across organizations, in order to understand what is providing value to any one organization, we need to identify what each organization is doing and calling project management.

- Second, we need to understand enough about the organization, its business orientation and environment to be able to assess the impact project management is having, isolating as much as possible contextual variables.

- Finally, we need to identify and document evidence of all forms of value, recognizing that value comes in many forms, only some of which are directly quantifiable.

Underlying this conceptual model is the inherent assumption derived from the literature that the value of project management is a function of what is implemented and how well the implementation *fits* the needs of the organization using it.

Given this model and PMI's authority to proceed, we turned to devising a methodology that would enable us to capture data to test this model. Chapter 3 provides a discussion of how this methodology was derived and how it evolved over time.

3

Methodology and Methods

INTRODUCTION

No one has successfully and rigorously addressed how to measure the value different functions add to an organization's operations. The challenges are many—largely stemming from the interconnectedness of managerial processes. Thus, this study set out to develop a method to inclusively investigate the question of value. Starting from a position where there is no clear approach or theoretical grounding for such a study, the decision was made early on that the study would need to create and test methods and instruments in a recursive fashion over the course of the project.

A full discussion of the theoretical, empirical, and methodological foundations and implications of these choices is beyond the scope of this chapter and will be elaborated in future academic publications. This chapter lays out the rationale for the study's approach and choice of methods at a fairly high level but with, we hope, enough detail to allow the reader to judge the rigor of the study design and to appropriately assess the validity of its conclusions. We begin by explaining the methodology of the study through discussion of the main rationale and philosophical assumptions that underlie the study, including ontological and epistemological views. Based on these underlying assumptions, we chose a mixed-methods approach incorporating both qualitative and quantitative data collection instruments grounded in deep, rich case studies, and utilizing various analytical approaches. We conclude with a phase-by-phase description of the research and methods.

METHODOLOGY

The term methodology refers to the rationale and the philosophical assumptions that underlie a particular study. It describes the epistemological and ontological assumptions driving the choice of methods used to answer the research questions. The purpose of this section is to discuss the key decisions we made and questions we had to answer in proposing a research approach that could effectively address the defined problem. It presents these considerations and the breadth of perspectives and positions that need to be balanced in contemplating a research project of this size and scale. The methodology considerations outlined in this section provide a way of framing the assumptions that underlie the methodological choices described in the next section of the monograph.

Initial Study Assumptions

Embedded in the original proposal for this research were a set of assertions about the study and what it would take for it to be successfully completed. These assertions framed the proposed approach that was felt to be necessary to conduct a research project of this size and scale, and to respond to the many research challenges that were identified at that time and have been subsequently expanded upon in Chapter 2. Making these assertions provided a basis for PMI to adjudicate the relevance and appropriateness of our proposed approach. They also served to guide the subsequent development of the research methodology as the research process itself got underway.

Nature of the Question—No Readily Available Theory

From the literature reviewed in Chapter 2, it is clear that pursuing value as a financial measure is insufficient, as too much of what project management contributes to is excluded in this approach. Solely focusing on the three prevalent approaches to examining financial assets (revenue, property, and equipment) would leave the study open to two fatal flaws:

- First, measuring the financial contribution of organizational functions has proven to be very difficult across a number of organizational disciplines and would leave the research vulnerable to pursuing what might be an impossible answer.

- Second, focusing only on financial measures would ignore the knowledge-based and intangible benefits that are currently being recognized in both project management and organizational strategy literature as fundamentally important to improving an organization's competitive position, even if the contributions cannot be financially assessed.

Ignoring the contributions project management can make to an organization's ability to contribute to strategy delivery, cultural change, transparency in communication, and soft-human factor benefits (e.g., intellectual and business intelligence development) would artificially reduce and simplify the nature of the value that project management contributes to organizations. Excluding these benefits either due to the operational complexity of identifying meaningful and comparative measures or the potential inability to quantify the measures would be a mistake.

The search for value to date has become a prolonged and unrealized quest because of this preoccupation with a single definition—or at least too narrow understanding—of what contributes value to organizations. Although demonstrable project management value is often discussed and even proclaimed in consulting and practitioner literature, the actual value resulting from investments in project management has been hard to define, let alone measure. The attempt to narrowly quantify value has been highly paradoxical; the more the search is focused on isolating a precise and discrete value of project management, the easier it has been for researchers of different perspectives to make sound, reasonable and devastatingly effective critical attacks. The result has been the initiation of yet more efforts to narrow and further refine a more precise measure. The result is not discussion and collective expansion of the body of understanding of this important topic, but instead disagreement and discord regarding the validity of any single definition. In some ways, this has meant that the more the quest is pursued, the less likely the achievement of success has become—and yet the more there are people with varying opinions on what "the" answer should be.

Given the apparently complex nature of thoughts about the value that project management may bring to an organization and the limitations that previous studies have experienced, there is a fundamental challenge as to how to approach researching such a question. There is no single theory—or even partial theory—existing today that effectively, convincingly, and defensibly explains what value means, how it is expressed and what the relationship is between the value of the project management initiative and the delivery of bottom-line value to the organization. As a result, this research cannot simply be about conclusively testing a single theory, but instead must emphasize the generation of theory based upon actual findings and data. This study must embrace the different contexts in which organizations exist, and the different dimensions of value that they may seek or encounter. Theories of value must be inductively developed based upon the circumstances encountered in different organizations. These theories, in turn, must be tested to assess their generalizability across different organizations and different contexts.

The nature of the question, therefore, drives the study towards a cross-disciplinary exploration of multiple definitions of value, taking into account the broad contextual landscape of organizations within which project management is implemented and the types of value these implementations might realize to different audiences within these organizations. Considering the different values that project management might bring to an organization, exploration must consider the raison d'être for the project management implementation from the perspective of each of the major participants (project managers, team members, project offices, management, and stakeholders).

Ensuring Credible, Reliable, Valid Results

One of the primary assumptions driving this research is that the results that emerge must be credible, reliable, and valid. Credible means believable, convincing, probable, and trustworthy. Reliable means that the data is suitable and fit to be relied upon. Valid means that another researcher could recover (if not replicate, as this is difficult, and potentially meaningless, in these types of studies) the study and achieve comparable results (Checkland & Holwell, 1998).

Yet we see from the literature review that this has been a problem to date with all of the project management value research and much, if not most, of the organizational value research conducted to date. Initiatives to measure ROI often fail because the measures they use are not deemed credible by either the academic or practitioner audience they are meant to serve. Often studies focus only on measuring the quantifiable costs and benefits and ignore the holistic evaluation of what was implemented, how well it was implemented and any intangible benefits that result. They choose this focus to try to avoid estimating values for intangible or unquantifiable benefits (and costs), and so stick with only the easily quantified cost and benefits. On the other extreme, ROI studies sometimes fail because of using overly optimistic estimates of benefits or underestimates of costs, resulting in low credibility of the results. Other research studying the value of IT to organizations has reported mixed and largely non-repeated results over the years (Kohli, 2003).

A second problem in almost all ROI research is that most organizational change initiatives are implemented under circumstances that mediate against the organization taking the time to conduct solid baseline statistical analysis of the situation. Most changes are undertaken when a change leader recognizes and can define convincingly the need to change. In project management, prior research (Thomas, Delisle, Jugdev, & Buckle, 2002) has shown that most investments are made in project management initiatives as the result of some form of "crisis" situation where the need to change the project management practices is clearly recognized by management. Given this reality, the existence of the baseline data necessary to measure the improvement in organizational functioning or returns attributable to the implementation of project management is not likely to be something that managers could readily report to researchers in most organizations.

Finally, measurement of the key variables is an important challenge to this study. Selecting any one approach to measuring value risks criticisms from various disciplines as to the definition and measurement of key variables, as well as the validity of the analysis techniques. Because organizations do not necessarily account for expenditures or measure outcomes in the same way, any study seeking to be able to compare findings across organizations must be prepared to deal with this issue; there must be an explicit allowance of different measures and perspectives, but also an approach to normalize both the measures used and the results being reported. This means that the study must be designed to include a wide array of perspectives in order to be able to triangulate results through more than one instrument or assessment technique. In this manner, not only should we be able to increase the likelihood of statistically valid correlations and qualitatively rigorous relationships being identified, but also that the correlations and relationships are relevant and defensible across multiple perspectives and inputs.

The assertion that we will collect data that will provide credible, reliable, and valid results leads to some requirements for the empirical methods selected. Prior studies of the value of project management have attempted to collect quantitative measures largely from surveys of single informants. These studies were not able to justify the credibility of the data collected or to collect sufficient data to answer the questions adequately across organizations. This meant that data collection approaches would of necessity form an important aspect of research design. We asserted that care needed to be taken to ensure that we collected data in a similar fashion across organizations, and where assumptions were made they would need to be carefully documented. Triangulation of data from a variety of sources would be necessary to ensure that the data collected is reliable and credible. Finally, to address the contextual nature of the definition of value, rich understandings of each organization would need to be generated.

To ensure the credibility and validity of our results, the following approaches were proposed in conducting the research:

- Continually check both our process and our results with academic and practitioner advisory groups and the participant organizations to ensure that there is a common and documented understanding of the process of collection and analysis.

- Devise data collection instruments and procedures that would allow all the research teams to collect consistent data across organizations.

- Use only credible sources for collecting and analyzing data and use triangulation (more than one data source) wherever possible.

- Where there is a choice among alternative valuations, always use the most conservative and document the choice.

- Ignore extreme data items and unsupported claims.

- Confirm calculations with stakeholders in each organization wherever possible.

Generalizabilty and Transferability

Another assumption contained within the proposal was that the findings needed to be generalizable across organization type, region, etc. In traditional quantitative positivist studies, generalizabilty refers to the ability of the research to make claims based on the study to populations outside the original study. In qualitative research, generalizabilty is typically measured by the degree of transferability of the findings of the study by the reader to situations outside of the original study.

Generalizabilty typically refers to quantitative analysis and comes in three forms (Runkel & McGrath, 1972). First is the assertion that the results predicted in the study will hold true in other situations. To responsibly make this assertion, the study results must be found in a variety of organizational settings. The second form of generalizabilty focuses on the measurements, looking to see if the same results are realized even when using a different form of measurement. The third form of generalizabilty relates to the subjects of the test situation and tests whether the results of the study are applicable beyond the group originally tested. This form of generalizabilty usually relates to the size and randomness of the sample tested. The challenges of organizational research in obtaining large scale, random samples often limit the generalizabilty of study results. However, the careful choice of theoretically justified rather than random studies is often used in management research to study questions of interest, and claims about generalizabilty are often made when the potential limitations of sample are taken into account. Finally, it should be noted that determining causal relationships requires utmost precision in both measurement and holding extraneous constructs constant. However, generalizable results require adding scope and variance to test how the results generalize. The solution is typically to perform a greater number of observations.

Transferability, on the other hand, is often used as a measure of the usefulness and generalizability of qualitative research. Qualitative researchers attempt to provide a highly detailed description of their research site and methods to allow the reader to identify how the situation is the same or different from their own. In comparing the specifics of the research situation with one in which they are familiar, the reader may be able to infer that the results would be the same or similar in their own situation.

Generalizable studies indicate that phenomena or relationships apply to broad categories of organizations. Transferable studies have strong face validity in that they resonate with knowledgeable readers and provide some of the "how" and "why" behind these results.

While we strongly believe that in-depth analysis of a controlled subset of organizations is essential in order to arrive at holistic and justifiable results, we also recognize that this potentially opens up the research to criticism as to the applicability and generalizabilty of the findings beyond the scope of the industries and types of projects evaluated. Conducting as many as 60 detailed case studies should provide for sufficiently generalizable results and allow for statistical analysis of relationships. Further, the original research proposal identified a potential third phase where a more comprehensive web-based data collection effort aimed at gathering data from a significant number (200 or more) of organizations could be carried out, if deemed appropriate. This effort would have allowed verification and validation of the local findings of the case studies and confirms their applicability in a more general context. Due to time and resource constraints discussed later in the chapter, this third phase has not been included as part of this project. Thus, the assertion that the study must be generalizable pushes the study design to collect sufficient data to make valid generalizable as well as transferable inferences.

Isolating the Project Management Influences

The question of isolation refers to efforts to identify the impacts of the project management initiative separate from all the other initiatives taking place in the organization at the same time, as well as other environmental and situational factors. The risk is that the research will not be able to unequivocally state which benefits are attributable to the project management implementation.

Addressing this challenge requires that all aspects of the organizations participating in the research be carefully documented and taken into account in the analysis of the results. While ignoring this complication would arguably increase the benefits identified with project management, it would not help us in the credibility of the benefits attributed to project management.

The proposal identified some common methods for addressing this challenge (as suggested by Philips, 1998; Philips, Bothel, & Snead, 2002) and committed to use them wherever possible to isolate the benefits project management from the benefits of other initiatives:

- Trend lines projecting the value of specific output variables, if the project management initiative had not been implemented, would be compared to actual data after the implementation.

- Organizational estimates of the total amount of improvement on key variables, and the apportionment or "adjustment" necessary to reflect the portion of the improvement attributable to the project management initiative, would be available

- All extraneous factors would be identified and their impact estimated. What remains would be attributable to the project management initiative. Dummy variables would be used to account for their level of input on cross organizations analysis.

- An understanding of the organizational environment and context (both internally and externally) would be monitored throughout the periods of study to understand and triangulate the impacts that internal initiatives as well as external market, economic, and competitive factors have in influencing the observed results.

While these were strategies that were outlined in the proposal, the pragmatic reality is that the dearth of rigorously collected organizational data across case studies during the actual research is likely to complicate or even make impossible this analysis.

UNDERLYING ONTOLOGICAL AND EPISTEMOLOGICAL ASSUMPTIONS

Our ontology helps us to identify that which we accept to be real and therefore what we can study. Naïve realism stresses the reality of empirical facts independent of our consciousness of them and is the basis of "scientific method" and the search for generalizable rules or laws. In contrast, subjectivists adopt a constructivist position that argues that we cannot know what is "real" independent of the context of that knowing. Ontology is important because it is the researcher's understanding of the nature of social reality, and will have serious impacts on the way we chose to scientifically analyze it. The ontological position that there is no one "right" way to define value or project management for that matter clearly suggests that we approach the research from what might be called a subjectivist or social constructivist ontological position. However, this is not to say that some members of the team and some of the methods utilized will not come from a more objectivist ontology. The very notion of counting or measuring anything requires a belief that there is something to measure.

Epistemology, on the other hand, determines what is or is not considered knowledge in a field. An ontological position of extreme positivism is associated with logical empiricism, and science based on the relations between observable empirical facts or objective structures. At the other extreme, social scientific knowledge is found in the interpretation of the meanings and constructions of social actors.

This research was based on a set of assumptions that drove us to particular choices about how best to conduct the study. These methodological choices further influenced the timeframe and specific choice of methods and design of instruments. Fundamental among these assumptions are the following:

- There is no one right way to measure value or project management outside of an organizational context.

- Both value and project management are multi-dimensional constructs and, therefore, a variety of disciplines across the management spectrum have contributions to make in answering these question.

- The data to answer these questions is not easily available in most organizations.

Ultimately this project is founded on a pragmatic approach to the ontological and epistemological choices made in the design of the research and the belief that multi-paradigm inquiry is not only possible but is necessary to "offer insights into the characteristic contradictions and tensions embodied in contemporary organization" (Reed, 1985, p. 201). We seek to "apply an accommodating ideology, valuing paradigm perspectives for their potential to inform each other toward more encompassing theories" (Lewis & Kelemen, 2002 p. 258), and to "respect opposing approaches and juxtapose the partial understandings they inspire. Pearadigm lenses may reveal seemingly disparate, but interdependent facets of a complex phenomena" (ibid). Thus, we actively seek multiple perspectives to apply to the complex and ambiguous phenomenon of how value is created in organizations. "Ideally, this strategy engages researchers more fully in a quest for understanding—an understanding that encourages tolerance, preserves theoretical diversity, and fosters non-obsessive uses of paradigm lenses" (Lewis & Kelemen, 2002, p. 264), and leads to the methodological choices described in the following sections.

METHODOLOGICAL CHOICES

The fundamental assumptions combined with recognition of the challenges addressed in the last section moved us to identify three fundamental methodological choices very quickly. First, this would be an inter-disciplinary, multinational study. Second, the study would require a mixed-methods approach. Finally, data collection would have to be situated within the organization and would require development of a deep rich understanding of each organizational participant from a variety of perspectives. We conclude this section of the chapter with a brief discussion of the philosophical foundations of the process to collaboratively generate theory grounded in empirical evidence from the field. This section reveals the considerations that went into each of these decisions.

Inter-Disciplinary, Multinational

One of the first conclusions reached from the literature review was that the nature of the questions we set out to answer was such that it would require the expertise of many different managerial academics to answer it. No single academic could be expected to bring to the table expertise in all of the managerial disciplines (accounting, industrial engineering, organizational performance, strategy and change, finance, project management, engineering, information technology, and complex systems, to name a few) and empirical methods that needed to be applied across industry types to address the complex phenomenon of interest.

Inter-disciplinary research is recognized as extremely important to address complex organizational phenomena (Martin & Turner, 1986; Lewin, 1988; Eisenhardt, 1989; Pettigrew, 1990; Dokter et al., 1991; Van de Ven & Huber, 1990; Easterby-Smith and Danusia, 1999; Merlin et al, 2000; Williams, 2008) such as the value of organizational initiatives. As previously discussed, the nature of this research question requires an interdisciplinary team working in a coordinated manner in order to address the question of value from varied organizational points of view. Additional benefits of such a team are that the diversity of theoretical points of view that are brought to the table encourages frame-breaking perspectives by "gathering and connecting diverse insights" (Dougherty, 1992, p. 181). While this approach may be less efficient than parceling the question out into smaller projects to be addressed by semi-autonomous teams, if rigorous study of the demonstrable value of the entire phenomenon across disciplines is the objective, it is the only effective means available to us.

The same sorts of considerations led us to recognize the need for international participation in the research team. The literature findings on the importance of understanding context to understand the value phenomenon and our desire to be able to generalize findings across geographical as well as industry boundaries clearly indicates a need to collect data from geographically dispersed organizations. The best way to do this was to build a geographically dispersed team of native language speakers to help us understand the disparate cultural contexts that will come into play in interpreting cross-organizational data.

However, it was difficult to coordinate and carry out this type of research under the current academic reward structures which emphasize individual performance, name recognition, and independent publishing, and lack effective mechanisms for managing such projects. In looking for guidance on how to build the team structure and many elements of the research design, we found only one article on the management of interdisciplinary research teams (O'Connor, Rice, Peters, & Veryzer, 2003). In designing the research, we relied heavily on guidance from this article. First, the article suggested that it is very important that such a team be carefully recruited according to the types of expertise required, the willingness to work collaboratively, a high level of tolerance for conflict and openness to new ideas and perspectives, and where the leadership/coordination role is recognized and valued. Second, since our objective is to "leverage the team's diversity and/or intellectual power to arrive at a common theoretical perspective, it becomes important to build in multiple coordination mechanisms for managing and developing that interpretation together" (p. 369). Not only did we have to develop a common vocabulary and approach to the research, but also relationships that will form the foundation for long-term discussions and work.

Third, in a study taking more than three years to complete, we needed to include mechanisms to ensure continuity of membership over the entire period of study, and ways of "promoting understanding, tolerance, and acceptance related to the variability of motivation and commitment" (p. 366). Fourth, we "need to consider the best ways to leverage the team for balancing the efficiencies of delegated data collection with the effectiveness of handling your own rat" (p. 356); this refers to the challenges that delegation creates in establishing a level of immersion and strong familiarity with the data. Finally, we needed to manage coding and interpretation in order to leverage multi-paradigm insights, while still building in mechanisms to drive towards an interpretation that provides at least temporary closure for the project (p. 356). Each of these pieces of advice was taken into account in the research design described in the third section of this chapter.

Mixed Methods

Given the inter-disciplinary nature of the study, it was clear that its design would require a mixture of qualitative and quantitative methods in order to capture the data and the analysis that each member of the team would need to feel comfortable with the results of the study. Both qualitative and quantitative data is required to throw real light on our research question. A wide variety of methods would best serve research into the question what value project management brings and organization. A mixed-methods approach would provide the coverage required to address such a wide and complex research question. At the time we started this project four years ago, there was very little published guidance on how to design this study. Today, there is published structure and a working definition: "Mixed methods research is, generally speaking, an approach to knowledge (theory and practice) that attempts to consider multiple viewpoints, perspectives, positions and standpoints (always including the standpoints of qualitative and quantitative research)" (Johnson, Onwuegbuzie, & Turner, 2007, p. 113).

In the general population of social science researchers, there is ambiguity with respect to the choice of appropriate research methods. Social science methodology typically clusters around (1) deductive approaches using quantitative research methods, or (2) inductive approaches using qualitative methods. However, contributions can also be made when (3) quantitative methods have laid the ground for inductive theory building, or (4) qualitative methods are used in deductive theory testing (Bitektine, 2008).

Mixing of methods is even more controversial. Some researchers believe that the assumptions underlying qualitative and quantitative methodologies are inherently opposed, and therefore that the two methodologies cannot be meaningfully combined. Others believe that the two approaches are best used in combination only by alternating between methods—typically using qualitative research for theory generation and quantitative methods for theory testing. Some researchers think that both qualitative and quantitative methods can be used simultaneously to answer a research question (a journal supporting the development of this approach to research, *Journal of Mixed Methods Research*, was founded in 2007).

Mixed method approaches to research make valuable contributions by applying what Johnson et al. (2007) call critical multiplism whereby research questions can be asked and answered from different perspectives. It is suggested that this approach improves the significance of the findings by increasing the richness of the data

(Bryman, 2007) available for interpretation, and thereby improving the usefulness of the findings (Collins et al. in Johnson et al., 2007). Mixed-method approaches are particularly prized for their ability to use both triangulation of data and method (Jack & Raturi, 2006). The suggestion is that using multiple methods allows the researcher to use one method "as a validation process that ensures that the explained variances are the result of the underlying phenomenon or trait and not the method" (Johnson et al., 2007, p. 113). We value the ". . . ability of qualitative data to offer insight into complex social processes that quantitative data cannot easily reveal" (Eisenhardt & Graebner, 2007, p. 26). By extending generalizability of the theory to those aspects of the social phenomena that are not amenable to quantification, theory testing using qualitative methods can reduce the need for "leaps of faith" when translating quantitative results to other less-measurable aspects of social process (Bitektine, 2008). Finally, mixed-methods studies have been suggested as the best way "to reconcile the seemingly contradictory demands of theory development and the application of rigorous research techniques" (Srnka & Koeszegi, 2007, p. 30). At the same time, mixed-method approaches are recognized as difficult to complete successfully. Bryman (2007) makes the following points that need to be taken into consideration when contemplating mixed methods research:

- Integration of data from both methods is difficult, and there are few good examples of integrative results;

- Specialists are required to collect and interpret the two types of data;

- Nature of the data means one set is more interesting than the other particularly to some researchers; and

- Audience of the results of the project may prefer one type of data over another.

The co-leads of this study are of the opinion that to study complex cross-disciplinary organizational phenomena such as value, it is both necessary and possible to design in a cross-method way to realize the benefits of critical multiplism, process, and data triangulation and improve the usefulness of the findings. Recognizing at the same time the difficulties raised by Bryman, we sought to address them in two ways. First, one of the co-leads was well trained and experienced in using both qualitative and quantitative methods. Second, the size and nature of the multi-disciplinary team ensured that we had the expertise in both methodologies to manage a complex cross-method study.

The decision was made then to pursue a cross-method approach to the research. The study is designed as largely a combined process of both qualitative and quantitative theory generation with small scale theory testing initiatives embedded in the final stages. We chose to start "from qualitative material and transform it into numerical data to be used in further quantitative analysis aimed at deriving generalizable results" (Srnka & Koeszegi, 2007, p. 33) as well as separately collecting quantitative data. Both qualitative and quantitative data will be analyzed separately *and* jointly to provide an overall picture of the value phenomenon. Adopting this generalization approach to mixed methods research design allows us to conduct discovery-oriented research that provides significant research insights while also allowing us to derive generalizable results from largely qualitative data (Srnka & Koeszegi, 2007).

Selecting an approach that requires both qualitative and quantitative measures and analysis in the same study also provides some unique requirements for the structure of the research team. All research team members were strong researchers in their own right with very strongly embedded research approaches arising from their own closely held ontological and epistemological assumptions. The study had to be designed such that they could bring their own specific research approach to the table while still operating within the larger study which may be based in different ontological assumptions. In addition to the concerns identified in the last section, all of the researchers selected for this study needed to be ready and willing to engage with researchers coming at the same question from often diametrically opposed epistemological and ontological approaches. This meant that not all the methods or methodologies applied in the project would be comfortable for all of the researchers. It was critical that all researchers recognized this overall project approach from the start and be ready to work through the inevitable conflict that mixed-method approaches entail. Developing the trust among these disparate researchers and the engagement that motivated these close working relationships was one of the key ongoing challenges of the project (discussed at the end of the chapter).

Multiple Detailed Rich Cases

In order to provide the interlinked, contextualized understanding of project management situated within the organization, a case study approach was chosen for this research. "A case study is an empirical inquiry that investigates a contemporary phenomenon within its real-life context especially when the boundaries between phenomenon and context are not cleanly evident" (Yin, 1994, p. 13). We believe that the importance of context in research such as this cannot be underestimated. Cases provide context: both by example and by corroboration of theory and proof to the contrary (Siggelkow, 2007). Cases allow the context of the real world to be present in the inductive formation of theory from data and the deductive theory testing of existing theory using empirical data. In this way, we set out to study the phenomenon of project management and the value it delivers as embedded within the context of the individual organization.

"The central notion is to use cases as the basis from which to develop theory inductively" (Eisenhardt & Graebner, 2007, p. 25). "Building theory from case studies is a research strategy that involves using one or more cases to create theoretical constructs, propositions and/or midrange theory from case-based, empirical evidence" (Eisenhardt, 1989). Case studies can be used to motivate (why and how does a phenomenon occur?), inspire (sharpen existing theory, inductively generate theory), and illustrate (ground theory in practice) (Siggelkow, 2007). ". . . [W]ith inductive theory building from cases producing new theory from data and deductive theory testing completing the cycle by using data to test theory" (Eisenhardt & Graebner, 2007, p. 25). "Although sometimes seen as 'subjective', well done theory building from cases is surprisingly 'objective,' because its close adherence to the data keeps researchers 'honest.' (Eisenhardt & Graebner, 2007, p. 25). The ". . . ability of qualitative data to offer insight into complex social processes that quantitative data cannot easily reveal . . ." (Eisenhardt & Graebner, 2007, p. 26) is of great import for this study.

There is some thought that within case study approaches, generalizability can be drawn from a small sample or, in some cases which present very rare phenomenon, one case (Siggelkow, 2007). While a single case can richly describe the existence of a phenomenon, multiple cases provide stronger basis for building theory (Eisenhardt & Graebner, 2007) because they serve as discrete experiments that serve as replications, contrasts, and extensions to the emerging theory (Yin, 1994). But "while laboratory experiments isolate the phenomena from their context, case studies emphasize the rich, real world context in which the phenomena occur" (Eisenhardt & Graebner, 2007, p. 25). "Multiple cases also create more robust theory because the propositions are more deeply grounded in varied empirical evidence" (Eisenhardt & Graebner, 2007, p. 27). The expected variation of what is considered a project management implementation within the cases for this study leads us to believe that there is generalizable value in the findings of both one case and also in the common areas that are demonstrated across many cases.

Case studies are often considered a qualitative research approach. However, in multi-case analysis studies, both qualitative and quantitative data collection and analysis methods can be applied. In fact, this approach ideally addresses a common complaint aimed at case studies that rely solely on one qualitative method of data collection, interviews (Eisenhardt & Graebner, 2007, p. 28).

In summary, the cross-disciplinary nature of this project requires broad team involvement. This, coupled with the use of mixed methods, thus requires rich, high-quality data that will provide depth of understanding. Expertise and breadth and quality of data in the dimensions to be investigated present the study with a decision to source a research team and data set that is international. From a quantitative perspective, there are a minimum number of cases that would provide statistically significant data. In order to gain suitable coverage and richness of cases in a timely manner, parallel collection of data from teams across the total sample space (internationally) is required. This, in turn, requires standardization of data-collection methods and instruments across researchers.

A Process for Collaborative Theory Generation Grounded in Data

In making the previous methodological choices, we found it necessary to start planning both for the content of the research and the process by which we would accomplish the project. In other words, methodological choices started to drive specific methods, some of which were introduced above. Our purpose in designing the research is to observe "phenomena with multiple methods to ground the theory development process in different versions of an existing reality" (Jack & Raturi, 2006, p. 356). Our aim is to create "theory by observing patterns within systematically collected empirical data" (Eisenhardt & Graebner, 2007, p. 30) by "recursively iterating between (and thus constantly comparing) theory and data during analysis, and theoretically sampling cases . . ." (Eisenhardt & Graebner, 2007, p. 30).

We did not, however, attempt to follow a structured grounded theory approach in its totality (see, for example, Glaser & Strauss, 1967; Glaser, 1992; Strauss & Corbin, 1998). We chose instead to "engage in systematic data collection and theory development processes that are reported with transparent description . . . .of cross case comparison techniques. The key here is to convey the rigor, creativity, and open mindedness of the research processes while sidestepping confusion and philosophical pitfalls" (Eisenhardt & Graebner, 2007). Standard data was collected from each participating organization by every case team. In addition, each researcher collected any additional data they deemed necessary to explore the value phenomenon from their own unique disciplinary/theoretical perspective. Cross-case comparison using both qualitative and quantitative methods formed the foundation for both theory generation and theory testing. The following, and final, section of this chapter documents the specific methods we employed to meet the requirements of this challenging research project.

RESEARCH PROCESS

Proposal Process

At the continued urging of both its membership and Global Corporate Council, PMI posted an international request for proposals (RFP) for research quantifying the value project management delivers to organizations in the summer of 2004, after funding a series of smaller research studies during the 1990s. Preliminary proposals were requested for 1 September 2004.

In August, the two co-leads discussed what it would take to answer this research question and conducted an initial literature review. The research study that emerged from these discussions clearly indicated that a project of this magnitude would require a broadly based team composed of experts from around the world. Attendance at the International Research Network on Managing by Projects Conference in

Turku, Finland allowed the co-leads to test the initial ideas for the study, build support for a team-based approach, identify potential research participants, and develop an initial conceptual framework for the proposal, as illustrated below. The proposal was submitted on 1 September 2004 with support from an internationally recognized cohort of project management academics and experts. The proposal asserted that quantifying the value of project management may too narrowly define the nature of the research that was required to fully understand how project management contributes to successful functioning of organizations. In essence, the proposal clarified and repositioned the nature of the research in order to address the dimensions our team felt was necessary to respond to the questions behind the question being asked in the RFP.

In mid September, PMI asked us to elaborate on our research in a full 20-page proposal to be completed by mid-October. Working with the original team members as well as expanding the team as necessary to incorporate the breadth of research perspectives and expertise, the co-leads developed a detailed proposal that was based on a strategy of learning our way to meaningful findings. The strategy of the study was to reduce uncertainty and increase our knowledge of both how to study value and the nature of value through a phased approach, as depicted in Figure 3-1. The project was designed around a series of four workshops where the team would work together in a collaborative environment to define and explore the research approach, while conducting data collection, analysis, and additional research in between the workshops. The methods for each phase of the research are described in detail in the following sections of this chapter.

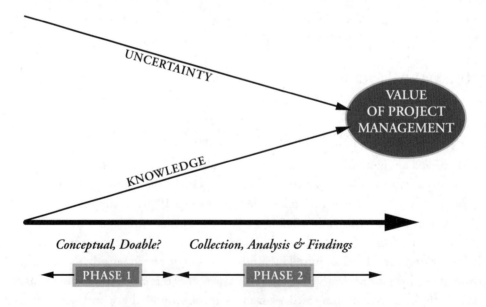

FIGURE 3-1—*Phased study approach of value and nature of value*

PMI provided a research grant to fund the costs of conducting the research through a contract between PMI and Athabasca University. The funding model outlined in the proposal was for a $950,000 grant to cover the expenses associated with the project, with nearly $1.3 million to be donated in kind through the time and efforts of the research team. All of the researchers on the project, including the co-lead investigators, volunteered their time as researchers to the project.

Contract negotiations began immediately and took almost six months to complete. Some scope changes to the original proposal, including adding China and South America as geographic regions within the research, were requested and negotiated. Topics discussed in detail in phone and face-to-face meetings over this period included: the nature of academically publishable, credible research; the difference between a research grant and contract research; the riskiness of this project, given past success rates for projects this type and the use of voluntary research efforts; the duration of the proposed project (three years) versus the perceived need for almost immediate results. The contract was signed and the project officially commenced in late May 2005, five months later than the originally proposed 1 January start date. The final contractual amount with PMI was $1.163 million. Along with donations-in-kind, the total cost for the project was almost $2.5 million.

Phase 1 – In Search Of Value

Phase Objectives

The objectives of the first phase of the project, "In Search Of Value," were to develop an initial framework for conducting the research of the project and confirm that the project was, in fact, conceptually possible to conduct. A number of challenges had been anticipated in conducting a research project of this magnitude, including: assembling and sustaining a comprehensive team of international researchers; identifying and securing organizations to participate in the research; developing effective instruments to successfully address and be able to answer the research questions; and being able to actually secure the data within the participating case study organizations. These challenges, and the approaches to addressing them, are discussed in the sections that follow.

Team Development

The first significant challenge was in assembling a team of sufficient size, depth, and breadth to conduct the research. The efforts of building a team had already begun with the proposal development process, but continued with the preparations for the first workshop, which was scheduled for 26-29 June 2005 in Broadway, United Kingdom.

The objective in establishing the team was to recruit well-respected and capable researchers who would be willing and able to make an effective contribution to the research. The criteria that were employed in selecting the team included:

- Broad international coverage within the team, in order to support and ensure that case studies from around the world could be conducted.

- Strong research reputations within the project management community, in order to ensure the results were credibly received.

- Broad subject interests within the domain of project management, in order to ensure that the exploration of project management practices and realization of value would incorporate as full and complete a perspective as possible.

- Broad coverage of relevant management and engineering research disciplines, including but not limited to: finance, accounting, organization theory, complexity theory, and engineering management.

- Different research perspectives and paradigms in order to establish and bring to the team a variety of theoretical lenses through which to view the study and its results.

- Ability to deal with the complex and ambiguous nature of the cross-discipline, multi-method approach.

- Cooperative research style, ability to collaborate and work well together for an extended period of time in conducting the research project.

- Willingness to contribute a significant proportion of their research time to this project over a three-year period.

An underlying principle in assembling the team was to fully assemble the participants from the outset. Given the size and complexity of the research, we recognized from the beginning that including additional participants as the research progressed would be disruptive and require a significant learning curve on the part of new participants, as well as adaptation by the rest of the team. As a result, a commitment was made to avoid this circumstance to the greatest degree possible. In reality, this was not able to be avoided, as will be discussed later in this section.

While the criteria for the construction of the team were, without a doubt, a tall order, the initial team that met in Broadway in many regards exemplified these criteria. While the team that met in Broadway brought a broad and diverse set of backgrounds, disciplines, and viewpoints, this was both a strength and also a challenge. The multiple viewpoints and perspectives led to comprehensive and lively discussion about how best to proceed with the research. One of the significant objectives of the first workshop was the integration of these different views into an agreed-upon view of the purpose and goals of the project and the processes to be adhered to.

Refinement of the Conceptual Model

Inputs to the meeting were the detailed proposal that had been submitted to PMI, as well as four key questions that we felt needed to be answered:

- Conceptually, what do we need to be able to understand to answer the value question?

- What do organizations implement and call project management?

- What elements of context are relevant to assessing the value that project management contributes to an organization?

- What different types of value does project management deliver to organizations?

The workshop employed both small-group and full discussions to explore these questions. The resulting discussions solidified the opinion of the team that the conceptual model outlined in the proposal provided a good starting point to elaborate from in defining a more comprehensive model that would reflect the full outputs of the workshop. The conceptual view of the team was captured and synthesized into what came to be called the *Broadway Model*, diagrammed in Figure 3-2 by Peter Checkland using a soft systems approach.

Empirically, the discussion focused on what data needs to be captured to provide evidence of these constructs in practice. Deliberations and brainstorming among the team identified a long list of potential data constructs that could be used to evaluate the context, project management practices, and realized value of organizations adopting project management. Also discussed were questions of sample size, regional distribution, industrial representation, case selection, random vs. theoretical sampling, and a number of other design issues.

The workshop concluded on a positive note, with the team feeling that a solid foundation for the research had been identified. We agreed that we now had identified the data that would allow us to study the value of project management. It was also recognized, however, that the data constructs identified could realistically only be fully assembled from each case study where there were no costs and no constraints to conducting the data, and where every participating organization had a rigorous consistency and alignment on the definitions used in the data being sought.

Recognizing that this "perfect world" scenario was far from the reality that we would find in organizations once we started researching and collecting the data, two major activities were identified as being required as a result of the workshop:

- Development of data constructs, and ultimately data collection instruments, that could be used to capture the defined data. Ideally, these constructs,

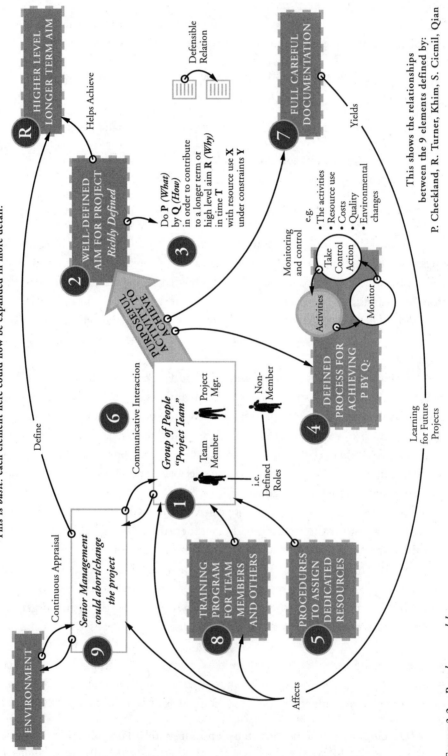

A CONSTRUCT OF PROJECT MANAGEMENT WHICH COULD YIELD QUESTIONS TO BE ASKED IN THE COMPANIES

This is *basic*: each element here could now be expanded in more detail.

FIGURE 3-2—*Broadway model*

variables, questions, and items should, wherever possible, incorporate strategies and use approaches that have been successfully employed in other research in order to optimize collectability and ensure points of alignment with other studies.

• Employment of the resulting data collection instruments in conducting a number of pilot case studies. This would allow the team to prove, test, and validate the instruments and collection approach, evaluate the degree to which the data was actually able to be collected, and explore the degree to which the resulting data provided a basis to answer the critical question of how project management provides value to organizations.

The result of the first workshop was an evolution of the original conceptual model proposed by the co-lead investigators, in light of the team's view described in the *Broadway Model*. A revised conceptual model (see Figure 3-3) was presented to the team and used as the basis for proposing data collection instruments.

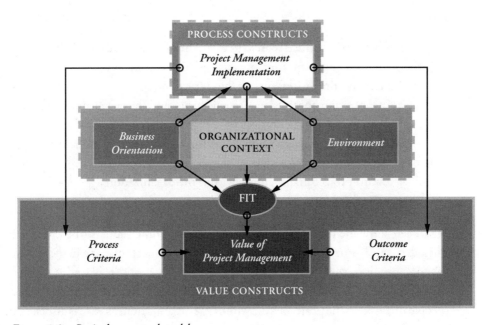

FIGURE 3-3—*Revised conceptual model*

Identification of Data Requirements

Based upon the revised conceptual model, the identification of the actual data requirements began in earnest. It was recognized that the research would require the design and assessment of a large number of data collection and analysis instruments. This was originally meant to be an interactive group design process facilitated over the internet. It quickly became a tedious coordination effort, and it was difficult for participants to be able to contribute in a meaningful way. The decision was made that the co-leads would draft an initial set of constructs that would be reviewed by the entire team. These reviewed constructs would then be used as the means of developing the data instruments to be used in the data collection of the pilot studies. The final instruments would then be revised based on the outcomes of the pilot studies and review of the instruments by the full research team during the second workshop.

Wherever possible, existing measures, constructs, and instruments were sought in the research literature in order to ensure the validity of measures and comparability of results once the study was completed. Where no existing measure could be found, measures were developed based upon principles found in the literature as well as the experience and understanding of the co-lead investigators and the research team of organizational practices and capabilities.

Three discrete constructs were developed to describe the data requirements from each organizational case study, based upon the fundamental dimensions of the revised conceptual model:

- **The organizational context constructs** attempted to understand the actual environment that the organization operates within. This included understanding broader contextual dimensions such as the culture and economic environment in which the organization operates, its strategic focus, and the overall demographics and performance of the organization. The organizational context also explored the role that project management plays within the organization, including the role of projects, experience of staff members in project management, and the attitudes toward project management within the organization.

- **The project management constructs** explored how project management had been implemented within the organization. Dimensions to be collected included the history of the implementation of project management within the organization, the structures and support organizations in place for project management, and identification of the demographics, skills, and expertise of the people involved in the project effort within the organization, as well as associated training and skills development efforts. The project management constructs also explored specifically how projects are managed within the organization, including the processes associated with the full life cycle of projects from idea through to value realization, and the tools, practices, guidelines, and aids that are available to stakeholders to assist in performing their roles.

- **The value constructs** identified the different dimensions of value that have been realized within the organization. The identification of value within the value constructs drew upon the evaluation framework proposed by Kirkpatrick (1998) and Phillips (1998), as discussed in the literature review. These constructs identified the specific means by which satisfaction, aligned use of practice, process criteria, outcome criteria, and return on investment would be measured.

Instrument Development

With the finalization of the data constructs, the next phase of preparing for the pilots was the development of the actual data collection instruments. This required the assessment of each measure defined within the data constructs, and determining where and how the measure would be collected in conducting an organizational case study.

The underlying strategy employed in defining the instruments was to determine where the information required to support the measure was most likely going to be able to found, and to determine the most appropriate means of securing that information. The result was the development of a comprehensive set of instruments that attempted to optimize the collection approach while also allowing for triangulation of responses wherever possible.

Data collection was to be accomplished in one of four ways:

- One-on-one interviews were to be conducted by the researcher either in person or over the telephone.

- Surveys were to be completed by stakeholders using either an online survey site (preferred) or a paper collection form (where circumstances, culture, or language constraints precluded the use of the online facility).

- Reviews of processes and archival project data were to be conducted by the researcher.

- Collection of archival organizational and project data was to be performed by the organization.

The data collection instruments and the core constructs that each is designed to collect are illustrated in Figure 3-4.

DATA COLLECTION INSTRUMENTS

ORGANIZATION DATA COLLECTION

Organization Data
PM Demographics
Demographics
PM Investments
Training
Practices & Tools

INTERVIEWS

Demographics
Education
Experience
History of PM
    Culture
PM Attitudes
PM Practices
Satisfaction
Perceived Alignment
Competencies
Training
Project Results

SURVEYS

Demographics
Education
Experience
Organizational
    Capabilities
Organizational
    Culture
Team/Project
    Culture
Human Resources
PM Attitudes
PM Practices
PM Role

PROJECT HISTORY

5 Projects/Year
10 Years

RESEARCHER DATA COLLECTION

Observations
File Review
    (Documented,
    Talked About,
    Done)
Interview Coding

FIGURE 3-4—*Data collection instruments*

The data collection was intended to ensure coverage of the conceptual model. Figure 3-5 illustrates the relationships between the conceptual model, organizational data sources, and the collection method.

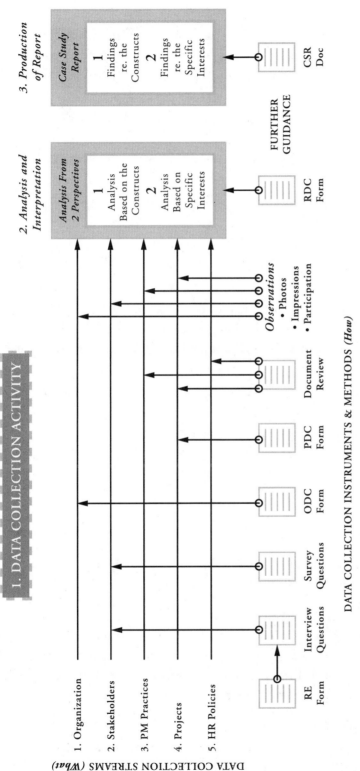

FIGURE 3-5—*Data collection approach*

Interview Questions

The interviews provided a structured approach to interviewing key organizational stakeholders within each case study. Each interview was anticipated to require 60 minutes to complete. The interview protocols include the following stakeholder roles:

- Project managers,

- Project management/project management office/center of excellence,

- Senior managers,

- Project sponsors, and

- Human resources.

Survey Questions

The survey questions were designed to provide a structured means of triangulating and validating the information gained through interviews, and providing additional information from a number of key stakeholder perspectives. Survey protocols include the following stakeholder roles:

- Project managers,

- Project team members/organizational employees,

- Project customers,

- Suppliers, and

- Subcontractors.

The survey for each stakeholder involved between 20 and 55 questions, and was expected to require approximately 30 minutes to complete.

Organizational Data Collection Form

The organizational data collection template was designed to support the collection of background and context information regarding the organization in a structured form. This form was designed to be collected by the case study organization, with assistance from the case study research team.

Project Data Collection Form

The project data collection form was designed to capture key project metrics for a sampling of historical projects within the case study organization. The form has been designed to be collected by the case study organization for each historical project being assessed, with assistance from the case study research team.

The organization was expected to identify their five most strategically important projects (as they define strategically important) completed in each year of the previous 10. It was recognized that because of the number of projects involved and the length of time, not all organizations would be able to provide a complete history. Part of the objective of this exercise was to identify what information could and could not be captured, and where information is not available, to identify the underlying causes of this missing data.

Researcher Data Collection Form

The researcher data collection form was designed to support capturing the case study research team's assessment of the organization in a consistent, structured format. This included confirming the espoused practices and theories-in-use of how the organization practices project management and a number of core attributes that define the context, structure, and capabilities of the organization. The form also provided a means of coding in a structured, qualitative fashion the information obtained during the interview process.

Ethics Review and Confidentiality Considerations

As with any research study, a key consideration was ensuring that the appropriate protocols were in place for the appropriate and ethical treatment of survey participants and ensuring the protection and confidentiality of data that was captured during the research process. This was complicated by the broad participation of researchers from around the world in both collecting and analyzing the data.

As the principal research institution, the ethics provisions of Athabasca University needed to be adhered to in conducting this research. As a result, the proposed data collection instruments were submitted to the Research Ethics Board for review and approval on 6 November 2005. The approval from the Research Ethics Board enabled conducting of the pilot assessments. Conditional approval was granted on 30 November 2005, subject to finalization of the data collection instruments.

Complying with the ethics policies of the university included ensuring a number of provisions were accommodated in conducting the research. These provisions are designed to ensure that no harm can come to research participants, whether in the form of physical or emotional duress or threats to their security or position in their organization. The organizations that were participating in the case studies, as well as each survey and interview participant, benefitted from the following provisions:

- All findings will be kept confidential. At no time will an individual participant's responses, or that of an organization, be revealed or associated with the person or an organization.

- The organization has a right to withdraw from participation in the research at any time. In the event that an organization withdraws, all data collected from the organization would be destroyed immediately.

- Each individual participant has the right to refuse to participate at any time. Participants in interviews, where culturally appropriate, would be asked to sign a form acknowledging their rights. Where not appropriate to request a signature, a copy of the form would be provided for the participant's records.

- All data captured from an organization would only be available in its raw form by the case study researchers collecting the data, and by the co-lead investigators.

- All data collected for data analysis would be stripped of information identifying the organization or the individual participants before being distributed to the data analysis team.

- The data collected by the research team would be maintained for a period of time to complete the research, and will be destroyed after 31 December 2010.

In addition, many of our case team leads had to apply for ethics approval from their home institutions in order to participate in the data collection efforts. In most cases, these secondary ethics approvals were based almost directly on the primary Athabasca University ethics approval.

Pilot Studies

Six pilot studies were initiated and four pilot studies were ultimately carried out to elaborate and test the conceptual model described above. The geographic distribution includes two in Canada and one each in China and the U.K., using a wide-ranging team of business and project management experts. Of the two case studies that were not completed as pilots, one case study was in the U.S. and another in both the U.S. and the U.K.; the latter case study was subsequently completed as part of the main data collection effort. One of the co-leads participated in all four of the pilot projects that were completed, which provided for some consistency and continuity across the pilot studies.

Each case study was designed to identify which capabilities and attributes exist within the organization from a normalized but evolutionary framework of capabilities. Data for each case study was collected through personal interviews, document reviews, project file reviews, organizational surveys, library research, and financial analysis. This multiple response methodology is used to provide triangulation across methods and study participants, and to include numerous perspectives on how the organization is perceived or rated on each measure. It is an approach recommended by a wide number of articles (Gray, Matear, Boshoff, &

Materson, 1998; Dawes, 2000; Tsai, 2002) to ensure that an organizational rather than individual picture is developed.

The results of the pilots were reviewed with the broader research team during the second workshop of the project, held in Montreal, Canada on 12-14 July 2006. Each pilot team presented the strategy adopted in conducting the case study, the results that they found, and a discussion of the successes and challenges that they encountered in conducting the case study and collecting the data within the organization.

The results of the pilot case studies demonstrated that most of the data needed is available within organizations if the identified sources of information can be accessed and the instruments are suitable for capturing the information being requested. Furthermore, the instruments have a unifying relationship across organizations and serve to provide a basis of making the kind of comparisons that would be required to answer the questions posed by this research project. Following the process outlined, the process is also recoverable—it should be possible for a researcher to replicate the findings within an organization using the same approach and protocols.

While the instruments proved reasonably effective, the greatest challenge identified by the case studies is that in many cases the information cannot be accessed. There were challenges collecting the organizational context data in three of the four organizations, as well as being able to capture the historical project information. In the case of one pilot study, the organization only undertook one project that spanned the previous 20 years, while for two of the other case study organizations, there was no history documented of project performance that predated the project management implementation being studied.

None of the pilot studies were able to calculate a return on investment that was clearly attributable to the project management implementation. Largely this was a result of difficulty in helping organizations meaningfully quantify either the benefits or the costs of their project management implementations. This level of data appears to be almost universally unavailable to the researchers across these pilots. The pilots were, however, able to identify and describe many meaningful and important benefits ascribed to project management, and several of these benefits were quantifiable.

Instrument Refinement

The other objective of the second workshop was the refinement and finalization of the data collection instruments for the main data collection process. The pilot case studies suggested that the overall constructs and instruments were appropriate and that the core data that will be required is available to us in most organizations. There were some specific challenges that were encountered in using the instruments, however, that needed to be addressed before proceeding with a more comprehensive data collection process. Many of these changes involved alignment or clarification of terminology, particularly in light of the different cultures across which data collection would be conducted.

One concern that had been raised by pilot case study researchers as well the larger research team was the amount of data required by the instruments, and the length of time required to collect the required data. Through a series of small-group sessions and larger work-group discussions, there was an attempt to rationalize and refine the data collection strategy. Ironically, however, the feedback during the workshop actually resulted in identification of additional data elements, rather than their subtraction.

The final objective of this workshop was to ensure that through the process of pilot review and instrument refinement, each and every potential case lead would have a complete understanding of the magnitude of the data collection effort and the appropriate and consistent approaches to data collection which were required for this project. We felt it was particularly important that each potential case lead was able to make an informed decision as to whether to commit to leading a case team. Our intent was that this in-depth review of the data and processes would ensure greater consistency in the data collected and less likelihood of case leads dropping out because the data collection was more onerous then they anticipated.

Following completion of the second workshop, the data collection instruments were refined and a finalized set of data collection instruments were published in anticipation of the main data collection process.

The results of the second workshop were also reviewed with PMI to confirm its satisfaction with the process to date, and to determine whether or not the next phase of the project would be undertaken. The decision to continue the project, recognizing that calculating ROI was likely to be nearly impossible, was confirmed at a meeting with PMI in Toronto on 11 August 2006.

Phase 2 – Understanding Value

Phase Objectives

The objectives of the second phase of the project, entitled "Understanding Value," were to conduct the broad data collection activities necessary to support the required analysis, and to evaluate the result of the research efforts in order to be able to answer the research questions developed as part of the proposal process. Building upon the insights gained during the first phase of the research project, phase two focused upon securing the appropriate team and organizational participation, collecting a sufficient cross-section of case study inputs and developing an analysis strategy that would allow for meaningful insights to be gained regarding the value of project management to organizations. This process is outlined in the following sections.

Setting Up Case Teams

Initiation of the second phase of the project required establishing research teams to conduct the case studies. Success in conducting the case studies depended upon securing the participation of teams that could provide the geographic and industry representation required. In addition, while it was expected that each team would use the data collection instruments in a consistent fashion to provide a common set of data, a second objective of each case study team was to bring their own research interests and perspectives to the table for their case studies.

A proposal process was used to identify and select the teams that would conduct the case studies. In this way, we were able to identify and select teams based upon ensuring an appropriate distribution of projects, ensure effective representation of different perspectives, and balance the types of organizations to be included within the case studies. Individual researchers and research teams submitted proposals that identified their interest in conducting case studies, including identification of the geographic region of the work, targeted industries, and specific candidate organizations. Proposals also identified the particular research lens that the teams proposed adopting in their research, over and above the collection of the common data using the established data collection protocols.

A total of 21 research teams were selected, proposing to conduct 71 case studies. This provided the research team with some buffer, in an effort to ensure that a targeted 60 case studies could be completed during Phase Two of the project.

A summary of the planned case studies is outlined in Table 3-1.

Region	Researcher	Case Studies
NORTH AMERICA	Thomas Mengel, University of New Brunswick	5
	Thomas Lechler, Stevens Institute of Technology	5
	Janice Thomas, Athabasca University	5
	Frank Anbari, George Washington University	1

NORTH/SOUTH AMERICA	Mark Mullaly, Interthink Consulting Incorporated	5
SCANDINAVIA	Erling Andersen, BI Norwegian School of Management	2
	Pernille Eskerod, University of Southern Denmark	5
	Jonas Soderlund, Linkoping University	3
	Vaidotas Viliunas, Vytautus Magnus University	1
UNITED KINGDOM	Tim Brady, University of Brighton	1
	Terry Cooke-Davies, Human Systems	1
	Svetlana Cicmil, University of the West of England	1
RUSSIA/EASTERN EUROPE	Maria Romanova, IBM	5
	Svetlana Cicmil, University of the West of England	3
NORTH AFRICA, MIDDLE EAST	Walid Bellassi, Athabasca University	3
	Fathi Elloumi, Athabasca University	5
CHINA	Ping Chen, Tsinghua University	6
	Shi Qian, Tongji University	3
	Xue Yan, Beijing University	3
	Zhai Li, Fudan University	3
SINGAPORE	Khim Teck Yeo, Nanyang Technological University	1
AUSTRALIA	Lynn Crawford, Bond University	4
Totals		71

TABLE 3-1—*Summary of the planned case studies*

Planned Case Studies

Contracts were ultimately drawn up between Athabasca University and 20 individual research teams. The purpose of these contracts was to define expectations around the work, as well as to ensure that the case study data collection was managed under the provisions required in the contract between PMI and Athabasca for the overall project, including those of confidentiality and assignment of intellectual property of the contracted products. Each contract provided a grant of US $6,000 per case study, half payable upon execution of the contract and the other half payable upon completion and submission of the identified work products.

Data Collection

With finalization of the contracts, the major effort moved to actually conducting the case studies. The pilot studies had already identified the challenge of securing participant organizations, and this became a priority for each of the research teams. Research teams relied upon individual contacts as well as the solicitation of local professional organizations and personal networks of academic and practitioner contacts to secure case study participation.

Workshop three, held in Esbjerg, Denmark on 13-17 August 2007, was a checkpoint in the completion of the data-collection process. It had been originally hoped that the data collection would be substantially complete by this point, and the focus of the project could turn to the analysis and compilation of the research findings. Given the challenges in securing organizations and the time required to conduct the case studies, many of the case studies were still incomplete at the time of the workshop.

A total of 42 case studies were presented during the workshop with teams outlining their current findings as well as the status and expectations regarding completion. Based upon these findings, the final portion of the workshop was used to begin to generate and evaluate initial hypotheses, in order to correlate the dimensions of value being observed with their different process and contextual drivers.

Confirmation of Strategy

An analysis of the current status of the case studies, including ensuring appropriate regional and industry participation, was conducted. As well, case study teams were asked to confirm their ability to deliver on the committed case studies, and some of the case studies were reallocated to other teams who had the capacity and ability to successfully complete them. At the close of the workshop, participants were dispatched to complete outstanding cases, work toward individual research questions and collaborate on overlapping cases, as well as submit data formally for analysis. Case leads were also encouraged to submit research papers using their unique value lens on their own case studies for presentation at the biennial PMI-sponsored research conference in Warsaw, Poland in July 2008. We attempted to use the November deadline for these papers to encourage an interim deadline for early completion of our data collection and analysis.

A review of the project was also conducted with PMI during the course of the workshop. In order to accommodate the desired timeline for marketing and dissemination of the research results by PMI, the project team was asked to confirm the originally proposed 4 August 2008 project completion. The project schedule was reviewed and evaluated to assess the ability to accommodate this request. While the project commenced five months after the initially targeted start date, and was experiencing some challenges in completion of the data collection, a strategy was identified that would allow us to still be able to deliver on the originally committed completion date. At this time, the optional online survey to test the theories generated by the first two phases of this study was explicitly removed from consideration for this project and all deliverables.

Preparation for Analysis

From the start, we planned that the individual case-team analysis would be supplemented by cross-case qualitative and quantitative analysis conducted by a smaller subset of volunteers. Shortly after the pilot projects were complete, as we finalized the plans for completion of the project, we realized we had not included provisions in the original budget for the focused analytic teams to come together to devise analysis strategies, conduct inter-coder reliability discussion of key constructs, and agree on a work plan for conducting the detailed analysis. We decided that funding at least one face-to-face meeting of this subteam would be crucial to this important activity, and that this was a scope omission that had to be corrected by spending contingency funds to make sure it happened early in 2008. This section documents the preparation for and outputs from this analysis workshop.

Preparation for Analysis Workshop

Two key activities were critical to the success of the analysis workshop. First, we had to have enough data available to allow the researchers to become familiar with what they could expect of the full data set, and thereby plan a strategy for the data analysis. Second, we needed to find a week when all members of our cross-case analytics team would get together in some corner of the world. Given that all case data were expected to be in by late 2007, we did not expect the first criteria to be a problem. Getting busy academics from around the globe together can be much more difficult, however. As it turned out, both requirements were challenging.

We began in November 2007 to finalize a date for this meeting, which was tentatively planned for February 2008. By the first week of January we realized we had both a date and a data problem. There was simply no week in February or March when the whole team could attend. We finally selected 16-20 March 2008 when all but one of the co-leads could be on site, provided the meeting was held in the U.K.

Data consolidation proved to be another challenge. It was clear by the first week of January 2008 that many of the case study teams were further behind than we expected them to be at that point, and many were only beginning to complete and enter the standard data-collection instruments. Those teams operating in non-English-speaking countries that had to translate both instruments and responses were finding this to be a time-consuming task. Our initial intention had been to send a complete, clean data set out to the analysis team members one month before the meeting so that they had time to become familiar with the data and trial some analysis techniques on their own before the meeting. Unfortunately, it was not until the first week of March that we had enough data to provide the analysis team with a subset of data to look at during the meeting.

The final preparation for the workshop entailed developing an agenda to guide discussions and preparing binders of handouts of background material for each participant. Each binder contained a guiding agenda for the meeting; a set of mind maps providing a definition for value, the context of value to an organization and within project management, and the relationship between value and the data collection tools; the value hypotheses developed by the team at workshop three in Denmark; and in-progress case study reports, value statements, and value quotations from the participating team leads (cases covered Serbia, U.K., Norway, Canada, Germany, and Denmark).

Analysis Workshop

The first two-and-a-half days of the workshop focused on the qualitative data sources. The midpoint was a joint meeting of both the qualitative and quantitative team, and the final two days focused on the quantitative sources of data. Many of the qualitative team remained available for questions (mostly regarding the interpretation of the data collection questions) during the quantitative meeting.

The qualitative team reviewed the case data materials presented. These materials were in the form of case reports and value statements and quotations. They considered where deviations in the completion of these document templates had already occurred and where they may yet occur, and further discussion identified a set of guidance notes that would be supplied to all case leads in order to ensure that a consistent set of case materials would be available for the analysis team to complete their analysis in time for the fourth workshop. A timescale was set for the completion of remaining case data by all teams. The work breakdown schedule, and responsibilities for the qualitative analysis, was agreed upon by the team.

The brief joint meeting allowed the qualitative team to identify to the quantitative team key questions that they would like to see considered in the quantitative data analysis.

The quantitative team reviewed the case data from the database of quantitative data input to date. Practicalities of sourcing data from this database were discussed and noted, data clean-up issues were listed and actioned, a requirement for a data dictionary was identified, and a date was set for a database freeze. Discussion continued around the best way to analyze the case data points according to their number and dimensionality, and also the most appropriate ways to visualize and summarize data for reporting purposes. The work breakdown schedule and responsibilities for the quantitative analysis were agreed upon by the team.

Analysis Strategy

Detailed methods of analysis will be discussed in two specific-methods chapters (Chapters 4 and 5) that discuss in detail the qualitative and quantitative approaches to conducting analysis within the study. This provides a means of exploring the analytical techniques used in each mode of analysis in detail, while presenting the results of the study in a more integrated fashion that reflects the multi-method nature and structure of the study. This section simply provides insight into the high-level analysis strategies that were defined by the analysis teams during the analysis workshop.

Qualitative Approach

As with any qualitative research, and especially in an undertaking of this size, we have collectively amassed a rich treasure-trove of qualitative data that will take some time to make sense of. The challenge for the qualitative cross-case analysis team was to devise an approach to this data that would allow us to focus quickly on the value contributions of project management and how they are realized by organizations. The decision had been made months earlier that we needed standardized ways of collating qualitative data in each case. Two specific instruments (the case study and the value statement worksheet) were developed after workshop three in Esbjerg, Denmark to allow the case-team leads, the closest researchers to the data, to make the first-level qualitative assessment and identification of the important insights from each case. These summaries and quotations would then form the basis for the qualitative cross-case analysis.

The second important decision revolved around how to share the work. We began by verifying that the set of research questions provided in the agenda for the workshop fully addressed our interests:

- Why do people implement project management? What are they trying to achieve?

- What do organizations do when they set out to implement project management? Who's involved? What does it take?

- What is project management? What do people talk about when you ask them about project management? What do they mention first? Where is the emphasis?

- What benefits (value) do participants report arising from this effort? Does this vary across organizations, roles etc? How do they support their assertions?

- How does what they've implemented work for them?

- What is the nature of the specific statements about "value" captured in the study?

Once we were sure that answering these questions would contribute to answering the global research questions, each researcher volunteered to complete the analysis for a question closest to his or her primary research interests. Each would independently write up their findings for their analysis to share with the rest of the team for synthesis into a paper on the qualitative findings that would be presented and discussed at the fourth workshop in June 2008.

Quantitative Approach

Quantitative analysis works both on the collected quantitative data, much of which provides a wealth of descriptive statistics and context to the study, and on derived quantitative data that can answer in more depth the key questions of the research project overall. Quantitative data also provides crucial triangulation of our findings.

As with any exploratory quantitative analysis, the first step is to present descriptive statistics in order to understand our data (percentage distributions and some bivariate relationships, e.g., Likert "satisfaction" box-plot against "tools" constructed variable or principal component). This first-level analysis gave us a solid understanding of the sample, any differentiating features, and identifies any outliers. Initial correlations also pointed to meaningful areas for further analysis.

The second level of analysis will consider the relationship between the implementation, context and value constructs defined in the model. Planning for this analysis started with consideration of the questions raised in the agenda:

- How do we measure implementation?

- How do we measure context?

- How do we measure value?

- How is implementation related to context?

- How is value related to context?

- How is value related to implementation?

- How is value related to fit?

Once an overall approach had been agreed upon, the work of actually conducting the analysis was divided up amongst the various team members. Given the nature of the work, it was expected that this would be a collaborative and interactive process that would culminate in the presentation of analysis results and findings at the fourth workshop.

Preparation of Findings

The final steps in the project were the integration of the various inputs in order to support the analysis, enable the development of findings, and allow for the summation of the research results contained in this research report.

The first step in this strategy was the completion of the data collection process. A completion date of 30 April 2008 was identified as the deadline for the submission of a full and complete set of data from each of the case study teams. This would include population of the full set of instruments for each case study into the consolidated database to support quantitative analysis, as well as the submission of the value statements, value quotations, and case study summaries required for the qualitative analysis.

Following the completion of the data submission, the next and final deliverable of the individual case study teams was the preparation of a comprehensive case study report. This was to be a research paper, suitable for journal submission, which presented the initial analysis and synthesis of the findings across the case studies conducted by that research team. As well, the paper was to present the particular analysis of the results based upon the specific theoretical, ontological, or epistemological research lens that the researcher chose to adopt. These reports provided both a basis for the integrated analysis and multiple perspectives of value, from multiple theoretical perspectives. Each of these analyses were presented in our final workshop in order to provide a rich framework in which to communicate the study results.

Finally, the analytical team would work to conduct the cross-case analysis, based upon the strategy identified during the analysis workshop in March 2008 in London, U.K. The result of this research was the development of papers by each of the qualitative and quantitative analysis teams. These papers were again prepared in journal format, expanding upon the methodological strategies outlined in this chapter while also presenting the cross-case findings that would establish the basis of the developing the overall research results.

Each of these strategies was targeted to be complete in preparation for the final workshop of the full research team, held in Lake Louise, Canada from 22-27 June 2008. During this workshop, the analysis papers of the individual case study teams were presented, along with the analysis results of the qualitative and quantitative analysis teams. Those research team members who were not responsible for the conducting of case studies served as peer reviewers, and provided feedback on the papers in order to optimize the quality and clarity of the presented results. The last stage of the workshop was the identification and synthesis of the key findings of the research project, in order to prepare for the development of this research monograph.

CHALLENGES

No research project is without its challenges. With a project of this size, scale, and complexity, challenges are not only inevitable but are often also significant in their magnitude.

This is a unique project on a scale that has not been seen in project management research previously. The research team for the project consists of an extensive network of over 48 leading researchers from over 15 universities on five continents. As such, it can be considered a risky project in project management terms and subject to a large number of project-specific challenges. Most of these challenges and risks have been discussed throughout this chapter. Thus, it is sufficient to only highlight them here. The purpose of this section is not to defend the research results, to make excuses, or to complain. Instead, these insights are offered for the benefit of future researchers in contemplating a research project that approximates the scope and magnitude of this one. Further academic writings on managing this sort of research project will be forthcoming and deal with these challenges in some detail.

Significant research challenges included:

- **Volunteer teams.** The full team participating in this project, including the co-lead investigators, was made up of volunteers. The funding provided by PMI paid for the expenses associated with actually conducting the research, including travel, workshops, project support, and research assistance. That said, each of the volunteers is a senior and respected researcher, each of whom have many other professional obligations and commitments. Maintaining the focus and efforts of the team over a four-year period was a challenge, and the reality was that allowances had to be made for the inevitable impacts and delays when these occurred.

- **Working at a distance.** This was an international team, with participation from researchers in almost every time zone from around the world. The result was that effective communication and collaboration was often a challenge. While the team employed numerous virtual technologies to support the project effort, including the use of intranet sites, online databases, instant messaging, online conferencing, and conference calls, dealing with a project of the complexity and subtlety of this one means that virtual communication tools are often not sufficient to fully explore meaning and establish effective communications. The workshops were essential in developing and sustaining a common and collective understanding of the research purpose and strategy.

- **Contractual funding and deadlines.** While the funding allowances were presumed to be generous and sufficient, a project of this scope, as noted before, is not without its risks. We learned early, for instance, that the buying power of US $6,000 varies substantially across both geographic economies and time. In project management terms, the primary driving priority of research is to ensure the optimal scope and quality of the finished product. At the same time, the nature of this project meant that there were significant schedule pressures placed upon the work in order to provide PMI with the results it sought in a time frame that it felt was necessary. The funding, while initially including a healthy contingency due to a favorable exchange rate between Canada and the U.S., quickly shrank with the significant and unexpected strengthening of the Canadian dollar. This required numerous rethinks of strategy. While we believe that we have been successful in meeting the scope expectations of this project on time and on budget, it has not been without significant headaches and numerous sleepless nights.

- **Magnitude of the data collected.** The sheer volume of data created in a research project of this magnitude is overwhelming. It is physically impossible for any one person to understand and be able to fully know the implication and relations of the full dataset. The use of individual case study teams, each of which became expert in their case studies, and the heroic efforts of the analysis teams in beginning to make sense of the full dataset, were essential in the beginning to establish meaning and make sense of the research findings. That said, this monograph does not represent the completion of this research, but is in fact only the end of the beginning. The research dataset that this research project has established promises to serve as the basis of significant future research.

- **Difficulty in securing organizational participation.** Securing organizational participation has been challenging from the outset. From the experience of the pilot case studies, we knew that obtaining willing participants would be a challenge. While the reasons varied widely across different organizations—ranging from time requirements to confidentiality concerns to the sheer workload they faced during the period of the research—the net result was still that it was significantly challenging to establish and maintain the commitments of the organizations that were involved. A tremendous debt of thanks goes out to each participating organization, as well as to the case study researchers who worked so hard to obtain and maintain access in order for this research project to complete.

- **Maintaining researcher independence.** One of the most significant challenges, and one of the key reasons for the delay in negotiating the initial contract with PMI, was ensuring the appropriate provision of intellectual property rights associated with the research. PMI, as the funder of this research, was the rightful owner of the work products of this research, and provisions were required to ensure the transfer of copyright ownership for the work to PMI, a requirement that had to cascade through every other contract associated with the project. At the same time, the majority of the team are academics for whom a core requirement is the publishing of research in academic journals and publications. This required that each researcher retain the ownership of the individual dataset they were responsible for creating, while making the full data set available to the co-lead researchers and the analysis teams in order to synthesize the case study results and develop the overall work products of the project.

- **Maintaining the core team throughout the project.** Four years is a significant amount of time, and a key challenge was maintaining the core team throughout this project. While team members have shifted job responsibilities, changed institutions, and dealt with the inevitable personal and family challenges that emerge over an extensive period of time, the team has nonetheless been able to maintain an astonishing degree of longevity. While some core team members had to step back and reduce their involvement in the project, the majority of team members contributing to the final research efforts were also involved with the project at its outset, and to them we owe our sincere thanks.

- **Integrating new members to the team.** At the same time, while we strove to maintain the integrity of the research team, it was impossible to avoid adding team members to the project. This proved to be a significant hurdle, and one that had to be cleared on several occasions. One strategy that proved effective was that the majority of new team members were introduced during or shortly before one of the project workshops, which allowed for them to develop a face-to-face level of familiarity and understanding with both the team and the projects. At the same time, however, this also often required revisiting decisions and explaining strategies and rationales multiple times throughout the project in order to maintain a consistent and universal understanding. In retrospect, however, this reiteration often proved as beneficial for existing team members in refreshing their understanding as it did for the new team members who were developing their knowledge of the project for the first time.

- **Maintaining momentum.** No project of this magnitude proceeds smoothly. Lives intrude, jobs intervene, and the ebb and flow of life means that, at times, enthusiasm waxes and wanes. Possibly the most significant responsibility of the co-lead investigators was maintaining the momentum and commitment of the team. At the same time, however, the establishment of co-leads meant that the lead researchers were also responsible for maintaining the momentum and enthusiasm of each other. The advantages of having co-leads was significant, and should by no means be overlooked. Repeatedly, we found that the back and forth of our interactions not only provided the momentum that we both required, but also resulted in a better work product. As the energy of one of us would flag, the other would be able to pick up and continue forward. Neither of us could have succeeded without the other.

- **Cross-disciplinary sense-making.** The primary value of this project was that it was a cross-disciplinary, multi-method project that interwove numerous theoretical, ontological, and epistemological lenses. It was also the project's greatest challenge. It is no doubt human nature that each of us brings his or her own lenses and perspectives to the table, and that each of us maintains a level of confidence and certainty in his or her virtues. Success in a project of this nature means being willing to let go of our personal perspectives, and having the courage to look at the project (and the world) through the lenses and perspectives of others without fearing that we will lose the sense of ourselves in the process. Numerous were the discussions, assertions, and arguments about the merits of one approach over another. The success of this project will be measured by the degree to which we were successful as a team in being willing not to advocate for one perspective in favor of allowing for multiple ones.

4

Qualitative Methods

INTRODUCTION

The primary qualitative method underpinning this project is that of multiple case studies. As per Yin (2002), a "case study is an empirical inquiry which investigates a contemporary phenomenon within its real-life context, especially when the boundaries between phenomenon and context are not clearly evident" (p. 13).

Each case study team collected deep, rich data from their organizational research sites, elucidating what the organizations implemented and call project management, their most recent implementation and the benefits (and costs) resulting from this implementation. Each case team conducted within- and cross-case analysis of its own particular cases. This analysis will be the focus of a special thematic edition of *Project Management Journal* coming out in early 2009.

The following chapter documents the qualitative methods applied to the cross case analysis of the full set of 60 case studies. This analysis was conducted by a subset of the main research team that included Ping Chen, Svetlana Cicmil, Pernille Eskerod, Zhai Li, Thomas Mengel, Mark Mullaly and Janice Thomas. The cross-case analysis was designed to address the following set of questions:

- What was the most recent implementation of project management in the case organizations?

- What aspects of that implementation had the most/least impact on project performance?

- What was the nature of the value statements made in interview responses?

- What tangible and intangible benefits are evidenced in the cases under study?

- What ROI can be calculated?

- How well does what has been implemented "fit" with what the organization needs?

Each member of the qualitative analysis research team took on one of these questions and examined the qualitative data using standard methods appropriate to the data to answer their particular question. Qualitative researchers identified more than 15 different methods of data analysis that are used in qualitative research. To date, the following methods were adopted by various researchers at different times and for different purposes in the analysis of the qualitative data.

ANALYTICAL METHODS

Constant Comparison/Grounded Theory

(widely used, developed in late 1960s by Anselm Strauss)

Here the researcher reviews the qualitative data looking for specific examples of an event or behavior (in this case, statements about the value of project management). Each incidence of such a statement is coded as to its meaning and intent. The resulting codes are then compared to find consistencies and differences. Consistency among codes leads to the identification of categories of codes with similar meanings. Eventually the coding structure "saturates" in that review of additional qualitative data does not produce any new codes or categories. Constantly comparing and reviewing the developing coding structure leads to identification of central categories (called axial categories) and often core categories of central focus to the investigation.

Analytic Induction

(key proponents: F. Znaniecki, Howard Becker, Jack Katz).

Researchers begin by looking at each event (in this case, the case study organization's implementation of project management) and developing an assertion about what value is being delivered and how. They then turn their attention to the next case study to see if it fits with the hypothesis developed in the first. If it doesn't, the hypothesis is revised to fit both cases or a new hypothesis is developed. This should result in a small set of hypotheses that accounts for all observed cases.

Logical Analysis/Matrix Analysis

(examples in Miles and Huberman)

Researchers begin by developing an analytical matrix of key data elements and descriptors of the cases of interest. Using this matrix or graphic as a starting point, color or other forms of coding are used to identify patterns in the data that help to explain the logic of the events of interest.

Quasi-statistics

(key proponent: Howard Becker)

Coding of qualitative data can be used to create counts of events or occurrences, or mentions of a specific benefit. These rough estimates of frequencies can be used as evidence for the categories created in qualitative data analysis or can, in fact, form the data for further quantitative analysis of the cases when combined with other quantitative data.

Content Analysis

(key proponent: R. P. Weber)

Content analysis determines the presence of concepts as well as their relationship and co-occurrence in texts. Existing categories and relations can be searched for, quantified, and analyzed to identify existing themes and properties (e.g., of authors, their context and culture, their message, and their audience). Conceptual (or thematic) analyses measure the presence and frequency of concepts; relational (or semantic) analyses measure the relationship of existing concepts amongst each other. Words in texts are counted and weighed to identify key words to be aggregated into concepts (Weber, 1990).

Both approaches within content analysis can be supported by commercially available software packages (e.g., Leximancer). Available standardized dictionaries can be used to significantly reduce the potential bias of the researcher when working with category schemes and codes. Computer-assisted counting, weighing, and concept identification processes also substantially increase scoring reliability and reduce coding inconsistencies. The process results in conceptual maps presenting relevant concepts, their relevance within the text, and their relationship towards each other; these maps are created using the absolute and relative count of words, categories, and terms as identified by the (computer-assisted) coding processes. Furthermore, the resulting data can be fed into further (computer-assisted) statistical analysis processes.

Metaphorical Analysis

(key proponents: Michael Patton, Nick Smith)

As part of the data analysis, various case team leads and members of the qualitative analysis team have developed or reported spontaneous participant-generated metaphors that seem to help us make sense of the data. This is a form of qualitative analysis that is often applied late in the analysis process to help describe the outputs of the research. At the time of writing this manuscript, this analysis is just beginning but already providing some interesting and colorful insights. Metaphors will be member-checked with participants as an ongoing part of the research process.

The following sections document the specific methods used to make sense of the qualitative data for each of the questions identified above.

MOST RECENT IMPLEMENTATION

This section, and the analysis discussed here, was contributed by Pernille Eskerod

Data in this analysis stem from case reports produced by teams conducting case studies in organizations around the world. Key informants in the case-study organizations have participated in individual interviews using a semi-structured questionnaire. For each case-study organization, the responsible team has developed a case-study report to sum up the data collected.

Explorations of the most recent implementation undertaken within the case studies are identified in case reports covering 51 organizations. In 22 reports, a single improvement effort was identified, while two or more efforts were identified in the reminding 29 reports. In total, 115 improvement efforts were identified. This analysis relies upon data that has been reported in the case study reports, in response to this descriptive and open question:

What was implemented in the most recent improvement effort?

The analysis aimed at two purposes: (1) to identify what kind of project management improvement efforts the companies have implemented, and (2) to investigate whether the improvement efforts varies according to region.

A meta-matrix was developed in which the improvement efforts were inserted together with company, country, and region identifications. The efforts were kept in an unedited form as they were represented by quotations from the reports. Hereafter, each effort was categorized. The analysis was carried out by applying a grounded theory approach (Glaser & Strauss, 1967; Strauss & Corbin, 1990) in which raw data from the case studies were coded and classified without using a pre-defined classification scheme. Instead, the categories were derived from the data on an inductive basis. By using this research approach, the data were allowed to speak for themselves and leave room for important variations in project management efforts that may not have previously been considered.

The data processing consisted of two analyses: a pilot analysis to gain insight into the data and viability of the planned approach, and a main analysis to generate the overall analysis results presented here. The pilot analysis was based on 22 case-study reports and 40 improvement efforts. The findings from the pilot analysis were discussed at a workshop in which case team members and project management experts participated.

Findings from this analysis are discussed in Chapter 7.

MOST / LEAST IMPACT ANALYSIS

This section, and the analysis discussed here, was contributed by Svetlana Cicmil

This analysis covers the complete qualitative data base of 60 cases available as of 1 July 2008. We had three aims for this inquiry: First, to identify, cumulatively, those elements within a range of formats and types of project management (methodologies) implemented in localities of the 60 case organizations that seem to matter most in terms of their direct impact on the performance of projects. Second, to help shed some light on, and differentiate between, those aspects of project management implementation that are perceived or evidenced as having worked well and/or met the expectations of those promoting the implementation of project management locally. This also involved identifying those aspects of the implementations that have disappointed in terms of their effectiveness and their ability to deliver promised or expected benefits in the specific organizational setting. This includes identification of some unintended consequences. Third, to illuminate practical relevance of the outcome for organizational members and decision-makers across industrial sectors and national borders.

Reflecting on the process of conducting this analysis, we find it important to highlight the following considerations for the reader. First, most of the time we had to rely on the information contained in the narrative of the individual case reports. The case report template consistently encouraged case-research teams to address the following question as explicitly as possible:

What aspects of the project management implementation have had:

a) the greatest impact on improving project performance?

b) the least impact?

Providing a consistent structure for responses through this question made the process of data systematization, coding, and analysis much easier in a majority of cases but not all. In order to decipher as accurately as possible what should be considered as relevant data to this question of "the greatest and the least," it was necessary to read almost all case reports in full and sometimes to consult individual case researchers. Once identified in the narrative, the relevant aspects were plotted against the corresponding codes under the category of either "the greatest" OR "the least," recording also the name of the case and industrial sector. The constructed color-coded data base also visually represented a cumulative distribution of aspects against "the greatest" and "the least" and further facilitated the analysis and comparison.

Second, it should be noted that in a number of case reports, information explanation / statements relevant to this question *did not refer explicitly to "impact on project performance"* but to some other "value related criteria" such as organizational performance, team coherence, and effectiveness of team work; motivation; safety; workload distribution; fit with organizational culture; fit with strategy; or simply to the key drivers behind the implementation of project management in the given organizational context. This is important to remember when making sense of the analysis and its conclusions.

Finally, *the most significant impact* was almost always understood or interpreted by respondents (and researchers) as "experiencing a positive consequence" while *the least impact* connected to either an "indifferent" or "negative" perception (e.g., "that aspect of the implemented project management methodology has not worked for us"). This did not necessarily have to be so (the most significant impact could, theoretically, refer to the most "disastrous"), but in our sample, it is the case.

Findings from this analysis are discussed in Chapter 7.

Value Statements

This section, and the analysis discussed here, was contributed by Thomas Mengel, Mark Mullaly, and Janice Thomas

Three types of analysis were applied to this data. First, the individual case-study teams were asked to identify all relevant quotes from the interviews that commented on the value the organization received from project management implementation. Then they were asked to do a first-level analysis of these quotations by identifying the value statement(s) exemplified in the quotes. Next, the value quotations and statements were submitted to two different types of coding and sorting activity.

In one set of analysis, the value quotations were subjected to a sophisticated content analysis using a computerized tool called Leximancer (Smith, 2007). This software compares the occurrences of various words and their relationship to each other to develop conceptual and relational analyses of the value quotes of the various stakeholders within the case study organizations. Findings from this analysis are discussed in Chapter 8.

The other coding analysis involved using a modified card-sorting routine using printed quotations with relevant identifying variables (quotation, quotation number, role of speaker, case organization) on a card. These cards were then hand-sorted by a team of three researchers into piles associated with particular types or levels of value identified in the literature review. This information was then re-entered into Microsoft® Excel spreadsheets that allowed for further coding and analysis of the nature of the quotations. Analysis included types of value realized by case, role, etc. Particularly relevant/informative quotations were identified for further analysis. The preliminary card-sort served as the foundation coding for identifying further coding structures and analysis using the traditional read, code, summarize, and sort codes approach. Exemplary quotations identified in this analysis are used throughout the monograph to provide depth to our findings.

ANALYSIS OF TANGIBLE AND INTANGIBLE VALUE REALIZED

This section, and the analysis discussed here, was contributed by Janice Thomas and Mark Mullaly

Organizations in our study had a particularly difficult time providing evidence of either the tangible or intangible benefits received from their project management implementations. However, in the value statements and the case reports, we noted many occurrences of both kinds of benefits for the case organizations. In order to "measure" the magnitude of these different benefits, we adopted a quasi-statistical frequency-counting approach. We first created a preliminary coding structure of the types of benefits the organizations reported grounded in the case reports. Two researchers then read each case and coded the benefits recognized. Each benefit identified was coded as being recognized in the case at a level 0 (not at all), 1 (a very little), 2 (to some extent), or 3 (to a very great extent).

Once the individual coding was completed, we compared our codings for each case. In many cases the coding was very similar. In some instances, one or the other researcher had overlooked a particular benefit all together (or sometimes seen one that on sober second thought was not visible in the case report). Sometimes, researcher background knowledge of the case, or the presentation of the case in workshops, needed to be used to substantiate claims for benefits. Ultimately we came to a common identification of both the benefits realized and the level at which they were realized for each organization.

The second stage was to categorize these benefits as tangible or intangible. Again, we used a 0- to 3-point scale. Coding was done independently and then discussed and confirmed. Finally, each case study was rated as to our understanding of the value trend for each particular organization. The rating scale here ranged from -2 to 2 where -2=actively destroying value by current investments, -1 =value of earlier investments being allowed to dissipate, 0 =unclear as to whether current investments in project management would deliver significant ongoing value), 1=current investments in project management expected to continue delivering some value, 2=current investments in project management delivers significant value and is expected to continue to do so. Ultimately, this data was analyzed qualitatively and fed into the quantitative analysis data set.

Findings from this analysis are discussed in Chapter 8.

CALCULATION OF ROI

This section, and the analysis discussed here, was contributed by Zhai Li and Janice Thomas

From the beginning of this project, the question of ROI and how we would measure it has been a consideration. Very few management studies in any discipline have been able to effectively measure ROI across organizations due to the measurement and data challenges we raised in the literature review. Nonetheless, we endeavored to capture the cost and benefit information from each and every organization in the sample that would allow us to calculate ROI. In reviewing the final data sets (and much earlier in data collection), it became evident that none of the organizations in our sample calculated the ROI for their project management implementation—few even collected cost information, let alone made any effort to quantify the benefits received. Those organizations that came closest to being able to calculate ROI were those that primarily did projects for customers (consulting, construction). These organizations reported the least interest in spending time trying to do so as they found the question almost nonsensical, in that they could not see any alternative to using project management. It is simply viewed as an essential good that needed to be invested in. The only interest exhibited in calculating ROI from this group of organizations came from those that sold project management services for a living and saw it as a useful marketing tool—but not useful enough for them to invest in capturing the data they would need to calculate it.

Despite this conundrum, we did make a concerted effort to find organizations that we might be able to construct quantifiable costs and benefits for in an effort to calculate ROI. In order to need the least possible data to calculate ROI, we attempted to compare the most conservative estimates of value (only those directly related to improving project process outcomes) to the direct costs of project management implementations. This approach was sure to underestimate the "true" ROI, as it excluded the benefits associated with increasing customer satisfaction, alignment, or organizational decision-making and strategy realization. Although these may be recognized and valued by the case-study organizations, they are the most difficult to quantify and for any one organizational function to take credit for. Figure 4.1 illustrates the types of quantifiable investment and returns, we expected to be able to examine.

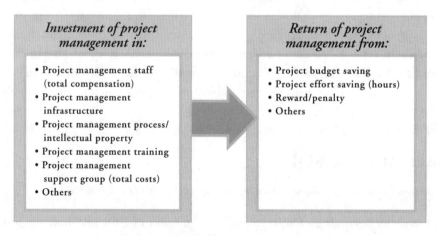

FIGURE 4-1—*Structure of minimal ROI model*

Our assumption was that this would require the least number of "reconstructions" and assumptions to be used to calculate the benefits or costs.

We started by reviewing the data from those organizations we expected to be most likely to have this data available to us–consulting and construction organizations. We then expanded our assessment to all organizations, looking for organizations that had provided enough data to quantify benefits and/or costs. We first targeted organizations where individuals made value assertions reporting quantifiable benefits. Many organizations were able to provide anecdotal evidence of some sort of benefit calculation, for example:

> *"By having a form [for change control] that everyone understands, predetermined criteria for submitting changes, predetermined requirements for the quality of information required on the change form, a predetermined approval matrix agreed upon, and some other basic [project management] behaviors, we were able to take approximately 20 hours off the effort to create and approve a change order. Remembering that many of the costs for this are for senior people, I would take a salary average of about $175/hr. If, during the year, each of the 60 projects averages 5 change orders (remember these are not all for money), then the monthly cost saving can be computed as $(20*\$175*5*60)/12 = \$87,500$ per month."*

However, when researchers pressed for the data upon which this assertion was made, it did not exist. Often the assertion was a "best guess" based on the individual's experience with the organization and reasonable assumptions (not measured) of average time savings.

Next we reviewed the full case data (from those organizations that had provided the fullest sets of data) on the understanding that a full dataset should provide us with the data from which we could make assumptions to drive calculations. Here we found that we could calculate quantifiable benefits from project process improvements for some organizations. However, no organization had a full set of data from which to calculate the complete list of project process improvement benefits. In addition, and more problematically, none of the organizations in our sample were able to provide evidence of the costs associated with their project management implementation. In most instances, costs associated with training, office space, and recruiting were not tracked separately for project management departments. The human resource budgets were most often tracked for the organization as a whole and there was no easy way to capture costs of the project management implementation. For implementations where the initial implementation extended back further than three years, this seemed to be a particular problem.

Ultimately, we were able to quantify some benefit realizations for a number of the organizations in the sample. Examples of these quantified benefits will be dispersed in the analysis as appropriate. We were not however able to calculate an ROI for any of the organizations in our sample. However, there are a couple of organizations that may be able to provide additional data in the future to allow more comprehensive calculations. In most cases, these are organizations that have only recently (within two years of data being collected) invested in project management implementations, have tracked their costs diligently, and are now beginning to track results.

Fit

This section, and the analysis discussed here, was contributed by Thomas Mengel

This analysis of 59 case reports was aimed at studying the "value and "organizational fit of project management implementations using different concepts of "value to determine the level of "organizational fit.

The first two value level constructs—satisfaction and alignment of practices—had initially been identified as criteria for the realization of value of project management. Furthermore, based on our understanding that project management may enable strategic fit, the value of project management can in part be identified as the extent to which the project management implementation enables that fit. Although the idea of fit is larger than simply being a measure of satisfaction and alignment (see Chapter 8 for a more detailed discussion), these concepts were initially identified as being potentially indicative of the degree to which fit can be measured. While they do not directly measure fit and can best be viewed as a proxy, they provide some initial insight to support this analysis. For this purpose, the two criteria combined into a concept of "Fit—Satisfaction/Alignment."

Furthermore, based on the observation of Shenhar and his colleagues (Shenhar & Dvir, 1996; Dvir et al., 1998; Raz et al., 2002) that various project configurations require different project management approaches, we have suggested a respective "Fit—UCP/PM" concept, which notes high organizational fit if a given Uncertainty-Complexity-Pace-context is matched by a flexible project management approach. In addition, we suggest the "Fit—Different Kinds" concept which indicates organizational fit in a case where the organization has either different kinds of projects and a differentiated and flexible project management approach, or only one kind of project and a respective clear and unified project management approach. We likely don't have organizational fit in cases where we either find different kinds of projects and a non-differentiated project management approach or we only find one type of project and a project management approach that is not geared toward this type of project.

Finally, a first scan of the various case studies available suggested that two factors not captured by the other criteria and concepts may play a major role for both creating value and contributing to organizational fit: the existence of a project management office (PMO) or the equivalent, and the delivery of extensive training to project management stakeholders. Hence, we suggest using the "Fit—PMO/Training" concept consisting of both the PMO and training criteria.

In the analysis, all criteria identified were scored based on the information in the case reports; subsequently, the values for the concepts used (the various fit concepts discussed above) were calculated based on the identified scores. Finally, two summarizing concepts were created to demonstrate three different levels of "organizational fit" (high, medium, and low).

The major results are presented graphically and discussed in terms of the major findings in Chapter 9.

Conclusions

A study of this magnitude creates a very great deal of data. In total, we have collected more than 440 interview transcripts and 60 case reports. In the interests of completing this monograph in a timely manner, the initial qualitative analysis included in this document have been based on the value statements extracted from the interviews by the case team researchers and the case summary reports prepared by the individual case team researchers to summarize the main findings from their studies. Each qualitative researcher has applied different data analysis techniques to explore the data and provide answers to pertinent questions. We hope that this short chapter has provided you with a feel for the types of analysis that inform the qualitative findings reported in the remainder of the monograph, where their contribution furthers our understanding of the construct of interest.

5

Quantitative Methods

This chapter was contributed by Dr. Terence Williams, except where otherwise noted.

INTRODUCTION

Chapter 3, *Methodology and Methods,* gives the overall structure of the methodology used in this study. Part of the multi-methodological study was a quantitative analysis of the data collected, and this chapter describes the methods used in analyzing this data-set.

Based on the conceptual model developed from Thomas and Mullaly (2005), shown in Figure 2-1, three basic areas of data were defined. This is further discussed in the "Identification of Data Requirements" section of Chapter 3.

- The organizational context constructs, looking at the environment within which the organization operates and the organizational environment within which the project management implementation occurred.

- The project management constructs, looking at how project management had been implemented within the organization, or what "project management" meant within the organization.

- The value constructs, looking at the different dimensions of value that have been realized within the organization, initially categorized into the five levels of value described in Chapter 2 (modified from Kirkpatrick, 1998 and Phillips, 1998). These are five different types of value, so the word "level" should be taken here to imply a nominal rather than an ordinal scale; in other words, they are simply categories of value, and one is not considered more or less important than another.

DATA

The work to develop data collection instruments resulted in a large set of instruments as shown in Figure 3-5. The data collected was held in a Microsoft® Access database, containing the following data instruments:

- Participant surveys, of five types depending on the role of the respondent. Respondents entered these directly into the database through a web-server (around 12-15 per organization, so of the order of 52x15 of these in total). The quantitative variables captured here ranged from 55 to 140 per survey, depending on the role of the respondent.

- Coded interviews undertaken by the researcher (around 10-12 per organization, so of the order of 52x10 of these in total). Around 100 quantitative variables were captured per interview.

- Research observations summarizing the whole company (from the researcher's view) (52 of these). This had many hundreds of data points, although many of these were multiple-choice check-points.

- Organizational data, data collected by the organisation, presumably filled in by the person responsible for the project management implementation, and therefore giving the organization's view of what was implemented and how it was implemented (52 of these). Around 340 variables were collected per observation, although a number of these were textual.

- Project Information, giving details of projects. This could in principal be anything from 0 to 60 projects per organization. However, the data collected here was very sparse, and what data was there tended to come from a small number of research teams. Given both the skew of the data within the case studies and the sparseness of many of the project summaries that were completed, most of this data was not used for this analysis, other than two sets of variables describing the degree to which the projects were considered to have delivered on various criteria, plus the risk/value ratings of the projects. Around 40 variables were collected per project.

The data was defined by a data dictionary that was developed to define the constructs, their sources, their variable names and their meanings. This dictionary ran to over 2,500 defined variables.

It is important to recognize that this is a vast amount of data from any single organization. While it was hoped that most of the data could be collected from most of the organizations, each individual case organization was able to provide different degrees of the data we sought. As a result, even though the majority of the instruments described above were collected from most case-study organizations, not every instrument was fully complete. The consequence is that for any given item or variable, there may be some organizations that did not provide a response or where the response was not in a usable form.

While there were a total of 65 case studies that were completed, there were 52 substantially complete case studies ultimately included in the frozen dataset that was used for analysis purposes, but some data did exist in some form for a total of 60 case studies. The result of different elements being missing from different cases, however, means that for each analysis the number of organizations reflected in any analysis (represented by "n") may not in fact be 60, or even 52, cases.

METHODS

Introduction

As was stated in Chapter 3, "the sheer volume of data created in a research project of this magnitude [was] overwhelming." However, the analysis workshop described in Chapter 3 developed a plan which subsequently formed the basis for the majority of the quantitative analysis work. Given the sheer magnitude of data that has been collected by this study, this will of necessity be a preliminary analysis of the data, focused specifically upon answering the research questions that the study posed. Further analysis will continue over coming months and years, but what is presented here certainly establishes the basic implications and findings of the data.

Core questions that were identified during the analysis workshop as being needed to be addressed and answered by the quantitative analysis include the following:

How do we measure implementation?

Implementation *(I)* is measured by multiple data points (e.g., software, practices, training, etc.) as per the project management constructs. Reduction of dimensionality is required using the hierarchy within the project management constructs. Using factor and/or principal components analysis, we were able to identify "types" of implementation efforts across organizations.

How do we measure context?

Context *(C)* is a problematic measure with a limited number of data points available, as there were many missing data items in the organizational spreadsheet that organizations were asked to complete. Where the data was missing, case leads were asked wherever possible to provide this information from further research and their own experience in the organization, if at all possible.

How do we measure value?

In looking at the Value construct *(V)*, we found that there were two natural ways to differentiate between value measurements. First, Levels 1 and 2 report on perceptual measures of satisfaction and alignment of practises. Levels 3, 4, and 5 include measures of both intangible and tangible benefits. We originally thought that the tangible benefits could not only be identified and defined but hopefully quantified as well. Through our data collection, we quickly realized that while these benefits were theoretically quantifiable, few of our organizations had the background data necessary to calculate hard dollar values for either benefits or costs. Thus, our approaches to how we would deal with Levels 1 and 2 value largely proceeded as expected. Our approaches to dealing with Levels 3, 4, and 5 needed some creative revisions.

Data points were identified and easily collected for each of value Levels 1 and 2. As with Implementation above, we needed to construct composite variables from the relevant data items to use in further analysis. We decided to try a number of approaches to data reduction in this construct, including: Picking most important; looking at variability within cases (include measures of agreement tables–but we have asymmetry); and principal component analysis. These steps were conducted after the descriptive analysis was reviewed to determine the most appropriate approaches. Ultimately, we sought to identify constructed variables for these two levels of value that provide some degree of variability across cases. For instance, at the simplest level, our cases may be categorized by their Level-1 satisfaction with project management currently implemented. It could also be possible to subdivide the sample into groups that were largely satisfied, largely unsatisfied, or neutral to the project management implementation, and look for differences in the benefits and value reported.

Many of the data items identified for each of value Levels 3 and 4 were available in only some organizations. In all organizations, we needed to correlate them to check validity. In particular, the project data we expected to use for measurements of project process outcome improvements was difficult to collect in many case-study organizations. The problem was that while many of them had good data since they implemented project management, their pre-implementation performance on past projects was sketchy at best. All levels of the organization perceived significant project performance improvement, but verifying these perceptions based on the project data was not possible. Therefore, in many cases we had to rely on perceptual indications that these types of benefits had been realized. We proposed that where there was consistent recognition of the benefit being realized from many informants, we could feel confident in its assertion. Qualitative analysis of the value statements derived from each case-study interview provided another triangulation point for this type of data.

We always anticipated that Level 5 value measures would need to be constructed. The value statements are likely to provide the first indication that ROI benefits are reported for each case. The next step was to attempt to quantify the ROI benefit recognized by the organization. To do this, we worked with organizational participants to identify specific costs and benefits and attempted to quantify them in a meaningful fashion. We did not find many organizations where good data was available to calculate ROI for project management investments. Many more organizational participants reported a strongly held belief that their project management implementation provided good return for the money invested than were able to even partially provide data to calculate it.

How is value related to context, implementation, and fit?

Regression of value on context and implementation on context gives some explanation of the degree to which context and implementation influence value. First steps were single regressions, followed by multiple regression analyses. Ultimately, an evolution of thinking about what is represented by "fit" (see Chapter 9) has precluded a more detailed exploration of the relations between value and fit, but this additional analysis is planned. We also expect to use structural equation modeling to understand the relationships between these constructs in greater detail in future analysis.

Plan Approach

Key to the plan for conducting the qualitative analysis was that this was to be an exploratory data analysis: there were no pre-conceptions about results before going into the analysis. Instead, the analysis process was geared towards looking for patterns and relationships within the data. This followed the general approach described in the section of Chapter 3 entitled "A Process for Collaborative Theory Generation Grounded in Data."

All data was included at the start of the analysis, and it was hoped that the use of multiple data sources would contribute to the robustness of the analysis and provide for the necessary triangulation of the data. As described in Chapter 3, the study was "designed to include a wide array of perspectives in order to be able to triangulate results through more than one instrument or assessment technique. In this manner, not only should we be able to increase the likelihood of statistically valid correlations and qualitatively rigorous relationships being identified, but also that the correlations and relationships are relevant and defensible across multiple perspectives and inputs" (p. 44).

The main method used was, therefore, Principal Components Analysis (PCA). This is a standard dimension reduction technique used where there are many inter-correlated variables. There are multiple textbooks on this technique, such as Everitt and Dunn (2001), or an older but authoritative one by Chatfield and Collins (1980). All variables are regarded as equal. The technique produces new variables, which are linear combinations of the original variables, such that first, the new variables are orthogonal (thus with zero correlation), and second, the first new variable explains as much of the variance as possible, the second variable explains the next most variance as possible, and so on. Thus, the first principal component is that linear combination of the original variables with the maximum variance, given that the sum of the squares of the coefficients is 1; the second principal component is that linear combination of the original variables with the maximum variance, given that the sum of the squares of the coefficients is 1 and such that it and the first principal component are uncorrelated, and so on. Note that the technique does not postulate an existent latent variable, rather it is exploratory. Put in simple terms, variables that tended to vary together, whether positively or negatively, would be grouped together, with that group of variables explaining the greatest degree of data being selected first. Once the first component was identified, additional components that varied together but were not correlated to the first component were then sought and identified.

The analyses were carried out in SPSS version 16.0. This gives various important outputs, but the three immediately relevant here are:

- "Component Matrices," giving the coefficients of the standardized variables in the equation for the standardized principal components (i.e., the correlations between the variables and the principal components). These show which variables were strongly weighted in the components, and enabled interpretation of the components. Generally, in explaining each component, we looked for values of 0.5 or above in these matrices; occasionally, when going into third- or fourth-level components, values became smaller and we sometimes relaxed this to look at values between 0.45 and 0.5 in order to interpret the components, particularly in evaluating the Construct-level PCAs as discussed later in this section.

- It gives a "Scree Plot", showing the relative amount of variance explained by each principal component. Figure 5-1, for example, shows the Scree Plot for the initial PCA of the 140 "Tools" variables. It shows that the first principal component has an Eigenvalue of 37, explaining 26.5% (=37/140) of the variance on its own; the next components have Eigenvalues of 10.5 and 8.5, respectively explaining 7.5% and 6% of the variance. Using these three variables alone would therefore explain 40% of the variance. The Scree Plot was particularly useful to inform decisions regarding how many components to select, together with the other PCA outputs discussed, based on:

  o Accepted guidelines for looking for discriminating components, including where Eigenvalues are above 1.0 or a sharp bend appears in the Scree Plot.

  o Pragmatic judgments about how much variance could be explained with only around 50 cases.

  o Recognition that beyond the level that was used, interpretability would become increasingly difficult.

- Non-standardized principal component scores are calculated for use in later analysis.

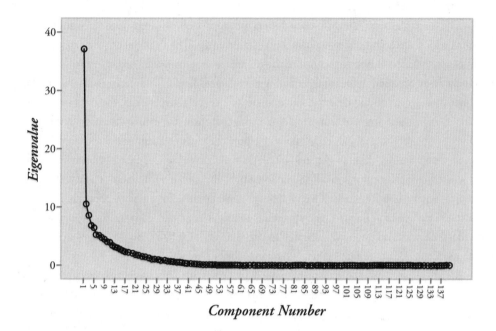

FIGURE 5-1—*SPSS scree plot*

Having reduced the dimensionality of the data, we could then explore the patterns within the reduced-dimensionality variables, by use of regressions between the constructs and cluster analyses within the constructs (see again Chatfield & Collins [1980] and Everitt & Dunn [2001]).

Plan Detail

In order to get an initial handle on the data, the analysis started with the structure in the data dictionary. This defined variables within

- Construct (context, project management implementation and value)

- Dimension (taking these three constructs into a lower level of detail)

- Criteria (taking the dimensions into a lower level of detail).

For example, the Project Management Implementation construct was divided into six dimensions: history, organizational infrastructure, people, practices, tools, and training; similarly, the practices dimension was divided into organization, portfolio management, program management, project management, project delivery, resource management, tools, and value realization. This classification followed the definition of variables developed in the mind maps described in the "Preparation for Analysis

Workshop" section of Chapter 3, which were the result of the development of the instruments over the previous workshops.

The use of a multi-method data collection approach resulted in the production of a number of different survey tools and instruments. This influenced the structure of the data produced. Therefore, data management was required in order to produce data that could subsequently be analyzed in a meaningful form. The main issue pertaining to data management was that for some forms of survey instruments, the data produced resulted in either single observations per organization or multiple observations per organization. As the analyses relied heavily upon the combination of data from different survey instruments, data structures with multiple observations per organization were aggregated using functions in SPSS version 16.0, and mean values were obtained before merging with the other data. This again was a pragmatically simple approach with the limited time available; a stronger approach would have been to have incorporated the standard deviations of views, or better to use the work by Wittkowski, Lee, Nussbaum, Chamian, and Krueger (2004) to show variability of views.

Missing data and the techniques used to deal with this were an important issue during analysis. Some of the survey instruments had large amounts of missing data for certain questions and for particular organizations. Therefore, informed decisions were made regarding the methods used to cope with the lack of data. For example, when there was a large amount of data missing for an organization, the organization was not included in the analysis. When there was not a large amount of missing data, missing values were replaced with the mean, as other strategies to deal with missing data would have resulted in the loss of a significant amount of data. When a large amount of data was missing for particular questions, then the likely outcome was that variable(s) were omitted.

Finally, a few data items which were essentially scoring data (e.g., tick-box variables with Likert-like headings such as "very poor, poor, . . .") were consolidated into single variables, with the individual options converted to scores.

Then each dimension of each construct was subjected to a PCA, and an appropriate number of components selected for each. Nineteen components in all were selected for the context construct, 19 for the Implementation construct, and 15 components for the value construct.

Taking the 19 components of the implementation construct as an example, these consist of seven sets of components, corresponding to the seven dimensions noted above. The seven dimensions were constructed by the project team as sensible ways in which to think about "implementation" but did not have empirical basis. Furthermore, the 19 variables are still likely to have inter-correlation (even though variables are uncorrelated within the six sets)–indeed, the discussion in Chapter 9 will show the intercorrelations between components within each construct, and identify some interesting relationships.

Even at this stage of analysis, however, 19 variables are still difficult to interpret or characterize. The next step therefore was to carry out PCAs of these components, giving clear characteristic components covering the whole of each construct. Each of these Construct-level PCAs, and the Variable-level PCAs and components on which they are based, are described in detail in Chapters 6, 7, and 8, which identify the findings associated with each major construct within this study.

At this point, we have identified the main characteristics within the implementation of project management, the context, and the value found. The next step is clearly to look for relationships between the constructs: to what extent are the components of implementation dependent upon context, or to what extent is the value found (in its different components) to be dependent upon implementation? The standard method to use here is linear regression. The main decision to make is the method used to choose the independent variables to incorporate. We used backwards elimination, where all variables are initially used in the regression calculation, and then removed one by one. The method looks first at the variable with the smallest partial correlation with the dependent variable. If it meets certain criteria, it is removed. Then the variable remaining with the smallest partial correlation is considered, and so on until no remaining variables satisfy the criteria. All variables remaining are, therefore, having an important effect in the regression equation, and of interest is not only the coefficients and (particularly) their signs, but also which variables actually made it to the final equation.

It should be noted here that there is significant potential for multi-colinearity caused by covariance of many of the input variables in these regressions. The most significant impact multi-colinearity could have in this analysis would be to create spurious relationships and possibly mask other significant relationships. In this first exploratory analysis, we chose to use the backwards elimination technique and then to cross-check all significant relationships with other qualitative and quantitative analyses to ensure that the relationships discussed were not spurious. Further, more sophisticated regression analysis will be conducted in the future to ensure that all of these potential relationships are teased out.

Constructing Project Management Value Scales

This section, and the analysis discussed here, was contributed by Dr. Thomas Lechler

The first step after exploratory analysis of the data is to identify and build a valid set of measures for the underlying constructs. A primary focus in this part of the analysis was to maximize the construct validity of scales associated with value. Ultimately, the purpose of scale construction is to design a questionnaire that provides a quantitative measurement of an abstract theoretical variable. This section provides a minimal introduction to the approaches used in scale development and details the methods used in this study for developing value scales. This portion of the analysis is largely aimed at developing quantitative measures for future use in large-scale survey explorations of value. However, the scales and their interpretations provide useful descriptions of the cases described in this monograph and help in theory generation.

Good scales possess both *validity* and *reliability*. A scale has validity if it properly represents the theoretical construct it is meant to measure. A scale has reliability if repeated measurements under the same circumstances tend to produce the same results. Validity and reliability are independent of each other. Validity is often thought of as the "accuracy" of the scale while reliability is its "precision." Scales that lack validity have systematic biases to them, while those that lack reliability have large random errors associated with their measurement. Obviously, a scale should be as valid and reliable as possible.

Project management research has traditionally been criticized for poor theory development and for lacking methodological rigor in measurement studies (Meredith, 2004). As with other disciplines, it is also clear that theoretically well-founded and rigorously developed construct operationalizations are a prerequisite for the beginning of a cumulative tradition. In spite of the importance of measurement development, which is vital to any empirical research study (Froehle & Roth, 2004), much project management research continues to lack rigorous development procedures as well as reliable and valid scales inventories. So far, few comprehensive scales inventories exist to measure constructs of interest in project management research and none exist to measure the value project management delivers to organizations. Such instruments, if valid and reliable, are vital to allowing empirical studies on project management to build on prior research and begin to build a consolidated empirical foundation for the field.

The first stage of scale creations is *item creation*, whose purpose is to create pools of candidate items for each relevant concept of interest. In constructing the data collection instruments for this research, we wanted to be sure that we collected more than one answer for each construct of interest. Thus we developed a moderately large number of items to measure each single construct. Wherever possible, we borrowed existing scales from published research to measure constructs of interest (for instance, we used published scales for measuring professional attitudes). The items within a scale were designed to be *interchangeable*, meaning that the response to one item has exactly the same theoretical meaning as the response to any other item within the scale. Each item was designed to be a different way to "ask" about the same theoretical variable. Some questions were written so that more positive responses indicate less of the variable in question (i.e., reverse coding), but we would expect that the magnitude of the correlations between items (whether positive or negative) would be relatively high throughout a scale.

The next stage involved *instrument testing*, whose purpose is to identify from the pool of candidate items a set of reliable and valid items to be used in later empirical studies. In our case this stage involved collecting data on all the items identified for all of the case studies in this study.

The final stage is *scale development*, whose purpose is to sort the candidate items into meaningful separate concept categories to display construct, convergent and discriminant validity (Moore & Benbasat, 1991). This stage consists of two steps, item identification and substrata identification. The goal in selecting scale items is unidimensionality, rather than internal consistency; this means that virtually all inter-item correlations should be moderate in magnitude. Factor analysis can play a crucial role in ensuring the unidimensionality and discriminant validity of scales, and did so in our analysis.

In total, 21 value scales are discussed in this monograph, including all different levels and perspectives of value coding. The scale development was implemented in two steps. These were based on individual responses (from both interviews and surveys), and not on aggregated responses on the unit level.

The first step was conducted with principal components analysis (described above) to test the dimensionality of the scale (face and convergence validity). The second step was conducted with Cronbach Alphas to test the scale's reliability. All scales fulfill the following criteria:

Factor Analysis (PCA):

- Kaiser-Mayer-Olkin: >0.8 (of course, not for two item "scales")

- Communalities of each item > 50% (e.g., factor loading >0.7, although in some rare cases a lower tolerance was allowed, depending on the reliability analysis)

- Explained variance >50% (in most cases over 60%; some scales could be improved marginally by deleting specific items).

Cronbach's Alpha (Scale Variance Analysis)

- Alpha should be clearly >0.75 (Some scales had to be accepted on this level due to low number of responses, etc. Most scales are >0.8 or >0.9).

Based on these tests, some items had to be removed. Due to the nature of the data collection for this phase, there are still many missing values, and in the aggregated data file representing the unit level, we have at best 51 cases and at worst 6 cases for our analysis.

Aggregation was conducted in several steps.

- For each respondent a scale value was calculated (please see definitions below)

- The scale values for each respondent group (project managers, customers, employees, suppliers, and subcontractors) were aggregated (averaged) to represent a scale value for each individual organization.

- The aggregated scale values for all respondent groups were merged in a single file, allowing the comparison ratings from different groups or perspectives. At the time of the monograph publication, much of this analysis is still preliminary. Many variables are not yet normal-distributed. Some adjustments to kurtosis and skew will have to be made in final scales.

The instrument development research outlined in this chapter and the scales discussed in Chapter 8 provide several important contributions to the field of project management over and above the interpretations they provide for this study. First and foremost, rigorously creating an overall scales inventory to measure the perceptions of the value delivered by project management implementations improves the capacity of the project management field to research and understand how value is created. The procedure described ensures high levels of confidence in construct and content validity of the scales. The method employed in this research has been found both helpful and rigorous and should motivate researchers to adopt this design in related empirical studies. The results obtained (i.e., the resulting value scales inventory) can now be used in various studies to investigate how value can be measured in research and practice.

Some words of caution are also appropriate here. The scales inventory development process described in this section is not yet complete. Without testing the overall scales on a large scale sample, only initial indications of reliability and validity could be obtained. However, the work to date contributes significantly by reporting on rigorous procedures of empirical study design and providing a foundation for future research in this area. A second noted limitation is related to the fact that our instrument development drew heavily on existing frameworks and theories related to value realization and thus potentially lacks other endogenous constructs that may pose relevance to the context of project management value realization. Researchers working in this area thus have to carefully decide whether or not to consider such factors in addition to the ones discussed here.

Multiple Analysis Of Variance (MANOVA)

This section, and the analysis discussed here, was contributed by Dr. Merlyn Foo

MANOVA highlights the main and interactive effects of categorical variables on multiple dependent interval variables. Using one or more categorical independents as predictors and more than one dependent variable, MANOVA analysis tests the hypotheses that there is no difference among the means of groups of variables on a particular data item.

There are multiple potential purposes for using MANOVA. In our case we chose to use MANOVA to compare groups of organizations categorized by how strongly they are described by the context, implementation or value components identified through PCA in an earlier analysis.

This analysis allows us to examine whether the differences we observe in the means of organizations' responses to certain sets of questions are statistically significant by testing for the significance of differences among categories or groupings of multiple dependent variables, whereby the groupings are based on categories of independent variables. In our case, the independent variables are grouped as follows:

- Group 1 = case studies with independent variable values in the bottom third of range of data.

- Group 2 = case studies with independent variable values in the middle third of the range of data.

- Group 3 = case studies with independent variable values in the top third of the range of data.

This analysis is conducted on the impacts of objectives and motivators for the implementation of project management, and is assessed against two sets of variables introduced in later chapters: implementation components (Chapter 7) and value components (Chapter 8).

Dummy variables are constructed based on the grouping criteria outlined above for each variable of interest. Thus, for each independent variable, each case study is assigned a value of 1, 2, or 3 depending on whether its independent variable value is in the bottom, middle or top third of the data for that variable. For example, if case study 36 has an Impl 1 value that is in the top third of the means of Impl 1, it is assigned a value of 3 in the new dummy variable for Impl 1.

MANOVA is then performed on the context and implementation components using the dependent value construct variables.

The MANOVA test results tell us if the different groupings produce significantly different effects on the dependent variables. F-tests are used for this purpose, and the traditional test to use when there are more than two groups formed by the independent variables is Wilks' lambda. We chose to interpret any difference that is statistically significant at the 0.05 level and has an observed power of greater than 0.9 (which gives us confidence in the significance of our results). The partial eta squared gives us an indication of the proportion of the total variability in the dependent variable explained by the variation in the independent variable.

Regression Analysis

Regression analysis is most often used to produce an equation that will predict a dependent variable using one or more independent variables.

However, it can also be used as an exploratory technique to help a researcher understand how the significant independent variables influence the dependent variables. When it is used in this way, researchers are not sure there is a relationship between the dependent and independent variables, and use a technique called step-wise regression to test which variables are influential.

Step-wise regression is used in the exploratory phase of research for the purposes of understanding how the data is correlated, as well as for theory generation. In stage one, the independent variable best correlated with the dependent variable is included in the equation. In the second stage, the next remaining independent variable with the highest partial correlation with the dependent, controlling for the first independent variable, is entered. This process is repeated until the addition of a remaining independent variable does not increase R-squared by a significant amount (or until all variables are entered, of course). Alternatively, the process can work backward, starting with all variables and eliminating independent variables one at a time until the elimination of one makes a significant difference in R-squared. Backward step-wise regression is used here to help us identify the implementation and context variables that are most correlated with the value-dependent variables.

We recognize that there are some controversies associated with using step-wise regression in terms of its potential to possibly overstate R-squared, as well as its potential to include lenient significance tests. However, as we are still in the process of exploring the data, and are using this exploration in order to generalize to the point of being able to produce theories for further testing in future more targeted statistical analysis, these methods provide means solid analysis of the case study data set in its present form. With this in mind, the reader is asked to read the statistics provided with an understanding of their limitations, while reviewing this interpretation.

P values and Statistical Significance

The P value is the probability of seeing a result as extreme as the one you are getting (a t value as large as reported) in a collection of random data in which the variable had no effect. A P value of 5% or less is the generally accepted point at which to reject the null hypothesis, or say that the results represent meaningful differences and are therefore representative of meaningful differences between the samples. With a P value of 5% (or 0.05), there is only a 5% chance that results you are seeing would have come up in a random distribution, so you can say with a 95% probability of being correct that the variable is having some effect, assuming your model is specified correctly. In most cases we use this cut-off. For a very few analyses we loosen this requirement to a 10% chance of the analysis coming from random results in order to highlight some interesting potential results that will require further data collection but deserve further study in the future.

Coefficients

In multiple linear regressions, the size of the coefficient for each independent variable gives you the size of the effect that variable is having on the dependent variable. The sign on the coefficient (positive or negative) gives you the direction of the effect. In multiple linear regression, the coefficient on each variable is the amount that the dependent variable would change for a unit change of 1 in the independent variable, holding all other variables constant. In other words, a coefficient of 0.25 means that for every change of 1 in the independent variable, the dependent variable would also increase by 0.25.

R-Squared and overall significance of the regression

The R-squared of the regression is the fraction of the variation in the dependent variable that is accounted for (or predicted by) your independent variables. The R-squared is generally only of primary interest if your main concern is using the regression equation to make accurate predictions. If the important thing is to recognize the correlation of the independent variable with the dependent variable, the P value is really more important as it tells you how confident you can be that each individual variable has some correlation with the dependent variable.

R-square is a tricky statistic. It has been known to artificially inflate the amount of variance explained when more variables are included in the final regression result. For this reason, there is also a variable known as the adjusted R-squared, which adjusts for the number of independent variables included in the regression equation. This is identified for each of the regressions discussed here.

CONCLUSIONS

While the main results are reported in forthcoming chapters, some work is currently ongoing and not yet completed. In particular this includes:

- A key data element which needs more explanation is the match between those elements of implementation actually carried out and those espoused in the organization but not observed by the researchers in actuality. Some initial analysis has been undertaken of these variables, but it is not mature enough to report here.

- All of this chapter has dealt with analysis of the quantitative data, while a separate chapter has dealt with analysis of the qualitative data. Chapter 3 has already stated that "mixed-method approaches are particularly prized for their ability to use both triangulation of data and method" (Jack & Raturi, 2006), and this report brings many aspects of these two sides together. However, an important next step is formally to bring quantitative and qualitative analyses together to leverage the maximum benefit from the data. Part of our strategy to do so is reflected in the following chapters. The next three chapters present the results for each construct, and Chapter 9 presents a discussion of the drivers of value that have emerged from this study. Each chapter integrates both the quantitative and qualitative results to provide a multi-method view of each construct as well as of the results of the study.

6

Context

Introduction

The objective of understanding the context of organizations is to explore the environments in which they are situated, and how the organizations structure themselves to respond to these environments. The exploration of context was a conscious effort to go beyond simply understanding what organizations implemented that they called project management, but why they implemented it. The conceptual model and research approach recognized that there were strong differences in how project management was implemented that needed to be understood. It was also speculated that these differences in context and implementation would have a strong influence on what value would ultimately be realized.

To understand context, then, it was necessary to explore the attributes of organization that went beyond what was done in terms of projects, and to explore how the organizations functioned at an overall level, in response to their internal strategies and their external environments.

There were two core questions that we sought to address in understanding context:

- How do organizations differ?

- What differences matter to project management implementations?

The following sections outline what was identified about the organizations we studied within our case studies, and situates them based upon their overall organizational attributes, in order to answer these questions.

Demographic Differences

In total, 65 organizations participated in this study. Unfortunately we cannot name these organizations. In return for access to sensitive and proprietary information, all of these organizations were guaranteed anonymity. However, if we could name them, you would recognize most of them. Many are global organizations. No matter where you are in the world, you drink their beer, use their computer systems, use computers built of their components, talk on their phone systems, take their drugs, work in their buildings, fill up with their gasoline. Some are near the top of their field, whether that is banking , engineering, or research. Some are regional examples of organizations found the world over, including government agencies, IT departments in large organizations, regional health authorities, national banks, engineering or IT consultants, or large construction firms. A small number are relatively small and/or relatively new to project management. Overall, the one thing all these organizations have in common is an interest in project management that leads them to donate significant time and effort to a research project of this nature.

In conducting the study, our goal was to include wide geographic participation from organizations that do projects:

- for customers

- to support their "real" business or function

- to develop new products or services, or to undertake research and development activities.

At the same time, we actively sought out similar organizations from different regional locations in order to facilitate comparisons across regions and cultures. Thus, we include in our study two national banks, five government infrastructure organizations, construction companies from four regions, and four large telecom providers. We also include IT shops embedded within large organizations situated in various regions.

The data in this section describes the organizations that were included in the research. This information is provided to help you understand the reliability of the findings, as well as the generalizability of the research to your own particular situation. The data presented here provides a simplified overview of the organizations included in the study. The research findings and conclusions in the remainder of this document are based on more detailed information gained from an investigation of case projects, the people involved in them, both throughout and external to the organizations, and researcher observations.

Size of Organizations

The smallest organization in our sample has only 15 employees and serves a relatively small geographic region. The largest employs over 100,000 employees around the world with annual revenues in the tens of billions. The average number of employees per case organization is 6,260.

Ownership Structure

Organizations participating in this study have a wide range of ownership structures, as depicted in Figure 6-1. The majority of the organizations studied are privately held corporations (29%), followed by government departments or agencies (23%), publicly traded corporations (16%), crown corporations (12%), limited partnerships (10%), sole proprietorships (6%), and joint ventures (4%).

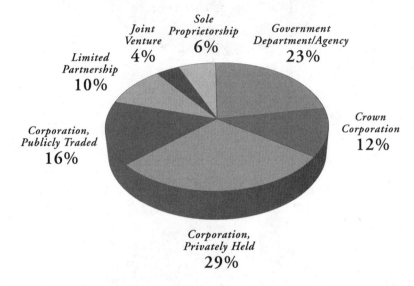

FIGURE 6-1—*Ownership structure of case organizations*

Organizational Structure

Case organizations represent a wide assortment of organizational structures, as shown in Figure 6-2. Just over one-third of the organizations are operationally structured (35%) in a traditional functional sense. Another third of the organizations are what we would call project driven (31%) with the organizational structure explicitly designed to accommodate project work. The final third is split between organizations that adopt a weak matrix (22%) or a strong matrix (12%) structure.

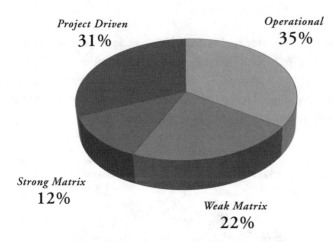

Project Driven
31%

Operational
35%

Strong Matrix
12%

Weak Matrix
22%

FIGURE 6-2—*Organizational structure of case organizations*

Regional Distribution

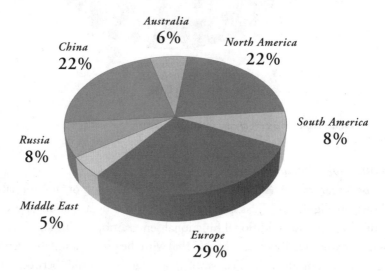

Australia
6%

China
22%

North America
22%

South America
8%

Russia
8%

Middle East
5%

Europe
29%

FIGURE 6-3—*Regional distribution of case organizations*

The regional distribution of the organizations participating (Figure 6-3) shows that we have a fairly comprehensive geographic coverage. Most of the organizations in the study originate in Europe (29%), followed by North America (22%) and China (22%). The rest of the organizations come from Russia (8%), South America (8%), Australia (6%), and the Middle East (5%).

Why this distribution, you might ask, especially as it does not reflect PMI's current membership? The answer, as we discussed in Chapter 3, is that this sample was chosen on a theoretical sampling basis to provide us with the distribution of organizations that will most fully describe what is happening with respect to project management the world over today. Thus, while it may not represent the current population, it does reflect the PMI membership growth rates and project activity levels in these various regions today.

Europe (29%) came to be the largest site of cases for two reasons. First, Europe is made up of a very large number of culturally diverse countries, many of which show a relatively high level of development in terms of the management of projects (as exemplified by cases in our study from the U.K., Norway, Sweden, Denmark, and Germany). Second, at the same time, Europe also includes a number of recent additions to the economic union that struggle with quite different challenges of emerging economies and economic reform (as exemplified by our Serbian and Lithuanian case studies).

North America (22%) is widely recognized as the origin of the academic study of project management and traditionally represents the largest share of PMI's membership (70% as of Dec 2007). Thus, it was important for the study to broadly cover representative organizations in this region. Note here that North America is represented solely by Canada and the United States. No case studies were conducted in Mexico.

China (22% of our cases) has only 358 PMI members as of December 2007. However, this is largely due to Chinese government restrictions on joining foreign professional associations. Other indicators of project management's importance in the region suggest that this region warrants the attention we paid to it in this study. Over the five years ending December 2007, the average annual growth in numbers of PMP credential holders in China was 67%, for a total of almost 20,000. At the same time, 103 schools in China are now providing masters degrees in engineering project management, reportedly the most popular and competitive masters program in China with 17,000 applicants annually. Finally, there are more large-scale projects (railroads, pipelines, airports, harbors) underway in China today than anywhere else in the world. By 2030, China will have built more new roads than the entire US highway system and have added one U.K.'s worth of electricity generating capacity. In fact, Chinese capital projects are driving a shortage of construction steel in North America today. At the same time that all these capital projects are underway, the Chinese economy is growing at a phenomenal rate, and along with it every other type of business project discussed here. Project management is huge in China and growing in importance rapidly.

Russia (8%), South America (8%) and Middle East (5%) are all rapidly growing economies with strong growth in both projects and interest in project management. Australia (6%) is a unique case example in its own right, as Australia has implemented national occupational standards and testing for project managers. This is a relatively unique government stance on project management that warrants including case studies in the sample.

Finally we should note the major omissions in case study collection. No case studies were collected in either Africa or India despite our best efforts to encourage case researchers from these regions. Their omission in no way indicates a judgment on their level of project activity or project management development, but simply comments on our inability to find researchers to cover these regions in a timely manner. Thus, study of these regions remains for future research.

Industry Distribution

Most of the case organizations in our study come from Construction (20%), followed by government (16%), high technology (14%), manufacturing (14%), research (13%), services (12%), and consulting (11%). On the basis of face validity, these certainly appear to be the industries you would expect to be included in a study of project management, and we have achieved a fairly even distribution among them.

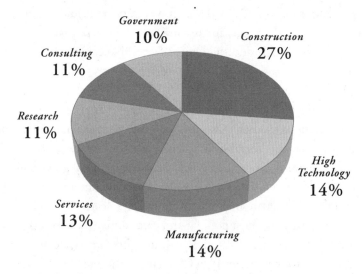

FIGURE 6-4—*Distribution of case organizations by industry*

In order to justify generalizations from a sample in quantitative terms, however, we must be able to justify that the sample is representative of organizations in the general population of organizations interested in project management. One way to check that our sample is generally representative is to compare the proportion of each industry grouping we have to the proportion of industry groupings represented in PMI's membership. This is, however, a bit more tricky than one might expect, as many PMI members identify more than one industry. Looking at the PMI data it appears that this happens most often when one is an IT professional working in an organization operating in another industry. Even if we adjust for this double counting, however, we still encounter some double counting of industries in the PMI data. However, it is likely closer to being comparable. The comparison allowing that adjustment is shown in Table 6-1.

Industry Grouping	PMI Membership	Our Sample
Construction	*14%*	*20%*
High Technology	*24%*	*14%*
Manufacturing	*19%*	*14%*
Services	*14%*	*12%*
Research	*7%*	*13%*
Consulting	*15%*	*11%*
Government	*6%*	*16%*

TABLE 6-1—*Comparing PMI membership and case study industry distributions*

Our sample slightly over-represents construction, research, and government and under-represents high technology, manufacturing, services, and consulting as compared to the PMI membership data. Given that the world is seeing the largest construction boom since the mid 20th century, and that PMI traditionally does not draw membership proportionally from the construction project management world, we would still assert that this sample is generalizable to organizations interested in project management today.

By Project Type

Another way of describing our case organizations is by the type of project they engage in. Only 48 organizations from our sample provided this information (see Figure 6-5).

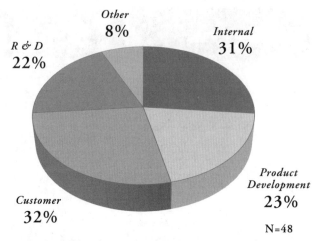

15 companies indicated 100% involvement in one type of project.

FIGURE 6-5—*Distribution of case organizations by project type*

Dividing the project types, we see the proportions of our case organizations that conduct the following types of projects: projects delivered for customers (32%), internal projects (31%), product development (23%), research and development (22%), and other (8%). While 15 organizations report engaging in only one type of project, the rest of our case organizations manage at least two types of projects.

Another way of describing the types of projects our case organizations engage in, by business project type, is depicted in Figure 6-6.

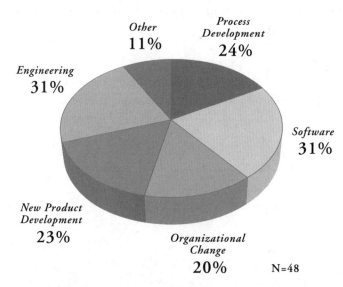

15 companies indicated 100% involvement in one type of project.

FIGURE 6-6—*Distribution of case study organizations by business project type*

Almost one-third of the organizations (31%) engage in software and engineering projects. Organizational change projects are reported by 28% of the organizations. Process development projects (24%) and new product development (23%) are the next most common type of projects. Again, 11% of organizations report engaging in some other type of project.

People

Another way to describe the organizations in the sample is to describe the people that work in these organizations. Here we look at two important characteristics of these employees: their education level and their project and project management experience.

Education

Table 6-2 summarizes the education levels of employees in the case studies. Education information was available for 40 organizations. On average, a high proportion (approximately 58%) of employees in these companies had a higher than college/university degree level of education.

%	Some High School	High School Diploma	Some College/ University	Certificate/ Licence	College/ University Degree	Some Graduate Education	Graduate Degree	Doctorate
Avg	5.4%	13.4%	11.9%	11.9%	34.5%	5.4%	14.6%	2.9%
min	0%	0%	0%	0%	0%	0%	0%	0%
max	84.0%	71.4%	95.7%	50.0%	78.8%	43.8%	94%	45.2%

TABLE 6-2—*Comparing education distributions for case study organizations*

Analysis for each case study is also possible. For example, in Case Study 17, 50% of the employees possesses a certificate or license, 30% have a college or university degree, and 20% have a graduate degree.

Project Management Experience

Another way to describe each case organization is by the average project management and average Project experience of their employees. On average, the employees in these case studies have about 8.5 years of project management or project experience, ±4.5 years. Three large organizations in an emerging economy (a national bank, a government department, and an IT consulting company) that are very early in their project management implementation reported the minimum average years (two) of either project or project management experience. One organization, one of the top 10 telecom services providers in the world, reported an average project experience of 18.5 years and project management experience of 16.5 years.

CONTEXTUAL SIMILARITIES

What Data Is Available?

In evaluating the contextual similarities that exist among organizations represented within the case studies, the first challenge is to understand the data that is available to help describe the contextual factors.

The structure of the data that emerged from the conceptual model provides an initial framework for this analysis. The data constructs associated with context comprised a number of different views of the case study organizations, reflected in the following summary:

- **Economic.** The economic aspects of the organization explored the overall economic environment in which the case studies operate. Specifically, this dimension explored a number of economic variables, including gross domestic product, current account balance, and inflation rate. This information was consistently sourced using the CIA World Fact Book.

- **People.** The people aspects of the organizational context explored the core demographics of the people working within the organization, including number of staff, age, years of service, and education. The people attributes also considered an understanding of the competency of staff within the organization, as well as the typical workload and typical turnover of staff. Finally, the data explored the extent that staff were familiar with working in project management or working within a project environment.

- **Cultural Aspects.** The cultural aspects of context captured within the case study investigation strategy focus heavily on an understanding of the overall culture that exists within the organization. This includes an understanding of decision-making, collaboration, leadership and power structures within the organization as a whole. From a project-specific perspective, this also included an exploration of the perceptions of projects and project work within the organization, and the attitudes towards project managers and project management. This included an understanding of the degree to which professional attitudes were evidenced in the organization, including personal development responsibility and a focus on continuing to improve their personal practices as well as those of the organizations they serve.

- **Projects.** The project aspects of organizational context explored the role that projects play within the organization. This included an understanding of the kinds of work done as projects within the organization, the types of projects the organization conducts and the numbers of projects that are started, delivered and cancelled in a year. As well, the project attributes included an understanding of the priorities associated with project success and the drivers of projects within the organization.

- **Organizational Attributes.** The organizational attributes within the case studies explored specific demographic information. This includes an understanding of the size, structure, ownership, and project structure the organization adopted. As well, the strategy of the organization, and the means of realizing these strategies, including investment in staff, attitude to innovation and commitment to developing new products and services, is explored. Finally, the other initiatives being undertaken within the organization in parallel with the project management implementation, including improvement activities like 6 Sigma, ISO 9000, total quality management, restructuring, supply chain management, and the implementation of enterprise resource planning solutions, is examined.

- **Strategic.** The strategic aspects of the organization explored the nature of the strategies of the organization and how these influence both the projects that are conducted and how project management is approached. We also explored the customer focus of the organization, including the number of customers and customer turnover, customer satisfaction, and the number of customer complaints.

What Contextual Components Emerged?

The structure of the contextual data provide an initial basis for the exploratory analysis of the resulting case-study data. Using each of the essential categories described above within the construct of organizational context provided a framework to explore the degree to which the data co-varied together, and to identify which variables provided meaningful explanations of the data that had been collected. This exploration begins with the exploratory analysis technique of principal components analysis (PCA), as discussed within Chapter 5.

PCA identifies unique linear combinations of variables. To become meaningful, the researcher examines the way individual variables "load" on the new component (high negative or positive loadings indicate which variables most influence the score of the constructed component). The researcher uses the loadings and data collected directly from the organizations to interpret the constructed components.

The following diagram provides an overall picture of the resulting principal components:

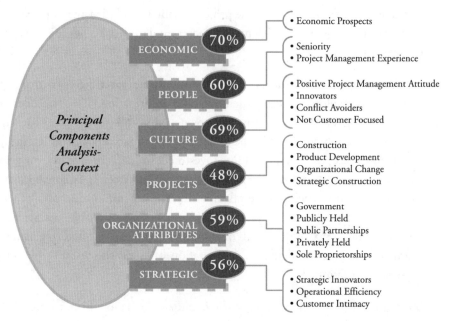

FIGURE 6-7—*Context principal components*

Each of the principal components is discussed in more detail in the following sections.

Economic

Four economic variables were used to measure the economic health of the country in which the organization is operating: the growth rate of gross domestic product (GDP), GDP per capita, the inflation rate, and the current account balance. The higher these variables are, the more robustly the economy is performing.

One component was obtained explaining a total of 70% of the variance:

- **Economic Prospects** (Percentage of variance explained: 70%; Eigenvalue: 2.809). This component loads heavily and positively on the relative economic performance measures GDP growth rate and inflation rate, as well as the current account balance, but negatively on GDP per capita. This component seems to be a measure of the stage of economic development of the region/country in which an organization is operating, whereby an emerging economy (e.g., China) has high GDP growth, high inflation, and high current account balance, but low GDP per capita. On the flip side, developed economies have low GDP growth, low inflation, and low or negative current account balance, but high GDP per capita.

    This component describes **Economic Prospects (Emerging Economy)** in that the higher this component is, the more likely that it describes an organization in a developing country or one in an emerging economy which is likely to have higher GDP growth, higher inflation rate, higher current account balance (i.e., higher export level) and lower GDP per capita.

People

Five variables were ultimately drawn on for the people PCA, which provides a description of the people within the case-study organizations in terms of age, years of service to the company, education level, project management experience level, and the workload of staff (expressed in hours per week). The variables together provide a picture of the overall workforce within a case-study organization.

Two components were obtained, explaining a total of almost 60% of the variance:

- **Seniority** (Percentage of variance explained: 37%; Eigenvalue: 1.854). This component loads heavily and positively on age, years of service, and education level, and loads negatively on workload. An organization measuring strongly in this component would likely have employees who are older, more experienced, better educated, and who work fewer hours (or who are possibly more efficient).

- **Project Management Experience** (Percentage of variance explained: 22.5%; Eigenvalue: 1.124). This component loads heavily on project management experience. An organization measuring strongly in this component would be one with a large number of employees who reflect a high level of experience in managing projects.

Culture

The culture of the organization draws on a number of distinct variables that collectively endeavor to provide an overview of the organizational culture represented within the case-study organizations. They include a number of key dimensions, including:

- The general attitudes towards project management within the organization, including:

  o Evidence of benefits from the project management implementation

  o The degree to which projects contribute to success of the organization

  o The degree to which project management contributes to the success of the organization

  o The degree to which contributions are recognized

- The risk attitude and culture of the organization, including the degree to which the culture could be described as being:

  o Conservative and risk-averse

  o Cautious

  o Innovative

  o Competitive

  o Entrepreneurial

  o Customer focused

  o Investor focused

- Attitudes towards collaboration and working together in the organization, including the degree to which:

  o The organization encourages risk taking and innovation

  o The organization allows expression of disagreement or concerns

  o The organization has a method of ensuring delivery of customer value

  o Staff value their project work

  o The organization has a method of ensuring that it is continually learning and growing its capabilities

Four components are obtained, explaining a total of 69% of the variance:

- **Positive Project Management Attitude** (Percentage of variance explained: 33.3%; Eigenvalue: 5.665). This first component loads heavily on the general attitudes towards project management, as well as a number of the attitudes regarding working together, particularly with respect to allowing expression of disagreement, ensuring delivery of customer value, and valuing project work. An organization measuring strongly in this component recognizes the contribution of project work to the organization and has a competitive, innovative, and customer-focused culture. It is an environment where staff value their project work, and ensure that their work products deliver customer value.

- **Innovators** (Percentage of variance explained: 17.9%; Eigenvalue: 3.043). This component loads heavily on competitive, entrepreneurial, and risk-focused variables, including the variables associated with risk-taking and innovation in how the organization works. Organizations that measure strongly on this component would typically value innovation highly and would have a high level of acceptance of risk-taking and a strong emphasis on growth and organizational learning.

- **Conflict Avoiders** (Percentage of variance explained: 10.2 %; Eigenvalue: 1.737). This component loads heavily on organizational culture descriptions of being cautious, conservative, and risk averse, and negatively loads on variables describing willingness to express disagreement and concerns and, to a lesser extent, risk-taking and innovation. Organizations that measure strongly on this component would typically be very cautious and conservative in their approach, and would be highly averse to expressing disagreement and conflict.

- **Not Customer Focused** (Percentage of variance explained: 7.9%; Eigenvalue: 1.348). This component loads negatively on variables describing the organization as being customer-focused and on having a process of collaboration that ensures the work results deliver customer value. An organization that measures strongly on this component is typically highly regulated, or focused more on the attainment of strategic or internal drivers than they are on delivering customer value.

Projects

The projects PCA draws on a number of discrete variables to describe the role of projects and the types of projects conducted by the organization. This includes a number of key dimensions, including:

- The nature of project work done within the organization, including:

  o Overall percentage of work done in projects

  o The number of projects conducted per year

  o The number of projects, strategic projects, and project management improvement projects started, completed, and cancelled per year

- The role of projects within the organization, including:

  o Internal projects, conducted to attain internal operating efficiencies

  o Product development projects, conducted to develop a product or service that can be subsequently delivered on an operational basis o Customer projects, where the project is the nature of the service being provided

o Research and development projects, which are intended to support pure and applied research efforts

- The types of projects conducted by the organization, including:

  o Process development projects

  o Software development and implementation projects

  o Organizational change projects

  o New product development projects

  o Construction and engineering projects

Four components are obtained explaining a total of 48% of the variance:

- **Construction** (Percentage of variance explained: 17.5%; Eigenvalue: 6.465). This component loads heavily on construction/engineering project work being conducted, as well as projects being done on a customer/consulting basis. There is also a significant positive loading on the number of projects conducted per year, and the number of project management improvement projects that are undertaken. An organization that measures strongly on this component would typically be a construction organization that conducts a large number of customer projects per year. They also conduct a number of project management improvement projects.

- **Product Development** (Percentage of variance explained: 10.9%; Eigenvalue: 4.040). This component loads heavily on new product development projects, as well as on the number of strategic initiatives that are undertaken in a year. An organization that measures strongly on this component would undertake a number of product development related projects, where product development is a core component of the organizational strategy.

- **Organizational Change** (Percentage of variance explained: 10.3%; Eigenvalue: 3.825).This component loads heavily on organizational change and process development projects. An organization that measures strongly on this component would typically be focused on conducting internal process improvement and organizational transformation efforts.

- **Strategic Construction** (Percentage of variance explained: 9.7%; Eigenvalue: 3.580). This component loads heavily on construction projects and the number of strategic initiatives undertaken per year. An organization that measures strongly on this component would typically be conducting large-scale construction projects for themselves, rather than on a customer basis, where the construction project is a strategic investment that the organization will be subsequently responsible for maintaining and operating.

Organizational Attributes

There are a number of variables that are used to characterize the organizational attributes of case-study organizations. These include:

- The organizational structure within which projects operate, including:

  o Operational/functional

  o Weak matrix

  o Strong matrix

  o Project-driven

- The type of organization, including:

  o Government agencies and departments

  o Crown/state-owned corporations

  o Privately-held corporations

  o Publicly-traded corporations

  o Limited partnerships

  o Joint ventures

  o Sole proprietorships

- The ownership structure of the organization, including:

  o Single owners

  o Partnerships (dual owners)

  o Narrowly held

  o Widely held

    o Municipal ownership

    o State ownership

- Other improvement initiatives that are being undertaken by the organization during the same period as the project management implementation, including:

    o 6 Sigma, ISO 9000 and total quality management implementations

    o Knowledge management

    o Process improvement and business process engineering

    o Supply chain management

    o Enterprise resource planning

Five components are obtained explaining a total of 59% of the variance:

- **Government** (Percentage of variance explained: 15.6%; Eigenvalue: 3.115). This component loads heavily on variables associated with state ownership, including government and crown corporations. It also positively loads on variables associated with supplier involvement, partner involvement, and other organizational improvement initiatives. Those organizations that measure strongly on this component are likely to be government departments or crown/ state-owned corporations. These organizations are also likely to be heavily involved with other stakeholders, and be engaged in a number of organizational improvement activities, of which project management is only one.

- **Publicly Held** (Percentage of variance explained: 13.3%; Eigenvalue: 2.659). This component loads heavily on variables associated with publicly held organizations, and loads negatively on variables associated with partnerships. Organizations that measure strongly on this component are most likely to be corporations that are publicly listed with a widely held share structure.

- **Public Partnerships** (Percentage of variance explained: 11.8%; Eigenvalue: 2.352). This component loads heavily on variables associated with publicly held organizations as well as loading positively on variables associated with partnerships structures. Organizations that measure strongly on this component are most likely to be organizations that are publicly traded or are owned by publicly traded parents, but are often special-purpose entities that have been created to establish a joint venture between more than one organization.

- **Privately Traded** (Percentage of variance explained: 9.7%; Eigenvalue: 1.948). This component loads on variables associated with narrowly held private ownership, and negatively loads on variables associated organizations that are operationally or functionally structured. Organizations that measure strongly on this component are likely to be private corporations with a single owner or very narrowly held ownership structure.

- **Single-Owner Structures** (Percentage of variance explained: 8.5%; Eigenvalue: 1.706). This component loads strongly on variables associated with sole proprietorships and single-ownership structures. Organizations that measure strongly on this component are likely to be those that have a single, individual owner.

Strategic

There are a number of variables which collectively construct the strategic PCA, and which together serve to describe the strategic focus and direction of the case study organizations. These include:

- The business model of the organization, determining the degree to which strategy of the organization is a product of:

  o Cost efficiency

  o Customer service

  o Customer Intimacy

  o Product leadership

  o Market dominance

- The means by which the strategic direction of the organization is determined, including:

  o Informally

  o Reactively, in response to competitive pressures

  o Reactively, in response to customer demands

  o Formally, on a decentralized basis

  o Formally, on a centralized basis

- The long-term and short-term strategic issues that the organization is facing, including:

    o Product development and innovation

    o Market share

    o Customer retention

    o Competitive positioning

    o Retention of staff

    o Change in products and services mix

    o Change in product and service quality

    o Change in markets

    o Change in customer share

    o Reduction in costs

    o Increase in sales

Three components are obtained explaining a total of 56% of the variance:

- **Strategic Innovators** (Percentage of variance explained: 39.3%; Eigenvalue: 12.568). This component loads heavily on variables associated with a strategic direction that is responsive to competitive pressures, as well as variables associated with a strategic direction of product leaderships. This component also loads heavily on the vast majority of variables associated with both long-term and short-term issues, and particularly those of competition, innovation, and market share. Organizations that measure strongly against this component are typically organizations that view themselves as highly competitive, very aware of their competition and their marketplace, and that are seeking a position of leadership within their market.

- **Operational Efficiency** (Percentage of variance explained: 9.2%; Eigenvalue: 2.959). This component loads heavily on variables associated with a business model of cost effectiveness, as well as informal strategic directions. This component also loads positively on variables associated with short-term strategic issues of reducing costs, and loads negatively on variables associated with short-term issues associated with innovation. Organizations that measure strongly against this component are frequently focused on cost reduction and operational efficiency as a dominant driver and the focus of the organization, with little emphasis on innovation or establishing strategic direction.

- **Customer Intimacy** (Percentage of variance explained: 7.5%; Eigenvalue: 2.407). This component loads very heavily on variables associated with customer intimacy and customer service. Organizations that measure strongly against this component demonstrate a strong focus on establishing and maintaining customer relationships, and most typically employ a strategy of ongoing customer retention and growth of customer share.

What Contextual Similarities Exist?

The contextual components that emerged from the PCAs above serve to help understand the nature of the organizations that are reflected within the cases studies conducted as a part of this research. That said, each component typically provides a number of potential dimensions by which any organization could be described. The next challenge was to reflect the typical configurations of the components–how components from each PCA come together to describe specific contexts that have been observed within the organization.

As discussed in Chapter 5, a Construct-level PCA was conducted of each of the constructs, using as input the components that were derived from the initial PCA. In essence, this second level of PCAs was intended to reduce the dimensionality of the data further by identifying the overall contexts that explain a significant proportion of the case-study organizations.

Conducting this Construct-level PCA yielded six clear components that collectively explain 64% of the variance in the contextual data associated with the case studies:

- **Operationally Efficient Strategic Construction in Developing Economies** (Percentage of variance explained: 15.9%; Eigenvalue: 3.030). This component loads heavily on components of operational efficiency as a strategic direction, as well as components associated with developing economies, a positive project management attitude, and a strategic construction focus. The component also loads negatively on components associated with employee seniority and publicly held organizations. Organizations that measure strongly against this component are those that are partnerships or organizations with narrowly held ownership structures, engaged in strategic construction projects in developing or high-growth economies. Typically, their staff is younger and less experienced, but has strong positive attitudes towards project management. The overall strategic focus of these organizations is operational efficiency.

> *Case study organization 74 is a construction company operating regionally within the Sichuan province of China. The company operates in a strongly competitive environment, and is responsible for both the development and subsequent operation of major hydroelectric projects.*
>
> *In 2006, the company had completed the first two projects and started operation, and been authorized to further develop another six projects. In order to be more effective and efficient in its developing and managing multiple projects, and operating the completed plants simultaneously, the company had undergone a 'management process reengineering' to improve and standardize its project management system.*
>
> *"The serious use of the project management methods and tools has improved our work efficiency and helped to raise our profile as a well-organized and disciplined company . . . We adopt project management concepts and methods not only for showing that we have followed the relevant regulations about adopting project management methods, we really want it to create value for our work, and the fact is it has created value for project outcomes."*
>
> — *Senior Manager, 74*

- **Innovative, Conflict-Avoiding Product Developers** (Percentage of variance explained: 12.5%; Eigenvalue: 2.373). This component loads heavily on components associated with innovation and a product development focus, but also loads heavily on components associated with conflict avoidance. Organizations that measured strongly against this component tend to be large, well established organizations that are more conservative, risk-averse and structured in their operations, but that have a dominant strategic focus on product development and innovation.

Case-study organization 75 is a large, publicly traded organization in the oil and gas industry in Canada. It operates in both regulated and unregulated industries, which establish different cultures internally and externally. The unit of analysis of this case study was the information technology business unit, which is responsible for all systems development, maintenance, and support in the organization.

The organization implemented a project management center of excellence in the late 1990s. There is an extensive, comprehensive, and detailed array of procedures and guidelines that are designed to cover all types of projects and all types of contingencies, from business planning through to implementation. Less emphasized are the process of collaboration, leadership and communication.

"The structure project management brings to the table adds value to the organization. In this organization and others, though, what they don't add on top of the toolkit is a relationship management piece—that's where the value is added."

— Project Manager, 75

- **Customer-Focused Product Developers** (Percentage of variance explained: 10.5%; Eigenvalue: 2.005). This component loads heavily on components associated with strategic innovation, product development and customer intimacy. The component also loads negatively on components associated with lack of customer focus, and has a positive loading associated with positive project management attitudes. Organizations that measure strongly against this component are typically organizations focused on product development and innovation that have a strategic focus on customer intimacy and customer service. Their staff are also typically positive about project management and value the role of projects quite highly.

> *Case study organization 44 is a division of a state government department in Australia responsible for the construction of social housing. It is organized based upon a project management model and delivers projects on a commercial basis, with its fees generated through services delivered.*
>
> *Working to very specific social issues in providing public housing to the underprivileged and those in need means that project management approaches need to be flexible, and soft skills are especially critical when dealing with clients and stakeholders in the wider community.*
>
> *"We build to a budget, but we also work to specific social needs; by definition, these can be in opposition. The budget cannot be our single point of reference."*
>
> —*Project Manager, 44*

- **Positive Project Management in Government** (Percentage of variance explained: 9.5%; Eigenvalue: 1.795). This component loads positively on components associated with government and positive project management attitudes. The organizations that measure strongly in this component are typically either government departments or organizations owned by municipalities or states, and whose staff has a positive attitude towards projects and the role of project management.

> *Case study organization 45 is a division of state government within Australia that is responsible for major infrastructure construction projects. There is no longer a mandate for the organization to deliver projects to government. The organization competes for projects with the private sector, and is now responsible for significant projects at both state and local levels.*
>
> *"We don't have a captive client base any more. But some clients come to us on a regular basis anyway. Clients don't have to come to us, so if they do it means they are happy. We have to keep improving, though, and continually monitor our performance. Our salaries are paid by clients."*
>
> —*Project Manager, 45*

- **Project Management Experience in Government** (Percentage of variance explained: 8.6%; Eigenvalue: 1.634). This component loads very strongly on components associated with government organizations, employee seniority, and project management experience. Organizations that measure strongly against this component are typically government entities, and have more senior and experienced staff who have a stronger level of project management experience.

Case study organization 29 is the information technology division of a department within the Canadian government. The organization established a project management office in 2001 to improve the management and delivery of projects and address a number of identified performance shortcomings.

Participants in the organization recognized the need to work within a project management framework that consisted of competent project managers and cross-functional project team structures, with supporting business processes and performance measures.

"The utilization of personal values as a basis for professional decision-making, prioritization, and leadership styles and behavior can be expected to contribute to the continued commitment of employees to the organization and, as a consequence, to the ongoing performance of the organization even when facing increased external and internal challenges."

—Researcher, 29

- **Organizational Change** (Percentage of variance explained: 6.9%; Eigenvalue: 1.311). This component loads heavily on components associated with organizational change efforts. Organizations that measure strongly on this component are typically engaged in significant organizational change projects, and are often organizations that are involved in large-scale internal change efforts, whether driven by strategic reasons or as a result of mergers and acquisitions.

Case study organization 20 is the information systems division of a government agency providing health services within Canada. In response to the increasing complexity and numbers of change projects in the organization, a project management capability was introduced several years ago.

The organization demonstrates a high customer and patient focus. Successful delivery of projects goes beyond delivering products and this is clearly acknowledged by senior management:

"It . . . gives them a sense of accomplishment, it gives them a sense of being connected to the enterprise, it gives them an opportunity to contribute and understand . . . how [their work] relates to the larger operation and to the success of the organization."

—Senior Manager, 20

ORGANIZATIONAL PROFILES OF CONTEXT

Each of our case study organizations included in the PCA analysis has been measured on each of the context components identified above. Figure 6-8 depicts those organizations that rank low (below one standard deviation from the mean) and high (above one standard deviation from the mean) on each context descriptor. The organizations are recorded in each cell (for example, *high-organizational efficient strategic construction in developing economies*) in numeric order–that is, there is no meaning embedded in where in the cell an organization appears. If it is in that cell, it is beyond one standard deviation from the mean.

Some organizations very clearly relate to a single context descriptor. The dark circles in Figure 6-8 identify these organizations. For instance, organization 77 registers highly as being described by *innovative conflict-avoiding project developers* and nothing else. Single-context descriptor organizations can be said to be most representative of the component they are associated with.

Some organizations ranked above or below one standard deviation from the mean on more than one context component. These organizations are described by more than one contextual component. Lines connect all of the instances of the same organization across the cells and should help you find the duplicates.

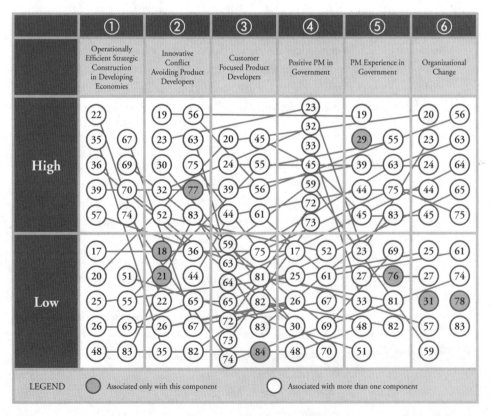

FIGURE 6-8—*Organizational profiles of context*

Figure 6-8 provides a number of insights into the sample organizations and the contexts they come from:

- Few of the organizations that rank above or below one standard deviation from the mean do so on only one context component. Only seven of the case study organizations that measure more than one standard deviation of the mean have only one context descriptor.

- Most of the organizations that rank either above or below one standard deviation from the mean on these context descriptors are also described by other context components at that level.

- Often organizations are most described by what they are not. Six of the seven organizations solely defined by one context descriptor are best described as being not that context descriptor.

- All but two context components have close to the same number of organizations above one standard deviation from the mean as below. This indicates a relatively normal distribution of organizations against this component.

- PCA3 (*customer-focused product developers*) and PCA 4 (*positive project management in government*) both have more organizations best described as not these components. This indicates that we have less organizations in the data set strongly described by these context components. Almost two-thirds more organizations are not described by these components than are strongly described by these components.

- There also appear to be patterns in how the context descriptors can be applied to the organizations.

  o Organizations that rank beyond the first standard deviation on PCA 1 (*operationally efficient strategic construction in developing economies*), also appear to rank low on PCA 2 (*innovative conflict-avoiding product developers*).

  o Organizations that rank beyond the first standard deviation on PCA 4 (*positive project management in government*) also appear to rank low on the PCA 5 (*project management experience in government*). This suggests that government experience in project management is inversely proportional to positive attitudes towards project management.

  o Organizations that rank above the first standard deviation on PCA 3 (*customer-focused product developers*) also rank high on PCA 5 (*project management experience in government*). This might, on first glance, seem odd, but looking at the organizations ranking this way, it appears that those in the government sector are providing innovative services and products to clients, and so rank in both categories.

o Organizations that rank above the first standard deviation on PCA 3 (*customer-focused product developers*) also rank high on PCA 6 (*organizational change*). This suggests that organizations operating in a context of customer-focused product development also engage in significant levels of organizational change initiatives.

o Many organizations in our sample could be described as being *not* PCA 3 (*customer-focused product developers*) and also be described by some other PCA component than any other contextual descriptor.

CULTURAL INFLUENCES AND IMPACTS

From the beginning, this study took seriously the potential impact culture (at the country, organizational, and professional levels) would have on both the data we would be able to collect and the findings of the study. One of the major contextual differences between the case organizations would simply be the differing national cultures these organizations operate in. Almost one-fourth of the case studies come from China; almost one-half come from what could be viewed as emerging economies (China, Brazil, Serbia, Russia, and the United Arab Emirates). With this distribution, simply assuming that cases adhered to a common Western business culture would not be reasonable. Each of the countries in our study brings with it a unique national culture that will impact how it views and values project management and in fact how it engages with this study.

Over and above the national culture, organizational cultures come into play in terms of how welcoming they were for the implementation of project management. Professional cultures as evidenced by beliefs about the role and function of project management within organizations were also expected to influence the type of project management tools introduced and the implementation approach. Accordingly, we consciously collected data on both organizational and professional culture, as well as national culture and history in the many regions represented by the case studies. This also includes consideration of the implications of national culture work such as Hofstede (2001)and Trompenaars (1997).

The principal components analyses discussed above shows that organizational cultural attributes around risk, conflict, innovation, and collaboration clearly differentiate the organizations in our study. It remains to be seen how specific cultural differences influence what gets implemented in terms of project management and what value those implementations deliver. Further study of the case data set with respect to how culture affects project management implementations will look at questions such as:

- How does seeing project management as a profession influence organization's project management implementations?

- Are there connections between risk aversion and any particular project management implementation?

- Are risk-averse organizations more likely to implement a full set of risk management tools and training?

- Are national cultures with a strong bent towards collectivism or national pride more or less likely to adopt a standardized project management implementation?

Questions at this level have yet to be pursued and will provide the basis for further analysis of this data set going forward.

Over the course of the study, the influence of culture became increasingly evident in everything from gaining access to organizations, working with the people within the case-study organizations, availability of data, and working with our fellow researchers. The following example explores how culture influenced the conduct of this research and provides some insights into how it might be an influence in the data that was collected.

Commitment: China versus Canada

As discussed in Chapter 3, gaining access to organizations was a difficult task for all our researchers; collecting the data once inside tended to be easier. Our experiences in two of the pilot cases illustrate the differences that culture made in conducting case studies in different regions.

In our first example, a project management office manager of a Canadian telecom heard an early presentation on this study and was keen to participate. We rapidly gained access, got approval for the study, and made plans for two researchers to travel 4.5 hours by plane to the site for a week to collect the case study data.

Once on site, we found an interesting dichotomy in terms of the level of commitment to the study. C-level executives in this organization were fully committed to participating and providing us with whatever data we needed to conduct the study. One interview with the senior participating executive went overtime. When the researcher tried to wrap up the interview, the executive resisted, stating that he wanted to be sure that we got all the data we needed for the study—even though he had been notified that his next meeting was waiting.

At the other end of the scale, project managers in this same organization failed to make scheduled interview times (even knowing that the researchers had traveled long distances) sometimes not even remembering the appointment, or attended but continually interrupted the interview to take cell phone and email pager messages. Clearly these project managers felt they were too busy to participate in the research study. The culture of project manager as external expert and hero did not value involvement in reflection or research. Organizational commitment from the top was not aligned with the actions of those further down the hierarchy. Not surprisingly perhaps, this organization did not complete the organizational data collection for this study, and so cannot be fully analyzed within our case-study sample.

While this is an extreme example of the attitudes towards this study, we can report that many of our case team leads in Western countries reported similar experiences. Many cited participants being rushed, committing to the study initially but losing interest as the amount of effort required of them became clear, and simply not providing the final data we waited for. Organizations appeared to be very interested in the results of the study and in participating until it became clear that answering these questions would require time and commitment. Many of our case leads reported entering discussions with organizations, gaining commitment to participate and having the organization retract that commitment at a later point, citing economic conditions or changes in circumstances. Clearly a commitment to participate in a research study was conditional on the participation being convenient for the organization.

In a Chinese case study conducted at roughly the same time, the experience was quite different. It took considerable time to help the organization understand the nature of the study and for it to commit to participate. Personal relationships between a senior researcher and the president of the company were used to gain access and have this organization participate as the first Chinese case study. However, once the decision to participate had been made, this intent was clearly communicated to all levels of the organization. Everyone we met with appeared interested in fully participating (or at least clearly understood that this was an organizational priority).

At our first data collection meeting in Beijing, a senior vice president flew 4 hours to participate. The manager of a construction project for one of the largest venues for the Beijing Olympics also attended this meeting just hours before he had to meet with the International Olympic Committee. He attended the first part of our research meeting and then politely asked if he could be the first interviewee as he had to travel across Beijing for this very important meeting in the afternoon. Clearly, we made that accommodation.

We had been concerned at the start of the project as to what proportion of the data we set out to capture would be available from the Chinese organizations. While this was a valid concern, some of the most complete datasets were provided by the organizations participating in China. This particular Chinese organization took its commitment to this study so seriously that it assigned three employees to review 10 years of project and organizational archives for three weeks in order to document the information we required. We in no way expected that level of effort from any of our organizations to capture the data. Over time it became clear that some of the data we asked for was simply not readily available in many organizations. This organization was one of the few to provide an almost-complete set of case-study data set to the study, for which we are very grateful. The commitment to participate, and in doing so participating as fully as possible, speaks volumes about the level of importance with which the research was viewed once the organization made the decision to be involved as a case study.

In China, much deliberation and consideration went into the decision to participate (even where personal relationships were being leveraged). However, committing to participate meant that the organization felt obligated to do everything in its power to help make our research project a success. Commitment was unilateral and complete. Case leads from other developing economies indicated that they had similar levels of commitment and support for the study from their case organizations. We also found this level of commitment in organizations that had a culture of collectivism.

Culture Summary

National culture and history as well as organizational culture clearly becomes very important to understanding not only what is implemented and called project management but also what holds value for people in these different settings. This is also reflected in the data that we collected and the level of participation that we saw. At our last full-team workshop, cultural differences at both the organizational and the national level were strongly reported by many of our case team leads as crucial to the understanding of the analysis conducted within and between the case studies they completed. The full research team deliberated on these cultural implications and the many ways that they could be studied. Some of the discussion pursued the national cultural differences that may be at play in the attitudes to the study and project management. A number of our research team members are particularly interested in these implications. We all agreed that this is an important additional question for further study within this dataset in later stages of this research.

Many in our team are interested in the cultural aspects of the quest for value and will be further assessing these impacts over the course of the next few months. One such analysis of our Serbian case studies concludes:

> *"Any discussion of perceived value and benefits of project management in a transitional economy therefore must take into account and be informed by its strategic role, political forces and instruments of power operating in the specific local context. The value and benefits accrued from the adoption and implementation of project management has a lot*

to do with bounded rationality in decision making (in predicting and interpreting the dynamics of the environment; risks); with the level of controllability and instability of people and environment (alignment, adaptation, culture, behavior, tasks/profession); sensitivity to context; social responsibility of decision makers (accountability, transparency); and mechanisms of power operating in the given organizational context. These are areas where further study and theorizing are necessary." (Cicmil, Djordjevic, Zivanovic, 2008 under review).

We agree wholeheartedly. This monograph presents high-level analyses across all 65 case studies using both qualitative and quantitative methods to explore project management implementations while taking into account the context within which they are situated. However, we recognize that the fully nuanced and theorized understanding of the impacts of culture on the practice of and investment in project management across organizations and nations will require richer and deeper analysis and will be an ongoing part of the study of this data set.

CONCLUSIONS

What can be seen from the sections in this chapter is that organizations that participated within this research study vary considerably, and on a number of different dimensions. Simply looking at the demographics and descriptive statistics associated with the case studies demonstrates the diversity contained within the data. The case-study organizations demonstrate geographic diversity, are drawn from a broad spectrum of industries, and encompass a full range of ownership and organizational structures. The projects represented include everything from traditional engineering and construction to complex organizational change, product development, and research and development efforts.

So what do the variations in the case studies tell us about our initial questions? Revisiting the two questions we began this section with yields the following conclusions:

- **How do organizations differ?** The answer is clearly that organizations differ broadly and diversely. Organizations exist within a broad array of contexts. They have different background, different histories, and different strategic goals. Each of the organizations represented within this research, however, in some way values project management. While this may to some degree also represent a source of bias, what it serves to reinforce here is that while organizations may be inherently different, they also universally appreciate some aspect of project management as a method that is appropriate within their context.

- **What differences matter to project management implementations?** This is a question that is much harder to answer. What we have identified so far is what differences exist, and that there are in fact meaningful differences that are important to understand. What we cannot yet say is which of these differences matter with respect to project management implementations. To do this, we need to look at the implementations that are in place within these organizations. The next chapter explores the observed implementations in detail.

7

Implementation

INTRODUCTION

Understanding implementation involves defining what has in actual fact been implemented that organizations refer to as project management. The specific question that this portion of the research has been designed to answer is:

- What do organizations implement that they call project management?

In doing so, we have taken a grounded approach to understanding the implementation of organizations. We have avoided specifically evaluating the various implementations against any one model, which by the admissions of most model authors are incomplete and not fully representative of the overall domain of project management. We have also avoided adopting a strictly maturity-based means of assessment, although a comparative understanding of maturity does emerge from the implementations that are described. Instead, we have endeavored to understand what in actuality has been implemented and the underlying motivations and objectives that led to those implementations. In doing so, we have used the broadest encompassing of project management possible, including dimensions such as process, training, and toolsets, as well as exploration of the full scope of project management, whether at the portfolio, program, or project level.

Of course, to collect data regarding implementations, it is necessary to make some assumptions regarding the range of implementations that are possible. This is particularly important in designing surveys and similar instruments, so of necessity there are some pre-defined frames within which implementation is being evaluated. This has also been complemented, however, with open-ended interview questions and qualitative reporting of both the implementations and the impacts and fit associated with those implementations in the case-study organizations, in order to provide as grounded and contextual a view as possible of what each organization has done.

LATEST PROJECT MANAGEMENT IMPLEMENTATION

This section was contributed by Dr. Pernille Eskerod

The aim of this section is to contribute to the understanding of what companies have done in terms of project management implementations in order to manage their projects. Based on a cross-case analysis, we present an overview of the latest project management improvement efforts implemented in these companies. Knowing what the companies have chosen to invest in will improve our understanding of what they value–or believe will deliver value in the future.

This analysis rests on data reported in the case-study reports, from this descriptive and open question:

- *What was implemented in the most recent improvement effort?*

Answers to this question are identified in case reports covering 51 case companies, based upon the number of case reports available at the time of this analysis. In 22 reports, a single improvement effort was identified, while two or more efforts were identified in the reminding 29 reports. In total, 115 improvement efforts were identified. A meta-matrix was developed in which the improvement efforts were inserted together with company, country, and region identifications. The efforts were kept in an unedited form as they were represented by quotations from the reports. Hereafter, each effort was categorized.

The analysis was carried out by applying a grounded-theory approach (Glaser & Strauss, 1967; Strauss & Corbin, 1990) in which raw data from the case studies were coded and classified without using a pre-defined classification scheme. Instead, the categories were derived from the data on an inductive basis. In reviewing the data, categories were defined arising from the case data descriptions. For example the category *Competence development*. By using this research approach, the data is allowed to speak for itself and room is left for important variations in project management implementation efforts to be identified that nobody had previously identified as important.

Data analysis consisted of two separate efforts: a pilot analysis and a main analysis. This approach was used in order to gain insight from the pilot analysis prior to the main analysis. The pilot analysis was based on 22 case-study reports and 40 improvement efforts discussed within them. The findings from the pilot analysis were discussed at a workshop in which case team members and project management experts participated. The pilot analysis identified three categories:

   o   Competence development

    o Models/tools/methods/standards

    o Governance structure/support units

Based on discussion at the workshop and analysis of the rest of the case-study reports, these three categories were later expanded into four:

    o Competence development

    o Models/tools/methods/standards

    o Governance structure

    o Support units

Further, the workshop participants offered suggestions on how to distinguish between the categories if a given effort was difficult to categorize. An example of this would be the improvement effort *Integrated and unified project management procedures of daughter companies*. The agreement in the discussion was that if the project management procedures were established on behalf of the daughter companies in order to accomplish projects in a better way, the effort should be classified within the category *Models/tools/methods/standards*. However, if the project management procedures were imposed on the daughter companies in order for the mother company to improve on the control of the work of the daughter companies, then the effort should belong to the *Governance structure* category.

Case Studies And Improvement Efforts Around The World

In Table 7-1, the number of case companies and improvement efforts in regions across the world is presented. The table shows that the improvement efforts are almost evenly distributed around the world and that only in Europe do we see a significantly higher percentage of improvement efforts than case studies.

	Asia	Australia	Europe	North America	Middle East	Russia	South America	SUM
# of case companies	10	4	13	11	3	5	5	51
Percentage of case companies	20%	8%	24%	22%	6%	10%	10%	100%
# of improvement efforts	23	7	32	26	5	13	9	115
Percentage of improvement efforts	20%	6%	28%	23%	4%	11%	8%	100%

TABLE 7-1—*Case companies and improvement efforts in each region*

Identified Categories

Based on the discussions of the pilot analysis and an analysis of the whole dataset, six categories were identified (in alphabetical order):

- Adjusting human resources/formal authority

- Competence development

- Incentive systems

- Models, standards, templates, software

- PMOs, support units

- Project governance structure

Table 7-2 presents the distribution of improvement efforts within the six categories. The numbers show that the efforts were not evenly distributed. 40% of the improvement efforts were related to new models, standards, templates, or software systems, while only 3% of the improvement efforts were related to new incentive systems.

Priority	Category	Total # of efforts	Percentage
1	Models, standards, templates, software	46	40%
2	Project governance structure	21	18%
3	PMOs, support units	16	14%
4	Adjusting human resources/formal authority	15	13%
5	Competence development	14	12%
6	Incentive systems	3	3%
		Sum: 115	Sum: 100%

TABLE 7-2—*Number of improvement efforts in each category*

The following table presents the distribution of improvement efforts in the six categories within the various regions.

	Asia	Australia	Europe	North America	Middle East	Russia	South America
Models, standards, templates, software	*11*	*3*	*14*	*7*	*2*	*5*	*4*
Project governance structure	*4*	*1*	*2*	*5*	*3*	*5*	*1*
PMOs, support units	*1*	*2*	*3*	*6*	*0*	*2*	*2*
Adjusting human resources/formal authority	*2*	*0*	*4*	*7*	*0*	*1*	*1*
Competence development	*2*	*1*	*9*	*1*	*0*	*0*	*1*
Incentive systems	*3*	*0*	*0*	*0*	*0*	*0*	*0*

TABLE 7-3—*Number of improvement efforts in each category and in each region*

The numbers are too small to conduct hypothesis tests based on statistical analyses. However, some tendencies can be seen.

The category *Models, standards, templates, software* has the highest frequency within the region in Asia, Australia, Europe, and South America, and is tied for highest frequency in both North America and Russia. It comes second in frequency count in the Middle East, but the difference is only one improvement effort (two as compared to three). The conclusion is that companies are most likely to invest in implementing new project management models, standards, templates, and software systems all over the world.

The category *Project governance structure* is the only other category represented in all regions, implying that project governance structure is considered important worldwide.

The categories *PMOs, support units* and *Adjusting human resources/formal authority* are more frequently implemented in North America (also when you adjust for the number of case studies in each region. This calculation is not offered in the text.).

The category *Competence development* is most frequently initiated in Europe. Of the nine scores, the seven improvement efforts are from Scandinavia. The suggestion is that Scandinavia invests more in project management competence development initiatives than the rest of the world.

The category *Incentive systems* is only reported in Asia. One of the improvement efforts was the establishment of a reward and penalty system in a Chinese construction company in order to encourage best practices. The same company established various competitions between the contractors on the construction sites in order to make the various teams compete with each other. Another incentive system consisted of a scoring system and an award system for project managers. This improvement effort was implemented in an IT company in China. The suggestion is that Asian companies focus on implementing new incentive systems, while this is not in focus anywhere else in the world. Of course, other regions may have incentive systems as well but they are not mentioned in the context of their latest improvement efforts.

APPROACHES IMPACTING IMPLEMENTATION

This section was contributed by Dr. Svetlana Cicmil

Overall, 38 aspects of project management implementation have been captured (and coded) from the 60 available case reports in an effort to find which had the greatest and the least impact. These were generated by careful study of the statements directly related to the principle question for this analysis:

What aspects of the project management implementation have had

a) *the greatest impact on improving project performance?*

b) *the least impact?*

This analysis was further informed by the full content of selected case reports and by research team presentations during the workshop at the end of June 2008. The cumulative list of 38 codes reflects all those aspects mentioned in the database that were identified as relevant, and which, in different combinations and coupling among themselves and with other unmentioned elements, should represent all that has been implemented as project management across the 60 cases.

A Reflection On 'Missing Data'

In two cases it was reported to be "too early to identify" aspects either with the greatest or the least impact. In these instances, none of the projects under the new regime had yet gone through a full cycle. It is evident in these examples that some doubts still persist in relation to the implemented project management procedures and bureaucracy, unnecessary extra work, etc., but some positive feelings and recognition of usefulness of project management in controlling time and budget have been acknowledged.

In 24 cases, no aspects had been identified as having the least impact. This means that it was not possible to ascertain the relevant information from the reports—either because it was not mentioned in the narrative at all, or because the respective case-study researchers stated that the respondents could not think of any aspect of project management implementation that could be confidently singled out as having the least impact. We discussed this at some length at the workshop, and agreed that there may have been some cultural biases that repressed speaking negatively about any aspect of the project management implementation. This is a topic for further research, but is not likely answerable from this data set.

The first step in the analysis was to look at the frequency and distribution of aspects separately for "the greatest" and "the least" category. Following from there, some comparative analysis will be presented and further conclusions made.

Aspects That Had The Greatest Impact On Project Performance

The number of identified "greatest" aspects per single case range from one to 12. In terms of frequency with which they have been mentioned as having the most significant impact on some aspect of organizational or project performance or benefit, the following "codes" lead the list:

- *Uniform or standardized project management procedures, processes, and systems; consistency.* This aspect of project management implementation was mentioned in 39 cases as having the greatest / most significant impact. The responses are proportionally distributed across the board, meaning that in a large number of cases (65%), standardization and/or consistency of the project management process is seen as contributing most significantly to improvements, better performance, or value accrued from the implementation of a given project management methodology in the local context. This aspect appears universally to have the most significant impact regardless of context differences in terms of the industrial sector, national culture, or position of the respondent. Interestingly, this aspect has also been mentioned rather frequently as the one with the least impact—which will be discussed later.

- *Structured and coordinated project communication system* was the next-most frequently stated aspect of project management implementation under this category. It was mentioned in 8 cases, half of which are manufacturing companies. It is opportune to note here that no reference has been made in any of the 60 cases to this implementation effort as "having the least impact."

- The three other aspects worthy of consideration in terms of frequency (with seven references each) are:

  o *Project management training itself* (organization-wide and relevant)

  o *Designated formal title and role for those in charge of projects (project managers) including their adequate training* (project managers are visible and their role, status, competencies and terms of reference are recognized, distinguished, and made transparent). This aspect was only mentioned in relation to "the greatest impact."

o *Project risk assessment and management procedures.* It seems that this aspect of project management implementation is specifically appreciated in the public sector and construction as having a significant impact.

Aspects That Had The Least Impact On Project Performance

The number of identified "least" aspects per single case range from one to nine. We can speculate about this lower number (as well as much lower frequency below) as being a consequence of the overall enthusiasm for project management implementation. Or it could be the fact that any form of project management implementation contains unique and potentially influential/beneficial aspects that it is much more unlikely that their impact is perceived as low. Also, as discussed above, there may be a cultural bias against commenting negatively on any organizational initiatives.

In terms of frequency with which they have been mentioned as having the least significant impact on "project performance," the following codes lead the list:

• *Structured and timely reporting on project progress to the client, sponsors, stakeholders;* (administration of documents, templates and checklists) This aspect of project management implementation was mentioned in 9 cases as having the least impact on organizational or project performance, or against other criteria of benefit or implementation rationale. There is no particular pattern of distribution but we note a high frequency among manufacturing and IT/software development organizations. This aspect has been identified as having the greatest impact in six cases. Two case organizations stated that reporting had simultaneously both the greatest and the least impact for them (a small IT consultancy and a larger IT company).

• Two other "least" aspects are worthy consideration in terms of frequency (six references each) are:

o *Uniform or standardized project management procedures, processes and systems; consistency.* Out of these six cases, four stated that this aspect had simultaneously both the greatest and the least impact in their environment.

o *Project management software; the implementation and compulsory use of software packages for project data management, scheduling, and control* is seen as having the least impact, mostly because of the packages' inflexibility to be scaled down and adapted to the needs of the specific project. This inhibits rather than supports project-related decision-making. This aspect has not been identified as having the greatest impact in any of the 60 cases.

Finally, it can be noted that in identifying and discussing aspects of project management implementation with the least impact, many statements implicitly or explicitly refer to "overall increase of individual workload" and "increased bureaucracy" as the reason for that impact.

Further Comparative Discussion

Within this analysis, there are three outstanding either "greatest" or "least" aspects of project management implementation to be explored for possible relationships and propositions:

- *Uniform or standardized project management procedures, processes and systems; consistency* is without doubt the most significant aspect of project management implementation universally across the 60 cases (the greatest impact in 39 cases). It is interesting to note that this aspect was in four cases mentioned as simultaneously having both the greatest and the least impact (two public sector, one construction and one manufacturing). This can be explained by the fact that a wide adoption of the project management methodology increases demand on resources (staff and cost), and that the benefit of having a consistent, coherent approach to managing the organization's projects and common, standardized language to "make sense" of projects across the organization and among various project stakeholders is sometimes in juxtaposition with the need for immaculate adherence to procedures. This can stifle creativity, increase the "unpleasant, worrying" feeling of additional control (and self-surveillance), and mechanizes work. In some cases, the implementation of a standardized and structured project management methodology was identified as excellent for project performance, but was not accepted, embedded, or understood as a business concept across the organization, thus causing friction, tensions and disappointment particularly among ambitious project managers. This partially explains why the aspect *Introduction and adoption of project management as an overall business concept idea/business philosophy* scores very low (6) as having the greatest impact which at the same time being stated in five cases as having the least,

- The aspect *Structured and timely reporting on project progress to the client, sponsors, stakeholders* (administration of documents, templates, and checklists) leads the list of those with the least impact. The respondents who identified this aspect as the least influential come from a variety of roles within organizations, including the clients and senior managers indicating "information overload through reporting" as a counter-productive aspect of project management. Out of six cases where this was identified as having the greatest impact, two also put it in the opposite category, similar to the above category of *Uniform and standardized project management* discussed above.

- However, we can generate further insights if we consider the second-leading aspect on the "greatest" list: *Structured and coordinated project communication system.* It is not surprising to see this aspect positioned as it is and to note that it was not identified as having least impact in any of the 60 cases of project management implementation. If we understand it as indicating in the relevant cases the implementation of a project management methodology which includes a well-though-out, meaningful project management communication system suited to the specific local environment, then its contrast with the over-formalized, frequently burdensome, and unnecessarily routinized and imposed project management reporting system becomes obvious and explains why *Structured and timely reporting on project progress to the client, sponsors, stakeholders* scores highly as an aspect with the least impact.

The discussion above highlights some avenues for further analysis within the study's data set by combining the qualitative and quantitative outcomes, as well as some issues for consideration by those involved in decision-making processes in relation to the choice, design, and method of implementation of a project management methodology suitable for the specific local context.

Concluding Remarks

Given the fact that none of the traditional elements of project management (planning and control tools and techniques, complex project management software, contractual strategies, etc) tops the list of the aspects of project management implementation with the greatest impact, it appears that the most significant aspects of project management are strategic and behavioral ones. These, if implemented as part of project management methodology, seem to have a high potential for filling in the gaps in the existing organizational behavior and operating procedures that are otherwise inadequate for facing the challenges of successful management of contemporary projects.

The qualitative analysis related to the question *What aspects of the project management implementation have had a) the greatest impact on improving project performance? And b) the least impact?* was facilitated by both quantitative and qualitative means of making sense of the question itself, the data and the outcomes. The findings will be most effective when compared or integrated with the outcomes of other strands of qualitative and quantitative analysis for the overall study. This analysis illuminates the potential conclusions, practical recommendations, and directions for further study.

FACTORS INFLUENCING IMPLEMENTATION

What Data Is Available?

The preceding sections have explored different aspects of what has been implemented in organizations under the broad heading of project management, discussing what was implemented and the degree to which these implementations were seen to have impact. In evaluating the implementations within organizations, there is a comprehensive collection of data that was available to the research team for each case-study organization that allowed for exploration of the various implementations that were represented. Again drawing on the conceptual model, a number of implementation-related constructs had been established within the various datasets. This provided a significant number of construct categories and variables to support exploratory analysis, which again first drew upon the techniques of principal components analysis described in Chapter 5.

The data constructs related to implementation are summarized in the following points:

- **History.** The historical aspects of implementation focus largely on an understanding of the underlying motivations associated with implementing project management within the organization, and a history of how that implementation was conducted. The history of the implementation includes a general understanding of when the implementation occurred and who was involved, and explores in detail both the motivations and means by which the implementation was accomplished. The motivations include the strategic drivers that led to the implementation (such as in response to competitive pressures, increasing projects, greater project complexity, or compliance with international standards or regulatory requirements) and the specific objectives associated with the implementation (including improving project performance, ensuring better delivery of business cases, gaining competitive advantage, or enhancing the credibility of the organization).

- **People.** The people aspects of the implementation explore the skills, experience and competency of the people within the organization, specifically with respect to involvement and management of projects. While the contextual constructs of the organization explored the general make-up and demographics of staff within the organization as a whole, these attributes specifically gain an understanding of employees and other resources involved in managing projects for the organization. This construct explores the people associated with project management in an organization, including an understanding of the different roles that exist, and the experience of staff within the organization in working in a project environment, managing projects, and in serving in their current roles. The people constructs also include an exploration of the competency of staff supporting and managing projects, and an assessment of their performance in working on projects.

- **Practices.** A significant source of data related to the implementations within organizations is grounded in an understanding of the practices associated with project management. As well as gaining a comprehensive understanding of the various perspectives of the implementation through interviews and researcher observations, there is a considerable amount of data that is collected regarding the specific practices that may be viewed as being related to project management within the case studies. This includes an understanding of the degree to which portfolio, program, and project management practices are defined and present, as well as processes associated with project delivery, resource management, and value (or business case) realization. Also explored is how project management is integrated with the other practices and management capabilities within the organization. Finally, each case study provided a comprehensive view of the degree to which these practices were documented within guidelines and frameworks, talked about by organization participants, and actually evidenced in the management of projects. This final dimension essentially provides a view of the espoused theories of project management within the organization as compared with those actually in use.

- **Training.** The training aspects of implementations explore the means of skills development and learning that are adopted by the organization in supporting the development of project-related staff members and other resources. Understanding of the training approaches includes an exploration of the topics of project management training that are delivered, the degree to which training programs are customized or tailored to the organization, and the means of delivery. Delivery itself includes an exploration of the media (e.g., in person, distance-based, or video) and who delivers the training (e.g., in house staff, external consultants, or institutions), as well as who within the organization receives the training. Training also explores the means by which requirements for training are established, and how the effectiveness of training approaches is evaluated in terms of organizational impacts and adoption of delivered programs. The adoption of informal development approaches, such as association participation, lunch and learns, coaching, and site visits, is also explored.

- **Tools.** The tools aspects associated with implementation explore the broad mechanisms by which the project management practices within the organization are delivered and supported. Data collected with respect to tools includes the various guidelines in which the practices of the organization are defined, including the use of procedure documents, checklists, job aids, and templates. As well, the use of software packages to support the management of projects within the implementation are explored, as well as the use of various databases.

- **Organizational Infrastructure.** The organizational infrastructure aspects of implementation employ a broad set of variables to explore the organization supports and structures that are associated with the project management implementation. Understanding of the organizational infrastructure includes identification of where within the organization that responsibility for the project management implementation resides. The relative authority of project managers and of any project management support groups in place are identified, as well as the role and involvement of senior management in the oversight of projects and the support of the project management implementation. The presence, responsibility, size, and funding responsibilities of any project management support groups are also explored. The costs associated with the project management implementation were also sought, including the ongoing annual support costs of maintaining the implementation. Lastly, an assessment of the perceived maturity of the organizational practices is evaluated.

What Implementation Components Emerged?

In conducting the principal components analysis (PCA), the above construct dimensions guided the grouping of variables for exploratory analysis purposes. Given the number of variables that were available for each group, however, variables were often further divided based upon sub-themes within that group. As an example, the variables associated with understanding the training approach of the organization were further grouped into an understanding of the topics of training provided, the delivery approach that is utilized, and the overall duration of project management training.

The following diagram provides an overview of the resulting principal components:

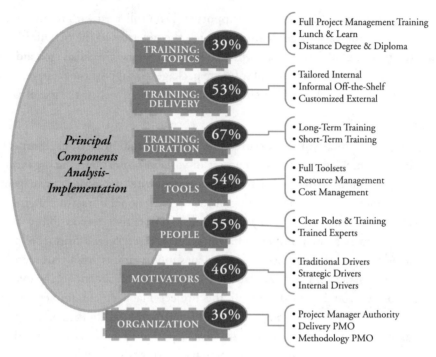

TRAINING: TOPICS 39%
- Full Project Management Training
- Lunch & Learn
- Distance Degree & Diploma

TRAINING: DELIVERY 53%
- Tailored Internal
- Informal Off-the-Shelf
- Customized External

TRAINING: DURATION 67%
- Long-Term Training
- Short-Term Training

TOOLS 54%
- Full Toolsets
- Resource Management
- Cost Management

PEOPLE 55%
- Clear Roles & Training
- Trained Experts

MOTIVATORS 46%
- Traditional Drivers
- Strategic Drivers
- Internal Drivers

ORGANIZATION 36%
- Project Manager Authority
- Delivery PMO
- Methodology PMO

Principal Components Analysis-Implementation

FIGURE 7-1—*Implementation principal components*

Each of the Principal Components is discussed in more detail in the following sections.

Training – Topics

The training – topics PCA utilizes a number of variables to understand the project management topics that are delivered within the training offerings of the case-study organization, including:

- The specific training topics offered by the organization in support of the implementation, including:

    o Portfolio management

    o Program management

    o Project management

    o Project delivery

    o Project governance

    o Value realization

- o Resource management

- o Organization integration

- o Team building

- o Risk management

- o Organizational methodologies

- o Government policies/legislation

- o Regulatory guidelines

- o Quality control

- o Leadership/advanced learning

- The means of delivery of training within the organization, including:

  - o Instructor-led

  - o Learner-driven

  - o Face-to-face

  - o Online

  - o Video

  - o Webcast

  - o Reading/Self study

- The degree of customization of training programs offered within the organization, including:

  - o Off-the-shelf

  - o Standard course adapted to the organization

  - o Customized organizational training course

  - o Project-specific training course

- Who delivers training within the organization, including:

    o Educational institutions

    o External consultants

    o In-house trainers

- The degree of informal training vehicles that are employed in supporting skills development and knowledge transfer, including:

    o Conference participation

    o Association participation

    o Internal conferences

    o Lessons learned

    o Lunch and learns

    o Coaching and mentoring

    o Communities of practice

    o Competition participation

    o Review meetings

    o Site visits

    o Self-learning

Three components are obtained explaining a total of 39% of the variance:

- **Full Project Management Training** (Percentage of variance explained: 22.7%; Eigenvalue: 9.749). This component loads heavily and positively on virtually all of the variables associated with project management training topics, as well as on the use of self-study and individual learning and informal techniques of coaching, mentoring, the establishment of communities of practice and participation in competitions. Organizations that measure strongly in this component typically utilize a broad and comprehensive approach to training, and provide training to their staff in a broad array of topics.

- **Lunch and Learns** (Percentage of variance explained: 8.7%; Eigenvalue: 3.379). This component loads heavily and positively on the use of informal lunch and learns as a specific approach to learning development, and also loads very negatively on the use of project-specific approaches such as review meetings and site visits. Organizations that measure strongly on this component typically emphasize informal training in general topics, and make more limited use of formal training and project-specific learnings and knowledge sharing.

- **Distance Degree and Diploma** (Percentage of variance explained: 8.1%; Eigenvalue: 3.468). This component loads heavily and positively on variables associated with the delivery of webcasts and videos as a training delivery method, and also loads positively on variables associated with delivery of degree- or diploma-based programs. Organizations that measure strongly on this component make use of distance-based degree and diploma programs as a primary means of employee development.

Training – Delivery

The delivery aspects of training are explored within this PCA, and evaluate the mechanisms utilized to support project-related learning within the organization. This includes:

- The degree of customization of training programs utilized by the organization, including:

  - o Adapted standard course

  - o Off-the-shelf

  - o Custom in-house course

  - o Developed by internal staff

  - o Developed by external consultants

- The means by which requirements and expectations of the organization are established for its training programs, including the degree to which they are defined through:

  - o Informal techniques and generalized understanding

  - o Interviews with project managers

  - o Interviews with senior managers and executives

  - o Perception of human resources staff

  - o Benchmarking against other organizations

o Adoption of another organization's curriculum

o Evaluation of lessons learned

- The overall effectiveness of the project management curriculum within the organization, and its perceived effectiveness relative to other programs offered by the organization.

Three components are obtained explaining a total of 53% of the variance:

- **Tailored Internal** (Percentage of variance explained: 36.4%; Eigenvalue: 9.089). This component loads heavily and positively on variables associated the use of adapted standard courses and courses developed or customized by internal staff. The component also loads heavily on the majority of variables associated with delivery approaches, and heavily on variables associated with formal gathering and incorporation of requirements associated with training, including the use of interviews, adoption of other curricula and evaluations of lessons learned. Organizations that measure strongly on this variable typically develop or adapt their training programs, based upon industry standard programs or programs that have been successfully delivered in other organizations. They make use of a broad array of delivery approaches, and make use of a formalized approach to training development.

- **Informal Off-the-shelf** (Percentage of variance explained: 9.1%; Eigenvalue: 2.278). This component loads heavily and positively on variables associated with the use of off-the-shelf training programs, and also loads heavily and positively on the use of informal techniques of defining training requirements. Organizations that measure strongly on this component are typically reliant upon standardized course offerings, with minimal consideration of specific requirements and no tailoring of the training delivery to the specific practices or project management implementation of the organization.

- **Customized External** (Percentage of variance explained: 7.6%; Eigenvalue: 1.898). This component loads heavily and positively on variables associated with the development of customized training courses and the use of external consultants to develop and tailor the curriculum to the organization. This component also loads negatively on the use of internal staff for course development and positively on the requirements for the curriculum being based upon the perception of human resources staff members. Organizations that measure strongly on this component are typically organizations that adopt customized training curricula, but rely heavily upon their development by external consultants. The training course development is often highly reliant upon mediation and co-ordination by human resources staff, with minimal input from project management staff or through evaluating lessons learned from previous projects.

Training – Duration

The duration of training evaluates the duration of training offered to support staff members in their various project management roles, including training programs with durations that are:

- Long-term (more than 6 months)

- Mid-term (1 to 6 months)

- Short-term (2-4 weeks)

- 1 week

- < 1 week

Two components are obtained explaining a total of 67% of the variance:

- **Long-Term Training** (Percentage of variance explained: 40.2%; Eigenvalue: 2.012). This component loads heavily and positively on variables associated with the delivery of longer-term training programs, particularly with variables associated with durations of one to six months or more than six months. This component also loads negatively on variables associated with delivery durations of less than one week. Organizations that measure strongly on this component typically make use of long-term programs, often delivered through diploma and degree programs.

- **Short-Term Training** (Percentage of variance explained: 27.6%; Eigenvalue: 1.380). This component loads heavily and positively on the variables associated with the delivery of short-term training courses, and particularly variables associated with durations of one week or less. Organizations that measure strongly on this component rely on curricula that consist of short-term workshops and training courses.

Tools

The tools PCA utilized a number of variables to explore the various mechanisms used to support definition and utilization of the project management implementation. These include:

- Guidelines that are used to define and support the project management implementation and its practices, including:

o Project management procedures

o Templates

o Checklists

o Job aids

- Software tools that are used to automate or provide administrative support to the project management implementation, including:

  o Scheduling software

  o Resource management software

  o Cost management software

  o Risk management software

  o Estimation software

  o Portfolio management software

  o Dashboard reporting software

  o Portal software

  o Collaboration software

  o Software interfaces

- Databases that are used to support the capturing, management and sharing of knowledge and information within the organization, including:

  o Knowledge management

  o Expert systems

  o Lessons-learned databases

  o Project archives

  o Reference sources

Three components are obtained explaining a total of almost 54% of the variance:

- **Full Toolsets** (Percentage of variance explained: 37.6%; Eigenvalue: 7.144). This component loads heavily and positively on the majority of variables associated with software tools and databases, and also load positively and heavily on variables associated with the use of checklists and job aids to define their practices, and to a lesser extent on variables associated with procedure documentation and templates. Organizations that measure strongly on this component have a broad array of software tools and databases to support their implementations and have typically invested heavily in establishing toolsets to support their implementations.

- **Resource Management** (Percentage of variance explained: 9.0%; Eigenvalue: 1.715). This component loads heavily and positively on variables associated with the use of resource management software and also load negatively on variables associated with the use of process documentation and templates to reflect their practices. Organizations that measure strongly on this component typically limit their use of software, and the focus of their implementation, to the management of resources. In many instances, their motivation for implementing project management was focused on more effective resource usage and control.

- **Cost Management** (Percentage of variance explained: 8.2%; Eigenvalue: 1.565). This component loads heavily and positively on variables associated with the use of cost management software. Organizations that measure strongly against this component are typically those that predominately make use of cost management software and techniques, and whose implementation is primarily one that views effective project management as effective cost management.

People

The People PCA provides an understanding of the people that support the delivery and management of projects within the organization, and embody the implementation itself. Several variables are drawn upon to evaluate those people involved in project roles including:

- Assessment of the competency of people in various roles within the organization, including:

  o Executives

  o Project managers

  o Project team members

- The formality of roles associated with project management in the organization, including:

  o The formality of organizational roles in support of projects

  o The formality with which project-specific roles are defined

  o The degree to which there is a career path in place for project management

  o The formality of training mechanisms available to support project managers

- The experience and training required of project managers in order to qualify for a position within the organization

Two components are obtained explaining a total of 55% of the variance:

- **Clear Roles & Training** (Percentage of variance explained: 32.4%; Eigenvalue: 2.593). This component loads heavily and positively on variables associated with there being clearly defined roles defined within the organization and its projects, and variables that are associated with a clearly defined career path and formal training mechanisms in place to support the development of project managers. Organizations that measure strongly on this component typically view project management as a core competency within the organization, and have invested in both developing their project management resources and ensuring that there is sufficient role clarity to enable them to be effective in their roles.

- **Trained Experts** (Percentage of variance explained: 23.0%; Eigenvalue: 1.836). This component loads heavily and positively on variables associated with a high degree of training and qualification expected in project managers within the organization. The component also loads heavily and positively on variables associated with the competency of staff in all roles within the organization, and loads negatively on variables associated with the definition of clear project roles within the organizations. Organizations that measure strongly on this component typically view project management as a skill to be hired. There are high expectations and qualifications associated with the project management role, and an overall expectation of competence within the organization. There are few structures or roles formally defined in support of projects within the organization, however, and project managers are expected to already have an appropriate level of expertise and typically are expected to perform effectively with few organizational supports.

Motivators

The motivators describe the underlying rationale and motivations that led to the implementation within the organization. There are a number of variables that are drawn upon in establishing the motivators PCA, including:

- The duration of the implementation within the organization

- The resources involved in the development of the project management implementation, including:

  o Internal development, with new staff hired to support the implementation

  o Internal development using existing staff resources

  o Development with a combination of internal and external resources

  o Developed by externally sourced contract resources, but managed and coordinated internally

  o Developed by external consultants

- The motivators underlying the initial development of the project management implementation, including:

  o Increasing project complexity

  o Increasing number of projects

  o Time pressure on projects

  o Market pressures

  o Competitive pressures

  o Maintaining appearance of being current

  o Best practices

  o Internationalization/globalization

- The overall objectives that the organization hoped to realize as a result of the implementation, including:

  o Improve project performance

  o Improve business case realization

    o Accelerate project delivery

    o Reduce the costs of projects

    o Increase organizational credibility

    o Gain a competitive advantage

    o Align with partner expectations or commitments

Three components are obtained, explaining a total of almost 46% of the variance:

- **Traditional Drivers** (Percentage of variance explained: 22.4%; Eigenvalue: 6.948). This component loads heavily and positively on variables associated with implementations responding to time pressures, competitive pressures, and a desire to appear as an organization to be current. This component also loads heavily on variables associated with implementation objectives of improving project delivery, accelerating project performance, increasing organizational credibility, gaining a competitive advantage, and aligning with external expectations and commitments. Organizations that measure strongly on this component have typically implemented project management in response to perceived (e.g., competitive) or real (e.g., regulatory or funding bodies) external pressures, and have objectives of improving traditional project delivery measures such as on-time, on-budget and to-specification performance.

- **Strategic Drivers** (Percentage of variance explained: 14.3%; Eigenvalue: 4.436). This component loads heavily and positively on variables associated with organizational project challenges, including an increasing number of projects, increasing time and competitive pressures, and increasing project complexity. Organizations that measure strongly on this component have typically implemented project management in response to strategic and competitive pressures. The motivation for the implementation is driven at an organizational level, and the implementation is in part seen as a means of competitive differentiation.

- **Internal Drivers** (Percentage of variance explained: 9.2%; Eigenvalue: 2.843). This component loads heavily and positively on variables associated with managing an increasing number of projects, but negatively on variables associated with external drivers such as competitive pressures or international standards or requirements. This component also loads positively on variables associated with improving project performance, but negatively on variables associated with objectives of gaining greater competitive advantage. Organizations that measure strongly on this component have largely been motivated to implement project management in response to internally motivated drivers, and see project management as a means of managing the magnitude and delivery of their internal workload, rather than being a source of competitive advantage.

Organization

The Organization PCA provides an understanding of the organizational supports and structures that have been established to support the project management implementation. There are also a number of variables that explore the recognition of the organizational role of project management and the relative maturity of the practices within the organization. Variables contained within the organizational PCA include:

- Senior management involvement in projects, including oversight of project management decisions and involvement on project steering committees.

- The authority of project managers within the organization, including:

  o The degree to which project managers are perceived as high-ranking members of the organization

  o The degree of functional/line involvement of project managers in addition to their project responsibilities.

  o The degree to which project managers are fully responsible for the projects they manage.

- The authority of project managers in the projects they are responsible for, including:

  o The degree to which project managers are involved in setting goals for the projects they manage

  o Whether project managers have exclusive authority over the technical aspects of their projects

  o Whether project managers have sufficient authority to deliver on the goals of their project

  o Whether project managers are able to change the objectives of the project in order to attain the goals of the projects they manage

- The authority of project managers over the staff and team members involved in the delivery of projects, including:

o The degree to which project managers have incentive authority over those they manage

o The degree to which project managers contribute to the performance assessment of those they manage

o Whether project managers have influence over the kind of awards (promotions, bonuses, etc.) that are given to the staff that they manage

- The presence of a project support group within the organization, and the role that the project support group fulfills in supporting projects within the organization, including responsibility for:

  o Being a center of excellence

  o Methodology and tool development

  o Methodology and tool promotion and support

  o Resource management

  o Project manager development

  o Project manager coaching/mentoring

  o Project reporting

  o Project control

  o Project delivery

  o Project oversight

  o Project prioritization and selection

  o Program management

  o Portfolio management

  o Project management maturity process

  o Project manager competency assessment

  o Project intervention/rescue

  o Benchmarking

  o Project audits

- The relative maturity of project management within the organization, including:

  o The degree to which the organization has assessed the maturity of its project management practices

  o The model used to assess project management maturity

  o The initial level of maturity assessed within the organization

  o The latest level of maturity assessed within the organization

Three components are obtained explaining a total of almost 36% of the variance:

- **Project Management Authority** (Percentage of variance explained: 17.0%; Eigenvalue: 10.522). This component loads heavily and positively on variables associated with project manager authority, including authority over project staff and degree of consultation in establishing objectives and goals for projects. This component also loads positively and heavily on variables associated with project managers being high-ranking members of the organization and having significant line or operational responsibilities as well as their project responsibilities. Organizations that measure strongly on this component typically are ones where project managers have a significant level of authority and are considered high-ranking members of the organization, and have direct authority and the ability to provide rewards, recognition, and incentives to those that they manage.

- **Delivery PMO** (Percentage of variance explained: 10.9%; Eigenvalue: 6.733). This component loads heavily and positively on variables associated with the role of the project support group. There is particularly heavy loading on variables associated with the support group being responsible for resource management, project manager development, and competency assessment, as well as project prioritization, project delivery, project control, and project oversight. This component also loads heavily on variables where the project support group would be responsible for project rescue and project audits. Organizations that measure strongly on this component are those who have a strong project support group that is typically both the organizational home of project managers within the organization and where the support group has direct accountability and responsibility for the delivery, management, and success of organizational projects.

- **Methodology PMO** (Percentage of variance explained: 7.9%; Eigenvalue: 4.919). This component loads heavily and positively on variables associated with the role of the project support group, where the support group is responsible for methodology and tool development, and ongoing promotion and support of the toolsets. This component also loads heavily and negatively on variables associated with project oversight, project delivery, and project control. Organizations that measure strongly on this component are typically those that have a project support group that is responsible for the ongoing development, promotion and support of project management practices throughout the organization, but is not responsible for the actual management and delivery of projects.

What Implementation Similarities Exist?

The implementation PCAs and the components within them help to identify the meaningful variations that exist within the various project management implementations within the case study organizations. While some dimensions may be expected, other structures and implementation aspects may be surprising or at least less familiar. Each aspect of the implementations on its own, however, serves to identify only a single dimension of the implementations being observed within organizations. Of greater value is understanding how the components within the PCAs integrate into an overall view of implementations on an organizational basis.

As previously discussed in Chapter 5, a construct-level PCA was conducted for each of the constructs. The implementation construct-level PCA provides an integrated view of all of the components that emerged from the individual PCAs discussed in the sections above, and provides an overview of the overall implementations that collectively explain the greatest amount of variation within the data; in other words, those combinations of components that describe the most common implementations observed within the case study organizations.

Conducting the construct-level PCA of the implementation components yielded five clear components that collectively explain 62% of the variance in the implementation data associated with the case studies:

- **Full Project Management, Traditional Drivers And A Delivery PMO** (Percentage of variance explained: 21.1%; Eigenvalue: 4.002). This component loads heavily and positively on components associated with full project management training based upon a tailored, internally developed curriculum. The component also loads heavily on components associated with the use of full toolsets, the establishment of clear roles, career paths and formal training frameworks, and where a delivery PMO is in place. Finally, the component loads positively on the motivation for the implementation being in response to traditional drivers. Organizations that measure strongly on this component typically have a strong project management implementation that the organization has invested heavily in developing. There is a strong delivery focus within the organization, and the organization has established a clear point of accountability for delivery with the project support group, as well as establishing role clarity, training structures, and defined career path for project management within the organization.

> *Case study organization 22 is a state-owned construction company based in Shanghai, China delivering major infrastructure projects. The organization is recognized as having significant technical and management knowledge, but faces strong competitive pressures and a shrinking local market.*
>
> *The organization has made significant investments in developing its project management capabilities since it was founded more than 20 years ago. Because of the extreme complexity and risks of the mega-projects it conducts as well as the high market competition pressure, the organization continues to improve its project management capability in order to realize the goals of projects and improve project implementation efficiency.*
>
> *"Employees in our company had different backgrounds, for example, people came from construction unit still accustomed to doing jobs they were good at before, but didn't take responsibility for their own job. Project management helped us to define everyone's duty."*
>
> *—Senior Manager, 22*

- **Long Term Training, Strategic Drivers And Project Management Authority** (Percentage of variance explained: 14.8%; Eigenvalue: 2.806). This component loads heavily and positively on components associated with long-term training approaches, strategic drivers for the project management implementation, and a strong level of authority associated with project managers within the organization. The component also loads positively on the use of customized external training, and negatively on the use of off-the-shelf training or informal lunch-and-learns. Organizations that measure strongly on this component have typically adopted project management for strategic purposes but place a heavy level of reliance upon the authority of the project managers to be able to deliver projects. They invest in the development of their project managers through intensive training programs, and project managers have a high level of seniority and influence within the organization.

> *Case study organization 35 is an extremely mature state-owned construction and engineering firm based in Beijing, China. The organization has constructed significant and complex projects throughout the country as well as overseas.*
>
> *The organization has continuously invested in efforts to improve its project management capabilities since the mid-1990s, in order to be more competitive in getting projects and increase project profits. The company has also organized extensive training in project management for staff. The Ministry of Construction also requests that all the project managers in construction companies must be certified (involving 3 levels), for which the candidate project managers must participate in certain training courses and pass examinations organized by the government.*
>
> *"Most of our project managers have been educated in engineering/ construction, so the company has provided various trainings in order to improve their management capability as well as to support them to pass the certification exam . . ."*
>
> —*Human Resources, 35*

- **Cost Management, Clear Roles & Informal Training** (Percentage of variance explained: 10.8%; Eigenvalue: 2.048). This component loads heavily and positively on components associated with cost management implementations of project management, as well as the establishment of clear roles and a career path for project managers. The component also loads strongly on the use of customized external courses and informal training approaches. The component also loads moderately on both internal and strategic drivers for the implementation, but quite negatively on traditional drivers for implementation. Organizations that measure strongly on this component primarily view project management as a process of cost management. There are clear roles and formal structures in place for project managers, and the focus is on developing internal project managers through approaches that primarily rely upon external providers and internal, informal approaches.

> *Case study organization 27 is an information technology services organization serving the financial services industry in Germany. It is the subsidiary of a financial institution, and provides project and outsourcing services to more than 2,000 customers.*
>
> *Projects are formally identified but rather informally managed. Formal techniques primarily emphasize cost, schedule, and risk management, and there is less emphasis on scope management, formal requirements definition or the management of stakeholder expectations.*
>
> *"[Project management] ensures the delivery of a project that at a minimum is on the level the client expects, and that we make money."*
> —*Sponsor, 27*

- **Internal Drivers And External Off-The-Shelf Training** (Percentage of variance explained: 8.8%; Eigenvalue: 1.664). This component loads heavily and positively on components that are associated with internal drivers for the implementation of project management, and that primarily employ off-the-shelf training delivered on an external basis. This component also loads negatively on resource management, full project management implementation and the hiring of trained experts. Organizations that measure strongly on this component typically have project management implementations that have been driven by a desire to manage internal complexities and scope of work, and have primarily done so through the training of internal staff as project managers. These organizations typically rely upon off-the-shelf training courses delivered by external providers, with little tailoring of approach to the organization.

> *Case study organization 43 is a large, project-based division of a state government department in Australia. The organization is responsible for the construction and engineering of major infrastructure projects within the state.*
>
> *The implementation of project management has been internally driven as a result of the growing number of projects and increased project complexity that it faced. The implementation involved the tailoring of standardized processes to the organization, and the provision of training by an external consulting firm.*
>
> *"They're very capable; we have very capable staff generally. I think the will is there, it's just that the bureaucratic processes get in the way. Allocating the time for development and evolution is the problem. A lot of the time people get stuck in the phase of crisis management, because of the workload and the lack of resources. I've been doing less courses and conferences over the last years because of our workload."*
>
> —Human Resources, 43

- **Trained Experts And Methodology PMO** (Percentage of variance explained: 6.7%; Eigenvalue: 1.282). This component loads heavily and positively on components that are associated with the use of trained experts to deliver projects and the presence of a support group that is responsible for methodology implementation. Organizations that measure strongly on this component typically view project management as a skill to be hired for, and have high standards for the project managers they recruit but little internal structure or development approach to support their continued progression. There are often internal processes and standards that are developed and maintained by an internal project support group, but delivery responsibility is the responsibility of the project manager with few internal structures to support delivery or create an environment to support the project manager.

Case study organization 59 is a state-owned research organization within Canada that competes with other research organizations within the country and internationally for research projects.

The organization is staffed by senior personnel who take great pride in their expertise and professionalism. Project management was introduced as a means of gaining better control of the research projects undertaken by the organization, and consisted of introducing and mandating the use of processes and templates within the organization.

"Every once in a while I'm asked to fill in something that looks like a very traditional project plan and I find it is a real waste of time. It takes me easily three days of productive work, but I have to do it because somewhere somebody on the top believes that it is important"
—Project Manager, 59

Organizational Profiles Of Implementation

Each of our case study organizations included in the PCA analysis has been scored on each of the implementation components identified above. Figure 7-2 depicts those organizations that rank low (below one standard deviation from the mean) and high (above one standard deviation from the mean) on each implementation descriptor. The organizations are recorded in each cell (for example, High—Full Project Management, Traditional Drivers, and Delivery PMO) in numeric order – that is there is no meaning embedded in where in the cell an organization appears. If it is in that cell, it is beyond one standard deviation from the mean.

Some organizations are clearly most strongly described by a single implementation descriptor. The dark circles in Figure 7-2 identify these organizations. For instance, organization 22 registers highly as being described by a Full Project Management, Traditional Drivers and Delivery PMO and nothing else. Single implementations-descriptor organizations can be said to be most strongly described by the component they are associated with.

Some organizations ranked above or below one standard deviation from the mean on more than one implementation component. These organizations are described by more than one implementation component. Lines connect all of the instances of the same organization across the cells and should help you find the duplicates.

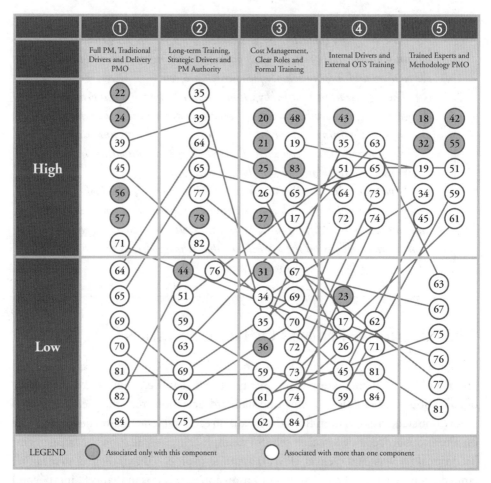

FIGURE 7-2—*Organizational profiles of implementation*

This figure provides a number of insights into the sample organizations and the implementations they come f rom:

- Many of the organizations that rank above or below one standard deviation from the mean do so on only one implementation component. Fully 20 of the case study organizations register solely on one implementation descriptor that is beyond one standard deviation of the mean.

- Most of the single implementation component organizations are described by a single "high" implementation. This suggests that their implementation is best described by a single implementation component seen in the data. The reader might remember that this was not the case in the context PCA organization profile in Chapter 6, where far fewer organizations were described by a single PCA. For those instances where organizations were described by a single context PCA, they were mostly *not* described by the component.

- Where an organization is described by multiple components, they are often described as *not* being reflective of the other component. In other words, the other components rank more than one standard deviation below the mean on the other components. This suggests that the organization's implementation does not fit neatly into any one implementation component that emerged from the PCA analysis. This could mean that the implementation is in itself quite unique or that it is not clearly differentiated. A closer examination of some of the organizations not being identified suggests that perhaps because it is early in the implementation and its final structure is still emerging.

- All but two implementation components have close to the same number of organizations above one standard deviation from the mean as below. This indicates a relatively normal distribution of organizations against this component. However, PCA 3 (*cost management, clear roles and formal training*) and PCA 5 (*trained experts and methodology PMO*) reflect skewed distributions. The distributions for these two components are more like one-third to two-thirds. PCA 3 has far more organizations reporting being *not* described by this component while PCA 5 has a larger number of organizations described by this component.

- Many more organization's implementations (24) are described as being one standard deviation above or below the mean on PCA 3 (*cost management, clear roles and formal training*) than any other component. The next highest association either 'high' or 'low' is for PCA 4 (*internal drivers and external off-the-shelf (OTS) training*) with 18 organizations. These components appear to be ones that organizations strongly resonate with, either as describing their implementation or as an implementation that they are *not*.

- There also appear to be patterns in how the implementation components describe the organizations.

    o Organizations that register high on PCA 1 (*full project management, traditional drivers and delivery PMO*), PCA3 (*cost management, clear roles and formal training*), and PCA 5 (*trained experts and methodology PMO*) are more likely than the rest of the high sample to be described only by that implementation component. This indicates that we have many single component implementations for these components.

    o More organizations are described as *not* PCA 3 (*cost management, clear roles and formal training*) than any other component. One half of the organizations in this category are associated with an above-the-standard deviation of another implementation component. Two organizations are best described by being *not* this implementation, and are also not described by any other component. The remaining six organizations are best described as *not* PCA 3 and *not* some other component.

IMPLEMENTATION MATURITY

Perceptions Of Organizational Maturity

A popular conception when evaluating the implementation of project management is the idea of project management maturity. The intent of assessing maturity is to measure both the progressive improvement of practices that exist at an organizational level with respect to an implementation, and the consistency with which they are applied within the organization. As noted earlier in this chapter, the assessment of project management maturity was not an express focus of this research study, and was not a dominant focus in the development of the implementation constructs. While there were many models of project management maturity that could have been applied to this study, the underlying intent was to take a grounded approach in understanding what organizations have in actual fact implemented, rather than imposing a pre-defined structure or model of project management against which case-study organizations would be compared.

There have been numerous debates and discussions regarding how best to evaluate maturity, the most appropriate models to use, and whether the idea of 'maturity' is even appropriate. Without wanting to either reopen or exhaustively address these here, the authors do recognize that project management maturity is a concept that is familiar to many in understanding implementations, and can provide a common frame within which to make relative comparisons of implementations.

Even within the research team, there were numerous views on the level of maturity that case-study organizations were perceived at. This is in part due to differing interpretations of maturity, as well as different cultural biases that emerge in how organizations are viewed and assessed. As well, the ratings of organizations against other maturity models (e.g. the Capability Maturity Model, or CMM) or the fact that an organization was ISO 9000 certified occasionally influenced the perception of project management maturity of the organization.

While the data collection strategy did not consciously embrace or incorporate a maturity model, the amount of data collected regarding organizational implementations within the case study is sufficient to infer a generalized sense of the maturity of an implementation. In other words, reviewing the implementation data that is available on each case study enables an assessment of what *level* of maturity an implementation could be interpreted to have attained.

Defining A Common Framework

The challenge of assessing maturity, however, is choosing a common framework that can be utilized. There are numerous maturity models present in the marketplace that purport to assess the relative effectiveness of project management implementation, and within these there are numerous scoring methods and reporting structures. Most models, however, with some adaptation adhere to the five-level structure originally outlined in the Capability Maturity Model for Software (Humphreys, 1992), arguably the most well-known of maturity models and a foundation for the development of many other frameworks.

Given the relative familiarity of a five-level model, a similar model was adopted as the basis of assessing the maturity of case studies within this study. The meaning of the levels used for the purpose of this assessment is described in the following points:

- **Level 1 – Ad hoc.** This level is associated with an informal and inconsistent approach to project management. In essence, Level 1 implies that there is no *organizational* implementation of project management; instead the processes that are utilized and the effectiveness of the results are the product of the experience and expertise of the individual project manager and teams.

- **Level 2 – Some Practices.** Level 2 suggests that there are some practices and capabilities defined and utilized at an organizational level, but that they are not complete or they are not consistently adhered to throughout the organization. While there is some level of organizational formality, it is not comprehensive nor is it fully applied.

- **Level 3 – Consistent Practices.** Level 3 represents a consistent and adhered to project management implementation. It suggests that there is a complete project management process in place, and that it is consistently utilized on all projects within the organization. For many organizations, this level of maturity is in fact the target level they seek to attain.

- **Level 4 – Integrated Practices.** A level 4 implementation would be one where there is not only a consistently defined and adhered-to project management process, but that it is fully integrated into the management capabilities of the organization. This does not presume only a project-driven organizational model, but does imply that the operational or functional management processes are aware of and integrated with those of project management and vice versa. Project management at this level becomes an integral management capability that is fully integrated within the organizational lifecycle.

- **Level 5 – Continually Improving Practices.** The final level of maturity would be one where there is a holistic, fully integrated approach to managing projects that exists within an ongoing cycle of continuous improvement. The idea of continuous improvement is one where there is a formal and consistently adhered-to process of continually learning from, evaluating, assessing, and improving the project management implementation.

It is important to note that while some aspects of some of the higher levels of maturity may be evidenced in some implementations, the assessment of maturity is at the level of the organization as a whole. A level of maturity is based upon performance of the entire unit of analysis, and the degree to which the practices described are formalized, adhered to and used consistently by all projects and by all employees. Even where some formal practices are evidenced that may suggest "good" project management, limiting their use to that of a project or a single project manager would suggest, for example, a level of 1.

Allowing For Discrete Differences

In assessing the maturity of case-study organizations, two fundamental challenges were encountered in endeavoring to make discrete distinctions between implementations:

- The first challenge was associated being able to accurately and consistently judge the maturity of an implementation, given that a formal maturity model was not used. A formal maturity assessment should utilize strict and consistent measures to be able to objectively determine the resulting maturity level of an organization's implementation. The approach used in interpreting maturity of the case-study organizations was based upon a comprehensive review of the reported process data as well as the case reports provided. These did provide a sound basis for assessing the overall level of maturity, but was not expanded upon to provide a more granular interpretation of individual capabilities or capability areas.

- The second challenge was that drawing distinctions between maturity levels would often find an organization in the "gray area" between one level and another. This is further complicated because, as has been evidenced in other maturity-based research (Mullaly, 2006), there are typically few to no organizations at the higher levels of maturity, with the vast majority of organizations clustered in the lower levels, particularly level 1 and level 2. To allow meaningful distinctions to be made, half-levels of maturity were also utilized. An organization that was at a level of maturity of greater than two (for example, with fairly well-defined processes) but not quite at level 3 (for example, not all projects consistently utilized the process), would then be assessed at a level of 2.5.

Observed Maturity In The Case Studies

The observed maturity in the case studies is illustrated in Figure 7-3:

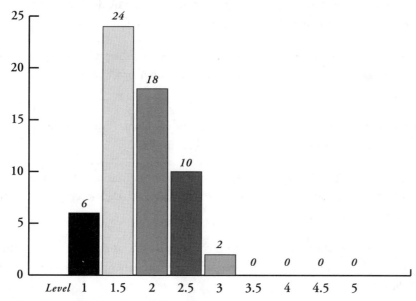

FIGURE 7-3—*Observed case study maturity levels*

The number of case studies included within this analysis is 60, which were the number of case studies for which both case reports and detailed implementation data were available. Overall, the distribution of maturity by level is articulated in Table 7-4:

Level 1	50%
Level 2	47%
Level 3	3%

TABLE 7-4—*Summary of observed maturity levels*

This distribution corresponds quite strongly to that seen in other studies (for example, the distributions cited in Mullaly (2006). It also highlights the varied distribution that does exist within the case-study organizations. Even though participation as a case-study organization implies that the organization has an interest in project management, which is an unavoidable source of bias in the overall research study, those organizations that did participate are still at a varied range of implementations. Moreover, even though there were a number of very strong practices and capabilities observed within the case-study organizations, for many organizations they are not fully and consistently utilized. This lack of utilization was observed to result from a number of different causes, including:

- The implementation itself being at an early stage of deployment within the organization, where it was not yet fully rolled out and being utilized.

- The implementation only being required on a subset of projects within the organization, where other projects adopted other practices or were managed in a more ad hoc manner.

- Customers and partners of the case-study organizations requiring different practices and approaches to be utilized on projects.

- Adherence not being enforced within the organization, or practices being established as 'guidelines' which are available for use rather than specifically being required.

- Employees within the organization consciously choosing not to fully adhere to the established practices associated with the implementation, or to circumvent the process.

Overall, the maturity results being observed align with observations elsewhere, and provide another perspective against which the value of the case study implementations can be assessed.

CONCLUSIONS

This chapter was designed to answer the following question: "What do organizations implement that they call project management?" As was indicated in the introduction, the planned approach to this study was to take a grounded approach to the investigation, understanding from organizations themselves what they have implemented, and why they have implemented what they did.

As with the context observed in the previous chapters, there are a range of implementations present. Different strategies are employed for training and employee development. Project managers are valued in different degrees within the case study organizations, and have different degrees of influence, authority, and power in the organizations that have been described. There are different approaches adopted in introducing project supports groups (such as project management offices), and these support groups differ in focus, structure, and influence. Finally, the maturity of the organizations varies considerably, from the very ad hoc and informal to approaches that are formally defined and consistently adhered to.

What this reinforces quite clearly is that there is no one way that project management is understood, and that there is no one model that is being adopted when project management is implemented. Organizations within the case studies employed very different strategies, based upon very different reasons and drivers. As a result, different implementations have emerged and been represented here.

One question, first posed in the previous chapter, still remains unanswered: "What differences matter to project management implementations?" An understanding of the implementations has moved us closer to being able to answer this question. We now understand the differences that exist within the organizations themselves, and what differences exist in how these organizations approach managing their projects. What still needs to be understood, however, is what matters about these implementations. To understand this, we need to also understand what these organizations value, and what value is being realized from organizations from their implementations. The next chapter explores in detail the value that has been observed.

8

Value

Introduction

The essential topic that this research set out to develop was an understanding of the value of project management. The fundamental theory of this study is that the value an organization realizes is a function of both the context it operates in and the project management implementation that it has undertaken. Neither dimension alone, therefore, would be sufficient to be able to determine the value that organizations receive from project management. Exploring both the context of organizations and understanding the implementations that they have adopted are necessary in being able to understand the kinds of value that organizations do in fact realize, and the underlying drivers that influence this realization.

The specific question that this part of the research is designed to answer is:

• What is valuable to organizations, and how is it measured?

To be able to assess value, it is necessary to understand the dimensions of value that organizations can realize from project management. It is equally important to understand how these dimensions of value are currently evaluated and measured. This chapter endeavors to explore the dimensions of value that can be associated with project management implementations, and the degree to which these different values are in fact being observed in the case-study organizations participating in this research.

Exploring The Measurement Of Value

Initial Measurement Strategies

There are a number of different dimensions of value that can be evaluated with respect to project management implementations, and in fact with respect to any organizational change initiative. As discussed in Chapter 2, this research originally adopted and adapted somewhat a framework suggested by Kirkpatrick (1998) and Philips (1998), which posited that value can be associated with five categories:

- **Level 1 – Satisfaction.** This category of value is associated with the degree that stakeholders realize satisfaction from the implementation.

- **Level 2 – Alignment.** This category of value is associated with the consistency and repeatability of the implementation; in other words, the degree to which the implementation creates a level of consistency, terminology, and understanding in the organization.

- **Level 3 – Process Outcomes.** This category of value is associated with the delivery of process efficiencies as a result of the implementation. In other words, was the process itself more effective? Did projects more effectively deliver to process measures of budget, schedule, and specification?

- **Level 4 – Business Outcomes.** This category of value is associated with the creation of actual business outcomes resulting from the implementation. Was the organization more efficient or profitable as a result? Did revenues increase, or costs decrease? Was there an improvement in competitive positioning, market share, or reputation of the organization as a result of the implementation?

- **Level 5 – Return on Investment.** This category of value is associated with the actual business case and cost-benefit analysis associated with the project implementation. In other words, what return was realized on the investment in the project management implementation?

It is important to recognize that while these categories are described as "levels," they are nominal, rather than ordinal. In other words, they are each discrete categories unto themselves. Each category is independent, and there is no inference that a level 2 value is more important or significant than that at level 1, or less important or significant than value at level 3. It is neither a maturity model or a discrete hierarchy of value, despite any potential temptation to consider it as such.

Direct vs. Derived Measures Of Value

As we proceeded with the above structure as an initial frame for understanding value, what emerged over time was a recognition that there were some dimensions of value that were being measured directly, while others could only be derived. Particularly as we commenced the analysis and working extensively with the data dictionary of constructs and variables that defined what had been collected, there emerged an appreciation that what was being evaluated and assessed within the instruments were the first four levels of the model proposed by Kirkpatrick and Philips. In other words, we had variables that directly captured either actual measures or perceptions associated with the categories of *satisfaction, alignment, process outcomes* and *business outcomes*.

There had always been recognition that the category of *return on investment* should also be able to be measured. As noted in Chapter 2, the principles of measuring ROI are straightforward, clear, and well understood. What is needed is to understand:

- What quantifiable benefits can be derived from the implementation?

- How do these compare to the costs of the implementation?

What became very clear, however, is that ROI is a measure that can only be *derived* from other measures that have already been collected. To do so would require determining which dimensions of value could be quantified, then developing strategies to actually quantify the resulting value that was realized and expressing that quantification in terms of monetary value. Second, there is a need to calculate the total costs associated with the implementation. Finally, the actually return on investment itself can be derived by comparing the quantifiable benefits to the defined costs.

What is important to distinguish here is that there are two fundamentally different types of measures associated with value:

- Those that can actually be measured directly.

- Those that must be derived from the measures that are available and have been captured.

Measuring Return On Investment

As a research team, we recognized that the measurement of return on investment was one that would need to be derived from the other measures in the study. As stated above, this is conceptually not particularly complicated. What is required is to have the underlying measures of value, and then to be able to quantify them.

What we did not expect, however, is the degree to which quantifiable measures of not just value but also cost would not be available within the case-study organizations. Only an extremely small number of organizations could in any way quantify the benefits that they realized from their project management implementation.

What is equally clear from these few examples is that the benefits are anecdotal; they are not actually a product of measurement, but of supposition on the part of interview participants within the case-study organizations. As will be discussed in the following sections, it is not that value was not being seen from case-study organizations. The very opposite is true; the vast majority of organizations both saw and were able to demonstrate clear value. What was not present, however, was an interest on the part of organizations in quantifying either the costs or the benefits of the project management implementation.

What emerged from the case studies that were conducted is a clear indication that the majority of project management implementations are not the result of business-case decisions, but are instead the product of other drivers. These drivers may be through reasons of competitiveness, the desire to better be able to manage a growing or more complex workload, the need to comply with regulatory or funding body regulations, or simply the desire to appear to be current. There were no case-study organizations that prepared a business case to justify their implementation, however, and even those organizations that should have been able to quantify costs and benefits did not have the data collection strategies in place to be able to do so.

Measuring "Fit"

One other concept of value that was present in the conceptual model was the idea of "fit." As expressed in the conceptual model, the idea of fit was an articulation of whether the actual implementation of project management within an organization is actually appropriate. Appropriateness, in this context, was intended to evaluate the degree to which the implementation is responsive to the environment and the business orientation of the organization.

In first relating the conceptual model of the research to the five-levels framework suggested by Kirkpatrick and Philips, it was first presumed that levels 1 and 2–*satisfaction* and *alignment*–could serve as proxies for an understanding of "fit." The presumption here is that if first, stakeholders are reflecting satisfaction with an implementation, and second, the organization is using the implementation consistently, then presumably the implementation must work for–or "fit"–the organization.

What was recognized in conducting and analyzing the case studies, however, is that positive value could be reported in terms of *satisfaction* or *alignment*, and yet an implementation could actually be inappropriate for the organization. This was reflected in case studies where:

- Organizations were satisfied with the results they were attaining from project management without valuing project management itself or being interested in adopting a formalized implementation;

- Organizations were very consistent in their implementation, but the implementation itself was viewed as completely inappropriate for the organization;

- Organizations where senior management stakeholders expressed high levels of satisfaction, while the project managers expressed both dissatisfaction and a desire for change; and

- Organizations where parent organizations expressed satisfaction with what was implemented and viewed the implementation as "done," but senior management in the subsidiary as well as project managers expressed high levels of dissatisfaction.

It is easy at times to view "alignment" as to what degree the implementation is actually appropriate for the context of the organization, however, it is in the context of this study simply a measure of consistency.

The idea of fit is a more complex one. At best, *satisfaction* can be a proxy for fit. As illustrated above, there is not necessarily consistency in how implementations are viewed by all stakeholders; while some stakeholders may be satisfied, others may not. Actual measurement of fit is more complex, and again is a derived value rather than something that can actually be measured directly.

To be able to measure fit requires first being able to answer the essential question "What implementations and context are associated with what value?" With an understanding of the value that an organization is seeking, and the context in which it operates, the appropriate implementation can be readily determined. This is, in fact, the underlying purpose of this research study–to be able to determine what context and implementations do deliver value, and the nature of the value that is actually being influenced. Once these influences are understood, then, it is possible to go back and evaluate whether organizations have, in fact, established implementations that are appropriate for their implementation and context, and are, in fact, realizing value. Again, however, the idea of "fit" can only be derived, it cannot itself be directly measured.

The results is that while fit is a concept that is contained within the original conceptual model, it is in the context of this research project something that we are endeavoring to demonstrate as a result of what we have collected, analyzed, and found. It is not something that has been measured directly, because it is not something that can be measured directly.

ASSOCIATING "FIT" WITH VALUE

This section was contributed by Dr. Thomas Mengel

This analysis is based on 59 case reports—and 43 value quotation summaries—studying the value and organizational fit of project management implementations. While most of the cases the submitted reports that contained sufficient data to extract the necessary information, some case reports provided data only on some of the concepts; these organizations were ranked based on the data provided. Eleven case reports did not provide clear information in regard to the concepts studied, and thus these organizations could not be included in this analysis. This analysis was first conducted by Thomas Mengel and then the coding was verified independently by another researcher before presentation here to examine inter-coder reliability. Coding on all constructs was very high (over 95%).

Concepts

Fit Satisfaction/Alignment

In our meeting in March 2008, the analysis team agreed that the first two value constructs—*satisfaction* and *alignment of practices*—could be used as proxy measures to identify organizational fit. At the final research workshop involving most of the research team, *satisfaction* and *alignment of practices* were recognized as primarily criteria for the realization of value (level 1 and 2 value constructs) and not "fit." What the idea of "fit" seeks to demonstrate is the degree to which what has been implemented in terms of project management is reflective of what is needed. Recognizing that they are at best a proxy measure, the concepts of *satisfaction* and *alignment of practices* do still give us some insight into the degree of fit being observed. This analysis combines the two criteria into a concept of "Fit—Satisfaction/Alignment" for further analysis.

Fit UCP/PM

Shenhar and his colleagues (Shenhar & Dvir, 1996; Dvir et al, 1998; Raz et al, 2002) have argued that not all projects are the same, and therefore need to be managed differently. Larson (2004) builds on this argument suggesting that various project configurations require "different project management techniques and styles for success" (p. 65) and that such a "contingency approach" (p. 65) requires a flexible management system. Shenhar's UCP model evaluates three dimensions of projects:

- Uncertainty at the time of initiation of projects

- Complexity—the number and variety of elements and disciplines involved

- Pace—speed and criticality of time

A detailed application of this model would require a much more detailed analysis of quantitative project-related information, which we leave for a later date. The analysis reported here is based on qualitative coding of individual project case reports pertaining to the UCP criteria, complemented by information indicating a high-risk environment. Given the information about the chosen project management approach, we assign each case a respective "Fit—UCP/PM" concept, which notes high organizational fit if a given high UCP context is matched by a flexible project management approach.

Fit Different Kinds

In addition, based on Shenhar et al.'s (2004) discussions and suggestions, we suggest the "Fit—Different Kinds" concept based on the following assertions:

- Where an organization has different kinds of projects, it may need a more "organic" (Shenhar et al. in Morris & Pinto, 2004, p. 1266) approach entailing different project management approaches.

- Where an organization has similar kinds of projects, a uniform—and sometimes "mechanistic" (ibid.)—approach may suffice.

Hence, we identify "Fit—Different Kinds" in cases where the organization has either:

- different kinds of projects and a differentiated and flexible project management approach; or

- only one kind of project and a respective clear and unified project management approach.

Organizational fit is likely not present in cases where we either find different kinds of projects and a non-differentiated project management approach, or where we only find one type of project and a project management approach that is not geared towards this type of projects.

PMO/Training

Finally, scanning the various case-study reports suggested that three additional factors may play a major role for both creating value and contributing to organizational fit, but which are not captured by the other criteria and concepts. These are:

- The existence of a project management office (PMO) or the equivalent;

- The delivery of extensive training to project management stakeholders; and

- Substantial communication opportunities being utilized by project management stakeholders in discussing project management issues, approaches, and models.

In conducting our analysis, we coded these variables from the case reports and value quotations against these factors. While the communication factor still appears to be meaningful, it did not contribute to differentiating concepts within this study. For the purposes of this analysis, therefore, we have utilized a "Fit—PMO/Training" concept consisting of only the PMO and Training variables.

Analysis

The case reports and value quotes were analyzed using the listed models and criteria. The information pertaining to the identified criteria were noted, analyzed, and interpreted as indicated below. While for some criteria the notes and their analysis is rather obvious, others are a bit more involved. For example, while criticism of interviewees on existing project management practices and approaches and respective suggestions for improvement may indicate some dissatisfaction, they may also indicate a level of satisfaction that is already above average and is in turn creating a desire for continued improvement.

For the criteria *satisfaction* and *alignment of processes,* a "satisfaction value" and "alignment value" was created based on the level of satisfaction and alignment respectively (high = 3; to some extent = 2; low = 1).

Finally, we created a "PMO value" and a "Training value" indicating the existence of a project management office (PMO, or the equivalent) and the level of training delivery (high = 1; low = 0).

Based on the models introduced earlier, we calculated (or determined) the FIT values for the various concepts as follows:

- Fit—Satisfaction/Alignment: Both criteria of *satisfaction* and *alignment of processes* (using the "satisfaction value" and "alignment value" respectively) have been considered with equal weight. Cases with an average between both satisfaction and alignment of 2.5 or more have received a value of 3; cases with the respective average being 2.0 have received a value of 2; and cases with an average below 2.0 have received a value of 1.

- Fit—UCP/PM: The value for this concept was 1 if an identified UCP was matched by a flexible project management approach column); it received a 0 in the case of mismatch. If no indication for UCP was given in the respective column, the value remained empty.

- Fit—PMO/Training: The value for this concept was calculated as the average between the "PMO value" and the "Training value," resulting in values between 0 (low fit) and 1 (high fit).

- Fit—Different Kinds: The FIT value for this concept was determined based on evaluation of whether different types of projects or different project management approaches Were observed. If different project management approaches were identified in correspondence to different types of projects, or if one type of project was matched by a respective single type of project management approach, the value was determined to be 1 (high fit); in other cases it was determined to be 0 (low fit).

Interpretation

The strongest concept in terms of data available and in terms of the original constructs of the research project clearly was the Fit—Satisfaction/Alignment concept. The resulting classification of case studies is presented in Table 8-1.

	Satisfaction/Alignment Fit Value		
	①	②	③
Case Study	19	30 64	17 29 71
	28	31 65	18 33 72
	34	32 86	20 35 73
	59	42	21 36 74
	67	45	22 43 76
	69	47	23 44
	70	48	24 49
	75	52	25 51
	84	53	26 55
	88	54	27 63

TABLE 8-1—*Detailed interpretation of fit*

Most organizations (25) according to this concept demonstrate a high (3) organizational fit of their project management implementation.

However, the other concepts identified appeared to meaningfully contribute to the overall interpretation. Hence, all concepts were cross-compared and combined as follows:

- First, the values of all four concepts of fit explored here (satisfaction/alignment, PMO/Training, different kinds, UCP/PM) were added and entered into a new resulting concept labeled "Fit—Sum of Concepts", resulting in values between 1.0 (very low fit) and 6.0 (very high fit).

- Second, a summarizing and simplifying new concept—"Fit—All Concepts"— was created that identified three levels of organizational fit based on the overall values of the other concepts explored here, as follows: Cases that had a high fit value in three or more concepts, including the "Fit—Satisfaction/Alignment" concept, received "high"; cases that had a high value in at least two other FIT concepts received "medium"; and the other cases received "low."

The main results (Fit—Satisfaction/Alignment, Fit—Sum of Concepts, Fit—All Concepts) are graphically presented and compared in Figure 8-1. The values for "Fit—All Concepts" have been set to 7 (high fit), 3.5 (medium fit), and 0 (low fit) to be better able to present the results in a legible and meaningful way.

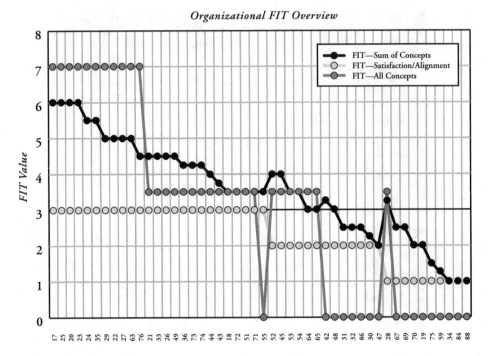

FIGURE 8-1—*Analysis of organizational fit*

Depending on how inclusive—in terms of the number of cases—or how granular the level of interpretation is chosen to be, the presented graph rather consistently presents a classification of cases based on their level 1 and 2 value—*satisfaction* and *aligned practices*—as well as on their "organizational fit" using the concepts discussed.

Further explanation of the case studies results in the following findings:

- 16 out of 25 cases which have a high "Fit—Satisfaction/Alignment" value (3) also demonstrate extensive delivery of training to project management stakeholders

- 13 out of 25 cases which have a high "Fit—Satisfaction/Alignment" value (3) also demonstrate the existence of a PMO (or its equivalent)

- Almost all cases (13 out of 14) that have a high "Fit—PMO/Training" value (1) also demonstrate a medium to high "Fit—Satisfaction/Alignment" value (2-3). Of these, 8 out of 14 cases demonstrate a "Fit—Satisfaction/Alignment" value that is high (3)

These findings suggest that extensive training and a PMO have an influence on the concept of organizational fit. At the same time, extensive training of project managers appears to have a greater influence on organizational fit than the existence of a PMO. This finding suggests that organizational fit may significantly be affected by concepts of "values" and "meaning" and the level and coordination of sense-making around common project management models and procedures that happens in organizations as a result of implementing project management (Mengel, 2008, and Eskerod & Riis, 2008, under review). Further studies—that would also in more depth and detail investigate the role of communication—should continue to investigate this cross-relationship.

Furthermore, all Chinese case studies have demonstrated high level 1 and level 2 values and subsequently scored high on the "FIT satisfaction/alignment" value (3). This suggests that either the Chinese have been consistently successful in implementing project management in a manner that specifically supports their needs in all types of organizations studied, or there may be some cultural bias in the data away from expressing dissatisfaction with the implementation. More comprehensive analysis of the concept of organizational fit and examining elements of national culture in conjunction with the identification of fit are likely necessary to fully understand this finding.

Finally, two research institutions—case studies 34 and 59—scored low on all criteria and concepts studied. This may be an indication of how difficult it is within this particular organizational context and culture to create organizational fit of project management in general. In particular, it seems to suggest challenges in realizing *satisfaction* and demonstration of *alignment of practices* within the "traditional" project management approach. Further analysis of these two cases is likely to prove fruitful.

Discussion

This analysis of 59 case reports and some of the 43 respective value quotation collections resulted in interesting implications with respect to "fit." While representing the majority of the case studies conducted in this research project, this analysis could only be based on 48 out of 59 case reports due to the lack of relevant information in the other reports. As an example, value quotations for 16 of the 59 case reports were missing. Hence, the findings of this study have been complemented by other analyses wherever possible.

This analysis resulted in four original codings of the data (Fit—Satisfaction/ Alignment, Fit—PMO/Training, Fit—Different Kinds, Fit—UCP/PM) and two summarizing variables (Fit—Sum of Concepts, Fit—All Concepts) related to organizational fit. In interpreting the results, three rather consistent levels of organizational fit could be identified for the 48 cases studied: high, medium, and low fit.

While the strongest concept was the "Fit—Satisfaction/Alignment" concept— based on the two levels of the value construct as identified in the overall research approach—the existence of extensive training for project management stakeholders and, to a lesser extent, the implementation of a PMO could be identified as factors of potentially significant impact on value creation and organizational fit arising out of our qualitative results.

Factors Influencing Value

What Data Is Available?

The previous sections have introduced some of the considerations and realizations associated with measuring value in this research study. As well, an elaboration of the concept of organizational fit of project management practices has introduced some possible perspectives by which the idea of fit can be explored. In evaluating the value of project management implementations within our case study organizations, the only data that can be collected is that which can be directly measured, as discussed earlier in this chapter. As a result, the data that is available to directly describe value in the case-study organizations are the four categories of value which represent actual measures, reflected in the following summary:

- **Satisfaction.** The satisfaction attributes within the case studies explore a number of dimensions related to stakeholder satisfaction. This included measuring the direct perception of satisfaction with the project management implementation from a broad array of stakeholders through interviews (with project managers, the managers responsible for the project management implementation, sponsors, senior executives, and human resources professionals) and surveys (of project managers, team members, project customers, subcontractors, and suppliers). Specific dimensions of satisfaction evaluated the degree to which stakeholders value working for/with the organization and satisfaction with project results, processes and the role of project management within the organization. Finally, this category evaluated what aspects of the implementation that they would like to see changed (e.g., more or less formality, consistency, structure, tools, documentation, or bureaucracy).

- **Alignment.** The alignment attributes within the cases studies focus on the degree to which consistent processes and approaches exist and are applied within the organization. This includes an understanding of the degree to which defined processes exist within the organization and are adhered to. As well, alignment evaluates the degree to which the resources are in place to manage and deliver projects, and the resource plan is in line with strategies and objectives. From a process perspective, the degree to which processes are documented, easy to understand, and actually applied in managing projects is captured. The idea of alignment also explores the degree to which the organization is aligned in support of its project management practices. This includes an assessment of structures and roles and responsibilities in the organization are clear and aligned with project needs, and whether project roles are adhered to at all levels of the organization. The overall clarity and consistency of organizational processes, decision making, structures and roles, are also evaluated.

- **Process Criteria.** The process criteria attributes within the case studies evaluate the value that is realized in terms of actual process improvements. This includes an assessment of the degree to which projects deliver on time, on budget and to objectives, and the degree to which the results of projects deliver on business cases, meet technical specifications, and are actually used by their intended customers. Process criteria also evaluate the degree to which reasonable processes for planning, management, and control of projects are in place and the degree to which project processes improve efficiency, multi-project coordination, project performance, and transparency of project efforts. The aspects of the implementation that are associated with the greatest and least impacts on process performance are evaluated. Finally, the actual project performance of completed projects is also reviewed.

- **Outcome Criteria.** The outcome criteria evaluate the business impacts that are realized as a result of the project management implementation. This includes an assessment of the degree to which the project management implementation has influenced overall organizational performance, including the degree to which the organization is more innovative or entrepreneurial, and whether there are improvements in the culture, communications, and knowledge management practices of the organization. Also evaluated is the degree to which the implementation has improved the realization of project benefits and enhanced business-case performance. Finally, the outcome criteria assess the degree to which the project management implementation is continuing to deliver value to the organization, the nature of the value delivered (tangible or intangible), and the specific changes to organizational performance that has been realized. Examples of these include improved customer retention, increased market share, reduced write-offs, the provision of new products or services and the ability to attract or retain employees.

What Value Components Emerged?

The structure of the value data significantly influenced the structure that was used in conducting initial exploratory analysis, particularly because the value dimensions were already derived from a pre-existing model. Using the categories that were defined above to explore the construct of value established a framework by which the value data could be evaluated and enabled identification of the essential components of value that were represented within the case-study organizations.

Figure 8-2 provides an overall picture of the resulting principal components.

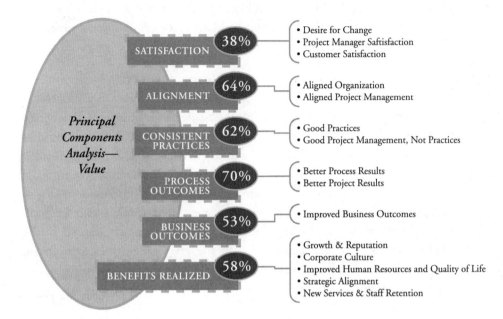

FIGURE 8-2—*Value principal components*

Each of the principal components is discussed in more detail in the following sections.

Satisfaction

The Satisfaction PCA evaluates the degree to which stakeholders are satisfied with the project management implementation. This involves evaluation of a number of discrete variables, including:

- Satisfaction in working with the organization, including:

  o The degree to which employees like working for the organization

  o The extent to which they feel they are a valued employee

  o The likelihood that they will leave the organization within the next 3 years

  o The degree to which they would recommend a job in the organization to someone else

- The extent to which participants would like to see changes within the organization, including:

- o More or less formality

- o More or less consistency

- o More or less training

- o More or less bureaucracy

- o More or less templates

- o Better templates

- o More or less documentation

- o Better documentation

- o More or less structure

- o More appropriate structure

- o More or less senior management involvement

- The degree of satisfaction with how projects are managed within the organization, including the degree to which participants perceive that:

  - o Projects are managed successfully within the organization

  - o Project management provides a high level of value to the organization

  - o Project managers are highly valued within the organization.

  - o Clients are consistently satisfied by the process by which projects are managed

  - o Clients are consistently satisfied with project results of projects managed by the organization

- The degree to which projects delivered by the organization improve stakeholder satisfaction, including:

  - o Sponsor satisfaction

  - o User satisfaction

  - o Project team satisfaction

  - o Client satisfaction

Three components are obtained explaining a total of 38% of the variance:

- **Desire For Change** (Percentage of variance explained: 18.7%; Eigenvalue: 9.921). This component loads heavily and positively on virtually all of the variables associated with a desire for change in the project management implementation of the organization. The component also loads negatively on variables associated with the satisfaction of project managers and employees in working for the organization, and variables associated with satisfaction with the delivery of projects. This component is in essence a negative assessment of satisfaction. Organizations that measure strongly on this component typically have employees who have a strong desire for changes to be made within the implementation. The view of organizational stakeholders is that projects are not successful, and the practices of project management are not effective when compared with those of other organizations. There is also a high sense of dissatisfaction expressed by organizational stakeholders, reflecting that they do not feel valued in the organization and would be disinclined to recommend employment in the organization to others.

- **Project Manager Satisfaction** (Percentage of variance explained: 10.9%; Eigenvalue: 5.862). This component loads heavily and positively on variables associated with project managers being satisfied with the management of projects within the organization. Organizations that measure strongly on this component have project managers who feel that projects are managed successfully, that project management provides a high level of value to the organization, and that perceive the project management role being highly valued. The project managers also report a high level of perceived satisfaction by customers in the process by which projects are managed and the project results that are delivered.

- **Customer Satisfaction** (Percentage of variance explained: 8.9%; Eigenvalue: 4.811). This component loads heavily and positively on variables associated with customer satisfaction with the delivery of projects. In particularly, the component loads heavily on variables associated with customer perceptions of the degree to which projects are successful, deliver value, and provide high levels of customer satisfaction with the project process and the results of projects. Organizations that measure strongly on this component are typically those who are successful in delivering on customer projects, and whose customers value both the project management process and the project results that are being delivered.

Alignment

The alignment PCA evaluates the degree to which organizational practices support and are consistent with the needs of projects within the organization. This includes assessment of:

- The clarity and consistency of decision-making within the organization

- The clarity and consistency of processes within the organization

- The clarity and consistency of roles within the organization

- The clarity and consistency of structures within the organization

- The degree to which participants view projects as adhering to organizational guidelines

Two components are obtained explaining a total of 64% of the variance:

- **Aligned Organization** (Percentage of variance explained: 50.7%; Eigenvalue: 5.069). This component loads heavily and positively on variables associated with the consistency and clarity of organizational processes within the organization, including the degree to which there are consistent decision making structures, roles, and processes in place. Organizations that measure strongly in this component typically report a high level of overall process formality and rigor in place, and operate with a high level of structure and formality.

- **Aligned Project Management** (Percentage of variance explained: 14.2%; Eigenvalue: 1.421). This component loads heavily and positively on variables associated with the degree to which projects adhere to organizational guidelines. Organizations that measure strongly on this component tend to have formal project management processes in place, which are consistently embraced and utilized by virtually all projects within the organization. These organizations tend to value the process of project management quite highly, and view the consistent management of projects as both essential and a significant source of value.

Consistent Practices

The evaluation of consistent practices draws on a number of variables that evaluate the degree to which the project management practices within the organization are aligned and consistently adhered to. This includes evaluation of:

- Whether project management practices are aligned with the organization, including the degree to which:

    o Organizational structures around projects are logical and aligned with the organization's needs

    o Organizational structures around projects are clear and unambiguous

    o Organizational decisions about projects are logical and aligned with the organization's needs

    o Organizational decisions about projects are clear and unambiguous

    o Project roles and responsibilities are logical and aligned with the organization's needs

    o Project roles and responsibilities are clear and unambiguous

- The processes of obtaining approvals is streamlined and effective, including the degree to which participants report requiring:

    o Excessive amount of time clarifying the intent of management regarding the projects managed

    o Excessive amount of time renegotiating project goals

    o Excessive amount of time securing executive sign-offs

- The extent to which goals, objectives, and outcomes for projects are clearly defined, including assessment of whether:

    o Project requirements are clearly defined

    o Scope of delivery is clearly defined

    o The success criteria for projects are clearly defined and understood

    o The business case for projects is clearly defined and understood

- The degree to which processes are clearly defined and understandable, and support for using them can be obtained, including the extent to which:

    o Project management knowledge is shared through codified forms like manuals or documents

    o Project management knowledge can be acquired easily through formal documents and manuals

- o Results of project and meetings ore documented

- o Project management knowledge can be easily acquired from experts and co- workers

- o It is easy to get face-to-face advice from experts

- The extent to which the processes and practices of the organization are valued in managing projects, including the extent to which:

  - o Formal project management process and procedures are rigorously followed in the organization

  - o Following formal project management processes help to better manage the organization's projects

  - o Formal project management processes and procedures add little value to the organization's projects

  - o Existing formal project management processes and procedures are not used to manage projects

- The quality and effectiveness of the project management practices within the organization, evaluating the extent to which:

  - o Project management practices and policies are clearly documented

  - o Project management policies and procedures are followed diligently

  - o The project management practices of the organization consistently exceed expectations

  - o The organization has superior project management practices

  - o The organization delivers successful projects despite poor project management practices

- Two components are obtained explaining a total of 62% of the variance:

- **Good Practices** (Percentage of variance explained: 52.0%; Eigenvalue: 20.837). This component loads heavily and positively on variables associated with the quality of project management practices. This component loads particularly strongly on variables associated with project management practices that are clearly documented and adhered to diligently, and where the quality of the practices are superior and consistently exceed expectations. The component also loads strongly on variables associated with ensuring effective resources are in place to successfully utilize the processes, effective knowledge-sharing practices, and the degree to which project management processes are valued in the organization. Organizations that measure strongly on this component typically have capable, well-documented and formalized practices that are consistently adhered to throughout the organization. They typically value the role of process, and express a positive view of the value that formal and consistent processes provide.

- **Good Project Management Not Practices** (Percentage of variance explained: 10.0%; Eigenvalue: 3.986). This component loads heavily and positively on variables associated with projects being successfully delivered despite what most would describe as poor project management practices. This component also loads positively on variables associated with formal project management processes and procedures adding little value to the organization, and on variables associated with spending significant amounts of time clarifying the management role on projects and regularly renegotiating project objectives. Organizations that measure strongly on this component typically have minimal process capabilities in place, and do not understand or value the role of project management practices. Project management is often seen as an overhead or source of bureaucracy rather than a source of value.

Process Outcomes

The assessment of process outcomes relies upon several variables in order to understand the degree to which projects deliver specific process improvements in managing projects within the organization, including:

- The degree to which projects deliver more effectively against their targets and objectives. This includes an assessment of project performance in terms of:

    o Attainment of scope

    o Attainment of driving priorities

    o Sponsor satisfaction

    o User satisfaction

    o Project team satisfaction

- The extent to which the project management implementation enables better process performance overall within the organization, including:

o Efficiency

o Better multi-project coordination

o Improved project control

o Greater project transparency

o Better project performance

Two components are obtained explaining a total of 70% of the variance:

- **Better Process Results** (Percentage of variance explained: 40.2%; Eigenvalue: 4.022). This component loads heavily and positively on variables associated with improvements in process effectiveness within the organization. In particular, this component loaded heavily on variables associated with improvements in efficiency, multi-project coordination, project transparency project control, and project performance. Organizations that measured strongly on this component typically view their project management implementation as having improved the processes by which projects are managed. They report increased effectiveness of their processes, better understanding of their processes by employees and other stakeholders, and more control over their project processes.

- **Better Project Results** (Percentage of variance explained: 30.3%; Eigenvalue: 3.027). This component loads heavily and positively on variables associated with improvements in the performance of projects themselves. In particular, this component loads heavily on variables associated with better project delivery in terms of attainment of scope, delivery against driving priorities, and delivery in terms of sponsor, team, and user satisfaction. Organizations that measure strongly on this component have reported significant improvements in their project delivery as a result of their project management implementation. They describe project management as improving how projects are managed, and their ability to successfully deliver projects as promised.

Business Outcomes

The assessment of business outcomes associated with the project implementation evaluates the degree to which projects deliver improvements in organizational outcomes, including:

- Improvement in the organizational culture

- Greater entrepreneurship

- Greater innovation

- More knowledge management/know-how

- More effective communication

One component is obtained that explains a total of over 53% of the variance:

- **Improved Business Outcomes** (Percentage of variance explained: 53.3%; Eigenvalue: 3.200). This component loads heavily and positively on all variables associated with improvement in organizational outcomes. This is particularly true of variables associated with improvements in entrepreneurship, innovation, knowledge management, and effective communication. Organizations that measured strongly on this component typically saw significant benefits at an organizational level as a result of their project management implementation. They typically report that project management is an essential contributor to organizational success, and has had a strong influence on the structure and management practices of the organization as a whole.

Benefits Realized

The benefits realized PCA consists of a number of variables that collectively evaluate the specific nature of the benefits realized from the project management implementation within case-study organizations. This includes assessment of:

- The maturity of project management practices of case-study organizations, as assessed by the research team

- The degree to which the project management implementation is expected to continue to deliver value to the organization

- The nature of value being realized from the project management implementation:

  o Tangible

  o Intangible

- The specific types of value that are being realized from the project management implementation, including:

  o Cost savings

  o Revenue increases

- o Customer retention

- o Increased customer share

- o Greater market share

- o Improved competitiveness

- o Reduced write-offs & rework

- o Attainment of strategic objectives

- o The launch of new product/ service streams

- o Greater social good

- o Improved quality of life

- o More effective human resources

- o Staff retention

- o Improved reputation

- o Improved overall management

- o Improved corporate culture

- o Improved regulatory compliance

Five components are obtained explaining a total of almost 58% of the variance:

- **Growth & Reputation** (Percentage of variance explained: 21.085%; Eigenvalue: 4.217). This component loads heavily and positively on variables associated with the delivery of tangible and intangible benefits. The component also loads heavily and positively on variables associated with the delivery of revenue increases, customer retention, and increases in customer share, as well as overall improvements in organizational reputation. Organizations that measure strongly on this component typically have reported significant increases in reputation and revenues, often through the attraction of new projects and customers as a result of successfully completing and delivering on previous initiatives.

- **Corporate Culture** (Percentage of variance explained: 12.9%; Eigenvalue: 2.582). This component loads heavily and positively on variables associated with intangible value and improvements in corporate culture. Organizations that measure strongly on this component typically have reported significant influences of their project management implementations on the organization as a whole, with significant improvements in collaboration, cooperation and communication within the organization. Organizations often report a strong sense of pride in the ability of the organization to deliver projects that have had a positive influence on the culture of the organization.

- **Improved Human Resources and Quality Of Life** (Percentage of variance explained: 9.6%; Eigenvalue: 1.928). This component loads heavily and positively on variables associated with more effective human resources and improved quality of life of employees. Organizations that measure strongly on this component typically have seen improvements in the effectiveness of employees within the organization and the overall quality of life reported by employees. Significant aspects of their implementation have often been focused upon improving culture, work-life balance, and employee workloads.

- **Strategic Alignment** (Percentage of variance explained: 7.8%; Eigenvalue: 1.565). This component loads heavily and positively on variables associated with improved strategic alignment of projects with the ability of the organization to more effectively deliver on its strategic objectives. Organizations that measure strongly on this component typically have reported a significant improvement in the role of project management enabling attainment of the organization's strategic objectives. For many organizations, this has resulted in improved selection of strategic priorities, launching of projects enabling the attainment of strategic objectives, including acquisitions, or, in some instances, project management being considered central to the success of the organization.

- **New Services and Staff Retention** (Percentage of variance explained: 7.3%; Eigenvalue: 1.461). This component loads heavily and positively on variables associated with the delivery of new products and services and improvements in staff retention. Organizations that measure strongly on this component have typically reported the ability of project management to enable provision of new projects and services, often where they are now able to either charge (or charge more for) their project management services, or they have obtained new revenue streams through consulting with other organizations in delivering project management improvement efforts. Organizations that measure strongly on this component have also reported improvements in how the project management role is viewed and the value placed on project managers, and have seen improvements in the ability to attract and retain project managers and other project employees.

What Value Similarities Exist?

The value PCAs and their components help to identify the discrete types of value that exist within the various implementations and contexts observed in the case-study organizations. What can be observed is that organizations are encountering significant value in each of the four categories of value that can be directly evaluated, and that there are multiple dimensions of value being observed within each category.

Understanding the degree to which these dimensions of value combine and interact is equally important to understand the value that is in actuality being observed within the case-study organizations. As discussed in Chapter 5, a construct-level PCA provides an integrated view of all of the components within that construct, enabling the identification of the meaningful groupings and clusters of value that emerge in actual practice.

Conducting the construct-level PCA for the value construct yielded six clear components that collectively explain 68% of the variance in the data associated with the case studies. These components describe the types of value that are typically reported as occurring together in our case-study organizations:

- **Aligned Practices, Better Processes and Business Outcomes** (Percentage of variance explained: 21.8%; Eigenvalue: 3.263). This component loads heavily and positively on components associated with improvements in project manager satisfaction and aligned project management practices. As well, the component also loads positively and heavily on components associated with improved process outcomes and overall business outcomes. Organizations that measured strongly on this component typically demonstrated significant improvements in overall processes and process capabilities, and placed a high level of value on the role of process in creating transparency and improving project collaboration. Organizations measuring strongly on this component also reported significant improvements in their overall organization performance directly attributable to improving their project management, including both increases in revenues and the ability to attract new project work based upon previous project successes.

> *Case study organization 36 is a state-owned organization in China providing design services for large scale civil and industrial building projects. The organization operates on a competitive basis, and with the decline of Olympic-related construction projects, is facing the need to compete for projects in other regions of the country.*
>
> *Project management is an assumed essential capability within the organization and within its industry, and was established to adhere to industry standards and common practices. The project management process within the organization is ISO 9000 certified, and consists of a quality manual, a guideline to designing work, and a book of various forms and templates. All the management system, structure, roles definition, processes, templates, and so on are covered in these three books. These three books are guiding the organization's daily works. New employees must be trained based on these three books.*
>
> *"The ISO certification demonstrates our standardized project management system and process, which can convince the customers of our management capability and help us to win the project contract in competitive bidding."*
>
> *—Senior Manager, 36*

- **Good Practices, Effective Human Resources and No Desire For Change** (Percentage of variance explained: 12.7%; Eigenvalue: 1.912). This component loads heavily and positively on components associated with both good project management practices and improvements in the effectiveness of human resources and the delivery of quality of life improvements to staff. The component also loads negatively and heavily on components associated with a desire for change. Organizations that measure strongly on this component reported extremely high satisfaction with their project management implementations, often reporting that they are at a level of process that is effective and appropriate and are simply managing its sustainment and ongoing evolution. These organizations also placed great emphasis in their project management implementations on the cultural and human resources aspects of project management, investing heavily in employee development and improving leadership, collaboration, and interpersonal skills. These organizations are reporting strong benefits associated with improved human resource effectiveness and improvements in overall quality of life and attainment of better work-life balance for their employees.

Case study organization 26 is a large and well-established engineering consulting firm based in Denmark. The organization has grown considerably in the recent past, and is strongly competitive in its industry, although new and international competitors are emerging.

The organization has moved from emphasis on strictly technical dimensions of projects to a much more holistic approach to solution delivery. Significant emphasis has been placed on the development of staff through comprehensive training, coaching, and mentoring programs. There is a strong senior management focus on employee development and the development of leadership, collaboration and holistic-thinking skills.

"How should I provide value when we deal with water resources and environment? Are the buildings sensible? Will the people who are going to work there have a reasonable indoor climate? This is how we think. Instead of thinking "building" we think "good work environment." [. . .] On the other hand, if [the project] had a negative value, I don't think we would participate."

—*Senior Manager, 26*

- **Better Project Results, Aligned Organizations and Corporate Culture** (Percentage of variance explained: 9.6%; Eigenvalue: 1.437). This component loads heavily and positively on components associated with the delivery of better project results. As well, this component loads heavily and positively on improvements in organizational alignment and the creation of more effective corporate cultures. Organizations that measure strongly in this component are typically reporting improvements in the organizational structures and roles supporting projects, and as a result, greater alignment between the organization and the projects they are delivering. Organizations measuring strongly against this component frequently report that projects are a significant aspect of how the organization delivers its work, and that their project management implementation has had a positive influence on the overall culture and effectiveness of the organization.

> *Case study organization 72 is a state-owned hydroelectric company that is responsible for the construction and operation of major hydroelectric power projects in China. On the strength of earlier project successes, the organization has won the right to conduct a considerable number of additional projects, and sees few competitive pressures in the coming two decades.*
>
> *The organization was responsible for one of the earliest implementations of formalized project management techniques in China. Development of the project management implementation was a result of World Bank funding requirements for early projects it was involved with. Today the organization is considered a leader in project management practices within China.*
>
> *"What we have learned from the [project] has become the most valuable wealth of the company. We learned and practiced, and we then shared our experiences in the whole industry. And I believe more or less our experiences have also contributed to the relevant institutional reforms in the industry."*
>
> *—Senior Manager, 72*

- **Good Projects, Not Process, Not Customer Satisfaction** (Percentage of variance explained: 8.7%; Eigenvalue: 1.300). This component loads heavily and positively on components associated with good project results but also those that reflect an absence of process capabilities in place. This component also loads negatively on the delivery of customer satisfaction. Organizations that measure strongly on this component are often more mature, formally established organizations that have heightened expectations around their projects and their ability to deliver projects successfully. While reported customer satisfaction is still higher than a median of 3 (on a 5-point scale), it is lower than other organizations within the case studies, and may reflect either more critical or demanding customers, or more of an focus on internal strategic drivers and less on direct customer demands and expectations.

Case study organization 21 is a division within the government of Norway that is responsible for overseeing construction and renovation of major infrastructure projects throughout the country.

As an internal government department, there is less of a customer emphasis on projects. However, even though the organization has some kind of monopoly position, there is a close attention paid to the projects by media and public, which strongly affects the work of the organization.

While there is a project model defined for the organization, there are very different practices observed within the organization currently. Older project managers view their role as being present on site and meeting with the construction managers, while younger projects place more emphasis on administration and overall process management.

" To move from administration to more control and management has been an important thing, in my view. There has also been a history of little coordination and little holistic thinking, and I believe our suppliers have experienced us in many different ways from project to project. This is risky for the organization, in my opinion."

—Project Manager, 21

- **Good Project Management, Not Process, Customer Satisfaction** (Percentage of variance explained: 8.3%; Eigenvalue: 1.243). This component loads heavily and positively on components associated with good project results with few consistent process capabilities in place, as well as on the delivery of customer satisfaction. Organizations that measure strongly against this component are typically very customer-focused, with customers reporting satisfaction with the projects and project services being provided. Many organizations measuring strongly on this component are also earlier in their project management implementations, and while some demonstrate some good process capabilities, they also report much less consistency and adherence to these processes within the case studies.

Case study organization 48 is the information technology division of a large industrial organization in Denmark. The organization is one of the largest organizations in Denmark, and prides itself on its close involvement with major suppliers such as Microsoft.

The division was historically very technically focused, and project management was not valued or recognized as an independent discipline. As well as the development of a project management model, much of the project management implementation has focused on training and certification of project management staff (to IPMA level C). Most recently, a greater emphasis has been placed on the leadership development of project managers.

There are still several models of project management in the organization, some of which are mandatory for larger and strategic projects, but formal project management is not applied on all projects within the organization.

"I think a lot of our customers think we have some very good [project managers]—it is my impression, so that way around there is appreciation."

—Human Resources, 48

- **New Services, Staff Retention and Growth** (Percentage of variance explained: 7.1%; Eigenvalue: 1.066). This component loads heavily and positively on components associated with the provision of new products and services and staff retention, as well as on overall improvements in the growth and reputation of the organization. Organizations that measure strongly on this component are typically those that deliver project services to customers, on either a consulting or construction services basis. Organizations measuring strongly on this component report increases in the value associated with their project management services, including an ability to either charge for their project management or increase their revenues associated with project services. As well, these organizations have frequently reported the ability to secure additional projects as a result of improvements in their reputation for delivery or successful delivery of previous projects.

> Case study organization 76 is an information technology consulting firm providing services to small- and medium–sized firms in Canada. The organization primarily focuses on infrastructure projects and managed services for its customers.
>
> The organization has invested significantly in the development of its project management capability in order to improve the effective delivery, reliability, and profitability of its projects. Project management was introduced by hiring experienced project managers for some large projects. As the effectiveness and value of project management was demonstrated, a formal project was initiated by the experienced project managers to develop a basic project management framework and set of templates. The result has been increased customer retention, profitability, and growth of the company, and the ability to actually charge customers for project management services.
>
> "The project management framework has taken the company to the next level. It is a stepping stone to much bigger work, bigger clients."
> —Project Manager, 76

Organizational Profiles Of Value

Each of our case-study organizations included in the PCA analysis has been scored on each of the value components identified above. The following figure depicts those organizations that rank low (below one standard deviation from the mean) and high (above one standard deviation from the mean) on each value component. The organizations are recorded in each cell (for example, High-Aligned Practices, Better Processes, Business Outcomes) in numeric order; there is no meaning embedded in where in the cell an organization appears. If an organization appears in a cell, it is beyond one standard deviation from the mean.

Some organizations are clearly most strongly described by a single implementation descriptor. The dark circles in Figure 8-3 identify these organizations. For instance, organization 57 registers highly as receiving Aligned Practices, Better Processes, Business Outcomes and nothing else. Single-component organizations can be said to be most strongly described as receiving the value component they are associated with.

Some organizations ranked above or below one standard deviation from the mean on more than one implementation component. These organizations are described by more than one implementation component. Lines connect all of the instances of the same organization across the cells and should help you find the duplicates.

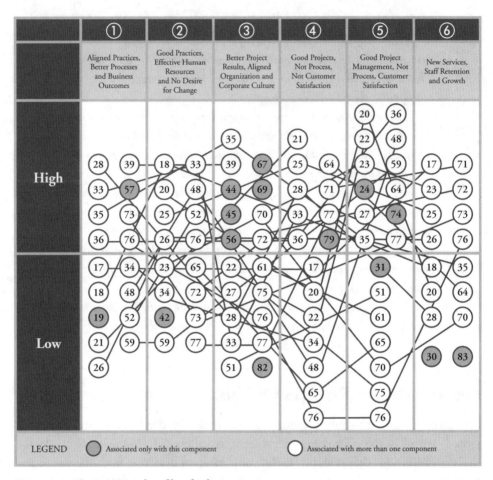

FIGURE 8-3—*Organizational profiles of value*

This figure provides a number of insights into the sample organizations and the value they report receiving from their project management implementations:

- Several of the organizations that rank above or below one standard deviation from the mean only do so on one value component. Fifteen of the case-study organizations register solely on one value descriptor beyond one standard deviation of the mean. Two-thirds of these organizations (9) report "high" receipt of a single value component. The other third of these single-value component organizations report a "low" rating on a single value component.

- Most of the case-study organizations report some combination of "high" and "low" positions on several value components. Many of the organizations that rank either above or below one standard deviation from the mean on one value component are also identified as *not* being described by the other value components. For these instances, this suggests that the organization's implementation does not fit neatly into any one specific value component that emerged from the PCA analysis. This suggests that the value that is being realized spans multiple components, or does not fit neatly into one of the dominant components that has emerged in the analysis.

- Five of the six value PCAs have a similar number of organizations reporting "high" or "low" rankings on each component. However, PCA 5 (*Good project management, no process, customer satisfaction*) has more organizations that are highly described by this component than are being strongly *not* described by this component–reflecting a skewed distribution (2/3 as compared to 1/3). These organizations are reporting weak process but good results largely as a result of the efforts of their good project managers (including possible reliance upon some heroics) and to some extent their efforts to improve project management. However, without processes identified and supported, their efforts are not institutionalized and likely would not survive losing their project manager resources.

- There also appear to be patterns in how the implementation components describe the organizations.

    o Organizations judged to be highly described by value PCA 1 (*aligned practices, better processes, and business outcomes*) tend to also be highly described by PCA 3 (*better project results, aligned organization and corporate culture*). Organizations in this group are receiving very positive benefits from their project management implementation from all four levels of the value model (*satisfaction, alignment, process* and *business outcomes*).

    o Organizations judged to be highly described by value PCA 2 (*good practice, effective HR and no desire for change*) tend to most likely *not* be described by PCA 1 (*aligned practices, better processes, and business outcomes*). This suggests that those that are happy with the results they are receiving and have low desire for change are not as likely to report solid aligned practices and processes or to be receiving organization-level benefits.

    o Organizations judged to be highly described by PCA 4 (*good projects, no process, no customer satisfaction*) tend to be *not* described by PCA 3 (*better project results, aligned organization and corporate culture*). It seems reasonable that these two value components would be inversely related, given their differing emphasis on process.

    o Organizations judged to be highly described by PCA 5 (*good project management, not process, customer satisfaction*) tend to be "low" on PCA 4 (*good projects, not process, not customer satisfaction*). While on the face of it, these components appear quite similar (if only to judge by their names) in actual fact, there are quite significant differences, as will emerge in Chapter 9. Organizations that are positively associated with value PCA 4 tend to have a limited view of project management. These organizations appear to have not consciously chosen to adopt a formal project management approach but have fallen into the need to manage projects. Project management in these organizations typically relies quite heavily on the skills and abilities of project managers in order to be successful. Organizations positively associated with value PCA 5, by contrast, are often working hard to be able to implement project management, but are often early in their implementation. What results are positive indications of improvement (both project results and customer satisfaction), but lower recognition of process as a result of the early phase of project management implementation.

CREATING MEASURES OF VALUE

How Can Value Measures Be Derived?

The previous sections introduce the variable-level components and construct-level components that have emerged from the exploratory data analysis conducted as part of this research project. Based upon an understanding of how the data co-varies and how variances in the database are explained, it becomes possible to identify specific scales that collectively measure discrete concepts within the case studies.

This section explores the specific measures of data that have been identified within the value-scale creation. It explains the scales that have been constructed, and the relative significance of each scale. Note that these scales for the most part reflect a refinement of the significant components identified above. The strong reliability and validity of these scale constructs serve to further support the durability of the research design and lay the foundation for the design of instruments for testing the theories arising from the exploratory analysis conducted in this monograph.

Constructed Scales Of Value

Satisfaction Scales

The satisfaction scales are those discrete measures of satisfaction that exist within the data collected for the case study organizations. The overall scales associated with satisfaction and the percentages of variance explained by each are illustrated in Figure 8-4.

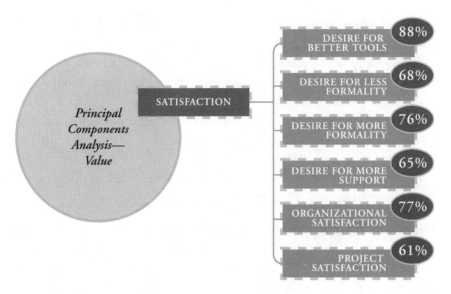

FIGURE 8-4—*Satisfaction scales*

The following scales have been constructed from the data as measures of satisfaction value:

- **Desire for Better Tools** (Percentage of variance explained: 88%; Chronbach's Alpha: 0.93). The scale is associated with a desire for better tools and measures the degree to which participants expressed a desire for better tools, documentation and templates associated with their project management implementation. Organizations that measure strongly on this scale reflect a strong desire within their organization to enhance the tools and practices that currently exist within the organization.

- **Desire for Less Formality** (Percentage of variance explained: 68%; Chronbach's Alpha: 0.93). The scale associated with a desire for less formality measures the degree to which participants expressed a desire for less structure, bureaucracy, and documentation associated with their project management implementation. This scale also measures a desire for a reduction in the consistency, formality, and level of senior management involvement in the projects they managed. Organizations that measure strongly on this scale reflect a strong desire to reduce the level of formality and bureaucracy associated with their implementations, often perceiving them to be very structured and rigid. These organizations typically view project management as bureaucratic overhead and the associated practices to be a source of additional work that is perceived as not creating or delivering value.

- **Desire for More Formality** (Percentage of variance explained: 76%; Chronbach's Alpha: 0.91). The scale associated with a desire for more formality measures the degree to which participants expressed a desire to increase the structure, documentation, and templates that exist within the organization. This scale also measures the degree to which more formality and consistency is seen as being valuable and desirable. Organizations that measure strongly on this scale reflect a strong desire to enhance the formality by which their projects are managed. They typically see their practices as being not sufficiently structured and detailed, and desire a greater level of consistency and an enhanced level of structure and control of the projects being managed within the organization.

- **Desire for More Support** (Percentage of variance explained: 65%; Chronbach's Alpha: 0.89). The scale associated with a desire for more support measures the degree to which participants expressed a desire for greater support for the delivery of projects, including more training and software tools. This scale also measures the desire for more senior management involvement in projects, and a greater desire for this involvement to be timely and relevant. Organizations that measure strongly on this scale reflect a desire for greater oversight and involvement from organizational executives in the projects that they oversee. They typically view their projects as having insufficient oversight and guidance, as well as desiring additional skills development opportunities and more appropriate toolsets.

- **Organizational Satisfaction** (Percentage of variance explained: 77%; Chronbach's Alpha: 0.84). The scale associated with organizational satisfaction measures the degree to which participants are satisfied with working for and being a member of the organization. This scale measures the degree to which participants enjoy working for their organizations, feel like valued employees, and would recommend the organization as an employer to others. Organizations that measure strongly on this scale reflect a strong environment where employees feel strongly valued and appreciated. Corporate culture is often quite strong in these organizations, and employees value being a part of the organization and take pride in being able to contribute to its success.

- **Project Satisfaction** (Percentage of variance explained: 61%; Chronbach's Alpha: 0.84). The scale associated with project satisfaction measures the degree to which participants expressed satisfaction with how projects are managed within the organization. This scale measures the degree to which projects are seen to be managed successfully, and that project management is seen to provide value to the organization. This scale also evaluates the extent to which project managers are seen as being valued, and whether project clients are satisfied with the process and results of projects. Organizations that measure strongly on this scale typically demonstrate a high level of satisfaction with how projects are being managed. Clients of these organizations, whether internal or external, view the process of project management as being effective and providing value, and are satisfied with the results that their projects are delivering. Project managers feel that their role is valued, and often have a high level of influence and authority over the projects that they manage. Overall project success is seen to be high.

Alignment Scales

The alignment scales are those discrete measures of alignment and process consistency that exist within the data collected for the case-study organizations. The overall scales associated with alignment and the percentages of variance explained by each are illustrated in Figure 8-5.

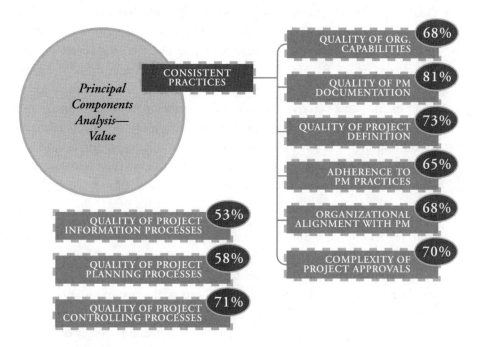

FIGURE 8-5—*Alignment scales*

The following scales have been constructed from the data as measures of alignment value:

- **Quality of Organizational Capabilities** (Percentage of variance explained: 68%; Chronbach's Alpha: 0.84). The scale associated with the quality of organizational capabilities measures the degree to which participants expressed a view that the organization appropriately supports its project management implementation. This scale measures the degree to which the organization evaluates its project management capabilities and capacity, and the effectiveness of its project management staff. The scale also evaluates improvement opportunities associated with its project management implementation, and ensures that the appropriate resources are in place to oversee the project management implementation. Organizations that measure strongly on this scale reflect a strong level of oversight of their project management implementation. The required capability and skill levels of project staff is formally understood, and there is an ongoing assessment and evaluation to ensure that employees embody the appropriate skill sets and have the ability to succeed in the projects they oversee. There is also an ongoing process of improvement by which opportunities to enhance the implementation are identified and improvement opportunities are formally incorporated into the defined practices.

- **Quality of Project Management Documentation** (Percentage of variance explained: 81%; Chronbach's Alpha: 0.88). The scale associated with the quality of project management documentation measures the degree to which participants expressed satisfaction with the documents that define the project management practices of the organization. This scale measures the degree to which participants perceive the practices as being appropriately documented, easy to understand, and easy to apply in managing projects. Organizations that measure strongly on this scale reflect a strong process capability to document practices in a clear, concise, and relevant way that allows project managers and team members to ensure effective adherence.

- **Quality of Project Definition** (Percentage of variance explained: 73%; Chronbach's Alpha: 0.88). The scale associated with the quality of project definition measures the degree to which participants expressed satisfaction with the process by which projects are defined and initiated. This scale measures the degree to which the requirements and expected scope of projects is clearly defined in advance, as well as the extent to which business cases and success criteria are clearly articulated. Organizations that measure strongly on this scale reflect a strong project initiation capability that ensures there is a formalized understanding of each project in place before it proceeds. There are typically strong processes in place associated with stakeholder management, and a clear and agreed-upon articulation of the expected outcomes of each project.

- **Adherence to Project Management Practices** (Percentage of variance explained: 65%; Chronbach's Alpha: 0.82). The scale associated with adherence to project management measures the degree to which participants expressed a consistent approach by which projects are managed. This scale measures the extent to which the project management practices of the organization are diligently and consistently adhered to, the extent to which these practices are documented, and the degree to which the practices of the organization are superior to those of other organizations. Organizations that measure strongly on this scale reflect a strong process capability that is clear and well-defined, and that is consistently adhered to by all projects. The organization often reflects a strongly process-oriented culture where employees value and appreciate the presence of a clear, well-defined process capability that they are expected to utilize.

- **Organizational Alignment with Project Management** (Percentage of variance explained: 68%; Chronbach's Alpha: 0.91). The scale associated with the organizational alignment of project management measures the degree to which participants expressed a view that the organization consciously aligns itself in a way that supports the projects it manages and the project management capability that is in place. Organizations that measure strongly on this scale reflect a strong organizational capability that ensures that the structures, roles, and responsibilities associated with projects are clearly defined, logical, and appropriate. As well, these organizations have a decision -making capability that ensures organizational decisions give consideration to and are aligned with the projects that they impact, and that there is a high level of integration of the project management practices with the larger management practices of the organization.

- **Complexity of Project Approvals** (Percentage of variance explained: 70%; Chronbach's Alpha: 0.79). The scale associated with the complexity of project approvals measures the degree to which participants expressed difficulty in securing project approvals within the organization. This scale is a negative measure of satisfaction, in that it measures how complex and difficult it is for project managers to obtain approvals. The scale measures the length of time associated with securing executive sign-offs, clarifying the goals of the project and clarifying the intent and purpose of the project management role relative to the project. Organizations that measure strongly on this scale reflect an organizational culture that is inconsistent or opaque in how organizational decisions are made. Project managers in these organizations typically operate in an environment that is characterized by a high level of ambiguity, and generally are forced to be highly reactive in their approach. Decisions are very difficult to secure, and both decisions and decision-making processes are often highly fluid.

- **Quality of Project Information Processes** (Percentage of variance explained: 53%; Chronbach's Alpha: 0.85). The scale associated with quality of project information processes measures the degree to which participants expressed satisfaction with how information about projects is communicated and disseminated within the organization. This scale measures the degree to which communications processes are defined in advance of the project. Also measured is the degree to which team members understand their role, know how to escalate problems should they arise, and know who they are able to go to for support. Organizations that measure strongly on this scale reflect a strong organizational culture where there is a high level of collaboration and cooperation, and where the importance of effective communications is understood and, more importantly, acted upon. The organizations typically are strong in confirming roles and responsibilities, and in ensuring appropriate lines of communication are in place.

• **Quality of Project Planning Processes** (Percentage of variance explained: 58%; Chronbach's Alpha: 0.76). The scale associated with the quality of project planning processes measures the degree to which participants expressed that the planning processes of the organization are seen to be effective. This scale evaluates the degree to which detailed project planning activities are seen to occur on projects, including the degree to which formalized and detailed schedules, budgets, resource, and work plans are established. Organizations that measure strongly on this scale reflect a strong process culture under which project managers ensure there is a detailed plan in place that clearly articulates the activities at a granular level, and defines the costs, timelines, and resource requirements for each activity. Detailed project plan information is typically also widely shared with members of the project team, and individual team members generally have the detailed information available to them to independently monitor and manage their individual work contributions to the projects they are involved in.

• **Quality of Project Controlling Processes** (Percentage of variance explained: 71%; Chronbach's Alpha: 0.87). The scale associated with the quality of project controlling processes measures the degree to which participants expressed that the process of project control on projects is seen to be effective. The scale measures the degree to which actual progress on the project is evaluated against the plan, and the extent to which all-important plan aspects (budget, schedule and resources) are both monitored and controlled. Organizations that measure strongly on this scale reflect a strong culture of managing projects, where there is a formalized tracking and management process and project progress is continually evaluated and assessed. These organizations typically highly value formal project management tools, and adopt a high level of discipline in monitoring and controlling project process.

Process Outcome Scales

The process outcome scales are those discrete measures of process efficiency and effectiveness, and the delivery of project results, that exist within the data collected for the case-study organizations. The overall scales associated with process outcomes and the percentages of variance explained by each are illustrated in Figure 8-6.

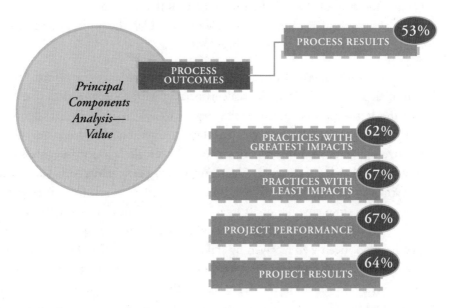

FIGURE 8-6—*Process outcome scales*

The following scales have been constructed from the data as measures of process outcome value:

- **Process Results** (Percentage of variance explained: 53%; Chronbach's Alpha: 0.94). The scale associated with process results measures the degree to which participants expressed satisfaction with the impacts that the project management practices have had on the organization. This scale measures the degree to which participants have reported greater efficiency and transparency, as well as the degree to which projects deliver more effective communications, client satisfaction, and multi-project coordination. Organizations that measure strongly on this scale typically place a high degree of value on process, and express a strong satisfaction with the improvement in process results that project management has provided them.

- **Practices with Greatest Impacts** (Percentage of variance explained: 62%; Chronbach's Alpha: 0.94). The scale associated with those practices with the greatest impacts measures the degree to which participants identified factors in their project management implementations that have had a positive influence on project performance. This scale measures the degree to which participants feel that project performance has improved as a result of the project management implementation. Organizations that measure strongly on this scale typically have made a number of positive improvements in their project management capability which are widely viewed to have had a positive impact. Rather than being a measure of the specific improvements that have been made, the scale serves as an overall assessment of the degree to which the project management implementation is seen as having been positive.

- **Practices with Least Impacts** (Percentage of variance explained: 67%; Chronbach's Alpha: 0.95). The scale associated with those practices that have had the least impacts measures the degree to which participants identified factors in their project management implementation that have not had a positive influence on project performance. This scale is a negative assessment of value in that it measures the degree to which participants feel that project performance has declined or not been impacted as a result of the project management implementation. Organizations that measure strongly on this scale typically have had a number of changes made in how projects are managed that have not been well received by stakeholders. Rather than being a measure of the specific improvements that have not resulted in impacts, the scale serves as an overall assessment of the degree to which the overall project management implementation is seen as having been negative.

- **Project Performance** (Percentage of variance explained: 67%; Chronbach's Alpha: 0.83). The scale associated with project performance measures the degree to which participants indicated that projects were typically successful within the organization. This scale is a measure of the degree to which interview participants indicated that projects typically deliver on time and on budget, and to which expected objectives and business outcomes are delivered. Organizations that measure strongly on this scale typically have a good track record in delivering projects successfully. They are seen by most stakeholders as delivering projects successfully and meeting overall project targets.

- **Project Results** (Percentage of variance explained: 64%; Chronbach's Alpha: 0.84). The scale associated with project results measures the degree to which participants indicated that projects typically deliver on their expected results. This scale is a measure of the degree to which survey participants indicated that projects typically deliver on schedule, on budget, and to the expected technical specification. The scale also measures the degree to which projects deliver on objectives and to which they attain their expected business value and changes in client performance. Organizations that measure strongly on this scale reflect a strong project management capability that routinely delivers projects on target. There is also very often a strong track record in ensuring that project results are utilized, and that the expected business outcomes and value of the initial business cases are realized.

Business Outcome Scales

The business outcome scales are those discrete measures of business results and organizational outcomes that exist within the data collected for the case-study organizations. The overall scales associated with business outcomes and the percentages of variance explained by each are illustrated in Figure 8-7.

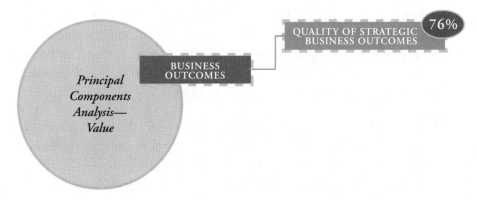

FIGURE 8-7—*Business outcome scales*

The following scale has been constructed from the data as a measure of business outcome value:

- **Quality of Strategic Business Outcomes** (Percentage of variance explained: 76%; Chronbach's Alpha: 0.85). The scale associated with the quality of strategic business outcomes measures the degree to which participants indicated that the project management implementation has delivered positive business impacts. This scale evaluates the degree to which the project management implementation has an impact on the culture of the organization and has resulted in the organization being more innovative and entrepreneurial. The scale also evaluates the extent to which participants are satisfied with the project management implementation and how projects are managed. Organizations that measure strongly on this scale are typically those that have implemented project management for cultural reasons, and have been successful in seeing positive improvements at an organizational level. Employees within these organizations often have a strong level of personal ownership, accountability, and commitment to the projects they manage, and are willing to take initiative to ensure their projects are successful.

TYPES OF VALUE BEING OBSERVED

What Kinds Of Value Are Being Observed?

The previous section outlines in detail the types of value that were observed within the case-study organizations. At an aggregate level, these characteristics of value can be categorized into two groupings:

- **Tangible Value.** Tangible value relates to specific value that can actually be measured. In the discussion of return on investment earlier in this chapter, it was clearly articulated that the only values that can be incorporated in a cost-benefit analysis are those which can be quantified and expressed in financial terms. Tangible value represents those dimensions of value which are most readily quantified, as typically they are both measurable and measured directly in financial terms. Examples of tangible value include increases in revenue, expansion of market share, and reductions in costs.

- **Intangible Value.** Intangible value relates to benefits that are also realized by an organization, but that are much more difficult to quantify. While intangible value is no less real, and can often be quite important to organizations and senior executives, its measurement is significantly more challenging. Even where strategies may exist to quantify intangible value, these are rarely consistent from organization to organization. Examples of intangible value include enhanced reputation, improvements in management capabilities, enhanced strategic alignment, and the attraction or retention of employees.

In evaluating value observed within this study, the case reports were comprehensively reviewed and coded as to the types of value being demonstrated. The following categories of value were identified, using the two groupings defined above:

- Tangible Value:

  o Cost savings

  o Revenue increases

  o Customer retention

  o Increased customer share`

  o Greater market share

  o Reduced write-offs & rework

- Intangible Value:

  o Improved competitiveness

  o New product/service streams

  o Greater social good

  o Improved quality of life

  o More effective human resources

  o Staff retention

  o Improved reputation

  o Improved overall management

  o Improved corporate culture

  o Improved regulatory compliance

To What Degree Is Value Being Realized?

In addition to evaluating the categories of value that were observed, it is also important to understand the degree to which that value is actually being evidenced. While one case-study organization may have observed a few cost savings in a limited subset of its operations, another organization may have yielded significant cost reductions. In order to make meaningful distinctions between organizations, levels of value were defined in order to enable a more accurate and consistent coding of realized value. These levels are defined in the following points:

- 0 – A coding of 0 indicated that no value was being realized.

- 1 – A coding of 1 indicated that some value was evidenced within the case-study organization, but it was marginal at best and did not represent a significant proportion of the realized value of the organization.

- 2 – A coding of 2 indicated that a significant level of value was being observed within the case study that was meaningful and important to the organization, and clearly observable.

- 3 – A coding of 3 indicated an extremely high level of value was being observed within the case-study organization.

Where Is Value Being Realized?

Evaluating the value results provided a perspective on the types of value that were most prevalent within the case-study organizations, the categories of value actually being observed, and the degree to which this value was being realized. While this provides useful information unto itself, equally important is to understand the underlying nature of the organizations associated with the value results. The following two sections provide an overview of the categories of tangible and intangible value that was observed within the case-study organizations, for each of the maturity levels discussed in Chapter 7.

Tangible Value

Realized Value

Maturity Level	⓪	①	②	③
Level 3			71	35
2.5	21 44 45 48 55 90	36 87	72 73	
Level 2	17 18 20 30 39 43 51 53 65	57 81	22 23 24 25 74 75	76
1.5	19 28 29 32 34 42 52 54 56 59 62 63 64 82 84 86	26 27 49 51 83	33 89	47
Level 1	88	31 60 70	67 69	

FIGURE 8-8—*Tangible value vs. maturity levels*

As can be observed in Figure 8-8, many organizations are not actually observing or demonstrating tangible value within their project management implementations. Thirty-two out of a total of 60 organizations assessed within this analysis had no tangible value evidenced.

Examples from some case study organizations where tangible value was evidenced are illustrated in the following quotations:

> *"We now bill an additional 20% for project management on all our projects."*
> —Senior Manager, 76

> *"Project managers have become good at selling additional services."*
> —Senior Manager, 76

> *"Improved project management should help with share prices because it will increase confidence in the market as we deliver on projects."*
> —PM Management, 75

Looking at those organizations where tangible value is observed, this analysis provides a number of significant observations:

- Tangible value is being seen at all levels of maturity. While many organizations do not report tangible value, of those that do there is little correlation between the maturity of the organization's implementation and the degree of value being evidenced.

- Even organizations that are at relatively low levels of maturity were able to attain high levels of tangible value. Some implementations that evidenced high levels of tangible value had very simple and straightforward implementations, a few of which involved minimal and superficial project management practices.

- Tangible value is most typically evidenced in organizations that conduct work for customers. Of those organizations that are demonstrating tangible value, the vast majority of them are either consulting or construction and engineering firms that conduct projects on a contract basis for their customers, although some are also departments of organizations that oversee large-scale construction and infrastructure projects.

- Even where tangible value is being observed within organizations, very few can actually quantify the value realized. What was surprising within those case-study organizations that did realize tangible value is that few organizations were actually able to articulate the degree of value that they had realized. While tangible value is inherently measurable and quantifiable, none of the case-study organizations had specifically take the time to capture the value associated with their project management implementation as a separate and segregated amount. All organizations demonstrating tangible value were able to articulate the value, and a few were able to anecdotally quantify scenarios to illustrate the value, but none had actually formally measured the value being realized. Moreover, there was no interest within these organizations in doing so. While they were very comfortable that their implementation had provided value, this level of knowledge was considered to be amply sufficient without benefit of further evidence.

Intangible Value

Realized Value

Maturity Level	⓪	①	②	③
Level 3			71	35
2.5		90	21 36 48 87	44 45 55 72 73
Level 2	30	51 53 57 65	17 22 23 24 25 39 75 76 81	18 20 43 74
1.5		34 47 49 51 54 56 59 62 64 82 84 86	19 26 27 28 29 32 33 42 52 83 89	63
Level 1	31 88	61 70	67 69	

FIGURE 8-9—*Intangible value vs. maturity models*

As can be observed in Figure 8-9, the vast majority of case-study organizations are realizing intangible value from their project management implementations, and a number of organizations are realizing significant amounts of intangible value.

Examples from case-study organizations where significant intangible value was evidenced are illustrated in the following quotations:

> *"Project management has a positive influence on creative thinking and enhances the organization's innovation capacity."*
> —*Sponsor, 24*

> *"Collaboration within and between teams has improved; silos within the organization have diminished."*
> —*Senior Manager, 76*

> *"It . . . gives them a sense of accomplishment, it give them a sense of being connected to the enterprise, it gives them an opportunity to contribute and understand . . . how [their work] relates to the larger operation and to the success of the organization."*
> —*Senior Manager, 20*

Exploring the intangible value being realized by organizations yields a number of important observations:

- Intangible value is evidenced by most organizations. Only three case study organizations, or 5%, reported no intangible value being evidenced. Almost two-thirds of case studies (38 out of 60) had evidence of intangible value rated at a level of 2 or higher, and 11 case study organizations demonstrated evidence of intangible value at a level of 3.

- The level of intangible value being observed appears to be tied to increasing levels of maturity. With only one exception, all organizations evidencing an intangible value level of 3 were at a maturity of at least level 2. As is illustrated in Figure 8-9, there seems to be a clear trend that increasing maturity of project management practices results in increasing levels of intangible value being realized.

An Integrated View

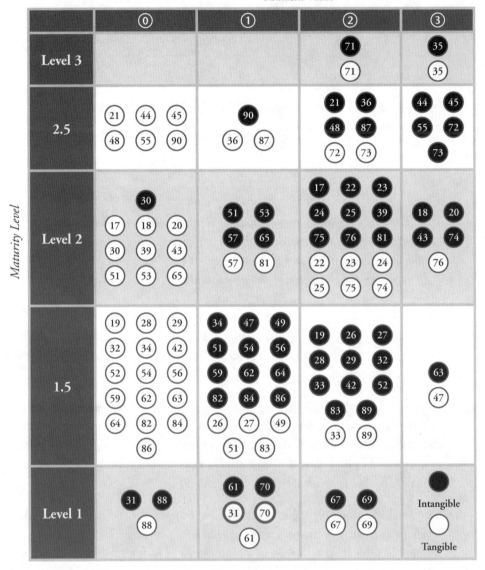

FIGURE 8-10—*Tangible and intangible value vs. maturity levels*

One final perspective on the relationship with observed value (tangible and intangible and maturity can be attained by adopting an integrated view that overlays both dimensions of value on the same chart, as illustrated in Figure 8-10.

Comparing tangible and intangible value together puts in stark contrast the degree to which intangible value is realized as compared to tangible value. While there are certainly organizations realizing tangible value, and at times are seeing considerable amounts, the majority of value that is being evidenced within the case-study organizations is intangible in nature. As well, there are higher degrees of intangible value at higher levels of maturity, where tangible value is being observed comparatively less.

TRENDS ASSOCIATED WITH VALUE

Exploring Trends In Value

As can be seen in the previous section, there is significant value being observed in the vast majority of case study organizations. What was also noted in a number of the case studies, however, was that while value had been demonstrated to date within the project management implementations, there were a number of organizations whose ability to continue to realize value was in question. Some of the comments from case reports and from research team members indicated that value was no longer increasing or was in fact declining. Examples of this included:

- Case-study organizations that indicated a high level of initial value being reported, but that were no longer seeing the same level of value.

- The implementation of project management within the organization viewed as being "done" or complete by senior management, with no subsequent investment, focus, or emphasis on the implementation.

- Declining discussion or emphasis on the importance of project management within the organization, either through a reduction in executive communications or through a decline in activities related to the implementation (for example, information sessions, training sessions, or project reviews).

- Reduction in use or adherence to the practices that had been implemented.

How Can The Degree Of Change Be Assessed?

To evaluate and attempt to corroborate these observations, each of the case reports for the case studies was assessed to evaluate the degree to which the implementation was continuing to be sustained and supported, and to evaluate the degree to which the implementation is likely to continue to create value in the future.

The resulting value trend was coded using the following levels:

- 2 – A level of 2 indicates that there is a strong trend towards the organization continuing to be able to realize value from its project management implementation. As well as evidence of value being evidenced to date within the implementation, there is a strong and continued emphasis on project management within the implementation, and the corresponding value is also expected to increase at a significant rate or continue to be delivered at a significant level.

- 1 – A level of 1 indicates that there is some increase in value that is continuing to be realized from the project management implementation. The project management implementation has demonstrated value to date and is expected to continue to deliver value at a more gradual level.

- 0 – A level of 0 indicates that the value of the project management implementation has either attained a plateau, or its continuation may be in question. A value level of 0 indicates a critical juncture for many of the case-study organizations that were observed. While they have realized value in their implementations to date, it is questionable whether further value will be realized. This may be as a result of a lack of continued emphasis and focus, changes in the competitive environment or structure of the organization, or a decline in support or activity related to the project management implementation. For some organizations, there is a risk that the value will, in fact, decline in the future.

- -1 – A level of -1 indicates that the observed value of the organization is declining, but is doing so at a moderate rate. There may have been strong value observed to date, but that level of value is not being sustained and is expected to continue to gradually decline over time.

- -2 – At a level of -2, the organization was observing a considerable decline in value. While value may have been observed previously in the implementation, the value being observed in the organization had declined significantly, and in many instances was being actively destroyed.

To What Degree Is Value Changing?

In exploring the value trend associated with the case studies, a number of additional insights emerge. Looking at where value has been and continues to be created, the majority of case-study organizations have a positive value trend, with 34 of 60 organizations having a value trend of 1 or greater, and five organizations having a value trend of 2. Additional insights can be gained from the following points:

- There are a number of organizations (22) which have a value trend is 0. What this indicates, as noted above, is that while they have already realized some value from their project management implementation, continued increases in value are in question. Based upon the observations of the researchers, there are significant questions as to whether or not additional value creation is possible. Some of these organizations have seen a decline in focus and attention on their implementations, while others are facing significant challenges elsewhere (for example, changes in market or competitive positioning) that call into question whether or not the value that has been realized to date can be sustained. For most of these organizations, stagnation or decline in value is not a foregone conclusion. For continued increases in value to be realized, however, this will likely require a change in strategy in their project management investment or a greater level of emphasis with respect to the organization's project management implementation.

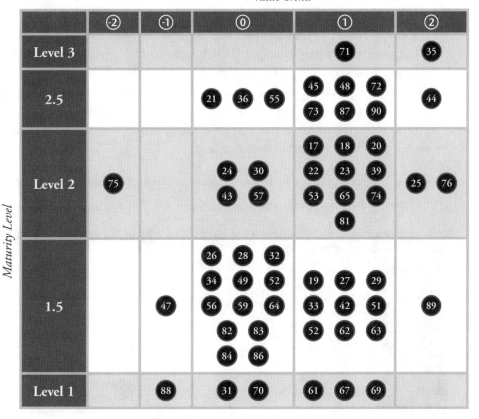

FIGURE 8-11—*Value trend vs. maturity levels*

- There are a small number of organizations (three within the case studies) which are seeing negative value trends. In each of these organizations, the nature of the current implementation means that the value being realized by the organization is declining or is, in fact, actively being destroyed. Two of these case studies are expanded upon in the next section, and illustrate some of the cautions associated with either de-emphasizing or significantly changing the focus and direction of the project management implementation.

- Those organizations that do demonstrate negative value trends are at lower levels of maturity. Two of those organizations are at a maturity level of 1.5, and the third is at a maturity level of 2. This suggests that not only was there a de-emphasis or reduction in focus on the implementation, but the implementations themselves were arguably incomplete and had not yet attained a level of consistency and repeatability under which the implementation could even be considered to be complete or "done."

- The greater the maturity of the organization, the more likely the value trend is to be positive. Looking at those organizations with a value trend of 0, there is a strong cluster of organizations that are at a maturity level of 1.5 – these organizations have implemented some practices, but arguably are still not at a point of stability or completion in the adoption of formalized project management practices. Organizations with a value trend of 1 demonstrate correspondingly higher degrees of maturity, with distributions of maturity primarily at levels of 1.5, 2 and 2.5, while organizations with a value trend of 2 are virtually all at a maturity level of above 2.

A further insight regarding the trends in value creation can be illustrated in Figure 8-12.

Value Trend

Maturity Level	‑2	‑1	0	1	2
Level 3				United States (71)	China (35)
2.5				China (72) China (73)	Australia (44)
Level 2	Canada (75)		China (24)	China (74) China (22) China (23)	Canada (76) Denmark (25)
1.5		United Kingdom (47)		Serbia (33)	Russia (89)
Level 1				UAE (67) UAE (69)	

FIGURE 8-12—Value trend of high-value organizations vs. maturity levels

The case-study organizations in Figure 8-12 are all high-value organizations. Each organization has tangible or intangible value scores of at least 2 in each dimension, or a value score of 3 in one of the two dimensions. As is illustrated, negative value trends are not exclusively associated with organizations that are realizing lesser value from their project management implementations. While the majority of organizations with high value are also demonstrating positive value trends, there is one organization that is at a value trend of 0, one with a value trend of -1 and one with a value trend of -2.

These observations can be expanded upon through exploring some specific organizational case studies (see Figure 8-13):

Value Trend

	⊘-2	⊘-1	⊘0	⊘1	⊘2
Level 3				United States (71)	China (35)
2.5				China (72) China (73)	Australia (44)
Level 2	Canada (75)		China (24)	China (74) China (22) China (23)	Canada (76) Denmark (25)
1.5		United Kingdom (47)		Serbia (33)	Russia (89)
Level 1				UAE (67) UAE (69)	

Maturity Level

FIGURE 8-13—*An exploration of specific cases*

Canada (75)

Maturity Level: 2; Value Trend: -2

Case study organization 75 is the information technology division of a major oil and gas firm in Canada. The project management implementation in this organization was initiated in 2000, and by 2005 the project management office had won awards. The initial implementation, which was highly valued by the organization, focused upon the creation of a center of excellence that was responsible for establishing and promoting a methodology and process for managing projects. The practices, training and coaching provided as a result of this implementation were well received, and arguably delivered a great deal of value in helping the information technology division to become a credible provider of projects to the organization.

In 2006, the focus of the project management office was changed to a control-focused project-delivery office. The project management office assumed responsibility for the delivery of projects, and became a centralized home for project management within the information technology division. In the last two years, however, the organization has struggled to retain project managers and has been challenged in its ability to deliver projects successfully. Much of the value perception within the organization is associated more with the historical implementation than with present-day capabilities.

Quotations from the organization regarding their implementation include:

> *"The value of project management is tangible. It's the structure behind the projects. We do better than industry benchmarks."*
> —*Project Manager, 75*

> *"Project management provides hard value: saving wasted dollars and effort and mitigating the risk of wasting dollars."*
> —*Senior Manager, 75*

> *"The value of project management is control."*
> —*Project Manager, 75*

As can clearly be illustrated from the quotations, there is still a strong perception of value amongst many stakeholders. What is notable about these comments, however, is the emphasis on issues of control, structure, and financial value. All of those aspects that are being emphasized focus on tangible, quantitative value, and there is none of the emphasis on leadership, excellence, and employee effectiveness that hallmarked the original implementation.

China (24)

Maturity Level: 2; Value Trend: 0

Case study organization 24 is a Chinese subsidiary of a major international telecommunications firm. Project management has been an essential discipline within the organization since it was established. The business units studied within the organization work exclusively in a project-driven mode. The earliest implementation was the introduction of basic project management practices at the time the organization was initially established. There is an extremely strong process focus within the organization; one project manager interviewed commented that the project management process was more important than the project management result. Overall, there is a strong belief within the organization that a strictly controlled project management process is the best guarantee of a high-quality result, and that the cost of prevention created by good, formal process is lower than that of remediation.

Most recently, the organization has implemented a change to its project management practice in 2006 as a result of being acquired by its current parent. This implementation saw the alignment of the organization's practices with those of the new parent, and the expansion of project management across the organization.

A quotation from the organization regarding their implementation is presented below:

> *"All divisions must work like a team to respond to customer needs. Project management contributes to team building and coordination. It greatly improved work efficiency and customer satisfaction."*
> —Project Manager, 24

Overall, there is a high level of satisfaction within the organization regarding its current implementation and the perceived value it brings. What brings this continued value realization into question, however, is the constant changing of processes. Each major organizational restructuring (there have been three in the organization to date, occurring approximately every two years) has led to a redefinition of project management practices. While the belief is that the current practices are effective, there is also a widespread perception that the documentation associated with the practices is ineffective, too complex, and too voluminous. As well, the continued emphasis on process for process's sake raises concerns about whether compliance with process will reduce the focus on project outcomes and the delivery of satisfaction on which the organization prides itself.

United States (71)

Maturity Level: 3; Value Trend: 1

Case study organization 71 is a high-tech division of a large engineering consulting firm based in the United States. The organization primarily specializes in the design and construction of highly specialized industrial facilities that require extremely specific and advanced structural provisions and environmental controls. The initial implementation of project management began over 20 years ago, and has been an ongoing focus of the organization.

The most recent project management implementation was a complete review and redevelopment of the project management practices of the organization. The primary goal of the organization was the unification of the best policies and procedures from each division in the organization into a single, unified body of knowledge that could support and serve all projects within this organization. This effort required between 30 and 40 person-years of effort over a two-year period.

A quotation regarding the organization's implementation is reflected below:

> *We would place this organization at the highest possible level of project management maturity. They have developed all of their own processes. They use appropriate software for every area of project implementation and control, and have customized the software extensively. Their results speak for themselves.*
>
> *—Researcher, 71*

The resulting process capability is an extremely involved, extremely complex one. This organization is one of only two within the case studies of this research project that were rated at a maturity level of 3, which is based upon an assessment of their current state of practices. They are in the process of piloting and evaluating the new process capability, and this is an organization that is likely to continue to increase in maturity as the resulting capabilities become used and integrated across the organization. While the development of their project management capabilities has required significant investment and expense, the organization is expected to continue to realize value through subsequent adoption and use, and continued refinement over time.

China (35)

Case study organization 35 is a construction firm based in Beijing, China, that is responsible for the construction of major public infrastructure projects. Originally a branch of the government, within the Chinese army, the division was transferred in its entirety into a state-owned civilian construction enterprise. The organization has a strong reputation throughout the country for its projects, and has been involved in some of the most complex and difficult construction initiatives undertaken in China.

The implementation of project management within the organization began in the 1990s, in response to government requirements and regulations. The organization has since continued to put efforts into the ongoing improvement and refinement of its project management practices. Most recently, the organization has undertaken a comprehensive review and evaluation of completed projects, compiling a book of project cases that outline their project management experiences and lessons learned. This is considered today to be one of the most effective training tools the organization has employed in developing its capabilities.

Quotations from the organization regarding their implementation include:

> *We've not only followed the government regulations, but we've been continuously establishing and innovating our own management system according to the company's development and the industry's situation."*
> —*Project Manager, 35*

> *"It was only since the adoption of project management methods that the company started to really reform its system and establish new management procedures and processes and to run as an economic enterprise. "*
> —*Senior Manager, 35*

There is little question about the value that has been realized as a result of the project management implementation. There are strong and well-defined practices within the organization, and the organization continues to thrive and grow in a challenging and competitive construction market in which other organizations are beginning to struggle and see a potential decline in future revenues. The adoption of lessons learned and the focus on continued improvement and enhancement of the organizations capabilities in the future is likely to see the value of the project management implementation continuing to grow significantly, as well as the overall maturity of the organization's implementation.

CONCLUSIONS

As was mentioned at the beginning of this chapter, the essential focus of this study is to be able to identify and explore the value of project management. This chapter posed the specific question "What is valuable to organizations, and how is it measured?"

We began by exploring a framework that defined value through the lenses of satisfaction, alignment, process outcomes, business outcomes, and return on investment. As we have seen, the first four measures are able to be directly assessed within the case-study organizations. The idea of return on investment, while simple in principle, and theoretically possible to be derived where direct value measures can be quantified, has proved extremely elusive. Each case-study organization contained with this study values project management in some degree and believes it to be in some way important. Nevertheless, none of the case study organizations that could quantify the benefits associated with their project management implementations have done so. Moreover, there are no case-study organizations that can directly and discretely measure the actual costs associated with their implementations. Finally, no project management implementations represented within the case studies have been initiated based upon a promised business case, or expressed an interest in determining a cost-benefit analysis.

One other dimension of value that has also been introduced is the idea of "fit." Put simply, this question asks to what extent what was implemented is what is needed by the organization, based upon the environment the organization operates in and the types of projects the organization manages. An introductory exploration of fit was provided in which Thomas Mengel explored a number of different potential concepts by which fit could be understood, and the degree to which they are being demonstrated in the case study organizations. At its essence, however, the concept of fit is the essential question that has remained over each of the previous chapters: "What differences matter to project management implementations?" Each chapter has explored some aspect of this question: the differences that exist within the organizations, the differences between implementations, and the differences in value.

What can be concluded from the investigation to date is that looking at differences in context, implementation, and value in isolation from each other cannot help to identify the differences that matter. To understand what differences do matter, we need to look at each of these constructs together. The next chapter explores how context and implementation together influence value, so that we can finally identify and answer the question of what differences do matter to project management.

9

Drivers of Value

INTRODUCTION

This chapter represents a presentation of the integrated analysis that has been conducted to date in exploring the drivers of value within this research study. Each of the previous chapters have presented what was found in the case-study organizations that illustrates the constructs of context, implementation, and value. Each of these constructs represents a piece of the overall whole that illustrates how organizations deliver project management value. Chapter 6 (Context) provided an understanding of the differences that exist between organizations. Chapter 7 (Implementation) explored what organizations implement that they call project management. Chapter 8 (Value) established a framework for how value could be evaluated, and what observations of value emerged from the case-study organizations.

The remaining question to be answered, and the one that this chapter explores, is: "What differences matter to project management implementations?" In other words, to what extent do context and implementation influence value? What are the contextual considerations associated with how project management is implemented? What are the implementation considerations that influence how value is attained? What values are realized by specific combinations of context and implementation? Finally, and perhaps most importantly, how can an organization determine its context, establish its value goals and identify the most appropriate implementation to realize those goals?

HOW DO ORGANIZATIONS CLUSTER TOGETHER?

Cluster Analysis of Context Construct-Level PCAs

This analysis explores how the organizations included within this research project cluster together based upon their context. The technique that is used for this analysis is called cluster analysis and was described in Chapter 5. Inputs to this analysis are the context construct-level PCAs explored in Chapter 6. SPSS uses this data to cluster the organizations into groups sharing similar contexts. Each cluster depicts a different structure in the data, representing a different naturally occurring grouping of context characteristics. Organizations in a cluster are more similar to others in the same cluster than to those in other clusters.

The context cluster analysis results are described in Table 9-1. The numbers in the table indicate how far away from the average the cluster is in that particular context descriptor.

	Operationally Efficient Strategic Construction in Developing Economies	Innovative, Conflict Avoiding Product Developers	Customer-Focused Product Developers	Positive Project Management in Government	Project Management Experience in Government	Organizational Change
	Mean	Mean	Mean	Mean	Mean	Mean
1 Unregulated Private Sector	0.1	-1.0	0.1	-1.6	-0.7	-0.4
2 Public Sector Service Providers	0.1	-0.8	0.7	0.4	1.0	0.2
3 Project-Based Organizations	-0.1	0.7	0.3	-0.3	-0.2	-0.4
4 Heavily Regulated Product Development	0.0	0.5	-1.6	0.5	0.4	-0.2
5 Private Sector in Emerging Economies	0.4	1.0	1.0	1.4	-1.3	0.9

TABLE 9-1—*Context cluster analysis results*

Cluster 1—Unregulated Private Sector

The first cluster groups organizations that are definitely described by not being either government descriptor: *Positive attitudes to project management in government* (-1.6); or *Project management experience in government* (-0.7). They were also described as not *Innovative, conflict-avoiding product developers* (-1.0). Seven organizations make up this cluster. Three are from the United Arab Emirates and four are from Denmark. An organization in this cluster operates in the private sector in a largely unregulated environment. Looking at the organizations in this cluster in more detail, it is also evidenced that they all share a view that project management is used primarily reflected by a cost management approach, and each organization has a strategic driver of operational efficiency.

Cluster 2—Public Sector Service Providers

The second cluster groups organizations that are described as not coming from a context of *Innovative conflict-avoiding product development* (-0.8) while at the same time being described by contexts associated with *Customer-focused product developers* (0.7) and operating in a government setting with high project management experience (1.0). Thirteen organizations are grouped together. Many are government departments or recently privatized former government departments. All of these organizations provide services to customers who are largely other government departments and only indirectly (though very consciously recognized in all cases) to the public. Three are from Australia, two are from Canada, two are from Norway, one is from the United States, and the rest (five) are from China.

Cluster 3—Project-Based Organizations

The third cluster appears to be largely described by the context of *Innovative, conflict-avoiding, product developers* (0.7) as well as being described to an extent by a context of *Customer-focused product development* (0.3). These organizations tend to be large, well-established organizations that are more conservative, risk-averse, and structured in their operations. They appear to have a dominant strategic focus of product development and innovation. They also share a customer focus and place high value on projects and project management.

There are 16 organizations in this cluster originating from China (3), the United States (4), Germany (1), Serbia (2), the U.K. (1), Australia (1), Canada (2), Denmark (1), and Norway (1). All but one are large organizations operating in project-intensive environments, and are charged with delivering traditional products in new and innovative ways. The one small organization in this group is growing rapidly and is the largest such organization in its market sector.

Cluster 4—Heavily Regulated Product Development

The fourth cluster contains organizations largely described by their lack of a context of *Customer-focused product innovation* (-1.6). However, they can also be described as being *Innovative, conflict-avoiding product developers* (0.5) working in a government environment where the organization holds both positive attitudes to project management (0.5) and strong project management experience (0.4).

Nine organizations are clustered together. They come from Brazil (2), the U.K. (1), Canada (3), and China (3). None are government organizations. However, all work on product development in heavily regulated markets, whether those are pharmaceuticals, construction, or energy. All of the organizations are large, and appear to evidence a strong level of bureaucracy and hierarchy.

Cluster 5—Private Sector in Emerging Economies

The fifth cluster is largely described as being *Innovative, conflict-avoiding product developers* (1.0), with a strong customer focus (1.0), operating in a government environment with strong positive attitudes to project management (1.4), and where there are large-scale internal change efforts driven by strategic priorities and merger and acquisition activity (0.9). These organizations are definitely not working in government environment described as having strong project management experience (-1.3)

Five organizations fit into this cluster. Three are from China, one is from Serbia and the last is from Lithuania. All represent new types of organizations developing in emerging economies that are implementing project management as a way to compete in this new business world. Two are relatively small organizations, while the others are large or are subsidiaries of global companies operating locally.

This initial grouping of the data highlights the kinds of patterns of context to be found by mechanically sorting the case organizations. This analysis recognizes five separate project management implementations that can be seen in the data. Each cluster contains a different naturally occurring grouping of context characteristics where organizations come from contexts that are more similar to each other than to any other context described in the data.

Cluster Analysis of Implementation Construct-Level PCAs

This analysis explores how the organizations included within this research project cluster together based upon their project management implementation. Similar to the analysis in the previous section, which explores the clusters that emerge within the context construct-level PCAs, this section explores how organizations group together based upon how they approach project management. Inputs to this analysis are the implementation construct-level PCAs described in Chapter 7. SPSS uses this data to cluster the organizations into groups sharing similar project management implementations. Each cluster depicts a different structure in the data representing different naturally occurring groupings of implementation characteristics. Organizations in a cluster are more similar to others in the same cluster than to those in other clusters.

The implementation cluster analysis results are described in Table 9-2. The numbers in the table indicate how far away from the average the cluster is in that particular project management implementation descriptor.

Clusters	Full Project Management, Traditional Drivers, Delivery PMO	Long Term Training, Strategic Drivers, Project Management Authority	Cost Management, Clear Roles, Informal Training	Internal Drivers, External off the Shelf Training	Trained Experts, Methodology PMO
1 Project Management As Strategic Competency	*1.5*	*0.8*	*-0.1*	*-0.3*	*-0.3*
2 Project Management In Response To Customer Demands	*-0.5*	*0.3*	*0.6*	*-1.0*	*-0.4*
3 Project Management As Not Cost Management	*-0.3*	*-0.3*	*-1.5*	*0.2*	*0.2*
4 Project Management as Cost-Focused Hired Experts	*0.2*	*-0.7*	*0.6*	*0.5*	*0.8*
5 Project Management as Cost Management	*-0.1*	*-2.0*	*0.8*	*0.7*	*-2.0*

TABLE 9-2—*Implementation cluster analysis results*

Cluster 1 – Project Management As Strategic Competency

Organizations in the first cluster can be described as having a full project management implementation (1.5) supported by a tailored internally developed training curriculum. This implementation also includes the use of a full toolset, establishment of clear roles, career paths, and formal training frameworks supported by a delivery project management office (PMO). This cluster is also described by implementations based upon strategic drivers for project management and incorporate long-term training and high project manager authority (0.8).

Eleven organizations are grouped together under this implementation. All of these organizations are involved in project-intensive industries, largely in engineering or construction applications. Many (7) are located in China. The rest of the organizations are from Australia (2), and one each from Canada and the U.S. These organizations have implemented a full set of tools and training to support project management, as they see project management as a strategic competency for the industry they operate in.

Cluster 2 – Project Management In Response To Customer Demands

Organizations in the second cluster are most described by a cost management (0.6) focus for their project management implementation. The organizations in this cluster are not described by implementations based upon internal drivers or the use of off-the-shelf training (-1.0) to train internal project managers. These organizations are also moderately described as implementing long-term training and high project manager authority (0.3).

Twelve organizations are included in this cluster. Seven are from Europe. The rest are from China (2), the U.K., and Brazil (2). All of the organizations in this group are private-sector organizations operating to make a profit. The profit focus may be an indicator as to why the emphasis in these project management implementations is on cost management. Many of these organizations carry out projects for customers. The customer projects, combined with the lack of a strategic focus for these implementations, may indicate that they are implementing project management in response to perceived or real market demand for such practices.

Cluster 3 – Project Management As Not Cost Management

Organizations in the third cluster are most described by what they are not. These organizations are described as being strongly not associated with a cost management-focused implementation (-1.5).

Twelve organizations are in this cluster. Five are from China, two are from the United Arab Emirates, two are from the U.S., and one each are from the U.K., Serbia, and Canada. All of these organizations have implemented project management to improve their ability to manage projects in increasingly demanding and fast-paced environments. While many of them work in regulated environments where project management is strongly encouraged, these organizations appear to have invested in project management as a means of improving their ability to compete and operate in their environment. While cost management may be seen as an aid to operational effectiveness, these implementations do not solely appear to be driven by these pressures.

Cluster 4—Project Management as Cost-Focused Hired Experts

Organizations in the fourth cluster report a project management implementation that is defined as not incorporate long-term training, strategic drivers, and high project manager authority (-0.7). These organizations have a cost-management focus with clear roles and informal training (0.6). Implementations are supported by off-the-shelf training provided by external providers (0.7). As well, these organizations are described as operating with project managers hired as trained experts, and have a methodology PMO (0.8). The organizations in this cluster clearly focus on providing a consistent methodology they expect to be followed, and their policies appear to have a strong emphasis on cost-management. Actual project managers are hired for their expertise and are expected to bring significant training with them from the outside.

Twelve organizations from all over the world reside in this cluster: Australia (3), Canada (2), Norway (3), U.S. (2), Denmark (1), and Lithuania (1). All of the organizations in this cluster come from context clusters 2—Public Sector Service Providers, and 3—Project-Based organizations, as identified in the previous section. Thus, all of these organizations are focused on delivering projects for customers.

Cluster 5—Project Management as Cost Management

Organizations in the fifth cluster are described by implementations that adopt a cost-management approach to project management, with clear roles and internal training (0.8). These organizations are also described by implementations based upon internal drivers and supported by external off-the-shelf training (0.7). In contrast, they are clearly not described as having a full project management implementation with a delivery PMO (-1.0). These organizations are also not described as having implementations driven by strategic drivers or including long-term training or significant project manager authority (-2.0), or implementations utilizing trained experts and a methodology PMO (-2.0). These organizations appear to be driven by a cost management focus, but without providing either trained experts or providing internal project managers with any centralized training or supports to get the job done. Project management appears to be seen here as a fairly straightforward activity having more to do with financial controls than managing complexity.

There are three organizations in this cluster. All three of these organizations are located in Canada and are privately held. Two of the organizations are fairly large, while the third is small. Two of the organizations are not very far into their project management implementations, having been undertaken for less than two years at the time data was collected. The third implemented project management initially over eight years ago. However, it too began a new and quite different project management implementation in the last two years. This cluster is very similar to Cluster 2 with its focus on cost management, but differs in the degree to which it negatively correlates with the strategic and cultural aspects of project management observed in other implementations.

This initial grouping of the data highlights the kinds of patterns of project management implementation to be found by mechanically sorting the case organizations. This analysis recognizes five separate project management implementations that can be seen in the data. Each cluster contains a different naturally occurring grouping of project management implementation characteristics where the organizations' implementations are more similar to each other than to any other implementation described in the data.

How Do High-Level Trends Of Value Vary With Context and Implementation?

Chapter 8 introduced some high-level trends of value associated with the case studies that were developed based upon a comprehensive evaluation of the case-study reports and associated data for each organization:

- Tangible value: The degree to which the organization is receiving concrete, quantifiable value.

- Intangible value: The degree to which the organization is receiving other positive and important benefits that are not directly quantifiable.

- Value trend: The likelihood of the organization to continue to be able to deliver its value as its project management implementation proceeds.

- Maturity, which is not a direct value measure *per se*, but is intended to reflect the current level of formality and consistency of the organization's practices, and is a benefit that for many case-study organizations was both sought and reported on.

Based upon the components of context, implementation, and value that have been identified and presented thus far, this section explores the interrelationship between the high-level indicators and trends of value derived from the research team and the components that have emerged from the analysis of the case-study data.

Interpreting The Diagrams

In each of the following diagrams, one of the constructs associated with this study is presented in the columns of the chart, and is compared to one of the dimensions of value that are described above. The value dimensions are presented in the rows of the chart. An organization's association of these two dimensions is presented by a marker in the relevant square of the resulting matrix:

- A solid-colored dot indicates that the organization has a positive association with the construct component it appears below.

- A black-colored dot indicates that the organization is not associated with the construct component it appears below. This has been used in instances where organizations are defined not by their positive association with a component, but are instead defined by a negative association. In other words, there is not a component that describes them, and instead they are described by the components they are not.

- Where an organization is associated with more than one component, this is illustrated by a line connecting all of the dots that identify that organization on the chart.

Exploring Tangible Value Influences

As noted in Chapter 8, the majority of organizations that demonstrate tangible value are those that perform project work on behalf of their customers. Typically, these are either consulting or construction and engineering organizations for whom project work is the nature of their business.

Context

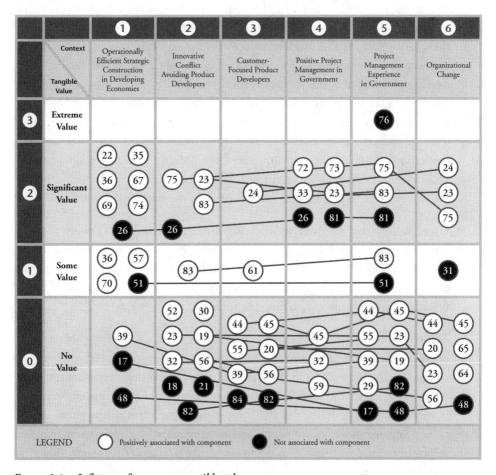

FIGURE 9-1—*Influence of context on tangible value*

In exploring the influence of context on the realization of tangible value, as illustrated in Figure 9-1, what is again reinforced strongly is the number of organizations that are not actually demonstrating tangible value from their project management implementations. Of those that are, however, some very interesting patterns emerge:

- Tangible value is being observed in all contexts. While there are patterns that emerge where contexts are more likely to demonstrate tangible value, all of the components illustrated here have at least one organization that is demonstrating significant tangible value.

- Those organizations that are most likely to demonstrate tangible value are those associated with the first context, *Operationally efficient strategic construction in developing economies*. This reinforces the observations about those organizations that are providing projects for customers, but introduces an additional level of nuance. As noted in the Chapter 6, a clear component that emerged in the context was those organizations engaged in "strategic construction"–specifically, those organizations that undertake projects for strategic purposes, where the organization is responsible for the subsequent operation of the facility they develop. A number of case-study organizations fall into this category, and what can be seen is that they are deriving a significant amount of tangible value from their implementations. Many of these organizations have been able to leverage their ability to credibly deliver projects to significantly enhance their reputations. This has, in turn influenced their ability to attract a significantly greater number of subsequent projects, where some case-study organizations in this component now have a pipeline of projects measured in decades.

- Organizations that are more functionally driven, or that do not deliver projects for customers, are less likely to realize tangible benefits. This can be observed in those components associated with product development, organizational change and *Project management experience in government*. The majority of these organizations are realizing no tangible value.

- The component entitled *Positive project management in government* has more organizations with a significant level of value being observed than those seeing no tangible value. On the face of it, this observation may be surprising. An exploration of the specific organizations associated with this component, however, reflects that the majority of these organizations are either state-owned organizations or divisions and departments of government that are responsible for construction and infrastructure projects. As a result, many of the tangible impacts that are observed in the strategic construction firms are also evident here.

Implementation

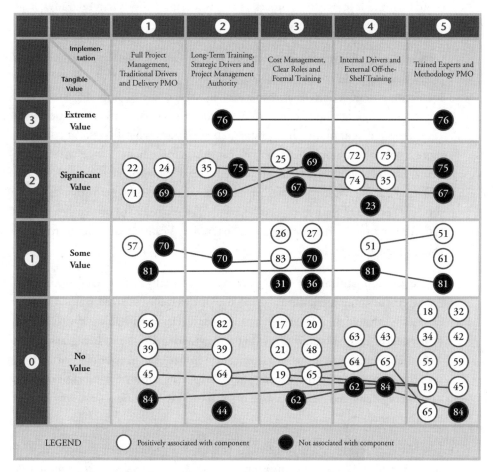

FIGURE 9-2—*Influence of implementation on tangible value*

In exploring the influences of implementation on tangible value (see Figure 9-2), there are again a number of interesting insights and observations that emerge:

- As with context, tangible value is being observed in all implementations. With one exception, each implementation component has at least one organization associated with it that is delivering significant value.

- Those organizations associated with *Full project management, traditional drivers and delivery PMO* and *Internal drivers and external off-the-shelf training* implementations are most likely to observe significant value being delivered as a product of their implementation. What is interesting about both of these components is they represent relatively formalized, process-based implementations of project management. Both components also leverage views of project management that rely upon externally accepted approaches and standards, and leverage both processes and training methods that take advantage of these common standards.

- Organizations with implementations defined as *Cost management, clear roles and formal training* and *Trained experts and methodology PMO* are only likely to leverage some tangible value. Only one organization in either of these components indicated significant tangible value being realized, although this was in combination with another implementation. These implementations are typically associated with a more minimalistic implementation of project management. Those with a cost-management implementation are often focused more on a view that project management is synonymous with management of the cost performance of the project. The use of trained experts and a methodology PMO primarily leverages external expertise, and these organizations have typically made limited structural changes to accommodate or support project management.

- While those organizations with implementations that are relying upon cost-management implementations or the use of externally sourced trained experts do attain some tangible value, significant levels of tangible value is being evidenced in those organizations that strongly identify as not being associated with these implementations. A significant number of organizations with strong negative associations to these components are seeing some or significant tangible value being delivered, and one such organization is realizing an extreme level of tangible value.

- Less tangible value is also evidenced for those organizations associated with the component *Long-term training, strategic drivers and project management authority*. While on the face of it this may seem counterintuitive, as this component is often also associated with more established implementations, what is distinct about organizations that align strongly with this component is that the motivations for their implementation are longer-term and often focused more on the organizational culture. While tangible benefits are not necessarily a focus of these implementations, it would be expected that intangible benefits would be higher.

Exploring Intangible Value Influences

Intangible value reflects value being observed within the case-study organizations that is less readily quantified, such as increases in reputation, improved staff retention, and greater strategic alignment. As noted in Chapter 8, the vast majority of case-study organizations are realizing some level of intangible value associated with their implementation.

Context

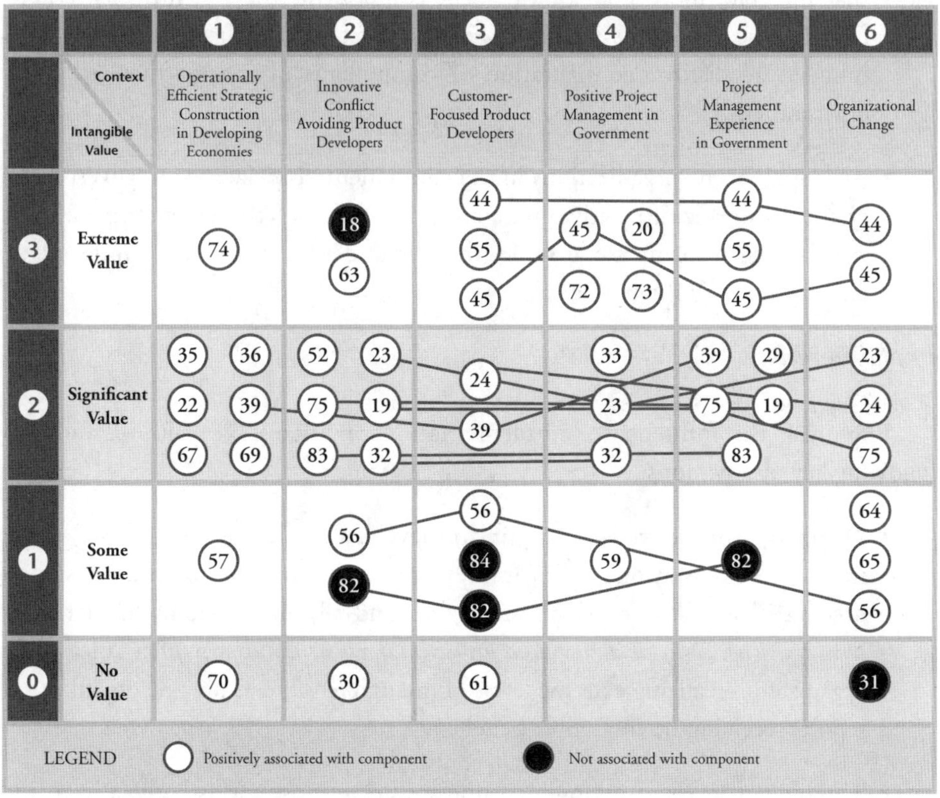

FIGURE 9-3—*Influence of context on intangible value*

Exploring the influence of context on intangible value (Figure 9-3) reveals a fairly broad distribution of value being realized across each of the contexts being observed:

- There are organizations in each context that are realizing significant levels of intangible benefits.
- Most of those organizations with a context of *Operationally efficient strategic construction in developing economies* are realizing high levels of intangible value as well as tangible value.
- A number of organizations that are realizing high levels of intangible value positively correspond with more than one context (as evidenced by appearing in more than one context; where this occurs, the linkages are indicated by a line joining each instance). This is true for each context component with the exception of the component associated with strategic construction. Those organizations in the strategic construction component tend to exclusively define their context within this component.

- While a number of organizations that are realizing value have implementations that integrate more than one context component, there is little pattern to how these components integrate. For the most part, each organization has a unique and distinct configuration of components of context that reflect its environment.

- Almost all of the organizations in the components associated with government contexts are realizing positive intangible value. Although there is one organization that is only realizing some value, the remainder are observing significant or extreme levels of intangible value.

Implementation

Exploring the influence of implementation on intangible value reveals the following key observations:

- Organizations are realizing significant levels of intangible (Figure 9-4) value in all implementations. Each implementation component has at least two organizations delivering significant value, and all but one component (*Long-term training, strategic drivers and project management authority*) has at least one organization realizing extreme levels of intangible value. Only one organization reports receiving no intangible benefits.

- The highest levels of intangible value are being most consistently seen in the components associated with *Internal Drivers and External off-the-shelf training* and *Trained experts and methodology PMO*. While each of these delivered some tangible value also, they are realizing proportionally higher levels of intangible value. Particularly interesting is the high level of value being observed in the component associated with trained experts, as while there is an organizational process defined, often there is less formalized structure in place and greater emphasis on the expertise of project managers.

- While it was speculated that the implementation component of *Long-term training, strategic drivers and project management authority*, because it was associated with a more strategic orientation, would demonstrate higher intangible value, this is not observed to be the case. While organizations associated with this implementation demonstrate some or significant amounts of value, other implementations are demonstrating consistently higher levels of intangible value.

- Unlike context, the majority of organizational implementations are reflected by a single component. There are proportionally fewer organizational implementations that are defined by multiple implementation components.

- The component associated with long-term training and strategic drivers is the only implementation component that is typically not observed as a single implementation type. All but one of the organizations associated with this implementation are also strongly associated with another of the implementation components.

- Organizations demonstrating significant levels of intangible value are associated with implementations based upon the components that they are not described by. Often, these implementations are negatively correlated with two or more components. While the implementations of these organizations do not strongly align with any of the implementation components that have emerged, there are specific components that categorically do not reflect their implementations.

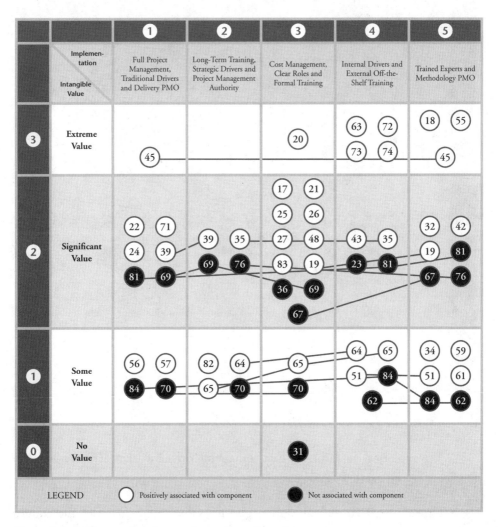

FIGURE 9-4—*Influence of implementation on intangible value*

Exploring Value Trend Influences

The value trends indicate a researcher assessment of the likely ability of organizations to continue realizing value from their implementations. As explored in Chapter 8, the value trend was evaluated on a scale of 2 (strong expectation of continued value realization) to -2 (strong likelihood of value reduction or value destruction).

Context

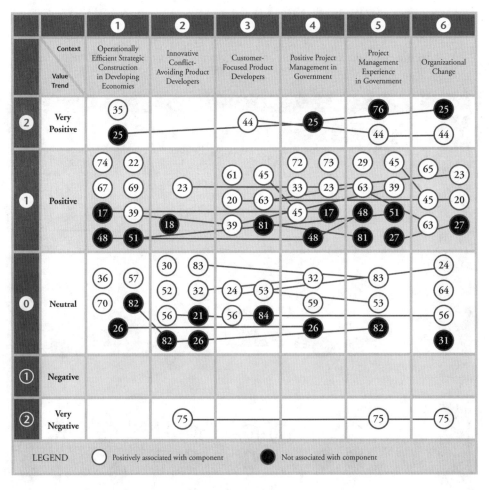

FIGURE 9-5—*Influence of context on value trends*

When exploring the influence that context has on value trends (Figure 9-5), the following key observations emerge:

- Organizations are demonstrating positive value trends in all of the context components observed within the study.

- The majority of organizations in all but one context are reflecting a value trend of neutral to positive, with a slightly higher trend in each towards a positive value trend of 1.

- The only context which is not correlated strongly with a positive value trend is the component defined by *Innovative conflict-avoiding product developers*. There is only one organization described solely by this component. The vast majority of organizations with this component show a neutral value trend, along with the only organization with a value trend of -2.

- The organization with a very negative (-2) value trend draws is not only associated with *Innovative conflict-avoiding product developers*, but also with *Project management experience in government* and *Organizational change*. While the organization is not governmental, it does operate in part in a highly regulated environment. It is the only organization in the research study to exhibit this pattern.

- One of the organizations with the most positive value trends (+2) does exhibit a similar pattern, being positively associated with the components of *Project management experience in government* and *Organizational change*. It also has a product development context, being strongly associated with the *Customer-focused product developers* component. There are two other organizations with this association, which are also demonstrating a positive value trend (+1).

Implementation

Exploration of the influence of implementation on value trends (Figure 9-6) results in the following observations:

- Every implementation has several organizations associated with a positive value trend. There are no implementations that stand out as influencing the creation or destruction of value.

- The one organization that is demonstrating the lowest value trend (-2) is defined by an implementation that is *not* associated with implementation components of *Long-term training, strategic drivers and project management authority* and *Trained experts and methodology PMO*. One of the organizations with the highest value trend (+2) has a negative association with these same components. This suggests that the significant differences between these two implementations may be more contextual than they are a result of the implementation. It may also, however, still be a product of implementation differences, as both implementations are defined by what they are not, rather than what they are.

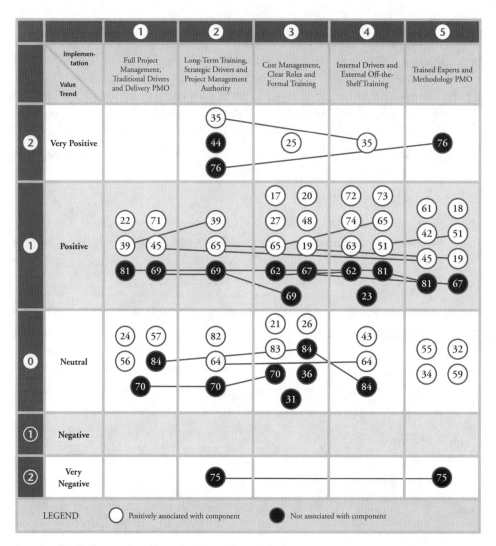

FIGURE 9-6—*Influence of implementation on value trends*

Exploring Maturity Influences

While not a direct measure of value, the exploration of maturity introduced in Chapter 7 provided an additional lens through which the case studies could be viewed. It could be argued that maturity level results from the implementation, as do the other dimensions of value. Maturity was also a concept that for many organizations was specifically sought as a goal of their project management implementation, and was described and reported on in several case-study reports as a value received.

Context

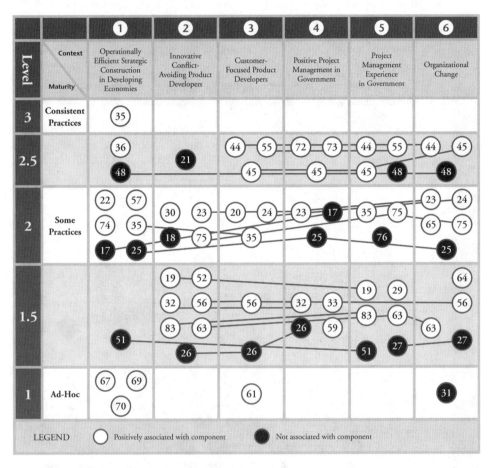

Figure 9-7—*Influence of context on maturity*

Comparing the influence of context against assessed maturity of project management (Figure 9-7) reveals the following observations:

- Maturity is being seen at all levels for the majority of the context components being observed. All context components have organizations with a maturity level of at least 2.

- While the component *Operationally efficient strategic construction in developing economies* is associated with organizations at the highest levels of maturity (level 3), it is also associated with organizations at the lowest levels of maturity. Three organizations at level 1 are directly associated with this component, and one other organization that currently appears as not being associated with the *Organizational change* component could arguably also be aligned with the other organizations here.

- The component *Innovative conflict-avoiding product developers* is the only context descriptor that is not associated with a maturity level of higher than 2, and has the largest proportion of organizations with a maturity level of 1.5.

Implementation

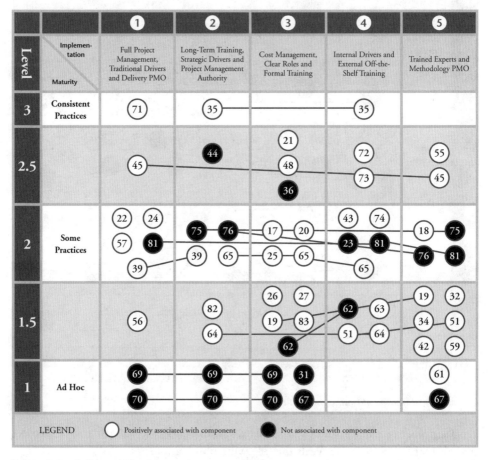

FIGURE 9-8—*Influence of implementation on maturity*

In evaluating the influences of implementation on project management maturity (Figure 9-8), the following observations emerge:

- All implementation components have organizations that are assessed at a high level of maturity. Every implementation component has more than one organization assessed at a maturity level of 2 and above.

- The highest levels of maturity (level 3) are associated with the implementation components of *Full project management, traditional drivers and delivery PMO, Long-term training, strategic drivers and project management authority* and *Internal drivers and off-the-shelf training.* Each of these components represents relatively complete implementations of project management, although interestingly they span the full range of motivations for implementing a project management capability.

- Comparatively lower levels of maturity are being observed in the *Cost management, clear roles and formal training* component, with most organizations having a maturity level of between 1.5 and 2. This is not atypical, as the implementations associated with this component are more focused on cost management than a more comprehensive implementation. A partial implementation is more likely to have a lower level of maturity.

- The lowest levels of maturity are being observed in the implementation component *Trained experts and methodology PMO.* On the face of it this may appear counterintuitive, as this is the only implementation component that has a methodology-focused PMO. Organizations in this component, however, typically place greater emphasis on the use of resources that are sourced externally, with few internal structures and supports being put in place to support the management of projects. The result is that even while there is an organization that theoretically advocates for a common process, greater project management emphasis is placed upon the knowledge and skills of individual project managers. As a result, these organizations are almost inevitably likely to reflect a lower level of maturity.

WHAT DIFFERENCES DO STRONGLY LOADING ORGANIZATIONS DEMONSTRATE?

Highlighting Organizations That Exemplify The Components

What the previous section has demonstrated is that there are relationships between both context and implementation and the value that organizations realize. What it has also served to highlight is that in order to gain greater insights into what specific patterns of context and implementation deliver value, we are going to need to explore the organizations at a more granular level.

In this section, we explore those organizations that exemplify each of the construct-level components that were identified in Chapters 6, 7, and 8. The descriptions of each construct-level component provided an illustration of one organization that exemplified that particular component. What we now want to do is look at all of the case studies that highly reflect each component, and to understand what similarities and differences may exist among these organizations.

As a part of the process of using principal components analysis as an exploratory analysis method, as described in Chapter 4, each case study is scored against each component that emerges in a principal component. For every component that has been identified, therefore, there is a score for each case-study organization. Moreover, these factor scores are automatically distributed against the overall sample of case studies. What this means is that a relatively uniform distribution of cases emerges based upon the following scores:

Distribution	Score
NEGATIVE (the case study is not strongly associated with this component)	LESS THAN 1 (more than one standard deviation below the mean)
1 STANDARD DEVIATION (the case study is in the median range of organizations associated with this component)	-1 to 1 (within 1 standard deviation of the mean)
POSITIVE (the case study is strongly associated with this component)	GREATER THAN ONE (more than one standard deviation above the mean)

This section explores in more detail how organizations that are positively associated with each component align or differ in terms of the other constructs against which they have been evaluated. In doing so, we explore:

- How organizations that are strongly associated with each context component distribute against the implementation and value components.

- How organizations that are strongly associated with each implementation component distribute against the context and value components.

- How organizations that are strongly associated with each value component distribute against the context and value components.

Interpreting The Diagrams—Organizations That Exemplify Context And Implementation Components

In each of the following diagrams, one of the constructs associated with this study is explored, based upon organizations that are strongly loading exemplars of that particular construct.

The construct being exemplified is presented in the columns of the chart, and is compared to one of the other two constructs. The construct that is being compared to is presented in the rows of the chart. If, for example, those organizations that are exemplars of context are being explored to identify the implementations that they are associated with, then the context components would be presented in columns, with its headings appearing at the top of the chart; the implementation components would be presented in rows, with its headings appearing along the left edge of the chart.

The diagram should be read vertically. An organization's association of the two dimensions is presented by a marker in the relevant square of the resulting matrix:

- All organizations have a positive association with the component that they appear below. Each chart is limited only to those organizations that are extremely positively associated with that component; in other words, those whose association is greater than one standard deviation from the mean.

- A solid-colored dot indicates that the organization has a positive association with the construct component it appears beside. The association of the construct component is greater than one standard deviation.

- An outlined dot indicates that there is an association with the component it appears beside, but this association measures within one standard deviation. In other words, the organization is not an exemplar of that component.

- A black-colored dot indicates that the organization is not associated with the construct component it appears beside. This has been used in instances where organizations are defined not by their positive association with a component, but are instead defined by a negative association. In other words, there is not a component that describes them, and instead they are described by the components they are not.

- Where an organization is associated with more than one component, this is illustrated by a line connecting all of the dots that identify that organization on the chart.

Relationships For Organizations That Exemplify The Context Components

Exploring Context and Implementation

This analysis (Figure 9-9) compares the influences that organizations which score strongly on each of the context components have on each of the implementation components. In essence, it identifies those implementation components that are most prevalent for organizations that are high in each context component.

Insights for each component are:

- Context 1—*Operationally efficient strategic construction in developing economies.* For those organizations that score highly on this context component, two

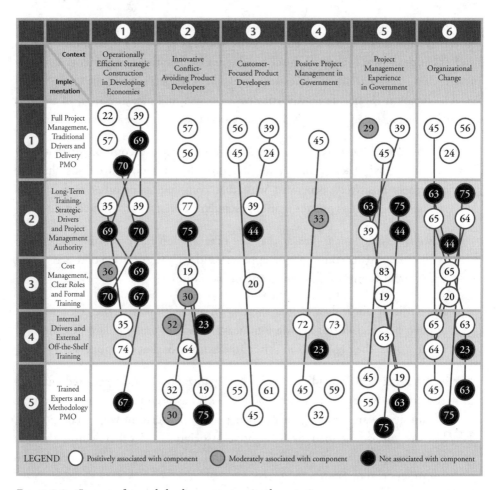

FIGURE 9-9—*Impacts of strongly loading context on implementation*

interesting insights emerge. First, there is a subset of organizations that score particularly on implementations 1 and 2: *Full project management, traditional drivers and a delivery PMO;* and *Long-term training, strategic drivers and project management authority.* As well, two organizations also score highly on implementation 4—internal drivers combined with external off-the-shelf training. What these essentially illustrate is that in delivering strategic construction projects in developing economies, there is a tendency towards full implementations, while the drivers underlying these implementations may themselves differ. For these organizations, however, project management reflects a traditional view that typically leverages recognized international standards and concepts. The contrary view, however, is taken by three organizations that, while measuring strongly on the context component, are identified by negative scores in the implementation components. These organizations are most particularly identified as not being associated with implementations 1, 2, and 3, which is nearly the inverse of the initial set of organizations. The reason for these differences emerge when we look at the maturity of these implementations—the negative correlations are associated with new implementations of extremely low maturity, while the positive correlations reflect established practices.

- Context 2—*Innovative conflict-avoiding product developers.* For those organizations that measure strongly on this context component, there is a surprising variety of implementations with which organizations indicate strong associations. Despite the consistent observations regarding value trends and maturity in the previous section regarding this component, the actual nature of the underlying implementations is very different for each organization, with at least one organization strongly associated with each implementation component. When moderate associations are taken into account, there seems to be a slight emphasis on implementations 3, 4, and 5—cost management; internal drivers and external OTS training; and trained experts with a methodology PMO. There are also two organizations that are negatively associated with implementations 4 and 5.

- Context 3—*Customer-focused product developers.* For organizations that measure strongly on this component, the predominant implementation associations are on implementation components 1 and 5: *Full project management, traditional drivers and delivery PMO,* and *Trained experts and a methodology PMO.* While both of these implementations typically embody a comprehensive project management implementation, they approach these implementations from very different perspectives. The full project management approach relies upon the development of internal project managers and the project support organization assumes responsibility for project delivery. The trained expert approach, by contrast, relies upon the individual expertise of the project manager, with little structural adaptation and a project support organization that may advocate for project management but does not necessarily have a strong ability to enforce adherence. Interestingly, one organization consciously bridges these two implementations.

- Context 4—*Positive project management in government.* For organizations that measure strongly on this component, the predominant emphasis is on implementation components 4 and 5: *Internal drivers combined with external off-the-shelf training,* and *Trained experts and a methodology-based PMO.* Interestingly, the difference in these implementations could be largely a cultural one. Those organizations that align on internal drivers and external training are based in China, while those that rely upon trained experts are North American.

- Context 5—*Project management experience in government.* Of the two government components, a much higher number of organizations measure strongly on this context component than they do on the component *Positive project management in government.* Organizations measuring strongly here, however, do not appear to have a common implementation with which they are typically associated. Each of the implementations has examples of organizations that are positively associated with them, and implementations 2 and 5 also have organizations that are negatively associated with them. Most of the organizations, however, are defined by multiple components working in tandem: whether defined by positive associations or negative ones, there is only one organization that is strongly associated with a single implementation component.

- Context 6—*Organizational change.* Organizations that measure strongly on this component, like the previous one, have organizations that also measure strongly in other implementation components. While there are several organizations that measure strongly on this component, there is very little consistency or alignment in identifying the type of implementation that they have adopted. There are also actually several overlaps with Context 5 with respect to organizations that have measure negatively against the implementation components.

Exploring Context and Value

This analysis (Figure 9-10) compares the influences that organizations that score strongly on each of the context components have on each of the value components. In essence, it identifies those value components that are most prevalent for organizations that are high in each context component. The diagram should be read vertically—within each context component, those value components that have a strong influence, some influence or negative influence on context are identified.

Insights for each component are:

- Context 1—*Operationally efficient strategic construction in developing economies.* Organizations that measure strongly on this component demonstrate a high degree of clarity in terms of where value is being realized. There are clear clusters of value associated with value components 1, *Aligned practices, better processes and business outcomes*; 3, *Better project results, aligned organization and corporate culture*; and 5, *Good project management, not process, customer satisfaction.* For some organizations, these components also cluster together, but they reflect a high degree of value being realized at an organization level as a result of the project management implementation. Interestingly, while there was more of a distinction at an implementation level between more and less mature organizations in this component, there is much less of one in terms of value.

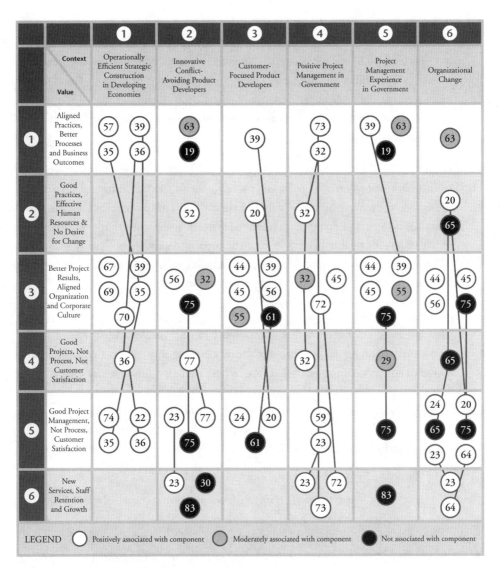

FIGURE 9-10—*Impacts of strongly loading context on value*

- Context 2—*Innovative conflict-avoiding product developers.* As with the implementations, those organizations that measure strongly on this component are yielding very different types of value. Each value component has at least one organization associated with it, but four value components also have organizations negatively associated with them. While the contextual component here is a constant, the underlying implementations and the specific value being delivered vary significantly. Organizations with the same context and value loadings are reporting distinctly different implementations.

- Context 3—*Customer-focused product developers*. The majority of organizations that measure strongly on this component have a strong association with value component 3, *Better project results, aligned organization and corporate culture*. There is also some positive association with value component 5, *Good project management, not process and customer satisfaction*, although one organization that measures strongly in this context is negatively associated with both value components 3 and 5.

- Context 4—*Positive project management in government*. Organizations that measure strongly on this component have very little discrimination in terms of where they are observing value. Every value component has at least one organization that is positively associated with it, indicating that they are seeing positive levels of value here. Many of the organizations are positively associated with multiple components of value, and this is one of only two components in which organizations have no negative value associations.

- Context 5 – *Project management experience in government*. Organizations that measure strongly on this component tell an interesting story. As in the implementation analysis, there is a strong correlation between this context and those of context components 2 and 3. Where there is a positive value association within organizations in this component, they are also likely to be realizing positive value associations in context 3, *Customer-focused product developers*. Where there is a negative value association, these organizations are also likely to be realizing negative value in context 2, *Innovative conflict-avoiding product developers*.

- Context 6—*Organizational change*. Organizations measuring strongly on this component are also realizing value in several of the value components. Predominant clusters for this component are 3, *Better project results, aligned organization and corporate culture*; 5, *Good project management, not process, customer satisfaction*; and 6, *New services, staff retention and growth*. At the same time, there are organizations measuring strongly on this component that have negative value correlations with value components 3 and 5. Differences in where value is observed largely appear to be based upon industry, with construction organizations largely positively associated with value component 3 and information technology organizations predominantly associated with value component 5.

Relationships For Organizations That Exemplify The Implementation Components

Exploring Implementation and Context

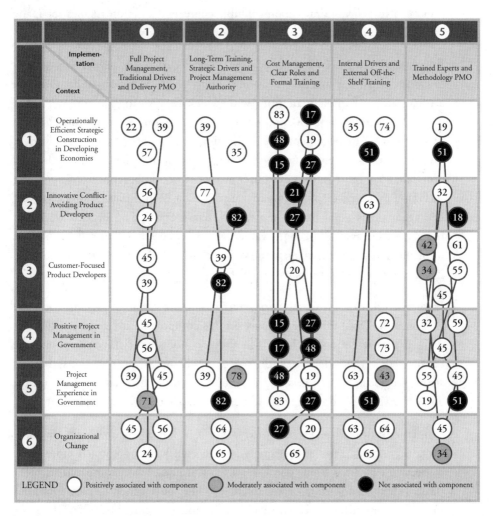

FIGURE 9-11—*Impacts of strongly loading implementation on context*

This analysis (Figure 9-11) compares the influences that organizations scoring strongly on each of the implementation components have on each of the context components. In essence, it identifies those context components that are most prevalent for organizations that are high in each implementation component. The diagram should be read vertically–within each implementation component, those context components that have a strong influence, some influence, or negative influence on implementation are identified.

Insights for each component are:

- Implementation 1—*Full project management, traditional drivers and delivery PMO.* Organizations that measure strongly on this implementation are drawn from a number of different context. Interestingly, most of the organizations, while positively associated in general, draw upon multiple contexts. Common themes for many organizations are a focus on product development and a government structure.

- Implementation 2—*Long-term training, strategic drivers and project management authority.* Organizations that measure strongly on this component demonstrate a broad array of implementations with which they strongly align. While the overall focus of this implementation derives from a longer-term, more strategic view of project management, the underlying contexts are actually quite varied. Two organizations are much-newer implementations that, while culturally motivated, are quite immature. Three are construction organizations operating in China that deliver projects on a customer basis, and have adopted project management as a means of strategic differentiation. The organization that has a negative association with value delivery is an engineering firm that has implemented project management very recently and is at a very early stage in its adoption of a project management frame.

- Implementation 3—*Cost management, clear roles and formal training.* Organizations that measure strongly on this component are interestingly more defined by the contexts with which they do not align with, rather than the contexts that they identify with. Virtually all of the organizations that are strongly associated with this implementation are also associated with multiple contexts, with only one organization clearly associated with a single context.

- Implementation 4—*Internal drivers and external off-the-shelf training.* Organizations that measure strongly on this component are much more likely to be aligned with a single context, which is unique when compared with the those other organizations that strongly align with other implementations. Only one organization is associated with multiple contexts. The others are clustered around contexts 1, 4, and 6. Again, this clustering appears to be based upon cultural lines. Those organizations associated with *Operationally efficient strategic construction in developing economies* and *Positive project management in government* are largely associated with state-owned construction enterprises in China, while those associated with *Organizational change* are associated with early implementations of project management.

- Implementation 5—*Trained experts and methodology PMO.* Organizations that measure strongly on this component demonstrate a considerable amount of diversity in terms of their underlying contexts. There is a strong association of different organizations with the majority of contexts represented by the case studies. Common themes still include contexts of government and product development, as in other implementations, but a significant number of organizations that are strongly associated with this implementation do not appear in other implementations. The association with government in this implementation is not overly surprising, given the reliance of many government organizations on the procurement of project management resources from external sources. What is interesting about this implementation is that a number of the contexts are associated with positive implementations and customer-focused orientations, which can be more challenging to support through externally sourced resources.

Exploring Implementation and Value

This analysis (Figure 9-12) compares the influences that organizations that score strongly on each of the implementation components have on each of the value components. In essence, it identifies those value components that are most prevalent for organizations that are high in each implementation component. The diagram should be read vertically – within each implementation component, those value components that have a strong influence, some influence or negative influence on implementation are identified.

Insights for each component are:

- Implementation 1—*Full project management, traditional drivers and delivery PMO.* Organizations that measure strongly in this implementation experience positive association with the value drivers in all instances. There are a number of different values that are being leveraged here, however. In exploring the details of the organizations identified here, many of the organizations associated with this implementation are based in China, and as a result seem to have focused on a much more traditional and comprehensive implementation. The value that these organizations realized, however, varies in part on not just the implementation but also the underlying context. Even within the same country, organizations associated with different industries are realizing different values.

- Implementation 2—*Long-term training, strategic drivers and project management authority.* Organizations that measure strongly on this component again show a broad distribution of value being realized. Organizations are strongly associated with realizing value in components 1, 3, 4, and 5. Each of these components also has organizations reflected as not receiving value, however. What is interesting in this component is that many of the organizations are realizing value in value components 4 and 5, both of which emphasize the delivery of good project results in the absence of consistent process. It would appear that several of the organizations in this component are relying more upon project manager authority rather than organizational capabilities to produce project results.

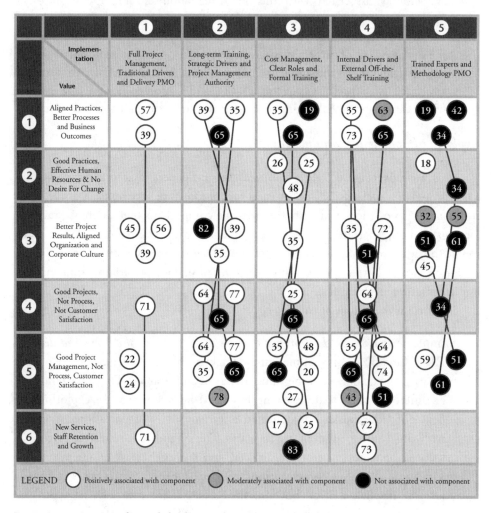

FIGURE 9-12—*Impacts of strongly loading implementation on value*

- Implementation 3—*Cost management, clear roles and formal training*. Organizations that measure strongly on this component again show a diversity of values that are being realized. Overall, however, organizations associated with this component predominantly tend to cluster around value component 2, *Good practices, effective human resources and no desire for change* and component 5, *Good project management, not process, customer satisfaction*. Organizations in this component are typically leveraging a subset of project management practices, and the results seem to fall into two discrete categories. Those organizations associated with value component 2 appear to be satisfied with the benefits that a limited project management implementation provides, and view their implementation as providing positive benefits in its current context. Those organizations with a positive association with value component 5 appear to typically rely on project manager expertise to compensate for internal process deficiencies, and place greater emphasis on the roles and structures within the organization than they do the underlying process. This is the only implementation in which multiple organizations are strongly associated with an implementation for which there is no desire for change.

- Implementation 4—*Internal drivers and external off-the-shelf training.* Those organizations that measure strongly on this component demonstrate a very wide level of diversity in the value being observed. The only value that does not have a strong association is that associated with positive human resources practices and no desire for change. Each of these implementations was in response to internal drivers, and there are a number of contextual similarities between the organization – in both types of projects and cultural backgrounds – but the values that these organizations realize is extremely diverse.

- Implementation 5—*Trained experts and methodology PMO.* Organizations that measures strongly against this component tend to be associated with an absence of value more than the positive delivery of value. Five organizations reflect strong negative value associations, and another two organizations only demonstrate moderate value being delivered. There are only three organizations that are realizing strong positive value, and the types of value being realized are different in each case.

Interpreting The Diagrams – Organizations That Exemplify Value Components

In each of the following sections, a diagram is included for each of the construct-level value components that are explored in this study, based upon organizations that are strongly loading exemplars of that particular value component.

The value component being exemplified is compared to the other two constructs—context and implementation. On each chart, the context components are presented in columns, with its headings appearing at the top of the chart. The implementation components are presented in rows, with its headings appearing along the left edge of the chart.

Organizations that are good exemplars of the value component are identified by their association with the two dimensions of context and implementation with a marker in the relevant square of the resulting matrix:

- All organizations have a positive association with the value component that is being presented. Each chart is limited only to those organizations that are extremely positively associated with that value component. In other words, only organizations that measure more than one standard deviation above the mean within the value component are included.

- A solid-colored dot indicates that the organization has an extremely positive association with the context component that it appears below and the implementation component that it appears beside. It is also an exemplar of both of these components.

- An outlined dot indicates that the organization has a positive association with the context component that it appears below and the implementation component that it appears beside, but the association for at least one of these isn't strong. It is not an exemplar of both of those components.

- A black-colored dot indicates that the organization is not associated with the construct component it appears beside. Negative associations on these charts always involve more than one component. In other words, an organization that is not positively described by a component is negatively associated with more than one component. When an organization is identified on the following charts by a negative association, it is always positively associated with the component the line points to (if the line is vertical, it is positively associated with the context component above it; if the line is horizontal, it is positively associated with the implementation component beside it). The organization is negatively associated with the components in which multiple organizational identifiers occur.

- Where an organization is associated with more than one component, this is illustrated by a line connecting all of the dots that identify that organization on the chart.

Relationships For Organizations That Exemplify The Value Components

Each of the following analyses compares the influences of context and implementation that are present for organizations that score strongly on each of the value components. In essence, they identify the relationship between context and implementation for organizations that are high in each value component. The diagram should be read holistically–each diagram (Figures 9-13 – 9-18) contains an illustration of the interrelationship of context and implementation for the identified value component.

Value Component 1 – Aligned Practices, Better Processes and Business Outcomes

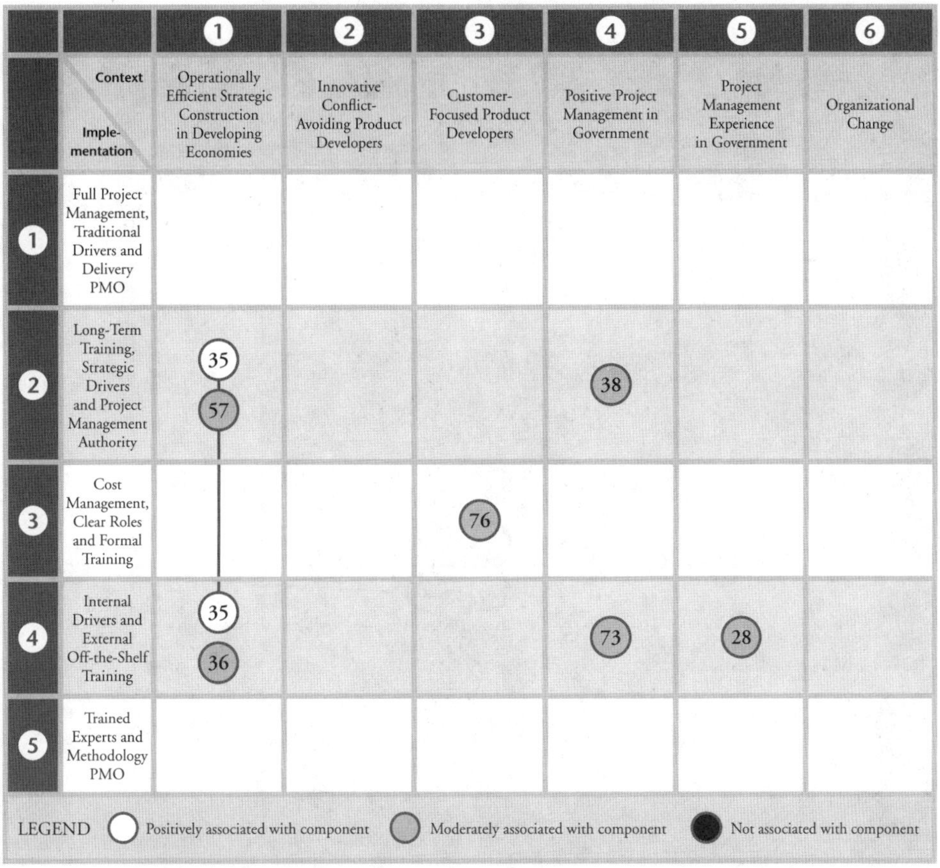

	Context	① Operationally Efficient Strategic Construction in Developing Economies	② Innovative Conflict-Avoiding Product Developers	③ Customer-Focused Product Developers	④ Positive Project Management in Government	⑤ Project Management Experience in Government	⑥ Organizational Change
①	Full Project Management, Traditional Drivers and Delivery PMO						
②	Long-Term Training, Strategic Drivers and Project Management Authority	35 / 57			38		
③	Cost Management, Clear Roles and Formal Training			76			
④	Internal Drivers and External Off-the-Shelf Training	35 / 36			73	28	
⑤	Trained Experts and Methodology PMO						

LEGEND ◯ Positively associated with component   ◉ Moderately associated with component   ● Not associated with component

FIGURE 9-13—*Impacts on context and implementation – Value Component 1*

While organizations that strongly measure on this component exhibit a number of different implementations, there are two fundamental implementations that are being observed in the majority of instances. The first implementation is component 2, associated with longer-term training strategies, strategic drivers, and authority being invested in the project manager. The other predominant implementation is component 4, associated with internal drivers and external off-the-shelf training.

Interestingly, the only organization that is positively associated with both context and implementation dimensions is positively associated with both implementations.

Value Component 2 – Good Practices, Effective Human Resources and No Desire For Change

	Context / Implementation	① Operationally Efficient Strategic Construction in Developing Economies	② Innovative Conflict-Avoiding Product Developers	③ Customer-Focused Product Developers	④ Positive Project Management in Government	⑤ Project Management Experience in Government	⑥ Organizational Change
①	Full Project Management, Traditional Drivers and Delivery PMO						
②	Long-Term Training, Strategic Drivers and Project Management Authority				33		
③	Cost Management, Clear Roles and Formal Training	26	26	25 48 / 76 20	26		20
④	Internal Drivers and External Off-the-Shelf Training			52			
⑤	Trained Experts and Methodology PMO				18		

LEGEND ◯ Positively associated with component   ◐ Moderately associated with component   ● Not associated with component

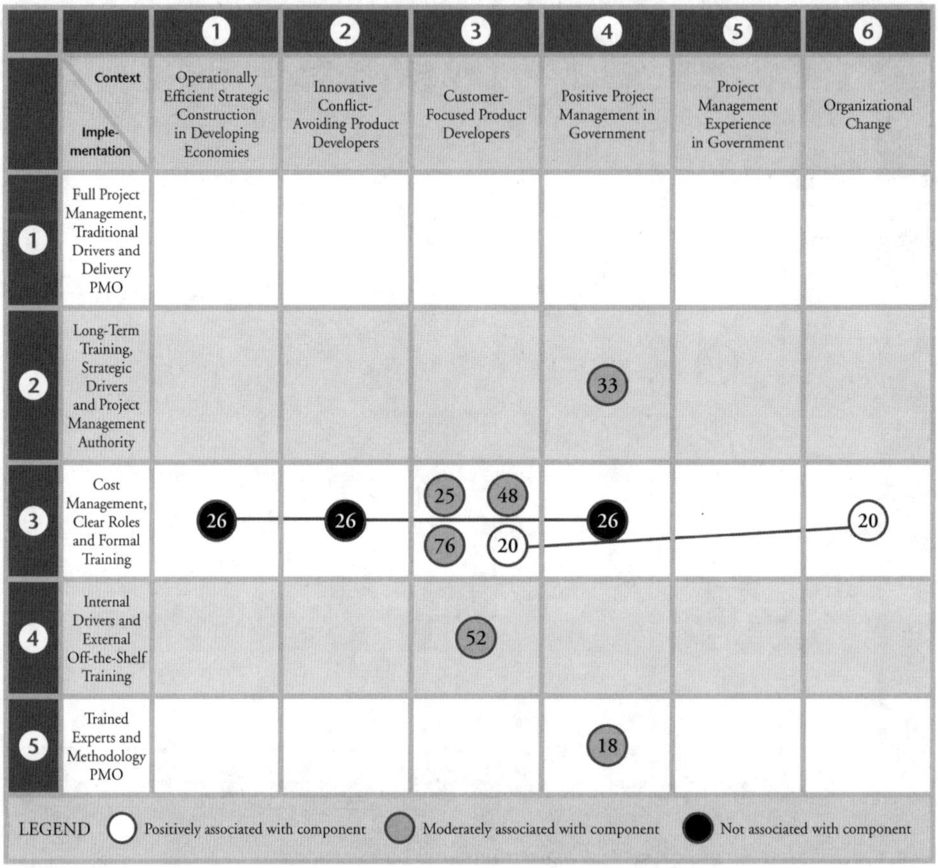

FIGURE 9-14—*Impacts on context and implementation – Value Component 2*

Organizations that strongly measure on this value component are predominantly utilizing a cost management implementation, with clear roles and formal training in place.

What is interesting about this implementation is that while there is a perception of good practices and no desire for change, it is most significantly associated with a relatively limited implementation of project management. While there are structural and training components in place that provide both a context for project management staff to operate in and a set of skills and abilities to draw on, the underlying process capability is relatively straightforward.

What does vary significantly here is the contexts in which organizations operate. The most prevalent one is arguably *Customer-focused product developers*, although for many organizations the association is less strong. As well, organizations are as likely to define their context by what they don't have an association with as those that they positively associate with.

Value Component 3 – Better Project Results, Aligned Organization and Corporate Culture

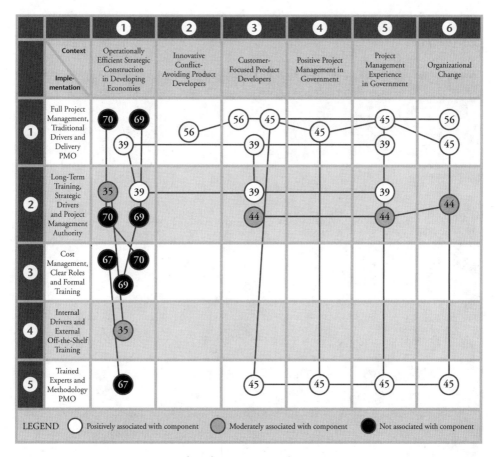

Figure 9-15—*Impacts on context and implementation – Value Component 3*

Organizations that measure strongly on this value component are very interesting, in that they vary on dimensions of both context and implementation.

From a context perspective, there are a number of organizations that are identified with context 1, *Operationally efficient strategic construction in developing economies.* What is significant about these is that their implementations are defined by what the organizations are not, rather than those implementations that they positively identify with. For each of these organizations, however, the project management implementations are both new and relatively immature.

From an implementation perspective, there are clusters of organizations associated with the component for *Full project management, traditional drivers and delivery PMO* and *Long-term training, strategic drivers and project management authority.* Each of these implementations draws on a number of contexts.

The majority of value is being realized based upon those organizations that strongly load on the implementation dimension, however, rather than those that negatively measure against the dimension of context.

Value Component 4 – Good Project Management, Not Process, Not Customer Satisfaction

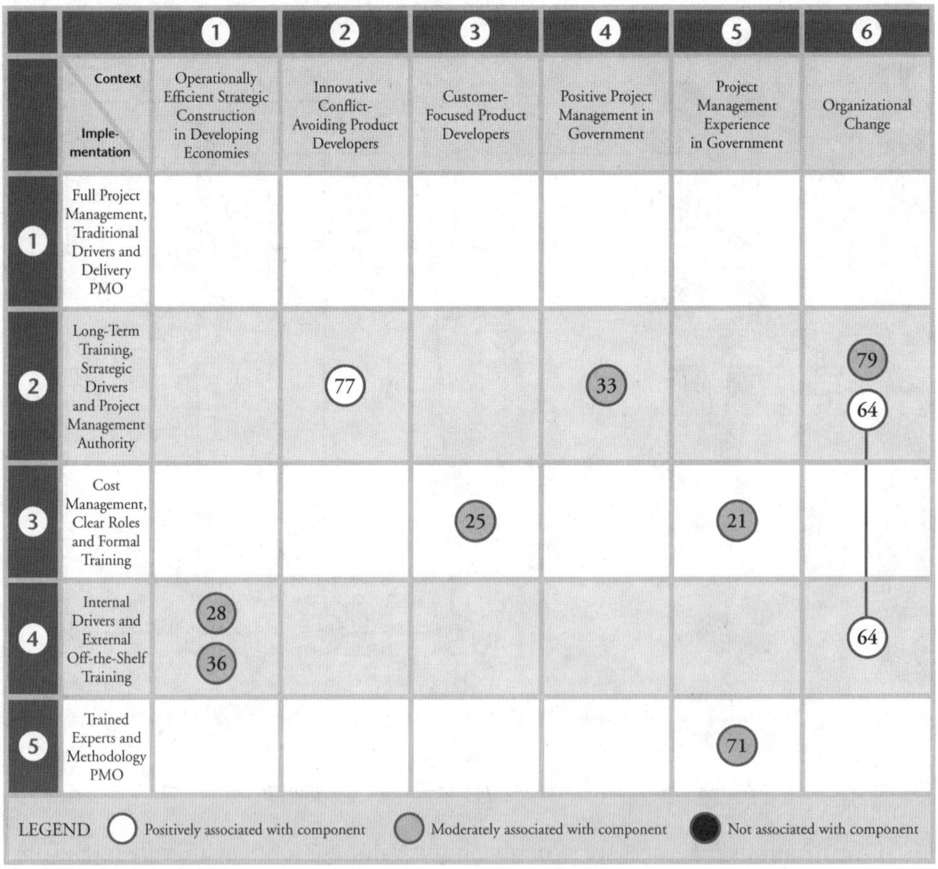

	Context → Implementation ↓	1 Operationally Efficient Strategic Construction in Developing Economies	2 Innovative Conflict-Avoiding Product Developers	3 Customer-Focused Product Developers	4 Positive Project Management in Government	5 Project Management Experience in Government	6 Organizational Change
1	Full Project Management, Traditional Drivers and Delivery PMO						
2	Long-Term Training, Strategic Drivers and Project Management Authority		77		33		79 / 64
3	Cost Management, Clear Roles and Formal Training			25		21	
4	Internal Drivers and External Off-the-Shelf Training	28 / 36					64
5	Trained Experts and Methodology PMO					71	

LEGEND ◯ Positively associated with component   ◒ Moderately associated with component   ● Not associated with component

FIGURE 9-16—*Impacts on context and implementation – Value Component 4*

Organizations that measure strongly on this component demonstrate a significant amount of diversity. They are associated with each of the context components, and almost all of the implementation components. Most significant is a context of organizational change, and implementations associated with strategic drivers and strong project management authority or internal drivers and external off-the-shelf training.

What is interesting about this value component is that many of the organizations do not strongly measure on either the context or implementation dimensions. While there is a correlation that appears, it is not as strong as for the other value components. As well, organizations are, with one exception, associated with a single context and single implementation.

What is unique about this dimension of value is the concept of "not process" and "not customer satisfaction." In evaluating the data, there is a level of statistical significance that supports this assertion. Compared to other organizations, there is less process and less customer satisfaction. The source for this, however, appears to be both a longevity of implementation and perception of process maturity that suggests a greater level of scrutiny that these organizations face. While not exclusively true, many of these organizations tend to be more established in their implementations, but as a result either perceive greater process capability than actually exists, face higher customer expectations, or else do not deliver projects on a customer basis.

Value Component 5 – Good Project Management, Not Process, Customer Satisfaction

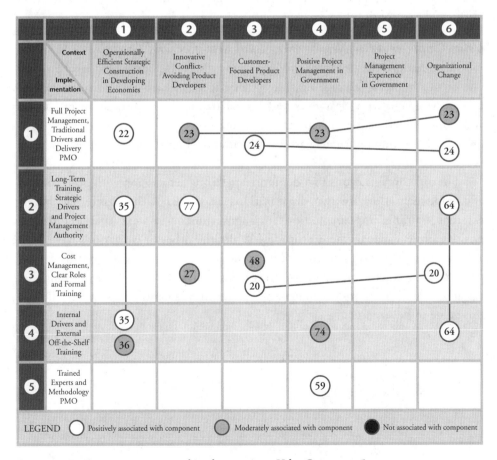

		① Operationally Efficient Strategic Construction in Developing Economies	② Innovative Conflict-Avoiding Product Developers	③ Customer-Focused Product Developers	④ Positive Project Management in Government	⑤ Project Management Experience in Government	⑥ Organizational Change
Context	**Implementation**						
①	Full Project Management, Traditional Drivers and Delivery PMO	22	23	24	23		23 / 24
②	Long-Term Training, Strategic Drivers and Project Management Authority	35	77				64
③	Cost Management, Clear Roles and Formal Training		27	48 / 20			20
④	Internal Drivers and External Off-the-Shelf Training	35 / 36			74		64
⑤	Trained Experts and Methodology PMO				59		

LEGEND ◯ Positively associated with component   ◔ Moderately associated with component   ● Not associated with component

Figure 9-17—*Impacts on context and implementation – Value Component 5*

Organizations that measure strongly against this component demonstrate the greatest level of diversity observed in terms of context and implementation. Organizations are positively associated with each implementation, and all but one of the context components.

What is consistent about each of these organizations is that, with one exception (74), they are responsible for delivering project management to customer organizations. The majority of them are either consulting or construction firms that deliver projects under contract. The implementations that they utilize, however, and the contexts in which they operate, are hugely diverse.

As with the previous component, the concept of "not process" is possibly a harsher judgment even though the statement is statistically supported by the data provided for these organizations. Exploring the organizations in more detail reveals that these organizations are seeking to concretely improve their project management practices, but are in fact quite early in their implementations. While some positive benefits are being perceived, and there is a concerted effort on managing well and delivering customer value, the processes are at an early stage of adoption and are not being utilized fully or consistently.

Value Component 6 – New Services, Staff Retention and Growth

Organizations that measure strongly against this component tend to align with one of two implementations: full project management with traditional drivers, or cost management with clear roles and formal training. The association of context and implementation for each of these organizations is not strong, however; each organization is only moderately associated with the context, the implementation, or both.

The only organizations that demonstrate strong association with both context and implementation are two organizations associated with an internal driver/ external training implementation in a government context that emphasizes positive project management attitudes. While the other organizations have been able to leverage growth and the ability to deliver new services as a result of their project management implementation, it is only these last two organizations that are at a level of maturity and longevity in their implementation that has allowed this value to be sustained.

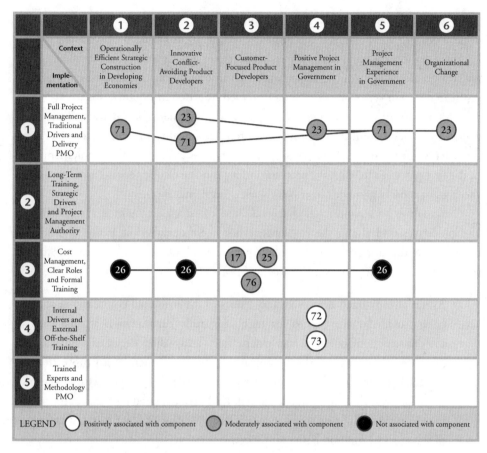

FIGURE 9-18—*Impacts on context and implementation – Value Component 6*

How Do Value And Implementation Change Based Upon Initial Objectives And Motivators?

Exploring The Impact Of Objectives & Motivators On Implementation and Value

As was illustrated in the previous section, there are a number of clusters and patterns emerging that explore the relationship of context and implementation with value. In terms of what has been presented to date, it is emerging strongly that both context and implementation drive value. While different values are being observed in organizations, it is different combinations of context and implementation together that are resulting in these values being delivered.

Interestingly, and to a certain extent not surprisingly, not every context and not every implementation delivers value–or the same degree of value–as others. In the initial conceptual model of the research project, the concept of "fit" was introduced as a means of determining the degree to which the implementation of project management was appropriate, given the context in which the organization operates. In other words, to what extent is the implementation appropriate for the context? What has been demonstrated in the previous sections, though, is that these relationships are not always clear cut, and the same combination of context and implementation can result in different types of value being observed in different organizations.

In terms of understanding how context and implementation deliver value, then, an additional level of understanding is required. Specifically, it is helpful to understand just what value the organization was hoping to realize as a result of its implementation in the first place. To do this, we need to understand the objectives and motivators that the organization began with in choosing their implementations.

An analysis was conducted that evaluated the degree to which the motivators and objectives underlying the implementation were observed as being significantly different for the dimensions of implementation and value that emerged from this study. This analysis involved the following approach:

- As has already been discussed, the results of the principal components analysis have provided factor scores for each-case study organization against each of the constructs of context, implementation, and value. Previous analyses have presented groupings of the organizations, by component, into those that are positively (more than 1 standard deviation), moderately (1 standard deviation), and negatively (less than one standard deviation) associated with that component. For the purposes of this analysis, a different grouping was necessitated as a result of the analysis method being employed.

  For a MANOVA analysis to be effective, the groups being analyzed should be evenly distributed in terms of the number of cases in each. For this reason, the case studies were regrouped into tertiles, which were segregated by factor score into even numbers for each component analyzed. The result is still three groups associated with each component, one of which has a high association with that component, one which has a moderate association, and one which has a low association. What is different is the number of case studies in each group; they are now evenly divided with one-third of cases in each group, rather than by standard deviation.

- For each case study organization, the underlying objectives and motivators for the organization was determined. This involved averaging the organizational responses to the following questions:

  o Identify the degree to which the following factors were motivators in initiating the project management implementation:

    - Increasing project complexity

- Increasing number of projects

- Time pressure on projects

- Market pressures

- Competitive pressures

- Maintaining appearance of being current

- Best practices

- Internationalization/globalization

o Identify the degree to which the following objectives were identified:

- Improve project performance

- Improve business case realization

- Accelerate project delivery

- Reduce the costs of projects

- Increase organizational credibility

- Gain a competitive advantage

- Align with partner expectations or commitments

- Adhere to recognized standards

- A MANOVA analysis was conducted in order to determine whether there were significant difference to key responses between the groups of organizational cases (high, medium, and low), based upon the different objectives and motivators underlying the implementation of project management within the case-study organization.

Impacts Of Motivators and Objectives On Implementation

Interestingly, the analysis of the influence of motivators and objectives on the resulting implementations produced no statistically relevant results. There is no statistically significant finding on the degree to which different objectives or motivators were associated with groups that were highly, moderately, or at a low level associated with that component.

What this suggests is that different implementations resulted from different objectives, and the same objectives could well result in a different implementation being adopted. In part, this helps to reinforce the hypothesis posed in the conceptual model of this study–that it is not implementation alone that delivers value. A further inference that results from this analysis is that, for a given objective, different implementations may be appropriate, given changes to the context of the organization.

Impacts Of Motivators & Objectives On Value

Examining the influence of the motivators and objectives on the value components that emerged in the case-study organizations helped us understand the degree to which specific objectives and motivators led to implementations which in turn delivered different degrees of value. In other words, to what extent was value realized in terms of what organizations started out seeking from their implementation, and are there common patterns that emerge between what was sought and what actually emerged?

Unlike the analysis of the influences of implementations, this analysis produced statistically significant results for each objective as well as for each motivator.

Only those associations that are significantly significant at the 0.05 level are discussed here.

Motivators

In exploring the relationship between the motivators and the value components, we examine the meaningful associations that exist between why organizations were prompted to implement project management, and the value that ultimately emerged from those implementations.

There are six statistically significant relationships that emerge between motivators and value, one for each value component:

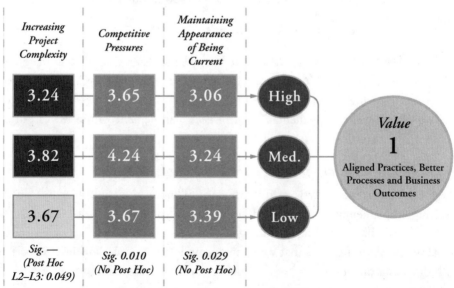

FIGURE 9-19—*Influence of motivators on value—Component 1*

- **Aligned Practices, Better Processes and Business Outcomes.** For organizations that are highly described by the component of aligned practices, better processes and business outcomes (which address three of the four categories of value evaluated within the research study), each of the significant motivators was lower than for organizations that were moderately or not described by the component. Increasing project complexity and maintaining an appearance of being current were at best considered neutral motivators, based upon a five-point scale, and were lower than for other organizations in the study. There was some agreement with competitive pressures being an influence, but this was as likely to be a motivator for organizations that are not described by this component as for organizations that are highly described here; by contrast, those organization with a moderate relationships to this component were much more likely to respond positively to a motivator of competitive pressures. The highest motivator for organizations that are highly described by this component was in fact the attainment of best practices. All groups scored highly on this motivator, but for those organizations that attained high levels of this value component, it was the highest-scored motivation.

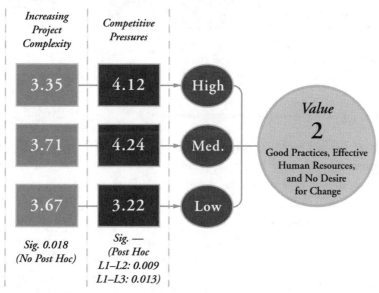

FIGURE 9-20—*Influence of motivators on value—Component 2*

- **Good Practices, Effective Human Resources, and No Desire for Change.** For organizations that are highly described by the value component of good practices, effective human resources, and no desire for change, a motivator of increasing project complexity was least likely to be described as a motivator of the implementation, but the score mean was close to neutral. A response to competitive pressures was a much stronger motivator for organizations that were highly associated with this component, but this motivator was higher still for organizations that were moderately associated with this component. The highest motivator for organizations that were highly described by this component was the response to time pressures on projects, and this was proportionally higher than for other organizations, but not to the level of statistical significance highlighted here.

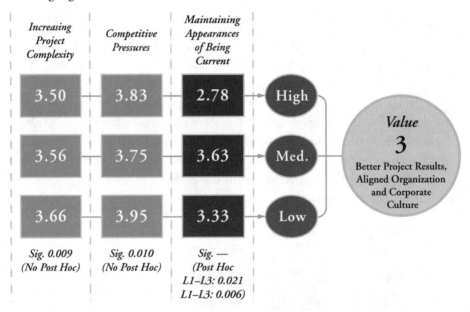

FIGURE 9-21—*Influence of motivators on value—Component 3*

- **Better Project Results, Aligned Organization and Corporate Culture.** For organizations that are highly described by a value component of better project results, aligned organization, and corporate culture, maintaining appearances of being current and responding to increased project complexity were least likely to be described as motivators for their implementations. Competitive pressures were more frequently identified as a motivator, although organizations that were only moderately associated with this component were more likely to see this as an influence. The strongest scored motivator for organizations highly described by this component was best practices, as was also the case for value component 2. There are again no differences between scores for best practices in the high, medium, and low groups.

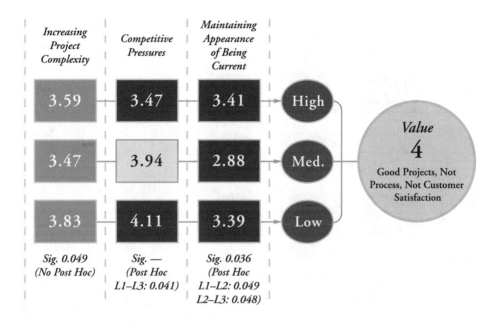

FIGURE 9-22—*Influence of motivators on value—Component 4*

- **Good Projects, Not Process, Not Customer Satisfaction.** For organizations that are highly described by the value component of good projects, not process, and not customer satisfaction, the motivators of increasing project complexity, competitive pressures, and maintaining an appearance of being current were all ranked roughly equally as motivators of the implementation. Each of these motivators, however, is ranked somewhere between "neutral" and "agree" based upon the five-point scale against which they were assessed. Of most interest here, however, is that organizations that were most highly described by this value component were those that ranked the motivator of *Maintaining an appearance of being current* highest. Although organizations least described by this component also ranked this motivator quite highly, both results are significantly above those organizations that are only moderately described by this component. What is useful to note, however, is that none of the motivators were ranked very strongly for organizations that are highly described by this component. It is a value that appears to have emerged as a consequence, as opposed to a value that organizations were consciously trying to attain.

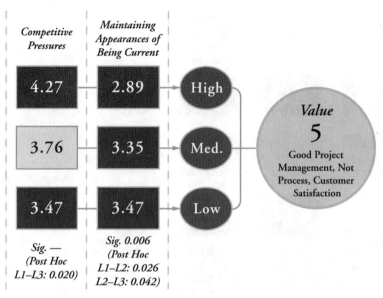

FIGURE 9-23—*Influence of motivators on value—Component 5*

- **Good Project Management, Not Process, Customer Satisfaction.** Organizations that are most highly described by the value component of *Good project management, not process and customer satisfaction* indicate that the strongest motivation for their implementation is the response to competitive pressures. In contrast to value component 4, which appears very similar at first glance, organizations that are highly described by this component are least likely to rank their motivation for implementation as *Maintaining an appearance of being current.* This reinforces observations made in other analyses discussed in this research study: While organizations that strongly identify with value component 4 may be viewed as having more cynical drivers for their implementations of project management, case-study organizations realizing value component 5 are genuinely striving to improve results, although they are often much earlier in their implementations.

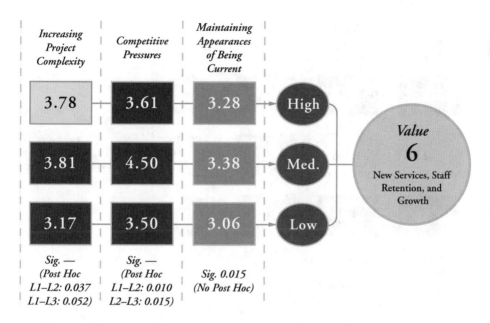

FIGURE 9-24—*Influence of motivators on value—Component 6*

- **New Services, Staff Retention, and Growth.** Organizations that are most highly described by a value component of new services, staff retention and growth are likely to most strongly identify a motivator of increasing project complexity. Organizations that are highly described by this component cite competitive pressures as providing a similar level of motivation, and are less likely to be described by a motivator of maintaining appearances of being current. While organizations that are highly described by this component are most significantly motivated by increasing project complexity and competitive pressures, organizations that are only moderately described by this component indicate a similar level of motivation with respect to complexity and a higher level of motivation regarding competitive pressures. This reinforces other findings regarding organizations that are highly described by this component, namely that in cases where organizations are now able to provide project management as a service or can now charge more for their project, this was not a specific intention or motivator, but instead was a value that emerged.

Objectives

In exploring the relationship between the objectives and the value components, we examine the meaningful associations that exist between what the organization was hoping to accomplish with its implementation and what value ultimately emerged from this implementation.

There are six statistically significant relationships that emerge between objectives and value, one for each value component:

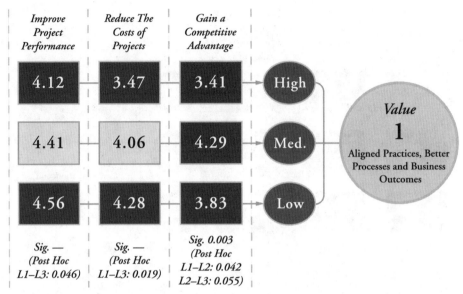

Improve Project Performance	Reduce The Costs of Projects	Gain a Competitive Advantage		
4.12	3.47	3.41	High	
4.41	4.06	4.29	Med.	*Value* **1** Aligned Practices, Better Processes and Business Outcomes
4.56	4.28	3.83	Low	
Sig. — (Post Hoc L1–L3: 0.046)	Sig. — (Post Hoc L1–L3: 0.019)	Sig. 0.003 (Post Hoc L1–L2: 0.042 L2–L3: 0.055)		

FIGURE 9-25—*Influence of objectives on value—Component 1*

- **Aligned Practices, Better Processes and Business Outcomes.** For organizations that are highly described by a value component of aligned practices, better processes and business outcomes, the objectives that are most significant (*Improve project performance, Reduce the cost of projects,* and *Gain a competitive advantage*) are all significantly lower than organizations who are least likely to be described by this component. While improving project performance is the highest-scoring objective cited by those organizations who are most highly described by this component, it is comparatively lower than in organizations that are receiving other values.

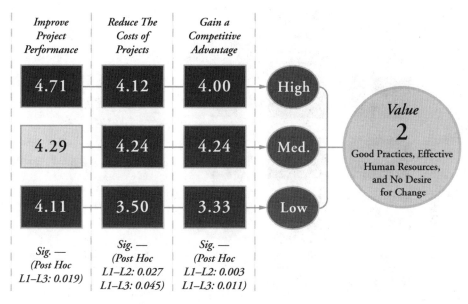

FIGURE 9-26—*Influence of objectives on value—Component 2*

- **Good Practices, Effective Human Resources, and No Desire for Change.** For organizations that are most highly described by this value component, the dominant objective influencing the implementation was improvement of project performance. This is higher than for those organizations only moderately described by this component, and significantly higher than organizations that this component least describes. Cost reduction and gaining a competitive advantage were also likely to be reported as objectives by organizations that are highly described by this component, but organizations that are moderately described identified these objectives as being more significant for them.

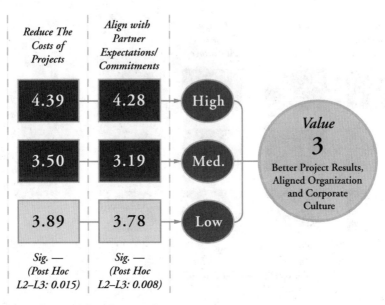

FIGURE 9-27—*Influence of objectives on value—Component 3*

- **Better Project Results, Aligned Organization and Corporate Culture.**
  For organizations that are most highly described by a value of better project results, aligned organization and corporate culture, reduction of project costs and aligning with partner expectations and commitments are the most significant objectives that are identified. These objectives are higher than those for organizations that are moderately or, to a lesser degree, not described by this value component. This is the only value component that reflects a significant objective of project cost reduction, and to an extent the value of "better project results" may in fact largely represent reducing project costs, or at least delivering projects on budget. This also contrasts with the second value component, which had an objective of improving project performance and delivers a value of "good practices." There appears to be a much stronger alignment between objectives and value associated with this component, at least with respect to enhancing financial results.

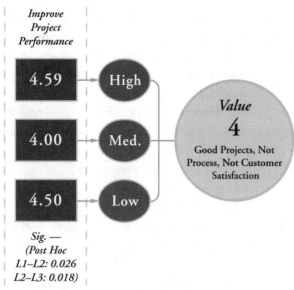

FIGURE 9-28—*Influence of objectives on value—Component 4*

- **Good Projects, Not Process, Not Customer Satisfaction.** Organizations that are most highly described by a value component of good projects, not process, and not customer satisfaction are most significantly associated with an objective of improving project performance, and this is the highest-scored objective associated with these organizations. Interestingly, though, organizations that are described the least by this component also reflect an objective of improving project performance to the same degree.

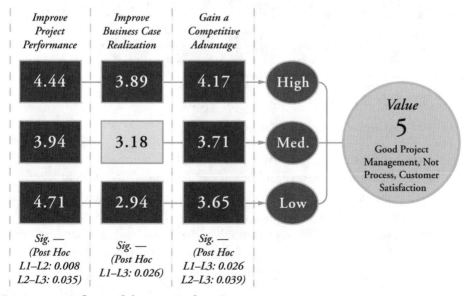

FIGURE 9-29—*Influence of objective on value—Component 5*

- **Good Project Management, Not Process, Customer Satisfaction.** Organizations that are most highly described by a value component of good project management, not process and customer satisfaction are–like value component 4–most likely to identify an objective of improving project performance. Interestingly, the results for this objective are almost inversed for the two components. This helps to reinforce the stark differences that actually exist between organizations that are described by the two components, even though the names of the components suggest much more similar implementations. As well as an objective of improving project performance, organizations that are highly described by this component also identify objectives of improving business-case realization and gaining a competitive advantage, both of which are significantly higher than organizations that are not described (and to a certain extent, moderately described) by this component. Overall, organizations that are highly described by this component appear to place a much higher degree of emphasis on increasing their external credibility, as well as improving not just the performance of their projects, but also the underlying business results.

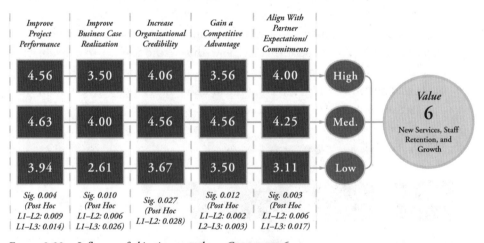

FIGURE 9-30—*Influence of objectives on value—Component 6*

- **New Services, Staff Retention and Growth.** One of the most interesting results emerges for those organizations with implementations highly described by a value component of new services, staff retention, and growth. This component has by far the highest number of statistically significant associations with objectives, identifying five objectives that have significant patterns. While all of these objectives rank quite strongly for organizations highly described by this component, those organizations only moderately strongly described by this component actually have higher average scores for each objective. Again, this reinforces that organizations that are realizing this value do not have a significantly different implementation, nor do they have a significantly greater emphasis on their improvement goals. The realization of values of new services and growth appear to be a byproduct of their implementations, and one that they have unintentionally realized, rather than being an outcome that was actively sought.

What Are The Drivers Of Value?

So far, our analysis has shown that there does not seem to be a particular value component that is recognized consistently from any one project management implementation or context to another for our case organizations. This further supports our study's thesis that it is the fit between the context (internal and external) that the organization operates in and the nature of the project management implementation which combine to deliver value for investments in project management. The previous sections have provided a number of interesting perspectives on helping to understand this influence, and offer useful insights and interpretations. Much of this analysis, however, has been based upon the components that emerged from the construct-level principal components analysis. We are now interested in building on this understanding by exploring what combinations of implementations and contexts influence what kinds of value realization using the variable-level components.

Regression analysis was used to identify the statistically significant relationships between our independent context and implementation descriptors and the dependent variables that describe the sets of value our case organizations are recognizing. These regression results are all explaining a reasonable amount of the variance in the case-study data (ranging from 7 to 80%, with most over 50%) and are highly significant at the 0.05 level (except a few where we introduce the insights generated from a lower 0.1 significance level). However, we must remind the reader that these regressions are based on a relatively small data set (54 organizations) and use an exploratory regression technique (backward step-wise regression) on highly summarized data, and so are only presented as an aid to generating theory about how project management implementations create value. As a result, these regressions should not be interpreted as a formula for value prediction. Future analysis will be conducted on smaller subsets of rigorously constructed scales that will explore more focused questions with respect to the value dynamics of project management implementation.

Fifteen regression analyses were conducted. The dependent variables in each case are the component measures of value as constructed by the PCA analysis of the value variables. Independent variables come from the detail-level component measures constructed from the PCA analysis of the context and implementation variables. Each regression is named by the dependent value PCA it is trying to explain.

Regression 1: Value PCA 1—Desire For Change

> *"Creating an office that focused specifically on project and programme management was a powerful sign of commitment by the organisation that they valued project management. It was an acknowledgement that the organisation doesn't yet have a high level of maturity, and that the environment is changing and people need to become more rigorous in their work. It's clear that the organisation values project management but may not fully understand what it is. And senior executive may not yet fully understand what adopting a project management methodology such as Prince 2 would actually mean to them in terms of the complexity that would be involved. At a higher level there are few staff with project management backgrounds. There is much more social work and social policy experience."*
>
> — *PM Management, 42*

R=.770   R-square=.594   R-squareadj = .538

#steps = 32	Unstandardized Beta	Std. Error	Standardized Beta	T	Sig.
Constant	0.008	0.089		0.093	0.926
Impl PCA 6—Traditional Drivers	0.281	0.130	0.265	2.168	0.035
Impl PCA 6—Strategic Drivers	0.233	0.106	0.219	2.185	0.033
Impl PCA 7—Delivery PMO	-0.253	0.117	-0.254	-2.165	0.035
Context PCA 4—Strategic Construction	0.335	0.100	0.318	3.332	0.002
Context PCA 5—Privately Held	-0.221	0.096	-0.208	-2.299	0.026
Context PCA 6—Strategic Innovators	0.532	0.124	0.501	4.278	0.000
Context PCA 6—Customer Intimacy.	-0.450	0.105	-0.423	-4.293	0.000

TABLE 9-3—*Regression results for Value PCA 1—Desire For Change*

54% of the variance in the Value PCA 1—*Desire for change* independent variable is explained by the variables listed in Table 9-3.

Positive increases in the desire for change result where organizations are increasingly described by an implementation that is driven by traditional or strategic drivers and there is a primary strategic focus on strategic innovation in a strategic construction context.

Decreases in the desire for change result where organizations are increasingly described by an implementation that is characterized by having a delivery PMO, and a context that has a strategy of customer intimacy and that have a privately held ownership structure.

The variables showing the strongest impact on Desire for Change are related to the organizational context variable related to the organization's strategic orientation (Strategic Context PCA 3—*Innovators and customer intimacy*).

Ultimately, this suggests that the desire for change (a negative measure of satisfaction) is strongly dependent on the context in which the organization operates and the motivations driving the project management implementation and has little to do with the nature of the project implementation itself. What this reinforces is that specific contexts and motivators are more likely to generate dissatisfaction for their project management implementations than others.

Observing the specific components identified by the regression that have an influence on the desire for change, there appear to be two possible explanations for this pattern:

- The first one, and the lesser influence, is the degree to which the desire for change is associated with traditional drivers. Organizations that measure strongly on this component are typically focused upon improving project delivery and accelerating project performance, often with objectives of improving the degree to which projects deliver on-time, on-budget, and to specification. The presence of traditional drivers, however, may also lead to the organization adopting more traditional implementations that derive from standards or represent off-the-shelf methodologies, without tailoring them to the organization's needs. This has, in fact, been observed in a number of organizations realizing this value within the cases studies. The risk is that this may result in a lack of perceived fit with the types of projects that the organization manages, and therefore result in a greater desire for change on the part of participants.

- The larger influence on the desire for change, however, is the context of the organization, and specifically the degree to which there is a differentiator of strategic innovation. Organizations that measure strongly on this component typically have a strong appetite for change and are driven by external influences rather than internal ones. As a result, the desire for change may simply reflect an appetite for continuing to evolve and adapt, rather than a specific dissatisfaction with the implementation that is being observed. At the same time, however, those cultures that characterize themselves as being innovative also tend to be more resistant to process, and the desire for change may also be a resistance to the structures that the implementation is trying to impose.

It is important to note that the observations associated with this regression only explain 54% of the variance in the data. As a result, there are also other influences and factors that will increase or decrease a desire for change that are not noted here.

Regression 2: Value PCA 1—Project Manager Satisfaction

> *"[The value of project management] is beyond description. If you don't become aware of and are conscious about where you are going in relation to the objectives and the changes you want and don't have an efficient project management, then I think things will slip even more than they usually do."*
>
> — *Project Manager, 25*

62% of project manager satisfaction with the management of projects in the organization is explained by the variables listed in Table 9-4.

Positive increases in project manager satisfaction result where organizational implementations are increasingly described by the use of training approaches, such as lunch and learns, distance degree and diploma opportunities, and informal off-the-shelf training. Increases also result in implementations that are increasingly motivated by internal drivers and strategic drivers. Increases in project manager satisfaction also result in those organizations that are particularly described as having high project management authority and a positive attitude to project managers, and to a lesser extent as having higher levels of experienced project managers.

Decreases in project management satisfaction result where the implementations of organizations are increasingly described as employing tailored internal training, customized external training, and in those structures that operate in government and public-partnership contexts.

The variables showing the highest influence on *Project manager satisfaction* are internal drivers, *Project management authority* and *Project management attitude.*

This regression suggests that project managers are most satisfied with the project management implementation when it increases or supports their authority, where there is a positive attitude to project management, and where the project management implementation is predominantly the result of internal drivers. Having experienced project managers within the organization also appears to have some positive influence.

R=.838   R-SQUARE=.702   R-SQUAREADJ = .624

# steps = 27	Unstandardized Beta	Std. Error	Standardized Beta	T	Sig.
CONSTANT	0.007	0.080		0.083	0.935
IMPL PCA 1— LUNCH AND LEARN	0.293	0.110	0.260	2.658	0.011
IMPL PCA 1— DISTANCE DEGREE & DIPLOMA	0.226	0.098	0.200	2.311	0.025
IMPL PCA 2— TAILORED INTERNAL	-0.253	0.105	-0.238	-2.396	0.021
IMPL PCA 2— INFORMAL OFF-THE-SHELF	0.370	0.123	0.349	3.017	0.004
IMPL PCA 2— CUSTOMIZED EXTERNAL	-0.431	0.109	-0.407	-3.963	0.000
IMPL PCA 6— STRATEGIC DRIVERS	0.313	0.150	0.295	2.082	0.043
IMPL PCA 6— INTERNAL DRIVERS	0.572	0.106	0.539	5.410	0.000
IMPL PCA 7—PROJECT MANAGEMENT AUTHORITY	0.810	0.098	0.801	8.228	0.000
CONTEXT PCA 2— PM EXPERIENCE	0.209	0.093	0.207	2.239	0.030
CONTEXT PCA 3— POSITIVE PROJECT MANAGEMENT ATTITUDE	0.545	0.129	0.514	4.241	0.000
CONTEXT PCA 5 – GOVERNMENT	-0.391	0.108	-0.368	-3.607	0.001
CONTEXT PCA 5— PUBLIC PARTNERSHIPS	-0.200	0.099	-0.189	-2.030	0.048

TABLE 9-4—*Regression results for Value PCA 1—Project Manager Satisfaction*

Observing the results of the regression, there are also some extremely interesting findings associated with training. Those training approaches that influence positive increases in project manager satisfaction are more informal or standardized, or those that are distance-based and result in a degree or diploma. At the same time, those training options that are associated with either heavily tailored internal courses or customized external courses have a negative influence on satisfaction. Two possible explanations that could provide an underlying explanation for this pattern are:

- The use of lunch-and-learns, distance education, and off-the-shelf training are often supportive of more flexible use of time. Lunch and learns are typically short, focused and rarely have a significant impact on the business day, and many distance-training vehicles are specifically designed to provide participants with scheduling flexibility. As well, off-the-shelf training programs are often offered by training providers on a repeat basis throughout the year, providing a greater number of scheduling options. Tailored internal courses and customized external courses may limit the number of scheduling options available for participants to attend, and the frequency by which courses are available. Where project managers view themselves as being busy and subject to considerable time pressures, more flexible training options may well be viewed more positively.

- Off-the-shelf informal courses and those that are offered on a distance basis are often built around more standardized curricula, and are more likely to align with external standards and common approaches. Tailored internal training in particular, and customized external training, are adapted in part to the specifics of the organization. While some level of adaptation could be argued to be reasonable and even necessary, an excessive amount of adaptation could result in education that departs significantly from standard process and terminology, and this is true for some organizations observed within the case studies. Greater emphasis on customized approaches at the expense of standards may also be having an influence on project manager satisfaction, as it can create barriers to introducing project managers from outside of the organization, particularly those that are certified or more experienced with industry standards and norms. This may also be reducing project manager satisfaction as approaches that are overly customized reduce their mobility and ease of transitioning into other organizations as part of their own personal career development.

Regression 3: Value PCA 1—Customer Satisfaction

> "[Project management] increases customer satisfaction. For example, at the beginning of a road construction project, the customer was dissatisfied, but we changed their impression through hard work and qualified [project management]procedure; at last, we made a good impression to our customer. Then we got the chance to work together in the second phase of the project."
>
> — Project Manager, 22

R=.444   R-square=.197   R-squareadj = .183

# steps = 38	Unstandardized Beta	Std. Error	Standardized Beta	T	Sig.
Constant	0.006	0.119		0.054	0.957
Impl PCA 4—Cost Management	-0.472	0.126	-0.444	-3.736	0.000

Table 9-5—*Regression results for Value PCA 1—Customer Satisfaction*

18% of the variance in Value PCA 1—*Customer satisfaction* is explained by the variable listed in Table 9-5.

This regression only explains a small amount of the variation but it is a statistically significant relationship. It suggests that project management implementations that focus on tools for cost management are likely to decrease customer satisfaction. None of the other variables describing the project management implementation or the context in which the organization operates were found to significantly influence customer satisfaction.

This correlation could reflect the possibility that implementations that focus on cost management tools are likely to result in better scope management and change control. This emphasis on controlling project scope may be perceived by customers as reducing flexibility and constraining the project results, which may result in customers not feeling that the organization is being responsive to their needs.

Another possible explanation associated with this regression is that organizations that strongly align with a cost-management implementation are often associated with more limited process capabilities that are not reflective of a full project management implementation. These organizations also often exhibit a level of complacency with their implementation, which was observed in earlier analysis exploring the relationship between implementation and value. This lack of process, or a more complacent attitude to process, could in itself be an explanation for a decline in customer satisfaction.

Regression 4: Value PCA 2—Aligned Organization

> *"It is now easy to train the new employees, just showing them the three books of established standards and templates, and explaining each book's function/usage. New employees can very quickly understand and follow the process."*
>
> — Human Resources, 36

> *"So we went about aligning processes and creating a benefit; through aligning processes one automatically also creates a profit."*
>
> — *Senior Manager, 27*

R=.849   R-SQUARE=.720   R-SQUAREADJ = .688

#steps = 33	Unstandardized Beta	Std. Error	Standardized Beta	T	Sig.
CONSTANT	-2.846E-16	0.069		0.000	1.000
IMPL PCA 1— LUNCH & LEARN	-0.309	0.086	-0.290	-3.600	0.001
IMPL PCA 5— CLEAR ROLES & TRAINING	0.666	0.082	0.666	8.087	0.000
CONTEXT PCA 3— POSITIVE PROJECT MANAGEMENT ATTITUDE	0.205	0.101	0.205	2.027	0.048
CONTEXT PCA 4— CONSTRUCTION	-0.179	0.081	-0.181	-2.213	0.031
CONTEXT PCA 6— STRATEGIC INNOVATORS	-0.195	0.090	-0.195	-2.166	0.035
CONTEXT PCA 6— OPERATIONAL EFFICIENCY	0.317	0.086	0.317	3.706	0.001

TABLE 9-6—*Regression results for Value PCA 2—Aligned Organization*

69% of the variance in Value PCA 2—*Aligned organization* is explained by the variables listed in Table 9-6.

Positive increases in the organizational alignment result where organizational implementations are increasingly described by increasing levels of role clarity and training. Increases in alignment also result where organizational contexts are characterized by increases in a positive project management attitude and a driver of operational efficiency.

Decreases in organizational alignment result where organizational implementations are increasingly described by the use of lunch-and-learn training activities. As well, decreases in organizational alignment result with contexts that are increasingly described as being driven by strategic innovation and that operate in the construction industry.

The variables showing the highest influence on organizational alignment are those associated with an implementation characterized by clear roles and training. This suggests that there is a strong flow-through from implementations that clearly define the structures, roles, and accountabilities associated with the project management process and the overall alignment by which the organizational processes and structures are defined. Clearly, this suggests that organizations that are positively inclined to support project management and whose project management implementation entails clarifying roles and responsibilities and training people on them will likely also realize greater organizational alignment in decision-making and processes. As well, operational efficiency has a strong influence here; this suggests that as well as the structures and roles discussed already, that part of alignment – at least for those for whom operational efficiency is a focus – is the establishment of formalized processes and control structures.

Regression 5: Value PCA 2—Aligned Project Management

> *"With the adoption and implementation of a more structured project management procedure over the years, customized to reflect changes in the local and EU law and in-house experience, the management of projects overall has become more mature."*
>
> — *Senior Manager, 28*

> *"People stick to that methodology quite strongly, more so than any other organization that I've been in."*
>
> — *Human Resources, 44*

R=.861   R-SQUARE=.741   R-SQUAREADJ = .658

#steps = 25	Unstandardized Beta	Std. Error	Standardized Beta	T	Sig.
CONSTANT	0.000	0.072		-0.009	0.993
IMPL PCA 2—TAILORED INTERNAL	-0.657	0.133	-0.657	-4.951	0.000
IMPL PCA 2—INFORMAL OFF-THE-SHELF	0.326	0.109	0.326	2.993	0.005
IMPL PCA 2—CUSTOMIZED EXTERNAL	-0.329	0.105	-0.329	-3.140	0.003
IMPL PCA 3—LONG-TERM TRAINING	0.295	0.102	0.292	2.881	0.006
IMPL PCA 5—CLEAR ROLES & TRAINING	0.279	0.116	0.279	2.401	0.021
IMPL PCA 6—TRADITIONAL DRIVERS	0.250	0.110	0.250	2.266	0.028
IMPL PCA 6—STRATEGIC DRIVERS	0.520	0.121	0.520	4.287	0.000
IMPL PCA 6—INTERNAL DRIVERS	0.781	0.103	0.781	7.566	0.000
IMPL PCA 7—DELIVERY PMO	-0.316	0.111	-0.337	-2.837	0.007
CONTEXT PCA 2—PROJECT MANAGEMENT EXPERIENCE	0.208	0.085	0.218	2.456	0.018
CONTEXT PCA 3—CONFLICT AVOIDERS	-0.460	0.091	-0.460	-5.029	0.000
CONTEXT PCA 5 – GOVERNMENT	-0.463	0.096	-0.463	-4.832	0.000
CONTEXT PCA 5—PUBLICLY HELD	-0.324	0.099	-0.324	-3.270	0.002
CONTEXT PCA 6—STRATEGIC INNOVATORS	0.903	0.125	0.903	7.205	0.000

TABLE 9-7—Regression results for Value PCA 2—Aligned Project Management

66% of the variance in Value PCA 2—*Aligned project management* (or the degree to which projects adhere to project guidelines and practices) is explained by the variables listed in Table 9-7.

Positive increases in the alignment of project management practices result where organizational implementations are increasingly described by the use of long-term training approaches and informal off-the-shelf training, and by the clarity of roles and supporting training. Increases in project management alignment also result in implementations that are increasingly described by drivers that are internal, strategic, and traditional (in declining order of influence). Finally, positive increases in project management alignment result in organizations that are increasingly described by contexts of strategic innovation and that contain experienced project managers.

Decreases in project management alignment result in organizations that are increasingly described by an implementation that has a delivery PMO, and by contexts that are increasingly described as having government or publicly held structures and a culture of conflict avoidance.

The variables showing the highest influence are a context of strategic innovation and an implementation that is motivated by internal and strategic drivers.

This regression analysis suggests that the organizations that have the highest realization of project management alignment are those that are driven to project management through a combination of strategic and internal needs and who come from a context where the culture is defined by strategic innovation.

There are again significant influences of training on this regression. Training that is off-the-shelf and long-term in nature has a positive influence, which would appear to support both an alignment with standardized approaches and also a sustained investment in promoting the development of project management capabilities in employees. The greatest negative influences on aligned project management practices, however, seem to be an implementation that focuses on customizing and tailoring project management training. If we can assume that customized and tailored project management training is more likely to be associated with similarly customized project management implementations, it appears that project management practice alignment is more likely to be realized in less-customized project management implementations that are also more likely to align closely with recognized standards and terminology.

Interestingly, while the implementation of a delivery PMO would typically be thought to be a vehicle for improving project management consistency, this regression appears to suggest that the opposite is true. This may be a result of delivery PMOs, while being central project support groups, having less of a focus on the establishment of process than they do on the actual delivery of projects. As well, the pressure to successfully deliver projects may be forcing compromises to be made in the implementation that again cause more inconsistent practices to appear. This may also be a recognition within the delivery PMOs that different project management offices require different practices. Finally, it may also illustrate that, despite some assumptions to the contrary, the focus of a delivery PMO is not on the creation of consistency within the organization.

Regression 6: Value PCA 3—Good Practices

> *"We've seen it in the past when perhaps an area did try to implement something without a formalized process and then called us to come in and then just busily work, so I think we're saving money from not having to do some of that rework by doing it right the first time"*
>
> — *Project Manager, 20*

63% of the variance in Value PCA 3—*Good practices* is explained by the variables listed in Table 9-8.

Increases in the establishment of what are described as good practices result where organizations have implementations that are increasingly described by a high level of project management authority and a motivator that is internally driven. Increases in good practices also result from implementations with increasing use of lunch-and-learn training sessions and cost-management approaches. Positive increases in good practices also result where organizations have contexts increasingly described by experienced project managers, a positive project management attitude, and an innovative orientation. Increases also result in contexts increasingly described by a strategy of customer intimacy.

Decreases in good practices result where organizations are increasingly described by an implementation employing customized external training, and where contexts are increasingly described by the presence of senior project managers, a strategy of strategic innovation, and being in the construction industry.

The variable showing the strongest positive influence on this regression is project manager authority.

This regression suggests that good practices are largely driven by the project manager's level of authority, but can be influenced by other implementation and contextual factors as well. Interestingly, the use of lunch-and-learns had a positive influence on promoting good practices, while the use of external, customized training does not. This may be a result of formal training courses being more infrequent, often being most prominently used at the start of an implementation. Lunch-and-learns are often by their nature more ongoing, which may provide more sustained focus and reinforcement.

R=.838   R-SQUARE=.703   R-SQUAREADJ = .626

#steps = 27	Unstandardized Beta	Std. Error	Standardized Beta	T	Sig.
CONSTANT	0.004	0.068		0.058	0.954
IMPL PCA 1—LUNCH & LEARN	0.240	0.097	0.249	2.477	0.017
IMPL PCA 2—CUSTOMIZED EXTERNAL	-0.189	0.086	-0.209	-2.213	0.032
IMPL PCA 4—COST MANAGEMENT	0.269	0.082	0.297	3.269	0.002
IMPL PCA 6—INTERNAL DRIVERS	0.355	0.080	0.392	4.467	0.000
IMPL PCA 7—PROJECT MANAGEMENT AUTHORITY	0.525	0.085	0.607	6.176	0.000
CONTEXT PCA 2 – SENIORITY	-0.345	0.078	-0.398	-4.443	0.000
CONTEXT PCA 2—PROJECT MANGER EXPERIENCE	0.194	0.076	0.224	2.538	0.015
CONTEXT PCA 3—POSITIVE PROJECT MANAGER ATTITUDE	0.271	0.096	0.299	2.837	0.007
CONTEXT PCA 3 – INNOVATORS	0.213	0.083	0.235	2.579	0.013
CONTEXT PCA 4 – CONSTRUCTION	-0.196	0.083	-0.219	-2.377	0.022
CONTEXT PCA 6—STRATEGIC INNOVATORS	-0.272	0.101	-0.300	-2.700	0.010
CONTEXT PCA 6—CUSTOMER INTIMACY	0.230	0.082	0.253	2.688	0.010

TABLE 9-8—*Regression results for Value PCA 3—Good Practices*

Also interesting in this regression is the combination of internal drivers of the implementation and a strategic context of customer intimacy. The positive influence of internal drivers is in itself not necessarily surprising; those implementations that are motivated by the internal needs of the organization rather than external factors, because they are directly benefiting the organization, could as a result see greater emphasis on both establishing and maintaining focus on using good project management practices. The strategy of customer intimacy, however, also suggests there is some external focus to these practices, suggesting that organizations see some linkage between good practices and an ability to more effectively serve their customers.

The final observation associated with this regression is that, while the previous regression was essentially defined by an inverse relationship between cost management and customer satisfaction, this regression sees good practices being influenced in part by a cost-management implementation and a customer intimacy context. While a potential influence on customer intimacy has been suggested in the previous paragraph, the role of cost management is interesting in the context of "good practices." As has been noted in other regressions as well as earlier analysis on the value drivers, an implementation of cost management is often associated more with a partial implementation of project management, with varied influences in both context and the value that it delivers. That it has been associated with a lack of process, but has a positive influence on increases in good processes, is therefore intriguing. Looking at the elements that characterize this value component, the primary emphasis is on processes that are clear, well understood, viewed as being effective, and, in particular, are consistently utilized. While cost-management implementations may not be viewed as fully embracing the discipline of project management, it is also possible that what practices are in place are being used consistently and are being seen as effective by internal stakeholders.

Regression 7: Value PCA 3—Good Project Management, Not Practices

> *"From the point of view of the researchers, project management is unnecessary, administrative burden, too much documentation, too much bureaucracy"*
>
> — *Project Manager, 59*

49% of the variance in Value PCA 3—*Good project management, not practices* is explained by the variables listed in Table 9-9.

Positive increases in good project management, not practices, result where organizations are increasingly described by implementations associated with tailored internal training and the use of trained experts. Positive increases are also influenced by contexts that are increasingly described by contexts associated with the attainment of economic prospects, a focus on organizational change projects, and an industry sector that is governmental.

Decreases in good project management, not practices, result from an implementation that is increasingly described as motivated by internal drivers, and increasingly described by contexts that have senior project managers and strategic drivers of operational efficiency and strategic innovation.

The variable showing the highest influence on good project management, not practices, is the seniority of project managers.

R=.756   R-SQUARE=.571   R-SQUAREADJ = .492

#steps = 30	Unstandardized Beta	Std. Error	Standardized Beta	T	Sig.
CONSTANT	-0.015	0.080		-0.187	0.852
IMPL PCA 2— TAILORED INTERNAL	0.251	0.117	0.277	2.136	0.038
IMPL PCA 5— TRAINED EXPERTS	0.436	0.109	0.481	4.003	0.000
IMPL PCA 6— INTERNAL DRIVERS	-0.487	0.128	-0.538	-3.796	0.000
CONTEXT PCA 1— ECONOMIC PROSPECTS	0.380	0.099	0.449	3.850	0.000
CONTEXT PCA 2— SENIORITY	-0.526	0.126	-0.609	-4.192	0.000
CONTEXT PCA 4— ORGANIZATIONAL CHANGE	0.366	0.109	0.408	3.346	0.002
CONTEXT PCA 5— GOVERNMENT	0.405	0.120	0.448	3.371	0.001
CONTEXT PCA 6— STRATEGIC INNOVATORS	-0.445	0.120	-0.492	-3.711	0.001
CONTEXT PCA 6— OPERATIONAL EFFICIENCY	-0.433	0.108	-0.478	-4.002	0.000

TABLE 9-9—*Regression results for Value PCA 3—Good Project Management, Not Practices*

This regression suggests that those organizations that evidence good project management but less of a process emphasis predominantly make use of trained experts within their implementation, and are correspondingly less likely to have senior employees to draw on internally. While the implementation is in part influenced by tailored internal training, this is correspondingly low. While it suggests some level of tailoring or customization of the implementation, organizations that make use of trained experts within the case studies we have observed are largely relying upon externally sourced project managers. As a result, there is likely to be far less emphasis on the use of or adherence to organizational practices, and more of an emphasis on personal expertise and project management heroics to successfully deliver project results.

The emphasis on government projects that predominantly involve organizational change in this regression also raises some cautions. Given that the regression suggests government and organizational change projects are likely to be strongly associated with increases in this value, it can be inferred that many government organizations are relying upon outside expertise to guide their organizational change efforts. Given the lack of organizational understanding, organizational expertise, and cultural understanding that external resources will have over internal employees, this may explain why there may be greater challenges associated with successfully delivering these project types.

Regression 8: Value PCA 4—Better Process Results

> *"The information management system has helped a lot in paperwork. I cannot image how messy all our paperwork would have been without it. Now with the system, it is a lot easier, it saves time, and makes it easier to trace the documents and historical files later."*
>
> — *Project Manager, 73*

77% of the variance in Value PCA 4—*Better process results* is explained by the variables listed in Table 9-10.

Positive increases in better process results occur when organizations have implementations that are increasingly described by motivators that are strategic or internal, and training approaches that emphasize a long-term focus and informal off-the-shelf content. Positive increases also result where contexts are increasingly described as having a positive project management attitude, organizational drivers of strategic innovation or operational efficiency, a culture that is not customer-focused and an ownership structure relying on sole proprietorships.

Decreases in better process results occur when organizations are increasingly described by an implementation that employs full project management training or customized external training, and that have a cost-management implementation. Decreases also result when organizations are increasingly described by a context with cultures of innovation and conflict avoidance, and that are in a government industry sector.

The variable showing the highest influence on better process results is an implementation of strategic drivers.

This regression suggests that there are many factors that influence whether or not an organization realizes better process results from its project management implementations. The strongest influence seems to be the nature of the drivers motivating the implementation. Organizations with strong strategic drivers (and,

R=.910   R-SQUARE=.828   R-SQUAREADJ = .769

#steps = 24	Unstandardized Beta	Std. Error	Standardized Beta	T	Sig.
CONSTANT	-2.334E-8	0.059		0.000	1.000
IMPL PCA 1— FULL PROJECT MANAGEMENT TRAINING	-0.232	0.095	-0.220	-2.435	0.019
IMPL PCA 2— INFORMAL OFF-THE-SHELF	0.254	0.094	0.257	2.694	0.010
IMPL PCA 2— CUSTOMIZED EXTERNAL	-0.186	0.085	-0.188	-2.191	0.034
IMPL PCA 3— LONG-TERM TRAINING	0.234	0.077	0.234	3.040	0.004
IMPL PCA 4— COST MANAGEMENT	-0.256	0.069	-0.259	-3.731	0.001
IMPL PCA 6— STRATEGIC DRIVERS	0.619	0.111	0.625	5.552	0.000
IMPL PCA 6— INTERNAL DRIVERS	0.385	0.078	0.389	4.968	0.000
CONTEXT PCA 3— POSITIVE PROJECT MANAGER ATTITUDE	0.433	0.109	0.437	3.982	0.000
CONTEXT PCA 3 – INNOVATORS	-0.248	0.080	-0.251	-3.110	0.003
CONTEXT PCA 3— CONFLICT AVOIDERS	-0.250	0.077	-0.253	-3.254	0.002
CONTEXT PCA 3— NOT CUSTOMER-FOCUSED	0.256	0.070	0.259	3.651	0.001
CONTEXT PCA 5 – GOVERNMENT	-0.474	0.084	-0.479	-5.634	0.000
CONTEXT PCA 5— SOLE PROPRIETORSHIP	0.169	0.067	0.171	2.527	0.015
CONTEXT PCA 6— STRATEGIC INNOVATORS	0.452	0.101	0.456	4.489	0.000
CONTEXT PCA 6— OPERATIONAL EFFICIENCY	0.313	0.084	0.316	3.744	0.001

TABLE 9-10—*Regression results for Value PCA 4—Better Process Results*

to a lesser extent, internal drivers) are most likely to see process improvements. Paradoxically, this regression suggests that organizations with full project management training including customized training, are less likely to see process results. This could be because organizations with this much training in place have already seen significant process improvements and so may not be realizing this type of benefit any longer from their project management implementation.

Conflict-avoiding and innovative cultures, government organizations and project management implementations focusing on cost management are also negatively associated with realizing this benefit. The cultural influences could have to do with process changes requiring some conflict and change while managing transitions that may make the conflict-avoiders uncomfortable, and that may also feel like unwarranted bureaucracy and rules to the innovators. Governments also tend to be more resistant to change than other types of organizations.

Finally, the negative influence of cost management on the attainment of better process results is worth noting. While cost management had a positive influence on attaining the value of "good practices" (value regression 6), it has a negative influence here. This again helps to support the suggestion that while a cost-management implementation may be perceived as well understood, used, and effective (good practices), it is not actually seen to be having an impact on improving efficiency, transparency and control, which are hallmarks of the value component of "good process results."

Regression 9: Value PCA 4—Better Project Results

> *"Being effective in delivering projects is the basis of this part of the Department. We need to demonstrate that we do it efficiently, not just to the client agencies but to Treasury, so they see a value in maintaining an organisation like us. We need to show that what we provide cannot be provided by private sector."*
>
> *— PM Management, 45*

68% of the variance in Value PCA 4—*Better project results* is explained by the variables listed in Table 9-11.

Positive increases in better project results occur where organizations are increasingly described by implementations that involve a methodology PMO, and by contexts that are increasingly described culturally as "innovators" and by an industry sector of construction.

Decreases in better project results occur where organizations are increasingly described by training that is short-term in nature, tailored and internal, and employing

R=.870   R SQUARE=.757   R SQUAREADJ = .679

#steps = 25	Unstandardized Beta	Std. Error	Standardized Beta	T	Sig.
CONSTANT	0.000	0.069		-0.005	0.996
IMPL PCA 1— DISTANCE DEGREE & DIPLOMA	-0.289	0.093	-0.274	-3.114	0.003
IMPL PCA 2— TAILORED INTERNAL	-0.365	0.115	-0.369	-3.168	0.003
IMPL PCA 3— SHORT-TERM TRAINING	-0.427	0.114	-0.427	-3.734	0.001
IMPL PCA 4— RESOURCE MANAGEMENT	-0.282	0.098	-0.285	-2.876	0.006
IMPL PCA 5— TRAINED EXPERTS	-0.508	0.097	-0.513	-5.231	0.000
IMPL PCA 6— STRATEGIC DRIVERS	-0.276	0.096	-0.279	-2.879	0.006
IMPL PCA 7— METHODOLOGY PMO	0.352	0.084	0.378	4.191	0.000
CONTEXT PCA 2— SENIORITY	0.297	0.105	0.314	2.839	0.007
CONTEXT PCA 2— PROJECT MANAGER EXPERIENCE	0.225	0.083	0.238	2.713	0.009
CONTEXT PCA 3— POSITIVE PROJECT MANAGER ATTITUDE	-0.232	0.111	-0.235	-2.097	0.042
CONTEXT PCA 3— INNOVATORS	0.492	0.121	0.497	4.075	0.000
CONTEXT PCA 4— CONSTRUCTION	0.175	0.085	0.179	2.059	0.045
CONTEXT PCA 5— PUBLICLY HELD	-0.746	0.112	-0.753	-6.633	0.000
CONTEXT PCA 5— PRIVATELY HELD	-0.339	0.083	-0.342	-4.107	0.000

TABLE 9-11—*Regression results for Value PCA 4—Better Project Results*

distance degrees and diplomas. Decreases also result where implementations are increasingly described by employing trained experts, being motivated by strategic drivers, and where the implementation is primarily one of resource management. Decreases in better project results also occur where contexts are increasingly described as adopting ownership structures of publicly held or privately held.

The variable showing the highest influence in this regression is a negative association with an ownership structure of being publicly held.

This regression suggests that organizations are likely to see the greatest improvements in project results where there is a methodology PMO to advocate a consistent approach, and project managers and employees have enough seniority in their workforce to know what they are doing. Project results are also positively associated with a culture of innovation, although interestingly this does not seem to have the same negative influence on process that has been observed in other regressions that have discussed the culture of innovation.

Similarly, organizations relying on trained experts are likely to see decreases in project results, suggesting that, as in other value discussions to date, while the use of trained experts can be a source of expertise, there is not a level of consistency associated with implementations that rely on this strategy. As well, this strategy can have negative impacts in that where trained experts are externally sourced (which has been frequently observed in the case-study organizations), there is less understanding of the organization and its culture, and projects may not either proceed as smoothly or transition as effectively as those guided by someone with greater internal understanding.

There are also decreases associated with a number of forms of project management training being made available. This could be a modeling problem, however, in that this analysis provides no way of ascertaining whether increasing training is causing decreasing project results or whether low project results are causing organizations to increase the amount of training they are providing. This is certainly an area that warrants further exploration.

One final note of interest is that the only implementation aspect that influences better project results is the presence of a methodology PMO, and the other drivers are largely contextual, drawing on the attitudes and experience of the employees in a project management role. This is a significant intersection of findings, in that while it does support the quality of the people managing projects, it also places importance on the existence of a support group that acts as a centralized advocate for the adoption and utilization of effective project management practices. In other words, project heroism and the strength of the people managing projects is not the only factor in project results being delivered, and the presence of a consistent process–and an advocate promoting its use–plays an equally important role.

Regression 10: Value PCA 5—Better Business Outcomes

> *"The value of [project management] to this organisation is in better work quality, satisfaction of targeted groups and realization of benefits, as well as team motivation, communication, and cooperation at all levels."*
>
> — *Project Manager, 28*

80% of the variance in Value PCA 5—*Better business outcomes* is explained by the variables listed in Table 9-12.

Positive increases in business outcomes result when organizations are increasingly described by implementations that employ lunch and learns, informal off-the-shelf training approaches, long-term training strategies, and full toolsets. Increases also result where implementations are described as increasingly motivated by strategic drivers and internal drivers, and where there is a level of project management authority. Positive increases in business outcomes also result from contexts that are increasingly described as having positive project management attitudes, a focus of strategic innovation and that operates in a sector of strategic construction.

Decreases in business outcomes result when organizations are increasingly described by implementations that employ customized external training courses, have cost-management implementations, and have resource strategy that utilizes trained experts. Decreases also result when organizations are increasingly described as having a context of low project management experience in its employees, a culture of conflict avoidance, product development project types, and a structure that is government, publicly held or privately held.

The variable showing the highest influence on better organizational results is an implementation that is motivated by strategic drivers.

This regression suggests again that the strongest determinant of obtaining better organizational results from a project management implementation is the driver that motivates the project management implementation. Organizations that have strong strategic drivers, supported by internal drivers, which exist in a culture that has positive attitudes toward project management, are more likely to realize higher organizational results than other organizations. Correspondingly, a culture of conflict avoidance and implementations that rely upon cost management and the use of trained experts are far less likely to attain improved business outcomes.

What this regression seems to quite positively support are a number of the themes that have been introduced in the other dimensions of value. In particular, sustained business outcomes appear to be a result of a full implementation of

R=.931   R-SQUARE=.867   R-SQUAREADJ = .803

#steps = 20	Unstandardized Beta	Std. Error	Standardized Beta	T	Sig.
CONSTANT	0.004	0.054		0.065	0.949
IMPL PCA 1— LUNCH & LEARN	0.302	0.093	0.287	3.254	0.002
IMPL PCA 2— INFORMAL OFF-THE-SHELF	0.332	0.112	0.335	2.956	0.005
IMPL PCA 2— CUSTOMIZED EXTERNAL	-0.306	0.080	-0.309	-3.814	0.000
IMPL PCA 3— LONG-TERM TRAINING	0.335	0.077	0.335	4.329	0.000
IMPL PCA 4— FULL TOOLSETS	0.289	0.089	0.291	3.241	0.002
IMPL PCA 4— COST MANAGEMENT	-0.397	0.073	-0.401	-5.415	0.000
IMPL PCA 5— TRAINED EXPERTS	-0.424	0.099	-0.428	-4.265	0.000
IMPL PCA 6— STRATEGIC DRIVERS	0.626	0.109	0.632	5.726	0.000
IMPL PCA 6— INTERNAL DRIVERS	0.239	0.112	0.242	2.135	0.039
IMPL PCA 7 – PROJECT MANAGEMENT AUTHORITY	0.152	0.069	0.161	2.191	0.034
CONTEXT PCA 2— PROJECT MANAGER EXPERIENCE	-0.246	0.082	-0.260	-2.980	0.005
CONTEXT PCA 3— POSITIVE PROJECT MANAGEMENT ATTITUDE	0.472	0.104	0.476	4.555	0.000
CONTEXT PCA 3— CONFLICT AVOIDERS	-0.501	0.086	-0.506	-5.832	0.000
CONTEXT PCA 4— PRODUCT DEVELOPMENT	-0.182	0.090	-0.186	-2.025	0.050
CONTEXT PCA 4— STRATEGIC CONSTRUCTION	0.152	0.068	0.154	2.240	0.031
CONTEXT PCA 5 – GOVERNMENT	-0.322	0.089	-0.326	-3.604	0.001
CONTEXT PCA 5— PUBLICLY HELD	-0.231	0.086	-0.234	-2.675	0.011
CONTEXT PCA 5— PRIVATELY HELD	-0.236	0.077	-0.238	-3.073	0.004
CONTEXT PCA 6— STRATEGIC INNOVATORS	0.350	0.099	0.354	3.530	0.001

TABLE 9-12—*Regression results for Value PCA 5—Better Business Outcomes*

project management practices, supported by an accessible and flexible approach to training. While lunch-and-learns and off-the-shelf training may seem more ad hoc and informal, they also seem to create a level of training flexibility that is valuable in maintaining a sustained focus and developing a longer-term culture of skills development. Combined with an attitude that views project management as positive and a source of value to the organization, and an underlying strategic focus that embraces and supports change, this appears to establish a broad-brushed portrait of what is required for sustained organizational success of a project management implementation.

Regression 11: Value PCA 6—Growth and Reputation

> *"Project management methods had really been pioneered in the [project]. [Our organization] really has a lot to boast about. People from all of the country come to learn from the [project's project management] experiences, and we are proud of our reputation and capability . . . Now, we are innovating again to develop an effective system for managing the cascade multi-projects in a rolling way."*
>
> *— Senior Manager, 72*

R=.581   R-SQUARE=.338   R-SQUAREADJ = .289

#steps = 35	Unstandardized Beta	Std. Error	Standardized Beta	T	Sig.
CONSTANT	-0.003	0.110		-0.028	0.978
IMPL PCA 6—STRATEGIC DRIVERS	-0.237	0.117	-0.225	-2.025	0.048
IMPL PCA 6—INTERNAL DRIVERS	0.341	0.119	0.323	2.868	0.006
CONTEXT PCA 1—ECONOMIC PROSPECTS	0.256	0.110	0.260	2.321	0.024
CONTEXT PCA 5—PRIVATELY HELD	0.409	0.118	0.387	3.456	0.001

TABLE 9-13—*Regression results for Value PCA 6—Growth and Reputation*

29% of the variance in Value PCA 6—*Growth and reputation* is explained by the variables listed in Table 9-13.

Positive increases in growth and reputation result where organizations are increasingly described by an implementation that is motivated by internal drivers, and where there the context is increasingly associated with economic prospects and a privately-held ownership structure.

Decreases in organizations characterized by *Growth and reputation* are increasingly described by a motivator of strategic drivers.

The variable showing the highest influence on growth and retention is the degree to which there is a privately held ownership structure.

In this regression, only the drivers of the implementation and the context have significant influences on the realization of value. In part, this regression suggests that organizations that are using project management to grow their reputation and position in the market in emerging economies are most likely to recognize this particular benefit, but this only explains 30% of the variance in the data. The rest of the variation in the data is the result of variables not included in this regression though possibly still captured in this data set. Further consideration will need to be given to identify variables that influence an organization's ability to capture this benefit over and above the contextual variables highlighted above.

The only other point of note in this regression is that while the value associated with this regression is increases in growth and reputation, it is internal drivers that are positively associated with its attainment and strategic drivers (which are predominantly a response to market and competitive pressures) are actually negatively associated with realizing this value. This is an interesting paradox, but reinforces observations in other regressions and elsewhere within the value analysis that there is a strong correlation between the degree to which the implementation is internally motivated and the overall improvements that occur. For many of the organizations in developing or growth economies that have seen significant improvements in organizational growth and reputation, their emphasis in improving project management was motivated and driven by internally generated needs. Growth and increases were not the driver of the implementation, but were, in fact, simply the byproduct of the implementation.

Regression 12: Value PCA 6—Corporate Culture

"One thing we try to do is learn from each other, focus on lessons learned at the end of each project. We develop a log sheet of situations and the risk factor, and what was the response by the project manager. Sharing that log sheet with other project managers allows us to learn. That's informal at the moment, but the corporate culture leads to sharing and learning from others' experience."

— *Project Manager, 44*

At 0.05 P significance

R=.292   R-square=.085   R-squareadj = .069

#steps = 38	Unstandardized Beta	Std. Error	Standardized Beta	T	Sig.
Constant	-1.036E-17	0.126		0.000	1.000
Impl PCA 4— Resource Management	-0.308	0.134	-0.292	-2.302	0.025

Table 9-14—*Regression results for Value PCA 6—Corporate Culture at 0.05%*

7% of the variance in Value PCA 6—*Corporate culture* is explained by the variable listed in Table 9-14.

At 0.1 P significance

R=.642   R-square=.414   R-squareadj = .306

#steps = 30	Unstandardized Beta	Std. Error	Standardized Beta	T	Sig.
Constant	-0.004	0.108		-0.034	0.973
Impl PCA 2— Tailored Internal	0.512	0.201	0.485	2.548	0.014
Impl PCA 4— Full Toolsets	-0.309	0.167	-0.293	-1.852	0.070
Impl PCA 4— Resource Management	-0.423	0.137	-0.401	-3.080	0.003
Impl PCA 6— Internal Drivers	-0.294	0.155	-0.278	-1.896	0.064
Impl PCA 7— Methodology PMO	0.324	0.122	0.327	2.657	0.011
Context PCA 1— Economic Prospects	0.285	0.129	0.288	2.214	0.032
Context PCA 4— Organizational Change	0.294	0.148	0.281	1.995	0.052
Context PCA 5— Privately Held	-0.279	0.124	-0.264	-2.245	0.029
Context PCA 6— Strategic Innovators	-0.502	0.145	-0.476	-3.474	0.001

Table 9-15—*Regression results for Value PCA 6—Corporate Culture at 0.1%*

31% of the variance in Value PCA 6—*Corporate culture* is explained by the variables listed in Table 9-15.

At a 0.05 level of significance, only one variable–the degree to which the organization is not described as having a resource management implementation–describes the positive increases in this value. At a 0.10 level of significance, however, a slightly different–and possibly more meaningful–picture emerges.

Positive increases in corporate culture result where organizations are increasingly described by an implementation that employs tailored internal training and a methodology PMO. Increases also result in organizations where context is increasingly described as being in an economy with high economic prospects and managing organizational change projects.

Decreases in corporate culture result where organizations are increasingly described by an implementation that employs full toolsets or has a resource management implementation and that is motivated by internal drivers. Decreases also result from contexts that are increasingly described as privately held and with a focus of strategic innovation.

The variable showing the highest influence on corporate culture is a training strategy of tailored, internal training.

While enhancing corporate culture through the implementation of project management is a focus for many case-study organizations within the research, this regression highlights some interesting insights. At a 0.05 level of significance, the only influence on this value is a negative impact of increasing levels of resource management. Interestingly, for many organizations focusing on enhancing corporate culture, the implementation of resource management strategies is an approach that is considered. It is, however, a mechanistic means of improving resource utilization that focuses more on control and the reporting of time than it does on enhancing collaboration and cooperation amongst staff.

At a 0.10 level of significance, this regression provides some additional insights that suggests that realizing corporate culture benefits are positively correlated with implementations that are not driven by getting internal control of projects or the use of resource management tools. Corporate culture benefits are positively correlated with those organizations in emerging economies that are dealing with a large number of organizational change projects. From an implementation perspective, the greatest influences are providing tailored internal training and establishing a methodology-oriented PMO. This final point, however, raises a point of caution – the adoption of tailored internal training is seen here to positively correlate with culture, but it has negatively influenced the realization of a number of other organizational values. There seems to be a very fine point of balance that must be found between customizing training to be responsive to the organization and reflective of its motives and desires, while not departing significantly from standards and consistently understood terminology and concepts.

Regression 13: Value PCA 6—Improved Human Resources and Quality of Life

> "Implementing formal project management has allowed the company to put people (employees) where there passions are . . ."
>
> — Human Resources, 76

At 0.05 P SIGNIFICANCE

R=.368   R-SQUARE=.136   R-SQUAREADJ = .105

#steps = 37	Unstandardized Beta	Std. Error	Standardized Beta	T	Sig.
CONSTANT	1.173E-8	0.123		0.000	1.000
IMPL PCA 6—TRADITIONAL DRIVERS	-0.311	0.134	-0.294	-2.329	0.024
CONTEXT PCA 6—CUSTOMER INTIMACY	0.298	0.134	0.282	2.233	0.030

TABLE 9-16—*Regression results for Value PCA 6—Improved Human Resources and Quality of Life at 0.05%*

11% of the variance in Value PCA 6—*Improved human resources and quality of life* is explained by the variables listed in Table 9-16.

33% of the variance in Value PCA 6—*Improved human resources and quality of life* is explained by the variables listed in Table 9-17.

At a 0.05 level of significance, the only variables which influence this regression are an increase in value as a result of a strategy of customer intimacy and a decrease in value as a result of an implementation that is increasingly motivated by traditional drivers. At a 0.10 level of significance, more context emerges by which to evaluate the regression.

Positive increases in human resource effectiveness and quality of life result from organizations that are increasingly described by an implementation that has a long-term training strategy, and by a context that is increasingly described as having a positive attitude to project management, a structure that is publicly held and a strategy of customer intimacy.

Decreases in human resource effectiveness and quality of life result from organizations that are increasingly described by an implementation that employs a training strategy of distance degree and diploma-based programs, a resource management implementation, clear roles and training, and that is motivated by

At 0.1 P significance

R=.694   R-square=.482   R-squareadj = .333

#steps = 26	Unstandardized Beta	Std. Error	Standardized Beta	T	Sig.
CONSTANT	3.169E-8	0.106		0.000	1.000
IMPL PCA 1— DISTANCE DEGREE & DIPLOMA	-0.315	0.148	-0.281	-2.133	0.038
IMPL PCA 3— LONG-TERM TRAINING	0.324	0.137	0.303	2.359	0.023
IMPL PCA 4— RESOURCE MANAGEMENT	-0.278	0.132	-0.263	-2.110	0.040
IMPL PCA 5— CLEAR ROLES & TRAINING	-0.326	0.162	-0.308	-2.012	0.050
IMPL PCA 6— TRADITIONAL DRIVERS	-0.840	0.183	-0.795	-4.599	0.000
CONTEXT PCA 2 – SENIORITY	-0.416	0.136	-0.412	-3.069	0.004
CONTEXT PCA 3— POSITIVE PM ATTITUDE	0.466	0.204	0.441	2.288	0.027
CONTEXT PCA 4— ORGANIZATIONAL CHANGE	-0.337	0.133	-0.322	-2.536	0.015
CONTEXT PCA 4— STRATEGIC CONSTRUCTION	-0.300	0.131	-0.287	-2.291	0.027
CONTEXT PCA 5— PUBLICLY HELD	0.459	0.155	0.435	2.966	0.005
CONTEXT PCA 5— PUBLIC PARTNERSHIPS	-0.241	0.132	-0.228	-1.820	0.075
CONTEXT PCA 5— PRIVATELY HELD	-0.265	0.130	-0.251	-2.038	0.047
CONTEXT PCA 6— CUSTOMER INTIMACY	0.415	0.136	0.393	3.055	0.004

TABLE 9-17—*Regression results for Value PCA 6—Improved Human Resources and Quality of Life at 0.1%*

traditional drivers. Decreases also result where organizations are increasingly described by a context of senior employees, projects that focus on strategic construction or organizational change, and structures that are either publicly held, public partnerships or privately held.

The variable showing the highest influence on human resources effectiveness and quality of life is the degree to which there is negatively a motivator of traditional drivers.

At the 0.05 significance level, a customer intimacy strategy is positively correlated with increasing human resources effectiveness and quality of life, and implementing project management to improve traditional project management indicators is negatively correlated. Loosening the significance level to 0.1 increases the influence of these variables and suggests that the organizational structure, type of projects, and type of training provided also significantly influence the attainment of quality of life. Implementations that are primarily characterized by only the formalization of processes, structures and toolsets, and working to get control of projects have a strong negative impact on quality of life and human resources effectiveness. Those strategies that take a more strategic view, however, whether in terms of the duration of the training strategy or the establishment of positive attitudes toward the work of project management, appear to result in organizations that recognize the importance of both employee effectiveness and the overall management of change as a long-term investment.

Regression 14: Value PCA 6—Strategic Alignment

> *"[Project management is of great value for the organization] because otherwise many things would not be launched or accomplished."*
>
> — *Project Manager, 17*

At 0.05 P significance

R=.614   R-square=.377   R-squareadj = .343

#steps = 36	Unstandardized Beta	Std. Error	Standardized Beta	T	Sig.
Constant	1.050E-16	0.106		0.000	1.000
Impl PCA 2—Tailored Internal	0.367	0.116	0.347	3.175	0.002
Impl PCA 3—Long-term Training	-0.349	0.117	-0.327	-2.976	0.004
Context PCA 5—Publicly Held	0.467	0.115	0.442	4.048	0.000

Table 9-18—*Regression results for Value PCA 6—Strategic Alignment at 0.05%*

34% of the variance in Value PCA 6—*Strategic alignment* is explained by the variables listed in Table 9-18.

AT 0.10 P SIGNIFICANCE

R=.779   R-SQUARE=.606   R-SQUAREADJ = .503

#steps = 27	Unstandardized Beta	Std. Error	Standardized Beta	T	Sig.
CONSTANT	9.340E-17	0.092		0.000	1.000
IMPL PCA 2—TAILORED INTERNAL	0.609	0.171	0.577	3.560	0.001
IMPL PCA 2—CUSTOMIZED EXTERNAL	0.210	0.114	0.199	1.843	0.072
IMPL PCA 3—LONG-TERM TRAINING	-0.506	0.116	-0.475	-4.349	0.000
IMPL PCA 3—SHORT-TERM TRAINING	-0.422	0.143	-0.396	-2.947	0.005
IMPL PCA 4—FULL TOOLSETS	-0.341	0.146	-0.323	-2.341	0.024
IMPL PCA 4—RESOURCE MANAGEMENT	0.383	0.127	0.362	3.008	0.004
IMPL PCA 6—INTERNAL DRIVERS	0.294	0.119	0.278	2.464	0.018
CONTEXT PCA 2—SENIORITY	0.378	0.122	0.374	3.091	0.003
CONTEXT PCA 3—POSITIVE PM ATTITUDE	-0.248	0.138	-0.235	-1.796	0.079
CONTEXT PCA 5—PUBLICLY HELD	0.342	0.136	0.323	2.512	0.016
CONTEXT PCA 5—PRIVATELY HELD	0.250	0.106	0.237	2.360	0.023
CONTEXT PCA 6—OPERATIONAL EFFICIENCY	0.365	0.142	0.345	2.568	0.014

TABLE 9-19—*Regression results for Value PCA 6—Strategic Alignment at 0.10%*

50% of the variance in Value PCA 6—*Strategic alignment* is explained by the variables listed in Table 9-19.

At a 0.05 level of significance, positive improvements in strategic alignment result from increases in tailored internal training in a publicly held ownership structure, while decreases result from increasing emphasis on a long-term training strategy. At a 0.10 level of significance, more context emerges.

Increases in strategic alignment result in organizations that are increasingly described by an implementation that employs tailored internal training, has a resource management implementation, and that is motivated by internal drivers. Positive increases also result from organizations increasingly described by a context of greater employee seniority, operating in publicly held and privately-held structures, and that employ a strategy of operational efficiency.

Decreases in strategic alignment result from organizations that are increasingly described by an implementation that employs long-term and short-term training and a full toolset. Decreases also result from a context that is increasingly described as adopting a positive project management attitude.

The variable showing the highest influence on strategic alignment is the degree to which there is a tailored, internal training approach in place.

At the 0.05 significance level, this regression tells us that 34% of the variation in *Strategic alignment* is realized in organizations in a publicly held environment implementing tailored but not long-term training. This suggests that tailored, targeted project management training can be used effectively in this environment to align project activities with strategic directions. As has been observed in other regressions, excessively tailored training approaches can have a negative influence on other measures of value. Specifically tailoring training to the context and environment of the organization, however, does seem to promote strategic alignment within the organization.

Loosening the significance cutoff to 0.1, we see that many other project management implementation activities around tailored and customized training and utilizing resource management tools are also positively correlated with delivering this benefit. What is interesting about these influences is that many of them, particularly resource management and a focus on operational efficiency, appear to be promoting strategic alignment through more mechanistic and control-oriented strategies. Other aspects of project management, including the employment of long-term and short-term training strategies, employment of a full toolset, and particularly the emphasis on a positive attitude towards project management, have a negative influence on the delivery of this value. This appears to suggest that the value of strategic alignment in this instance is more driven by a process-based focus on operational efficiency, rather than more humanistic approaches to organizational alignment.

Regression 15: Value PCA 6—New Services and Staff Retention, and Growth

> "Our goal with the career ladder program is that some individuals will stay a year or two longer, since they consider this program so attractive. There are no restrictions to this, however. We also have a goal to raise the knowledge in the industry, so we are only glad if we can contribute to this."
>
> —Senior Manager, 21

AT 0.05 SIGNIFICANCE

R=   R-SQUARE=   R-SQUAREADJ =

#steps = 37	Unstandardized Beta	Std. Error	Standardized Beta	T	Sig.
CONSTANT	4.656E-17	0.130		0.000	1.000

TABLE 9-20—Regression results for Value PCA 6—New Services and Staff Retention, and Growth at 0.05%

No implementation or context variables were seen to significantly influence the dependent variable Value PCA 6—*New services and staff retention, and growth at* the .05% cutoff.

AT 0.1 P SIGNIFICANCE

R=.307   R-SQUARE=.094   R-SQUAREADJ = .062

#steps = 37	Unstandardized Beta	Std. Error	Standardized Beta	T	Sig.
CONSTANT	0.00	0.126		-0.002	0.998
IMPL PCA 7—METHODOLOGY PMO	0.259	0.131	0.261	1.973	0.053
CONTEXT PCA 5—GOVERNMENT	-0.264	0.140	-0.250	-1.889	0.064

TABLE 9-21—Regression results for Value PCA 6—New Services and Staff Retention, and Growth at 0.1%

With this looser cutoff point, as shown in Table 9-21, it appears that the variables explaining the variation in this dependent variable are the degree to which there is a methodology PMO and that the organization does not operate in a government context. What is important to note, however, is that this regression only explains

6% of the variance in this value, and only a small number of organizations reported realizing this value.

Looking at the actual organizational case studies that have been able to realize a growth and the ability to offer new products and services as a result of their project management yields some interesting insights. There are a number of organization that have been able to either offer new services (primarily project management itself) or have been able to begin charging (or charging more) for the project management services that they provide. For each of these organizations, they value seems to have been one that has been a "happy accident" rather than being a positive focus or a conscious point of strategic emphasis. While this has occurred frequently enough that this value emerged as a discrete component in the exploratory data analysis, it is in very rare instances a value that organizations sought to realize. As well, the implementations associated with organizations realizing this value are not necessarily exceptionally robust or comprehensive. As a result, there are very few specific or repeatable trends that lead to the emergence of this value. What these organizations have in common is simply that they have become good enough at managing projects (at least in the eyes of their customers) that they are now able to charge for a service that was often once included as an overhead.

Regression Conclusions

Figure 9-31 summarizes the regression results discussed in this chapter.

Clearly these are early findings that will need to be refined and elaborated on with further explorations of this data set. However, they do point to some fairly significant insights that can be useful immediately.

Most importantly, what these regressions clearly demonstrate is that value is a product of both context and implementation. The drivers of each regression contain both contextual and implementation components. Context alone does not deliver the value observed, and neither does implementation. Only together do they collectively contribute to the creation of value.

WHAT ARE THE IMPLICATIONS IN REALIZING VALUE?

As the sections in this study have demonstrated, project management is delivering value for many of the case-study organizations included in this research study. The nature of the value, however, and the nature of the context and implementations delivering that value, vary considerably. Looking at the findings and observations associated with the drivers of value, a number of key considerations emerge that are important to keep in mind as organizations explore how to attain or maximize the value from their project management implementations.

	1	2	3	4	5	6	7	8	9	10	11	12	13	14	15	Count - All Regressions	Count - Positive Impact On Regressions	Count - Negative Impact On Regressions
	Value PCA 1 - Desire For Change	Value PCA 1 - Project Manager Satisfaction	Value PCA 1 - Customer Satisfaction	Value PCA 2 - Aligned Organization	Value PCA 2 - Aligned Project Management	Value PCA 3 - Good Practices	Value PCA 3 - Good PM No Practices	Value PCA 4 - Better Process Results	Value PCA 4 - Better Project Results	Value PCA 5 - Better Business Outcomes	Value PCA 6 - Growth & Reputation	Value PCA 6 - Corporate Culture	Value PCA 6 - Improved HR & Quality of Life	Value PCA 6 - Strategic Alignment	Value PCA 6 - New Services & Staff Retention			
Percentage of Variance Explained	54%	63%	18%	69%	66%	63%	49%	77%	68%	80%	29%	31%	33%	50%	6%			
Impl PCA 1 - Full PM Training								-0.22								1	0	1
Impl PCA 1 - Lunch & Learn		0.26			-0.29		0.25			0.29						4	3	1
Impl PCA 1 - Distance Degree & Diploma		0.20							-0.27				-0.28			3	1	2
Impl PCA 2 - Tailored Internal		-0.24			-0.66		0.28		-0.37			0.49		0.58		6	3	3
Impl PCA 2 - Informal Off-the-Shelf		0.35			0.33			0.26		0.34						4	4	0
Impl PCA 2 - Customized External		-0.41			-0.33	-0.21			-0.19	-0.31				0.20		6	1	5
Impl PCA 3 - Long-term Training					0.29			0.23		0.34			0.30	-0.48		5	4	1
Impl PCA 3 - Short-term Training									-0.43					-0.40		2	0	2
Impl PCA 4 - Full Toolsets										0.29		-0.29		-0.32		3	1	2
Impl PCA 4 - Resource Management									-0.29				-0.40	-0.26	0.36	4	1	3
Impl PCA 4 - Cost Management			-0.44				0.30		-0.26	-0.40						4	1	3
Impl PCA 5 - Clear Roles & Training				0.67	0.28								-0.31			3	2	1
Impl PCA 5 - Trained Experts								0.48	-0.51	-0.43						3	1	2
Impl PCA 6 - Traditional Drivers	0.27				0.25								-0.80			3	2	1
Impl PCA 6 - Strategic Drivers	0.22	0.30			0.52			0.63	-0.28	0.63	-0.23					7	5	2
Impl PCA 6 - Internal Drivers		0.54			0.78	0.39	-0.54	0.39		0.24	0.32		-0.28		0.28	9	7	2
Impl PCA 7 - PM Authority		0.80			0.61					0.16						3	3	0
Impl PCA 7 - Delivery PMO	-0.25				-0.34											2	0	2
Impl PCA 7 - Methodology PMO										0.38			0.33		0.26	3	3	0
Context PCA 1 - Economic Prospects							0.45				0.26	0.29				3	3	0
Context PCA 2 - Seniority						-0.40	-0.61		0.31				-0.41	0.37		5	2	3
Context PCA 2 - PM Experience		0.21				0.22	0.22			0.24	-0.26					5	4	1
Context PCA 3 - Positive PM Attitude		0.51		0.21		0.30		0.44	-0.24	0.48			0.44	-0.24		8	6	2
Context PCA 3 - Innovators						0.24		-0.25	0.50							3	2	1
Context PCA 3 - Conflict Avoiders					-0.46			-0.25		-0.51						3	0	3
Context PCA 3 - Not Customer Focused								0.26								1	1	0
Context PCA 4 - Construction					-0.18		-0.22		0.18							3	1	2
Context PCA 4 - Product Development										-0.19						1	0	1
Context PCA 4 - Organizational Change							0.41						0.28	-0.32		3	2	1
Context PCA 4 - Strategic Construction	0.32									0.15			-0.29			3	2	1
Context PCA 5 - Government		-0.37			-0.46		0.45	-0.48		-0.33					-0.25	6	1	5
Context PCA 5 - Publicly Held	-0.21				-0.32				-0.75	-0.23			0.44	0.32		6	2	4
Context PCA 5 - Public Partnerships		-0.19											-0.23			2	0	2
Context PCA 5 - Privately Held									-0.34	-0.24	0.39	-0.26	-0.25	0.24		6	2	4
Context PCA 5 - Sole Proprietorship								0.17								1	1	0
Context PCA 6 - Strategic Innovators	0.50				-0.20	0.90	-0.30	-0.49	0.46		0.35		-0.48			8	4	4
Context PCA 6 - Operational Efficiency				0.32				-0.48	0.32					0.35		4	3	1
Context PCA 6 - Customer Intimacy	-0.42				0.25								0.39			3	2	1

FIGURE 9-31—*Summary of regression analysis*

Exploring The Impact Of High-Level Value Trends

The exploration of the high-level value trends against context and implementation reveal the following insights:

- Tangible value is most evident in those organizations for whom the delivery of projects is the nature of their business, and particularly those that operate in a consulting or construction and engineering field. Even here, however, there are key considerations to keep in mind:

  o Tangible value is most significantly present in growing economies, which enjoy lower barriers to entry and less competitive friction than in established economies. While competition is still present and a factor to be considered, it is less of a hurdle to be overcome and organizations in growing economies report sufficient overall economic activity that even poor players can remain in business, while organizations that significantly enhance their reputation for project delivery are often experiencing extreme growth.

  o Organizations with minimal implementations or those that heavily leverage external resources at the expense of internal structures are less likely to demonstrate tangible value, and the resulting value tends to be lower.

  o Tangible value is less evidenced in organizations where the implementation is responding to longer-term or strategic and cultural drivers.

- Intangible value is being evidenced by virtually all of the case-study organizations. Some specific considerations are:

  o Those organizations that are realizing significant or extreme amounts of intangible value are frequently defined contextually by a combination of components; with the exception of those that engage in a strategic construction context, they often draw upon aspects of multiple context components. Equally important, however, is that there are few patterns to these contexts. While value is being leveraged in each case, it is being realized by organizations that often differ quite significantly.

  o Virtually all organizations associated with government contexts are realizing significant levels of intangible value.

- While positive value trends are observable in every implementation, there are some contextual impacts that seem to influence the ability of organizations to continue to realize value from their implementations:

○ The context of *Innovative conflict-avoiding product developers* is one that is rarely associated with the continuing delivery of value in the case-study organizations. While these organizations may have observed value in the past, there is some question about their continued ability to deliver value. This difference appears to be a product of the context, and is not reflected to the same degree in any implementation components.

○ The organization with the lowest value trend (greatest value destruction) is associated with the component of *Innovative conflict-avoiding product developers* and two other components. Three other organizations are associated with these components and another product development component, *Customer-focused product developers.* These organizations have a positive value trend, and one of the organizations has a value trend of +2.

• Positive levels of maturity are being realized in every implementation, and almost every context. The only exception to this is once again the context component of *Innovative conflict-avoiding product developers*, which does not have any organizations with a maturity above Level 2. As well, the implementation component with the lowest maturity is that of *Trained experts and methodology PMO*, reflecting a greater reliance upon externally-sourced resources rather than internal structures. Even though a PMO exists to support the methodology, these implementations are typically more heavily influenced by the personal approaches of individual project managers than they are by the practices and capabilities of the organization itself.

• The context component of *Innovative conflict-avoiding product developers* has emerged throughout the above analysis as one that is experiencing challenges. To an extent, this is not surprising, as highly innovative cultures can be less accepting of attempts to create structure and introduce formalized process. As well, the culture of conflict avoidance that emerges suggests implementations that are unwilling to impose structure or confront those that may fail to use it. As a result, it is unsurprising that less consistent implementations emerge. What is also useful to highlight there, however, is that while organizations in this context component have observed value, all but one of the organizations in this component are either likely to lose value or have an implementation whose ongoing viability and ability to deliver value is being questioned.

Exploring Relationships For Organizations That Exemplify The Construct Components

The explorations of the relationships of context, implementation and value for organizations that exemplify each of these components reveal the following insights:

- Implementation is clearly defined for organizations associated with only some of the contexts:

  - Those organizations that have a context of *Operationally efficient strategic construction in developing economies*, but only where there is a level of maturity associated with the practices. Those organizations that are much earlier in their implementations have unclear and, in actual fact, very simple implementations that do not correspond strongly to any of the implementation constructs that emerge in the research.

  - There are also clear implementations associated with the contexts of *Customer-Focused Product Developers* and *Positive project management in government*.

- From the perspective of value, there is a clear association between the contexts of *Project Management experience in government* and the two product-development contexts of *Innovative conflict-avoiding product developers* and *Customer-focused product developers*. Those which exemplify organizations in the government and conflict-avoiding contexts are likely to be negatively associated with the delivery of value, while those that exemplify the government, regulated, and customer-focused contexts are those which are positively associated with the delivery of value.

- There are a number of insights associated with those organizations that exemplify the different implementation constructs, including:

  - Clearest context and value associations are visible for full project management implementations (*Full project management, traditional drivers and delivery PMO*), even though there are a number of contextual and cultural differences between organizations that are associated with this implementation. Many organizations have adopted implementations that reflect a full and formalized implementation for traditional reasons, despite a range of backgrounds, cultures, and project types, and are clearly realizing specific dimensions of value as a result.

  - The implementation of cost management (*Cost management, clear roles and formal training*) is one of the most challenging implementations, in that there is no clear pattern of context associated with the implementation, and many case-study organizations are defined by the context they are *not* associated with, rather than the one they align with. This implementation also is most likely to be associated with values that reflect the most complacency in terms of value being realized, being associated with either good practices and little desire for change (*Good practices, effective human resources and no desire for change*) or a perception of good project management with minimal process capabilities (*Good project management, not processes, customer satisfaction*).

o The trained expert (*Trained experts and methodology PMO*) implementation is the most problematic in terms of value delivery. For the majority of organizations strongly associated with this implementation, organizations are likely to be negatively associated with the delivery of value. The reliance upon heroics and the expertise of the individual project manager over the creation of established capabilities seems to not deliver the same levels of value as other implementations being observed in the case studies.

• Organizations that exemplify the different dimensions of value provide a few meaningful insights:

o There are few strong associations that emerge for component 1 (*Aligned practices, better processes and business outcomes*) and component 2 (*Good process, good human resources and no desire for change*). Organizations that report realizing these values do not have a strong correlation with either context or implementation, but for both there are patterns that emerge that are mostly aligned along different implementations. Value component 2 tends to be associated with less formal or complete implementations (mostly associated with a cost-management implementation), while value component 1 associates more with implementations responding to internal or strategic drivers.

o The third component of value (*Better projects, aligned organizations and corporate culture*) has two clear groupings of organizations that report this value being realized. One grouping is strongly aligned with a context that reflects strategic construction organizations in developing economies, but that negatively is associated with a number of the implementation components. As discussed earlier, these are organizations that tend to have less well-defined and more immature implementations. The other grouping is strongly aligned with implementations associated with either traditional or strategic drivers but that are less differentiated by context.

o The fourth and fifth components of value (*Good projects, not process, not customer satisfaction* and *Good project management, not process, customer satisfaction*) differ largely in the degree to which the organizational implementations are actually delivering customer satisfaction; on the surface, the other dimensions of these components appear to be very similar. Looking at the organizations themselves, however, those organizations in the fourth component (not customer satisfaction) tend to be more established, have project management implementations that have been in place for a more extended period, and tend to have much more critical customers. These implementations, however, also tend to be less robust and employ fairly common approaches, even where internally the organizations view them quite positively and unique to the specific organization. Organizations in the customer satisfaction component (component 5) tend to be much more customer oriented, and also tend to enjoy more robust implementations, but are relatively early in their implementation. As a result, these implementations are comparatively less mature and less consistently applied, but have the potential to deliver greater value in the future.

o The final component of value (*New services, staff retention and growth*) appears at first glance to predominantly favor full implementations or cost-management implementations. Certainly each of these organizations–while with newer and less robust implementations–have been able to deliver new services (often project management itself) and grow their organizations as a result of their project management implementations. The strongest association with this component, however, are two organizations that clearly draw on a reasonably comprehensive implementation that stemmed from internal drivers, based upon external standards and training, and appear in the context of *Positive project management in government*. These two organizations represent large-scale, state-owned engineering organizations that have leveraged their implementations in order to grow and enhance their reputation exponentially within their marketplace.

Exploring Relationships Of Motivators & Objectives With Implementations And Value

The analysis of the influence that motivators and objectives had on the project management implementations that were initiated and the values realized by the case-study organizations provide some useful insights. Ironically, some of the most interesting results in this analysis were associated with what was not significant:

- The fact that none of the implementations differed significantly based upon their underlying motivators and objectives is extremely interesting. What this in essence reveals is that regardless of the implementation, an organization was as likely to be motivated by the same factors or working towards the same objectives as other implementations in other organizations. Even where similar objectives exist, organizations may adopt different implementations to attain them. A corollary to this would be that where different objectives exist among organizations, they may in fact adopt similar implementations. This continues to raise questions about "fit," and reinforces that it is not simply implementation that influences value, but the intersection of context and implementation.

- The motivators that were statistically significant in each value component were actually very similar. While implementations were assessed against eight different motivators, three emerged consistently in the majority of the value components: increasing project complexity, competitive pressures, and maintaining an appearance of being current. While organizations also reported the other motivators as being relevant for their individual organizations, the results here reinforce what was observed in the implementation analysis: there is little significance of the motivators among value components. In particular, the motivators that were most strongly ranked within organizations that highly described a component were not necessarily those identified as having the most statistically significant differences across the groups within that component. While organizations that were highly described by a value component may have had other motivators that were ranked higher, these tended to score the same for all groups, suggesting they had similar levels of importance for most organizations. As well, those motivators that had statistically significant differences were often associated with those motivators that scored much lower for the organizations strongly described by that component. What this implies is that the highest ranking motivators tend to be very similar across organization, and the majority of differentiation is in secondary motivators.

- The most variance, and the most meaning, actually emerged from the underlying objectives that led to the implementations being explored. Unlike for the motivators, what the analysis of the objectives does reinforce is that implementations that are being more effectively described by different values were, for the most part, in response to different objectives. This continues to reinforce the underlying theory put forth by this research study, that for the value that an organization is trying to realize, there is a unique combination of context and implementation that is appropriate. What it also highlights that is potentially significant, however, is not simply that different combinations of context and implementation lead to different values, but that it is the objective of an organization–the value it wants to attain–that will determine the best implementation for its context.

- The last point that is worthwhile exploring here is that there are two value components that appear to be less a deliberate response to objectives, and more an unintended consequence of the implementations that occurred. The component of *Good project management, not process, not customer satisfaction,* as has been noted elsewhere, appears to in many instances emerge most in response to organizations that have partial implementations, do not have unique implementations, or that have implemented project management as something that was seen as necessary, rather than something that was consciously thought of as delivering value. As well, the component of *New services, staff retention and growth* appears to be most often described by organizations that, while they are now able to expand their services and grow their organizations as a result of their project management implementations, did not in fact start out with this as an initial objective.

Exploring The Regressions Of Implementation and Context On Value

Additional observations regarding the regression results are presented in the following points:

Contextual Influences on Value

- The role of economic prospects has a strong influence on a number of the aspects of value being observed here. As a context component, economic prospects influence three of the 15 prospects presented here, each of which are positively correlated with value. While there are certainly advantages to operating in a developing economy in terms of economic activity and reductions in competitive friction, a number of case-study organizations have been able to demonstrate significant material value from their project management implementations. This is particularly true in a number of tangible dimensions of value, such as growth, increase in reputation, and increase in market share and customer retention. Many of the influences driving the project management implementations in these contexts, however, are related to ensuring compliance with financing organizations such as the World Bank. The influence of these requirements, and the transition that has been observed in a number of organizations from compliance to valuing the project management implementation that results, warrants further exploration and investigation.

- Cultural attitudes significantly correlated with value realized from a project management implementation in nine of 15 regressions reported here. The most prevalent cultural attitude within the regressions is the component associated with *Positive project manager attitude*, and it influences positively six of the eight regressions in which it appears. This influence on value seems to indicate that delivering value is in part a product of believing that project management provides value; where project management is viewed as being a valued organizational contributor, strong value is being evidenced consistently.

- Organizational strategy is significantly correlated with value realized in 10 of 15 regressions reported here. Of these, the driving priority of strategic innovation is certainly the dominant strategic influence, and is present in eight of the 15 regressions. Interestingly, in four of these, the strategy of strategic innovation has a positive influence, and in four there is a negative influence. While it is the most prevalent strategic driver within the case-study organizations, there are as many negative associations (reluctance to use process, aversion to structure) as there are positive (willingness and desire for change). Operational efficiency, by contrast, has a positive influence on three of four regressions, although each of these are more mechanistic and process-focused; in other words, a strategic driver of operational efficiency appears to drive alignment and process for the sake of alignment and process. A strategy of customer intimacy, while least prevalent within the case-study organizations, positively influences the regressions associated with *Good practices* and *Improved human resources and quality of life*, while negatively influencing only one (*Desire for change*, itself a negative measure of satisfaction).

- Ownership type is significantly correlated with value realized in 12 of the 15 regressions reported here. Interestingly, ownership type as a context is most likely to negatively influence value delivery. The component associated with government negatively influenced five out of six regressions; the component associated with publicly held organizations negatively influenced four out of six regressions; and the component associated with privately held organizations negatively influenced four out of six regressions. In the context of government organizations, issues of politics, avoidance of media exposure, and perceptions of excess bureaucracy are driving these results, as with short-term accountability and reporting issues in public organizations and a lack of structure and process in privately held firms. While these observations are supportable by both the regressions and case-study organizations, however, they are also frequent stereotypes associated with these organizational structures, which may in part be reinforced here, even by their organizational participants. Further investigation into the influences and underlying causes is certainly warranted.

- Project type is significantly correlated with value in eight of the 15 regressions reported here, and each regression in which project type is an influence is largely associated with one project type, with the exception of two regressions where two project types appear. This suggests that part of the contextual influence that determines what values are possible is the types of projects conducted by that organization, and that these types of projects may then further influence the appropriate implementations that support these values. Additional investigation and analysis would be of benefit here.

Implementation Influences on Value

- The drivers motivating the investment in project management are significantly correlated with the value realized in 12 of the 15 regressions reported here. While these drivers vary in focus–with project management being driven in response to traditional, strategic, and internal motivators–they figure prominently in how value is driven for many of the organizational case studies reflected here. These drivers reinforce the rationale for the investment in the first place, and therefore emphasize what was most important to the organization at that time. As such, it may be that these drivers may, in part, be a proxy for top management support of the implementation. As well, these motivators may play a significant influence in ultimately determining the basis of fit–what implementation is appropriate for organizations in a given context–based upon the actual values that organizations are attempting to realize. This will require further analysis.

- Training of various types is significantly correlated with value realization, but not always in a positive direction. Training components influence the value realized in 11 of the 15 regressions conducted here. Upon reflection on these results, it seems clear that the causality for this correlation may be confounded in this model. It is possible that increasing training or certain types of training decreases the value realized, but it is also possible that in organizations realizing very little value (just starting to implement project management, for instance) that one of the first things they may do is invest heavily in training for their project staff. Similarly, organizations that invested heavily in the past in training but have since stopped may still be reaping the value increases based on those investments. The timing of the investment and the value realization, therefore, becomes critically important, and may be influencing some of the results being observed here. This question definitely requires further analysis, specifically with respect to the timing of various implementation events relative to the realization of value in organizations. While these observations may hold true for other elements of the regressions analysis, it is the inconsistency of the findings with respect to training in these regressions that most seems to highlight this concern as well as make us suggest further investigation is warranted.

- The role of the PMO is providing interesting contributions to value within the regressions observed here. Five of the value regressions are influenced by PMOs in the analysis presented here. Of those, the two instances of a delivery PMO have a negative influence on value delivery, while the three instances of a methodology PMO have a positive influence on the delivery of value. While the delivery PMO is the prevalent model in the majority of case-study organizations within this research, it is clearly not delivering value in a number of contexts. In particular, while there is a perception that a delivery PMO will be a source of ensuring consistent practice, it would appear that the pressure of project delivery is leading delivery PMOs to sidestep process consistency in favor of project delivery. Those organizations that have a methodology PMO, by contrast, not only are observing greater process consistency but also positive influences on corporate culture and better delivery of project results.

- The distinction between adopting clear roles and structures, and the appropriate development of internal resources to support project management, plays an interesting juxtaposition to the use of trained experts. These two different resourcing models each influence value in three of the components presented here. The creation of clear structures and internally capable staff positively influences two value regressions (*Aligned organization* and *Aligned project management*) while negatively influencing one value regression (*Improved human resources and quality of life*). The adoption of trained experts, who are typically externally sourced, as capable project managers but who have few organizational capabilities on which to rely, negatively influences two regressions (*Better project results* and *Better business outcomes*) and only positively influences one (*Good project management, not practices*). Given the widespread use of external trained experts to deliver projects, these findings suggest some caution on the part of organizations, and certainly warrant further investigation.

- Cost-management tools are identified in four regressions as significantly influencing value realized. In three cases, they are reported to negatively attain value (*Customer satisfaction, Better process results* and *Better organizational results*) and only in the case of the value PCA related to *Good practices* did it correlate positively with value realization. As has been demonstrated in both the regressions and previous analyses, cost management has proven to be a problematic implementation. The only area where it is contributing value here may be solely due to the fact that cost management implementations, where they exist, are more straightforward and therefore tend to be better documented, better understood, and more consistently adhered to. In most instances, however, a cost-management implementation appears to add little to value, and in fact reflects a complacency regarding project management in general and process in particular within several of the case studies observed here.

CONCLUSIONS

As we indicated at the beginning of this chapter, its purpose was to explore the drivers of project management value that were evidenced within this research study. In doing so, we have brought together the component constructs of context, implementation, and value that were identified in the preceding chapters, and explored how these intersect within the case-study organizations. In particular, we have sought to answer the question that has been sustained through each chapter: "What differences matter to project management implementations?"

The resulting analyses have comprehensively reviewed this question from a number of perspectives. We have explored how the organizations within the study cluster together. The chapter has also explored the influences of context and implementation on the realization of tangible and intangible value, as well as the value trends and maturity that emerged from the study. The insights of organizations that exemplify each of the constructs–context, implementation and value–have been explored in detail. As well, the exploration of fit opens the question of what value was initially sought, not just what value was, in fact, realized. This chapter has identified those objectives and motivators of project management implementations that most influenced each of the components of value seen within the study. Finally, and most importantly, we have explored through regression analysis the specific influences of context and implementation that can be observed within each of the value components.

What has emerged in this chapter is not only clear insights into the diverse types of value that organizations are realizing from their project management implementations, but the wide variety of contexts and implementations that lead to those values. Clearly, value is being realized by the vast majority of organizations that participated in this study. What this chapter also clearly demonstrates, however, is realization of the underlying thesis of this research study–that it is not context or implementation alone that delivers value, but the contribution of both of those constructs together. Project management is not any one specific practice or model, and project management is not appropriate in only narrow and specific contexts. Project management value is the result of the implementation that is most relevant for an organization, given both its context and the objectives that it sets for its project management approach. Finally, and most importantly, this research study has advanced exploratory theories of which implementations and which contexts lead to specific value results, providing an initial basis for organizations to begin to evaluate their own environment and objectives, and enabling them to begin to choose the most appropriate implementation for their circumstances.

10
Conclusions

OVERALL CONCLUSIONS

At this point in our exploration of project management value, we are very satisfied that the analysis presented to date generates many useful and practical theories on how project management value is created in organizations. The specific conclusions on context, implementation, value and the interaction of all three of these constructs are provided at the end of Chapters 6, 7, 8, and 9, and will not be repeated here. This chapter provides a summary of the findings at a high level, and introduces the study limitations and future directions.

Reconfirming Original Expectations

At the outset of this research study, the proposal submitted to PMI indicated that in order for it to be successful, the study needed to provide unequivocal and compelling evidence of the value organizations recognize when project management is appropriately implemented.

In particular, we identified a number of requirements that would need to be met:

- **Establish a strong, international, multi-disciplinary team.** We identified from the outset that for a project of this scale and magnitude to be successful, we would need to establish a strong team that could successfully work together for an extended period of time in a largely virtual collaborative mode. It was extremely important for the team to be comprised of international participants, to ensure that the views and perspectives of project management in different cultures and national contexts would be reflected from the perspective of the researcher, as well as ensuring a broad participation of international organizations as case studies. Finally, the team needed to be multi-disciplinary, drawing on a breadth of fields, disciplines and research perspectives in order to present a comprehensive and rigorous view of project management practices in their broadest possible sense.

- **Adopt an approach that addresses the problems of earlier studies.** In designing the research strategy for this project, careful note was made of efforts to demonstrate value–not just of project management, but in a range of fields, disciplines, and organizational functions. We carefully examined previous value studies to understand their strengths as well as their limitations, and to adopt an approach that would be both rigorous and defensible. The approach that resulted was a comprehensive, context-rich view of the manner in which project management has been implemented within organizations, the fit of that implementation with the context of the organization, and the value that is being received. In particular, the research was designed to take into consideration the contribution and interplay of these factors in order to develop generalizable theories of the various dimensions of value that project management is observed to deliver.

- **Define a cohesive and integrated research strategy that explores the overall phenomenon of project management.** The design of the study was intended to be holistic in nature, viewing how project management was situated in organizations as an overall whole. This was viewed as far preferable to attempting to infer value by aggregating separate and isolated activities and investigations. Because project management itself is an integrated activity, the impact of the whole must be understood in that context. This approach means identifying and evaluating the clusters of behavior and activity that collectively make up that whole as an overall organizational project management capability.

- **Design an integrated, multi-method design that develops common, credible, and defensible measures of tangible and intangible value.** It was recognized from the outset that value cannot be simply measured in dollar terms, and that an investigation of the value of project management must embrace an understanding of both tangible and intangible impacts. Both the methods and the measures were designed to support the identification of tangible and intangible understandings of value, integrating qualitative and quantitative techniques in a mixed-method approach that would be credible and defensible to the greatest number of audiences possible.

- **Leverage PMI's investment through matching funds and donations-in-kind from other institutions and organizations.** Even with the sizable initial funding provided by PMI, successful completion of this study was going to require the leverage of additional funds as well as donations-in-kind. This began with the nature of the study itself, which was conducted on a strictly volunteer basis. None of the researchers on this study, including the principal investigators, were paid for their time in conducting this research project. The research funds were dedicated to the expenses of conducting a research project of this scale. Every institution and organization involved in this study generously contributed through donations-in-kind associated with their time and effort in participating in this study.

Determining The Value Of Project Management

Overall, we are extremely comfortable stating unequivocally that project management delivers value to organizations. This has been amply demonstrated in this monograph, and is revisited and summarized in these conclusions. We are confident that in approaching this study we have accomplished what we originally set out to achieve:

- An international team of more than 48 researchers contributed their time and effort to this study, as members of the research team, as case-study investigators, and as members of our analysis teams. The project results reflect a broad range of organizations involved in a variety of different types of projects with different strategies, different ownership structures, different cultural contexts, and different objectives and approaches to their project management implementations. What has resulted is a broad cross-sectional view of project management as it is practiced around the world.

- The research study adopted a sound multi-method, multi-paradigm approach. The study was not strictly qualitative nor was it strictly quantitative. These paradigms were integrated in a fashion that led to a truly multi-method study. At times, the qualitative investigation and analysis influenced the quantitative investigation, and the quantitative results provided structure and guidance to the qualitative results. We have worked to address the challenges of previous studies, and have been able to present results that are statistically significant, qualitatively rigorous, relevant, and defensible.

- We have adopted a research approach that is cohesive and integrated. The strategy that was adopted does not look at project management through a single lens, nor does it adopt a specific model or structure. What has resulted is grounded in the organizations that were studied, exploring the full dimension of project management as it is practiced, providing a comprehensive view of the cultures in which it operates and a broad assessment of the values that were delivered. In all, comprehensive and informationally rich case studies of 65 organizations from around the world provide a powerful, comprehensive and integrated view of how projects are managed organizationally and the value that it delivers to these organizations.

- There is strong reliability and validity in the results both within and across different research paradigms. The findings and conclusions presented here have been evaluated through a significant number of approaches and research techniques and a variety of investigative lenses, as discussed and explored in detail. The level of reinforcement of results through different approaches has been particularly gratifying, and a rewarding confirmation that the results do triangulate from a number of perspectives. It has also been a pleasing confirmation of the appropriateness of the research strategy.

- Overall, more than US$380,000 of additional funds were leveraged over and above PMI's initial investment of US$1.2 million. As well, donations in kind of more than US$1.2 million have been secured through the volunteer investment of the full research team and the contributions of the case-study organizations.

Understanding Tangible Value

More than half of our case study organizations demonstrate tangible value being realized as a result of their project management implementation. The other slightly smaller group of organizations do not indicate any tangible value being realized.

Even more intriguing is that none of the organizations that should have been able to quantify the degree of tangible value that has been attained have actually formally done so. Those organizations that demonstrate tangible value are those that primarily deliver projects for customers (typically consulting and construction and engineering firms, but also departments and divisions that oversee infrastructure and construction projects). While they should be able to compile and demonstrate the magnitude of tangible benefits that have been realized, they do not.

Fundamentally, this creates a significant challenge in measuring one of the fundamental dimensions of value that this study started to explore at the outset: return on investment. Even where organizations could calculate return on investment because there are tangible benefits that could be quantified, they are not doing so. The underlying cost and benefit data that would be required is not being collected, and for these organizations the answer is not considered meaningful. Without some form of baseline and tracking of costs and benefits, it was not possible for us to construct an ROI profile for any of the organizations in retrospect. Only a very small handful of organizations could even attempt to quantify the benefits that they had received, and these quantifications were nothing more than anecdotal summaries of assumptions regarding savings and productivity improvements.

This resistance to calculating return on investment seems to arise from a number of different factors, including:

- A lack of interest in the answer. None of the organizations in the case studies presented in this research began their project management through a business case that promised some degree of return on investment. For most of these organizations, the project management implementation has emerged over time and continues to expand and change in response to environmental or business demands. Even identifying when the project management initiative began in many organizations is not possible. For many organizations, the idea of understanding what the return on investment would have been is information that does not particularly interest them. It is simply a necessary investment in organizational effectiveness.

- There appears to be, in some regards, a fear of accountability. The realization of savings and efficiency gains can also lead to expectations of cost reductions and the forced realization of benefits from operating budgets. As well, the idea of measurability in general appears to create a generalized concern regarding accountability that leads to organizations not choosing to establish formal measures.

- There is a perceived complexity to the measurement of ROI. While the theoretical principles of measuring ROI are relatively straightforward, there are a number of implications and a level of formality associated with measuring ROI that means for many organizations, there is little desire to do so.

- The cost in terms of time and effort to calculate ROI is often considered not being worth the effort. While the principles of ROI measurement may indeed be simple, the formal establishment of a measurement framework to do so is not trivial. The establishment of this formality, and the effort required to ensure consistency of adherence and use by their organizations, is often far greater an investment than many organizations choose to make for the perceived benefits of doing so. In other words, there is no ROI to be gained from measuring ROI.

One final and important comment about tangible benefits is that many organizations did report concrete tangible drivers for their implementations that excluded ROI. Reasons for this included establishing credibility in the marketplace, responding to regulatory pressures, or simply responding to the increasing numbers of projects or internal complexity in managing projects. In many instances, these were characterized as essential to being able to compete, to stay in business, or to be able to function within their marketplace. While ROI was typically not the focus of the implementation, other tangible underlying factors were often prominent in those organizations exhibiting tangible value.

Exploring Intangible Value

Most organizations demonstrate intangible value as a result of their project management implementations. As well, these dimensions of value were the most frequently cited as being important and significant by the case-study organizations.

Most of the executive quotations on the value of their project management implementations commented on intangible rather than tangible forms of value.

The delivery of intangible value encompasses a number of different dimensions, including:

- Improvements in decision-making

- Enhanced communications and collaboration

- Improvements in effective work cultures

- Alignment of approaches, terminology, and values within the organization

- Overall effectiveness of the organization and its management approach

- Improved transparency, clarity of structures, roles, and accountability.

As well as being the dimension of value that most organizations considered to be most important, this study also demonstrated that there is a correlation between the realization of intangible value and the maturity of the implementation. The majority of those organizations realizing intangible value were at a higher level of maturity.

As well, the greater interest in intangible value helps to reinforce the lack of interest in the measurement of return on investment in most organizations. Not only is intangible value the greatest value that is being realized, it is often for organizations what highlights the most important aspect of their implementations and the results that they desired and attained from it.

Understanding The Impacts Of Maturity

As was noted earlier, the assessment of project management maturity was not a conscious focus of this study, and there was no specific maturity model that was employed or adopted. What was also noted, however, was that maturity of different implementations can be inferred as a result of the comprehensiveness of the data that was collected. As well, for many organizations, improvements in maturity can be perceived as a value in itself, particularly where there is a significant emphasis on process outcomes.

What clearly emerged from this study is that value appears to increase in proportion to the maturity of the project management implementation that is encountered. In particular, greater levels of intangible value were reported in organizations that have a higher level of maturity.

Tangible value, however, was seen at all levels of maturity. There was certainly tangible value—and considerable amounts of value—that were observed by organizations at high levels of maturity. Tangible value, however, was demonstrated at all levels of maturity. Even organizations with very immature implementations–or ones that were established for largely cynical motives–were able to attain significant tangible value.

One key conclusion from this study, therefore, is that there appears to be a threshold of maturity that enables the realization of intangible value. Tangible value can be attained at almost any level of maturity, and is primarily a result of the nature of the organization and the delivery of customer projects. The attainment of intangible value requires a base level of capability and a reasonable level of robustness to be established for it to be realized. As well, continued increases in maturity of the project management implementation appear to lead to greater levels of intangible value.

Establishing The Role Of Culture

Another key finding emerging from this research study is the significant role of culture in determining both the project management implementation that is appropriate and the value that can be realized. As has been observed repeatedly in this study, the value that is attained is a result of not just context or implementation, but the intersection of both together. Context itself is not a determinant of value, and neither is implementation. As well, there are not as yet hard and fast rules that correlate context and implementation.

As the regressions demonstrated, similar implementations appear in the generation of different values and are implemented by organizations operating in quite different contexts. It is the contextual basis an organization begins with, and the value that they hope to realize, that together can determine the most appropriate implementation. The regression analyses reported in Chapter 9 provide an initial basis to guide this interpretation, helping organizations to understand what aspects were observed to have the greatest levels of influence both in contributing to the attainment of value as well as limiting it.

Differences in culture, however, are broad, and this breadth needs to be understood. One of the repeated observations within our research team was that we need to be careful about how we define and use the term "culture," because there are very different types of culture that are being observed and that have a meaningful impact within organizations.

In particular, there were three different types of culture that had a dominant influence on the results of this study:

- **National Culture.** National culture, at its broadest, represents the influences of economic, political, and social dimensions on how people and organizations operate. There were a broad number of influences that national culture had on organizational implementations, which were observed from a number of key perspectives:

o There were very different approaches to project management implementations that resulted from the values and norms present in different national cultures. This was exhibited in cultures that strongly embraced tradition and rules, for example, and that demonstrate very strong adherence to formalized process, and valuing of process for itself. Other national cultures with strong emphasis on individual values and overall quality of life emphasized cultural and leadership dimensions, and willingly made aspects of implementation optional, even where attainment of more consistent approaches was seen as an overall objective. Still other cultures embraced values of innovation and entrepreneurism, and as a result observed little compliance with processes and rules or acceptance of consistency.

o As a result of these differences in national culture, very significant differences were observed in what was being implemented, as well as in the value resulting from these implementations. As an example, full and traditional implementations of project management were seen both in mature and established industries, as well as in emerging economies where these implementations were required by either parent multinationals or external funding bodies. In the more established and mature industries, many organizations that were studied – while they have received value in the past– are now beginning to see circumstances where the continuing attainment of value is in question or, in fact, declining. In emerging cultures, however, while the implementations and their rationale were initially questioned and challenged, they are now being embraced and adhered to rigorously and being held up as not just organizational but, in fact, national sources of pride and accomplishment.

o Even how this study was approached demonstrated significant differences in national culture, reflected in organizational and individual attitudes. In China, for example, despite being approached by a researcher well known to the organization, one organization considered very carefully whether to participate before finally agreeing. Once the decision was made, however, every effort was expended to support the research project. An executive flew four hours to oversee interviews, 15 person-days of work were conducted to review project archives, and an interview subject participated in discussions on the same day that they were to host the International Olympic Committee for an inspection of a construction project for the Beijing Olympics. By contrast, numerous participants in North American organizations missed interview appointments, routinely checked their messaging pagers during meetings and would interrupt interviews to receive cell phone calls.

- **Organizational Culture.** Organizational culture also had a significant influence on case-study organizations. The values, norms, and structures of the organization were observed to have significant influences on both how projects were approached and overall how the practice of project management was viewed:

  o A significant organizational cultural difference that emerged was in an orientation toward process vs. results. A number of organizations, particularly those with a strategic emphasis on operational efficiency, place a great deal of emphasis on process and adherence to standards. As was observed in the analysis of value, a number of process dimensions that emerged focused on the appreciation of process, consistency, and efficiency as values in and of themselves. Other organizational cultures placed much greater emphasis on results, particularly those with more of a strategic innovation or customer-intimacy focus. These organizations valued the results associated with project management, particularly improvement in project results or the attainment of overall business outcomes, while at times being quite flexible – and sometimes even dismissive – of the need to embody a consistent process.

  o Attitudes towards project management also varied considerably in different organizational cultures. As was demonstrated in Chapter 9, a significant influence on the attainment of value is a product simply of having a positive attitude towards project management. In these contexts, organizations valued the roles that projects play, the influence of project management as a discipline, and the importance of the project manager role. By contrast, many organizations demonstrated quite low attitudes towards project management. As noted in the discussion about tangible and intangible value, many organizations with low attitudes towards project management still were able to realize tangible value. The attainment of intangible value, however, appears to by much more strongly correlated with creating and maintaining a more positive attitude toward project management throughout the organization.

- **Project Management Culture.** As well as the observations regarding organizational attitudes toward project management, there were also strongly observed project management cultures observed in case-study organizations that stood separately and distinctly from the organizations they existed within. Although influenced by organizational culture, there was an observed project management culture that could be understood and assessed independently:

o One of the key differentiators of project management culture observed within organizations was in how project management was viewed, and specifically how the role of project management was viewed. This perception tended to take one of two forms. In some organizations, project management was seen as primarily a tool for control, with a strong process emphasis and a rigorous emphasis on structure, control, and policing. By contrast, for many organizations, project management was viewed as a leadership discipline. Project managers were seen as organizational leaders, and significant emphasis was placed upon coaching and mentoring and the development of personal leadership abilities.

o A marked influence on project management culture was the presence of experienced project managers within the organization. As was noted in a number of the analyses, the role of seniority and experience has a significant role on many implementations, as well as the realization of value out of those implementations. While some organizations, particularly those in emerging cultures, were able to realize significant value from less experienced and skilled employees, for the most part there was a strong correlation between experience and ability of the project managers and the ultimate value that was received, although as noted this was particularly true where this expertise was developed and cultivated within the organization.

o Professionalization attitudes also had a strong influence on the perception of project management culture, and the degree to which organizations received value from their implementations. One of the key components that emerged in the component of *Positive project manager attitudes* was the degree to which project managers adopted and exhibited attitudes associated with professionalism: a commitment to their role, identification of improvement opportunities, contribution to continued process development, and commitments to ongoing personal development. As the overall influence of this component demonstrated, organizations that have employees who adopt more of the attitudes associated with professionalism typically observe greater impacts in intangible value, in both project results and the attainment of business outcomes.

Sustaining Project Management Value

Almost every organization that participated in a case study within this research project received some degree of value, whether tangible, intangible, or both, as a result of their project management implementation. For many of these organizations, the level of value that was realized was quite high. What was intriguing, however, and was explored in considerable detail in Chapter 8, was that many organizations whose project management implementations had delivered value had no assurance of this value being sustained. For a select few organizations, value was declining or, in fact, being destroyed.

There are a number of organizations in this study that appear to be at an "inflection point" in their implementations. A significant number of organizations that had realized value from their implementations were assessed at a value trend of 0, indicating that there was some question as to whether value would continue to grow or the organization would begin to see value decline. The cause of this varied, and included attitudes that perceived project management as being "done" and something that required no further investment, changes in the market or competitive conditions of the organization, changes in oversight and involvement by executives or parent organizations and loss of key resources that were originally responsible for the implementation.

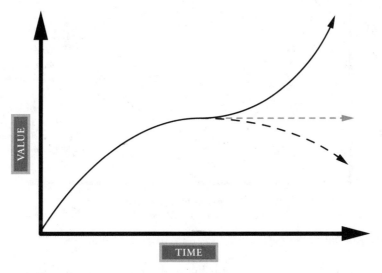

FIGURE 10-1—*Inflection point in project management value*

The idea of an inflection point is illustrated in Figure 10-1, which was contributed by Mimi Hurt and Janice Thomas in presenting the results of their case studies at Workshop 4. The diagram suggests that while implementations tend to realize value in the first stages of an implementation, its continued creation over time is in question. Implementations will reach a point where the value will plateau, and in some instances will decline. A key question that warrants further exploration and analysis for organizations is what will allow for the continued creation of value. Based upon some cases, it was suggested that a renewal and refinement of implementations occur in order to simplify, optimize, and enable continued sustainment of the implementation, but more data is needed to be able to support this inference.

Another observation was that while organizations demonstrate value today, and are actively investing in their project management, they are in fact destroying value. One example that was cited in Chapter 8 as being particularly illustrative of this was an organization that saw considerable value being created initially, but because of a change in leadership of the project management implementation–and a corresponding shift in strategic focus and emphasis of the project management implementation from a center of excellence to a delivery model–was seeing value decline. While there is an increasing effort on the part of this organization to improve its implementation and sustain the benefits it initially realized as well as creating new ones, the overall viability of the implementation is in question, and value is currently seen to be destroyed.

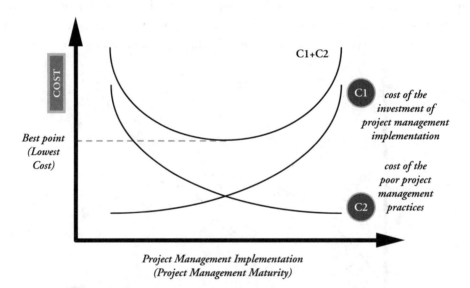

FIGURE 10-2—*Creating value and removing value destroyers*

The idea of the destruction of value is illustrated in Figure 10-2, a diagram borrowed from economics that was contributed during our fourth workshop by Shi Qian, one of the members of our research team from Tongji University in China. What it suggests is that there is a cost curve associated with project management implementations (C1), and a benefit curve associated with reduction in costs (losses) caused by poor project management practices (C2). At some point the two curves cross. At this point, the cost of improving project management is higher than the benefits to be realized from such improvements, as measured simply by cost reductions associated with poor practices. The U-shaped curve (C1 + C2) suggests that in the early stages of improving project management maturity, the cost of doing so is less than the cost to the organization of continuing to manage projects poorly. However at some point, continuing to invest in project management (and maturity) has a diminishing return on the gains from reducing losses due to poor project management, and in fact destroys value. Investing beyond this point is only rational and logical where some other benefits exist that warrant the additional investment. What this does serve to highlight is two key principles: There is a cost associated with bad practices, and the degree to which these costs diminish is proportional to the degree to which they are replaced with appropriate practices. Both of these points reinforce the idea of "fit," and ensuring the implementation of project management practices is appropriate and relevant to the organization.

One of the key conclusions that this observation supports, therefore, is that what is implemented – and what is sustained – must be carefully calibrated to the value that the organization is trying to attain. Not all implementations will provide value in any given organization simply because they delivered value elsewhere.

Sustaining Value – An Ongoing Focus

Building upon the thoughts and observations in the previous section, another conclusion highlighted by this study regards the focus that is required to sustain value. Sustaining value is not simply a product of making sure that the right implementation is in place for the value that an organization seeks to deliver. Where value is being sustained and is continuing to grow, there is ongoing focus on the project management implementation and ongoing improvement efforts are underway–even in organizations that have been investing in project management for over 20 years.

What this reinforces is that organizational project management implementations are rarely able to be completed and called finished. Organizations that stop focusing on attaining the value from their implementation, or feel that they are "done," stop demonstrating value. Equally importantly, the act of not enhancing value appears to, in fact, destroy value. In order to sustain the realization of value, there needs to be a continued emphasis on the use and improvement of the project management implementation.

One additional question that also needs to be asked, however, is on the nature of the value decline. What this study has demonstrated is that there are certainly case-study examples where the reported value of the implementation is declining, and there are many more where the continued sustainment of value is in question. What is unclear, and warrants further analysis, is whether this value is actually being lost, or whether organizations are perceiving a loss of value. To explore this point in more detail, it is helpful to revisit the idea of an inflection point as discussed in the previous section. At the outset of an implementation, as improvements are made, the perception of value increases is typically quite high. Once the implementation reaches a stage of familiarity, however, does the organization then risk losing value, or does it simply take for granted now the value that it has attained? In other words, does this familiarity, in essence, produce contempt? While it is not possible to gain further understanding of this from the data that has been collected, we believe that this is a fruitful path for additional investigation.

"Fit" As An Essential Determinant Of Value

From the outset, this study posited that the idea of "fit" was important: that the internal and external context of an organization would determine what implementation would be able to deliver value. In other words, fit measures the degree to which a project management implementation provides what an organization needs, based upon the context in which it operates and the value that it is trying to create.

What is clear from this analysis is that the value of project management implementations are fundamentally determined by the concept of "fit." Chapter 9 showed that contexts on their own are not determinants of value, and neither are implementations. This research study saw organizations create value even as organizations in a similar context and environment either lost value from their implementation or did not realize the same degree of value. We also saw organizations of very different context use the same implementations to create very different dimensions of value. Finally, we saw organizations use implementations that had been successful for other organizations they considered similar to themselves fail to realize the same degree of success within their own implementation. Fundamentally, the degree of value that organizations realize is determined by how well what is implemented meets the needs of the organization.

The measure of fit, however, is a problematic one. At the outset of this study, we attempted to infer fit from the degree of satisfaction and alignment that were being observed. What became clear very quickly, however, is that an aligned and consistent implementation does not necessarily deliver fit: organizations can very consistently apply something that doesn't work for them. The dangers of "best practices" and benchmarking are exactly those being highlighted here: organizations adopting the surface appearances of implementations that have worked for others, hoping that they will realize the same results, appear destined for disappointment.

While fit can be inferred by satisfaction, this is still simply an inference. Satisfaction is at best a proxy measure. Where a number of stakeholders from different perspectives all express a strong degree of satisfaction, the likelihood of fit being present is higher, but this is still a proxy for fit and not a measure of fit itself.

As was discussed in Chapter 8, we believe that the measure of fit is one that can only be derived from assessing other measures. To measure and assess fit, we first need to be able to understand what implementations result in what values for a given context. From that, we can assess the context of an organization, understand what value the organization was trying to create, and determine whether the implementation is appropriate in that context to deliver on the desired value. Until now, however, the necessary prerequisites for determining fit have not been present. We have not had sufficient statistically rigorous data to know with certainty which implementations create which dimensions of value for which implementations.

The results of this study pave the way for a more rigorous and defined means of measuring and assessing fit. What this research study has done is to comprehensively evaluate the contexts, implementations, and values received for a broad cross-section of organizations from around the world. Through the analysis presented here, we have been able to demonstrate that value is, in fact, the result of an appropriate implementation being deployed for a specific context. We have also been able to explore and infer what contexts and what implementations are associated with which specific value dimensions. The regressions that were presented in Chapter 9 lay the groundwork for being able to truly define fit, and define a promising basis for allowing organizations to determine what implementation is appropriate for them, given who they are as an organization and the objectives that they seek to maintain.

As discussed at the outset, fit is an essential dimension of assessing value. What we have demonstrated in this study is that fit is also the key determinant of creating value. Finally, we have begun the work of generating a theory of fit, which can be further explored and refined as this important research continues.

STUDY LIMITATIONS

While we believe that this study has made an important and positive contribution to the research and practical understandings of project management value, we also recognize that it–as does any research–has its limitations. Conducting research of this nature is extremely difficult and complex. Even with the efforts of a research team of this size, and as comprehensive a strategy as the one devised here, the results are of necessity bounded and constrained by their limitations and challenges. Particular limitations to be aware of are:

- **Small sample size.** This study is ultimately constrained by the number of organizations that participated in the research. The analysis of 65 organizations, while significant, is insufficient to reliably develop definitive quantitative conclusions from the analysis work that has been conducted. From the perspective of qualitative research, this would be considered a very large study, while from a quantitative one–by the measure of the number of organizations studied–it is a small one. The exploratory analysis presented here is extremely promising, and shows a good level of significance. At the same time, however, definitive conclusions require a much broader sample to be collected.

- **Different organizations, natures, and project types.** As well as the number of organizations, this study also involved an incredible diversity of organizations, with very different natures and project types. In any study that is trying to arrive at definitive conclusions, one wants to control the variables to the greatest degree possible. This study did the exact opposite. We deliberately incorporated a broad array of organizations in order to ensure as broad relevance as possible, and to compare and contrast organizations from a number of perspectives.

Combined with the number of organizations, this approach results in extremely rich exploratory analysis, but prevents the presentation of definitive assertions or conclusions for all categories in the data.

- **Complex data structures.** While the unit of analysis was the organization, the data that was collected and the sources of data collected were extremely diverse. Data was collected at the level of the organization, person, project, and economy. Observations were collected from executives, project managers, customers, team members, sponsors, suppliers, subcontractors and the researchers themselves. Integrating these multiple perspectives into a single view of the organization is, of necessity, extremely difficult to do, and while it allowed the research team to triangulate observations and confirm perceptions, it also led to an extremely complex process of analysis that resulted in raising as many new questions as there are conclusions being drawn.

- **Large data set.** Apart from the complexity of the data structures, the research study also produced an extremely large data set for analysis purposes. From a qualitative perspective, the amount of data collected is significant. From a quantitative perspective, the data set is immense. One of the principal objectives of quantitative analysis is to have a manageable level of dimensionality within the data. The number of variables, many of which measured and evaluated similar concepts from different perspectives, created significant challenges in reducing the dimensionality of the data to a level where meaningful analysis was possible. In doing so, the summarization that is necessitated in getting to statistically significant findings also results in reducing or eliminating the nuances that can be so valuable in making appropriate interpretations.

- **Confounding of cause and effect.** The case studies that are presented here represent a slice in time. Each case study was collected over a period of between one and six months, and provides a snapshot of what has been implemented, the context of the organization and the value the organization is receiving. The value that results—or does not result—is interpreted based upon the context and the implementation. What is not always clear, however, is whether what is implemented was done to try and create the observed value, or because the desired value was not being realized. If project performance was poor, and therefore training is increased, should the presence of training efforts be interpreted as a means of improving project performance, or did the presence of training mean that project performance is low? While trying to infer cause and effect is a challenge to any research, it is equally a challenge in this study. Introducing additional data coded from the case-study reports in the future may allow us to evaluate the stage and timing of the implementation in ways that will allow us to get closer to understanding the direction of the causality.

- **A broad array of interpretations.** One of the strengths of this project was the size and diversity of the team, but it was also one of its challenges. With a team of 48 researchers working around the world, it was extremely difficult to maintain a consistent and aligned interpretation of the data collection instruments and a consistent level of standardization in the reporting of case study results. As a result, not all instruments were collected in the same way and not all findings were reported in a consistent fashion, necessitating numerous follow-ups with the researchers – and sometimes within the case-study organizations themselves–as the analysis was conducted.

One thing that is important to note, however, is that many of the limitations discussed above are also the strengths of the study, and were a conscious part of the design of the study. The structure of the study, the nature of the data collected, and the number of case-study organizations targeted were all conscious decisions that were in part made to address the weaknesses and limitations of earlier studies. That they can represent limitations here is perhaps inevitable, but they are also the sources of strength in this study. As an example, the principle of triangulation of data sources allowed a much richer picture of the organization to emerge, and allowed researchers to verify observed phenomenon, even as it led to greater degrees of complexity in conducting the quantitative analysis on the data. As another example, the number of case-study teams led to inevitable differences in interpretation of some of the data collection instruments. At the same time, we had far fewer interpretation differences in the data we are using than we would if we were using self-reported data from these 65 organizations. While it is important to understand the limitations of any study, it is equally important to understand the rationale for why these initial assumptions and strategies were adopted.

FUTURE RESEARCH

This research project has been long and involved for everyone that was a part of it. The project engaged 48 primary research participants, 65 organizations, 18 case-study team leads, qualitative and quantitative analysis teams, and numerous additional case-study researchers over a period of more than four years. While what has been produced is significant, and represents a considerable contribution to the project management literature, it is only the start of an ongoing program of research that now becomes possible. Some of the additional research that underpins our findings but could not be reported in detail in this monograph will be published soon in a dedicated edition of the *Project Management Journal.*

Broadly, we see three major streams of work stemming from the research that has been presented here:

- **Testing of Exploratory Theories.** What this monograph has done is to present the research that was conducted, and the analysis and conclusions that emerged from the study. What these represent are a number of exploratory theories regarding the value of project management, and particularly the concept of fit: the degree to which what is implemented meets the needs of an organization given its environment and its objectives. To be able to prove out the exploratory theories that have been developed here requires a much larger and more focused data collection effort. It is the intention of the researchers to expand the data collection beyond the 65 organizations reported here. This will involve large-scale data collection of ideally several hundred organizations from around the world. Likely conducted online and through self-reported data, this would involve organizations conducting and reporting using a focused data collection strategy that would enable the broad-based analysis required to support appropriate theory testing.

- **Additional Analysis on the Existing Data Set.** This research has generated one of the largest and most complex data sets in the field of project management research. More than a dozen instruments were used to collect organization information against 256 questions and more than 2,500 discrete variables. Each question posed could itself become the basis of at least one – and often more than one – comprehensive research paper, and would represent a significant line of inquiry that could continue to advance the understanding of project management over an extended period of time. Continuing this research effort will allow exploration of a number of significant and meaningful topics, including, but not limited to, those of:

    o Cultural impacts (national, organizational, and project management) on value

    o The role of professional attitudes in project management maturity and generating value

    o Influences of training, project management support structures, and models on value delivery

    o Differences and similarities across industries and types of projects

    o Strategies for effectively managing project management implementations

    o Exploring the differences between "theories in use" and espoused theories of project management

- **Exploration of Additional Topics.** Over and above the additional research that is enabled from the current data set, there are a number of additional topics that have been identified as a result of questions raised within this research. While the current dataset would be helpful in exploring and generating early theories regarding these topics, appropriately addressing them would require still further investigation, data collection, and analysis. Potential topics of exploration include:

  o An understanding of the strategies and approaches that allow project management–and project management value–to be sustainable.

  o An exploration of the causes and drivers of the destruction of project management value.

  o Investigating how to better align the expectations of executive management and project management.

  o Investigating the perception and reality of declines in value.

Overall, this research effort, while substantial, has really only just begun. The potential reach and influence of this study is potentially significant for the field of project management, and for management research as a whole. What has begun with this study has the potential to drive and to influence a range of investigations in the project management research field for many years to come. We look forward to contributing to what is certain to be an exciting and productive period of research in the coming years.

Appendix A
Case Study Summary

Organization:		Attributes:
Name: 17		Region: Europe
Entity: Group IT		Country: DENMARK
		Industry: Financial

DESCRIPTION:

Based in Denmark and operating multi-nationally from Copenhagen this organization carries out work in the financial sector. The Group IT is responsible for IT projects, undertaking mainly internally driven project work.

The organization has a widely held ownership structure and operates within a moderately competitive environment. As the largest bank in Scandinavia, this organization has the largest market share and is growing faster than its main competitor. The predominant culture in this organization is cautious and customer focused.

Project management has been a part of this organization since 1996 and there is a maturity of project management in the organization classified at 2 of 3 for this research. The most recent project management improvement implemented by this organization from 2000 to 2007 was a project management model, PM4U. The implementation was to replace a formal control model (initiated in 2000) that facilitated cross-national projects but that had not encouraged suitable project leadership. The current project management implementation is thought to be well suited for this organization at this time. PM4U is mandatory on larger projects. A project model for software development is also being used by the organization but it is not coordinated with PM4U. A respected view of project management exists within the organization.

The perceived value trend for the organization is positive demonstrating few tangible, but definite intangible, benefits.

Case 17 experienced value benefits:

Tangible	*Intangible*
• Increased Customer Share	• Attainment of Strategic Objectives
	• More Effective Human Resources
	• Staff Retention
	• Improved Reputation
	• Improved Corporate Culture

Organization:		Attributes:
Name: 18 Entity: Construction Division		Region: Europe Country: NORWAY Industry: Government — Transport

DESCRIPTION:

Based in Norway and operating nationally this organization carries out work in the government transport sector. The construction division is responsible for construction projects, undertaking mainly product-driven project work.

The organization has a single (government) ownership structure and operates within a moderately competitive environment. Although there is no formal competition for this organization, being a government institution, there is close scrutiny from media and politicians that puts pressure on project management to be successful and compete with similar private-sector organizations. The organization has a project-based organizational matrix. The predominant culture in this organization is investor focused.

Project management has been a part of this organization since the 1960s and there is a maturity of project management in the organization classified at 2 of 3 for this research. The most recent project management improvement implemented by the organization, in 2006, was a Project Management School and the Project Model (a standardized stage-gate project model). The implementation was put in place to ensure consistency across methods and maintain suitable skills for project management employees. Many of the organization's projects do not have the same project management staff throughout; they are very long, quite diverse, and of high interest to many stakeholder groups. The current project management implementation is thought to be well suited for the organization at this time by keeping projects on budget and proceeding as planned. A cooperative view of project management exists within the organization.

The perceived value trend for the organization is positive demonstrating no tangible, but considerable intangible, benefits.

Case 18 experienced value benefits:

Tangible	*Intangible*
	• Greater Social Good
	• More Effective Human Resources
	• Improved Reputation
	• Improved Corporate Culture

	Organization:	Attributes:
	Name: 19 Entity: National Part of the International Organization	Region: Europe Country: NORWAY Industry: Communications

DESCRIPTION:

Based in Norway and operating internationally this organization carries out work in the communications sector. The national part of the international organization is responsible for product development projects, undertaking mainly, although not exclusively, product-driven project work.

The organization has a widely held ownership structure with the government still owning a substantial part. It operates within a very highly competitive environment. The organization is one of the fastest growing providers of mobile communications worldwide; it is 7th largest in the world at the time of this research. The predominant culture in this organization is one of ambitious growth and investor focus.

Project management has been a part of the organization since 2000 and there is a maturity of project management in the organization classified at 1.5 of 3 for this research. The most recent project management improvement implemented by this organization was a Project Management School and Project Model. The implementation was put in place primarily to improve selection and management of strategic projects. The current project management implementation is thought to be well suited for the organization at this time; there is strong understanding for those involved in project management but no broad project management understanding and culture within the wider organization. A cooperative view of project management exists within the organization.

The perceived value trend for the organization is positive demonstrating no tangible, but definite intangible, benefits.

Case 19 experienced value benefits:

Tangible	*Intangible*
	• **Attainment of Strategic Objectives**
	• **More Effective Human Resources**
	• **Improved Overall Management**
	• **Improved Corporate Culture**

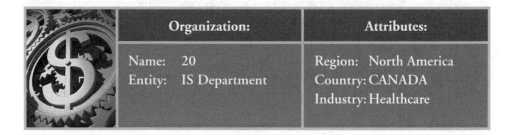

Organization:		Attributes:
Name: 20		Region: North America
Entity: IS Department		Country: CANADA
		Industry: Healthcare

DESCRIPTION:

Based in Canada and operating regionally in one province this organization carries out work in the healthcare sector. The IS department is responsible for IT projects, undertaking mainly, although not exclusively, internally driven project work.

The organization has a state ownership structure and operates within a medium competitive environment. The department has no competition in itself as it provides IT/IS services internally to the organization. The predominant culture in the organization is customer focused.

Project management has been a part of the organization since 2004 and there is a maturity of project management in this organization classified at 2 of 3 for this research. The most recent project management improvement implemented by the organization, in 2006, was a Project Management office (PMO). The implementation was put in place to implement a comprehensive project management implementation and formalize project reporting and delivery. The PMO also provides a centre of excellence in project management and supports/coaches project managers. The current project management implementation is thought to be well suited for the organization at this time; aligned use of practices are reported and demonstrated on a high level. Projects adhere well to guidelines and consistently deliver on objectives as well as on schedule; less so on outcomes and on budget. This is clearly perceived as an improvement in the organization's project management implementation. The implementation of the PMO is consistently perceived as a crucial and valuable step of project management implementation. A cooperative view of project management exists within the organization.

The perceived value trend for the organization is positive demonstrating no tangible, but considerable intangible, benefits.

Case 20 experienced value benefits:

Tangible	Intangible
	• Attainment of Strategic Objectives
	• Improved Quality of Life
	• More Effective Human Resources
	• Improved Reputation

Organization:		Attributes:	
Name:	21	Region:	Europe
Entity:	Construction Supervision Division	Country:	NORWAY
		Industry:	Government

DESCRIPTION:

Based in Norway and operating nationally this organization carries out work in the government sector. The construction supervision division is responsible for consulting and assisting in civil engineering projects, undertaking mainly product-driven project work.

The organization has a state ownership structure and operates within a highly competitive environment. The organization, although having exclusive rights to the construction of public buildings, contracts out the construction work. Close attention is paid to the projects it manages by the public and media. The predominant culture in the organization is stakeholder focused.

Project management has a well established history in this organization and there is a maturity of project management in this organization classified at 2.5 of 3 for this research. The most recent project management improvement implemented by this organization, in 2006, was a Project Management School and Project Model. The implementation was put in place to improve the project management capability of the organization, particularly in educating a wide range of employees in project management.

In some cases this education has been awarded academic credit. The current project management implementation is thought to be well suited for the organization at this time. A cooperative view of project management exists within the organization.

The perceived value trend for the organization is neutral demonstrating no tangible, but definite intangible, benefits. The neutral value trend results from somewhat ambiguous result statements in the organization coming from different levels and generations of employees.

Case 21 experienced value benefits:

Tangible	*Intangible*
	• **Attainment of Strategic Objectives**
	• **Greater Social Good**
	• **More Effective Human Resources**
	• **Staff Retention**
	• **Improved Overall Management**
	• **Improved Corporate Culture**

Organization:		Attributes:	
Name:	22	Region:	Asia
Entity:	Whole	Country:	CHINA
	Organization	Industry:	Construction management

DESCRIPTION:

Based in China and operating locally from Shanghai this organization carries out work in the construction management sector. The whole organization is responsible for construction projects, undertaking mainly customer-driven project work.

The organization has a state ownership structure and operates within a medium competitive environment. There are two main competitors in this organization's market; all competitors focus on mega-municipal infrastructure projects and differentiate on type of infrastructure building constructed. The organization has about a third of the market share and despite its competitive advantages it faces high pressure from emerging competitors. The predominant culture in the organization is customer and investor focused.

Project management has been a part of this organization since 1988 and there is a maturity of project management in this organization classified at 2 of 3 for this research.

The most recent project management improvement implemented by the organization, in 2006, was self-developed software for pre-period project management. This software offers detailed instructions about early stage procedures and methods. The implementation was put in place to improve project management capability by improving project implementation efficiencies and the realization of project goals. The current project management implementation is thought to be partly appropriate for the organization at this time; with internal discrepancy as to whether rules and regulations related to the construction industry provided the most helpful instruction for the project management implementation, or whether the intra-organizational templates and files about project management procedure, e.g., the Project Charter and Standard Implementation Manual, etc., are the most important tools. A strong cooperative project management culture exists throughout the organization with no encouragement for innovation.

The perceived value trend for the organization is positive demonstrating definite tangible and definite intangible benefits.

Case 22 experienced value benefits:

Tangible	*Intangible*
• **Cost Savings**	• **Attainment of Strategic Objectives**
• **Revenue Increases**	• **Greater Social Good**
• **Customer Retention**	• **More Effective Human Resources**
• **Greater Market Share**	• **Improved Reputation**
	• **Improved Regulatory Compliance**

Organization:		Attributes:
Name: 23		Region: Asia
Entity: IT Business Unit		Country: CHINA
		Industry: IT

DESCRIPTION:

Based in China and operating nationally from Shanghai this organization carries out work in the IT sector. The IT Business Unit is responsible for IT projects, undertaking mainly customer-driven project work.

The organization has a state ownership structure and operates within a very highly competitive environment. The organization is a pioneer (10 years ago this organization was a startup) and leading provider for software and financial processing solutions in China. It does not have any strong competitors at this time. The predominant culture in the organization is entrepreneurial, customer and investor focused; success and failure are both tolerated.

Project management has been a part of this organization since 1999 and there is a maturity of project management in this organization classified at 2 of 3 for this research. The most recent project management improvement implemented by this organization, in 2004, was CMM3 certification and a QA Department. The implementation was put in place to improve customer satisfaction in terms of quality of deliverables and to facilitate less experienced project managers in the control of projects within budget and schedule. The current project management implementation is thought to be well suited for the organization at this time; as a project-based organization almost every employee in the company was involved in the project management improvement. A respected view of project management exists within the organization.

The perceived value trend for the organization is positive demonstrating definite tangible and definite intangible benefits.

Case 23 experienced value benefits:

Tangible	*Intangible*
• Customer Retention	• Greater Social Good
• Increased Customer Share	• More Effective Human Resources
	• Improved Corporate Culture

Organization:		Attributes:
Name:	24	Region: Asia
Entity:	R&D Business Unit	Country: CHINA
		Industry: Telecommunications

DESCRIPTION:

Based in China and operating nationally this organization carries out work in the telecommunications sector. The R&D Business Unit is responsible for R&D projects, undertaking mainly customer-driven project work.

The organization has a partnership (dual owners) ownership structure and operates within a very highly competitive environment. The organization operates in an unstable climate of constant reorganization, mergers, and reacquisitions. Innovation is not encouraged. The market place in this sector is extremely competitive and the organization is the leading company in China. Its main competitor is an international organization. The predominant culture in the organization is customer and investor focused.

Project management has been a part of this organization since 2002 and there is a maturity of project management in this organization classified at 2 of 3 for this research. The most recent project management improvement implemented by the organization, in 2002, was a project management system introduced directly from the foreign parent organization. The implementation was put in place because of intensified competition and the complexity of projects undertaken in the organization. The current project management implementation is thought to be well suited for project management organization at this time. This organization makes great efforts on improving its project management as it regards project management to be very important to its success. A respected view of project management exists within the organization.

The perceived value trend for the organization is neutral reflecting internal desire for greater formalization and some differences in satisfaction levels between project managers and senior management. The organization is demonstrating definite tangible and definite intangible benefits.

Case 24 experienced value benefits:

Tangible	*Intangible*
• Reduced Write-offs and Rework	• More Effective Human Resources
	• Improved Overall Management
	• Improved Corporate Culture
	• Improved Regulatory Compliance

Organization:		Attributes:
Name: 25 Entity: Sales Department		Region: Europe Country: DENMARK Industry: IT

DESCRIPTION:

Based in Denmark and operating nationally from Copenhagen in the public-sector this organization carries out IT work. The sales department is responsible for IT projects, undertaking mainly customer-driven project work.

This organization has a municipal ownership structure and operates within a medium competitive environment. This organization is the largest IT public-sector provider in Denmark with 60% of the market share. It has several international competitors, one of which it also partners. Competition in this sector is expected to increase. The predominant culture in this organization is innovative and competitive.

Project management has been a part of this organization since 1980 and there is a maturity of project management in this organization classified at 2 of 3 for this research. The most recent project management improvement implemented by the organization, between 2004 to 2007, was development of a new project management model, allowing for multiple project programs for customers, A common frame of reference has been implemented—a uniform approach to the processes, methods, instruments, attitudes, and behavior for managing projects. The implementation was put in place to cope with the challenges of managing a program of projects. The current project management implementation is thought to be well suited for the organization at this time; common frame of reference, knowledge sharing, high quality, customer satisfaction, etc. One of this organization's project managers was awarded "Project Manager of the Year" in 2007. A respected view of project management exists within the organization although the attitude is more combative to recent change.

The perceived value trend for the organization is strongly positive demonstrating definite tangible and definite intangible benefits.

Case 25 experienced value benefits:

Tangible	*Intangible*
• Reduced Write-offs and Rework	• Improved Competitiveness
	• Attainment of Strategic Objectives
	• New Product/Service Streams
	• More Effective Human Resources
	• Improved Reputation
	• Improved Overall Management
	• Improved Corporate Culture

Organization:		Attributes:	
Name:	26	Region:	Europe
Entity:	Odense Regional Site	Country:	DENMARK
		Industry:	Engineering

DESCRIPTION:

Based in Denmark and operating nationally this organization carries out work in the engineering sector. The Odense Regional Site is responsible for consulting projects, undertaking mainly customer-driven project work.

The organization has a narrowly held ownership structure and operates within a medium competitive environment. The organization has one main and one smaller competitor; it holds a 15-20% market share and pursues rapid growth and excellence in its services. The predominant culture in the organization is one of rapid growth and is competitive.

Project management has been a part of the organization since 2000 (they have managed projects since 1945) and there is a maturity of project management in the organization classified at 1.5 of 3 for this research. The most recent project management improvement implemented by the organization, in 2007, was a series of seminars intended to develop competence in projects that give profit and customer satisfaction. The implementation was put in place to disseminate and anchor the project management implementations, seven best practices in the organization, and to improve the organization's project budget bottom line by 2%. The current project management implementation is thought to be well suited for the organization at this time; promoting competitive business, projects are the organization's business and project management is essential. Project management is driven by best practices, which in turn drives quality. A cooperative view of project management exists within the organization.

The perceived value trend for the organization is neutral as the results of this most recent implementation have yet to be realized. At the time of this research, the organization is currently demonstrating moderate tangible and definite intangible benefits.

Case 26 experienced value benefits:

Tangible	*Intangible*
• Customer Retention	• Improved Competitiveness
	• Attainment of Strategic Objectives
	• More Effective Human Resources
	• Staff Retention
	• Improved Reputation
	• Improved Corporate Culture

Organization:		Attributes:
Name: 27 Entity: IT Subsidiary		Region: Europe Country: GERMANY Industry: Financial

DESCRIPTION:

Based in Germany and operating nationally this organization carries out work in the financial sector. The IT Subsidiary is responsible for IT projects, undertaking mainly product-driven project work.

The organization has a state ownership structure and operates within a very highly competitive environment. Product leadership and market dominance are important to the organization. The predominant culture in the organization is innovative and competitive.

Project management has been a part of this organization since 2001 and there is a maturity of project management in the organization classified at 1.5 of 3 for this research. The most recent project management improvement implemented by this organization, in 2002, was a project management support group. The implementation was put in place to improve the benefits and reduce the costs of IT-related projects with the project management support group serving as a centre of excellence promoting the methodology and providing support. The major objectives of the project management implementation were to increase transparency, particularly when coordinating and working on multiple projects. The current project management implementation is thought to be well suited for the organization at this time; projects and project management is perceived to be key to the organization's strategic success—roughly

50% of the employees work effort is put into project work. The organization can be characterized as primarily innovative, competitive, and customer focused. A respected view of project management exists within the organization.

The perceived value trend for the organization is positive demonstrating moderate tangible and definite intangible benefits.

Case 27 experienced value benefits:

Tangible	*Intangible*
• **Greater Market Share**	• **Attainment of Strategic Objectives**
• **Reduced Write-offs and Rework**	• **More Effective Human Resources**
	• **Improved Reputation**
	• **Improved Corporate Culture**

	Organization:	Attributes:
	Name: 28	Region: Europe
	Entity: Local Authority Department for Construction	Country: SERBIA
		Industry: Government/Local Authority

DESCRIPTION:

Based in Serbia and operating locally in the town of Topola this organization carries out work in the government/local authority sector. This Local Authority Department is responsible for construction projects, undertaking mainly product-driven project work.

The organization has a state ownership structure and operates within a moderately competitive environment. As a public-sector organization it is in competition with other public-sector organizations for resources and (political) decision-making. It competes for international development funds. The predominant culture in the organization is customer focused.

Project management has been a part of this organization since 2001 and there is a maturity of project management in the organization classified at 1.5 of 3 for this research. The most recent project management improvement implemented by the organization, between 2001 and 2007, was a 12-stage PLC-based Project and Program Methodology. The implementation was put in place to facilitate the acquisition of international development funds and the delivery of agreed project objectives. The current project management implementation is thought to be partly appropriate for the organization at this time; the process of reflection, both individual and collective, is seen as important in project management development and implementation. The organization recognizes key perceived critical success factors in project work and the successful management of projects lies in good, integrated team work, frequent meetings, regular tracking of project realization, and innovative problem solving. A cooperative view of project management exists within the organization.

The perceived value trend for the organization is neutral demonstrating few tangible but definite intangible benefits. The neutral trend occurs as project management was implemented to meet external priorities and there appears to be resistance in the organization to the level of implemented formality.

Case 28 experienced value benefits:

Tangible	*Intangible*
• Cost Savings	• **Attainment of Strategic Objectives**
	• **More Effective Human Resources**
	• **Improved Reputation**
	• **Improved Corporate Culture**
	• **Improved Regulatory Compliance**

Organization:		Attributes:
Name: 29		Region: North America
Entity: IT Division		Country: CANADA
		Industry: Government

DESCRIPTION:

Based in Canada and operating nationally this organization carries out work in the government sector. The IT Division is responsible for IT projects, undertaking mainly customer and internally driven project work.

The organization has a state ownership structure and operates within a very highly competitive environment. The predominant culture in the organization is conservative, risk averse, and cautious.

Project management has been a part of the organization since 2001 and there is a maturity of project management in the organization classified at 1.5 of 3 for this research. The most recent project management improvement implemented by the organization, in 2001, was a PMO. The implementation was put in place to achieve better alignment of departmental resources in support of business objectives and program delivery. The current project management implementation is thought to be well suited for the organization at this time; the PMO has consistently been discussed as a crucial and valuable step within this project management implementation. A cooperative view of project management exists within the organization.

The perceived value trend for the organization is positive demonstrating no tangible but definite intangible benefits.

Case 29 experienced value benefits:

Tangible	*Intangible*
	• **Attainment of Strategic Objectives**
	• **Greater Social Good**
	• **More Effective Human Resources**
	• **Improved Overall Management**
	• **Improved Corporate Culture**

Organization:		Attributes:
Name:	30	Region: North America
Entity:	Engineering and Operations Unit	Country: CANADA
		Industry: Energy

DESCRIPTION:

Based in Canada and operating nationally this organization carries out work in the energy sector. The Engineering and Operations Unit is responsible for engineering projects, undertaking mainly product-driven project work.

The organization has a widely held ownership structure and operates within a moderately competitive environment. The predominant culture in the organization is competitive, entrepreneurial, and customer focused with a background of cautious and risk averse behaviors. The organization has gone through various recent mergers and acquisitions and is concerned with integrating various organizational cultures.

Project management has been a part of the organization since 2001 and there is a maturity of project management in the organization classified at 2 of 3 for this research. The most recent project management improvement implemented by the organization, in 2006, was based on the PMBOK®. The implementation was put in place in response to an increasing number of complex projects and aimed to improve the transparency of project information and raise the level of success in business case realization. The current project management implementation is thought to be well suited for the organization at this time; improvements in project transparency, particularly in the early phases, enable the level of success in business case realization through projects to be raised. A cooperative view of project management exists within the organization.

The perceived value trend for this organization is neutral as it is currently demonstrating no tangible and no intangible benefits reported in the case study.

Organization:		Attributes:
Name:	31	Region: Europe
Entity:	Whole	Country: SERBIA
	Organization	Industry: Consultancy

DESCRIPTION:

Based in Serbia and operating locally in Belgrade this organization carries out work in the consultancy sector. The whole organization is responsible for construction projects, undertaking mainly customer-driven project work.

The organization is private and family owned and operates within a medium competitive environment. Local competition is low in this sector as demand is substantially greater than supply. All competitors provide similar services. The predominant culture in this organization is investor focused.

Project management is not a fundamental part of the organization but it has been present since 2000. There is no belief in project management in the organization. It is implemented project management only because regulations say it must; however, the regulatory consultancy package has value as a sales stream. Consequently, there is a low maturity of project management in the organization classified at 1 of 3 for this research. The most recent project management improvement implemented by the organization, in 2006, was improving project management capacities by sending staff to seminars. The implementation was put in place because compliance with FIDIC international standards is required by some of its clients and funding institutions and the provision of project management is a lucrative revenue stream for the organization. The current project management implementation is thought to be well suited for this organization at this time. A dismissive view of project management exists within the organization.

The perceived value trend for the organization is neutral demonstrating moderate tangible but few intangible benefits.

Case 31 experienced value benefits:

Tangible	*Intangible*
• Revenue Increases	• Improved Competitiveness
	• New Product/Service Streams

Organization:	Attributes:
Name: 32 Entity: Whole Organization	Region: Europe Country: LITHUANIA Industry: Security

Description:

Based in Lithuania and operating regionally this organization carries out work in the security sector. The whole organization is responsible for construction projects, undertaking mainly customer and internally driven project work.

The organization has a widely held ownership structure and operates within a very highly competitive environment. Its market is developed and highly competitive with more than 50 companies providing the same services as this organization. The organization is one of the biggest and most rapidly developing. The predominant culture in the organization is competitive and customer focused.

Project management has been a part of this organization since 2004 and there is a maturity of project management in the organization classified at 1.5 of 3 for this research. The most recent project management improvement implemented by the organization, from 2004 to 2007, was the ISO project management standard. The implementation was put in place to ensure higher effectiveness of project management approaches, to reduce project duration, and to fit with market needs. The current project management implementation is thought to be partly appropriate for the organization at this time; management considers project management works for them (satisfaction, gain in time) and for the company, and they feel it from the outcomes of the projects and financial results of the company. A cooperative to dismissive view of project management exists within the organization.

The perceived value trend for this organization is neutral. It was implemented for external reasons, and is demonstrating no tangible but definite intangible benefits.

Case 32 experienced value benefits:

Tangible	*Intangible*
	• **Attainment of Strategic Objectives**
	• **Improved Overall Management**
	• **Improved Corporate Culture**

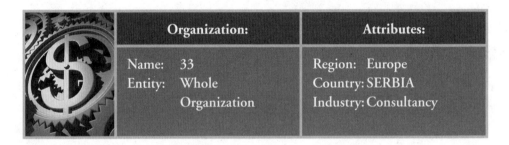

Organization:		Attributes:
Name: 33		Region: Europe
Entity: Whole Organization		Country: SERBIA
		Industry: Consultancy

DESCRIPTION:

Based in Serbia and operating locally in Belgrade this organization carries out work in the consultancy sector. The whole organization is responsible for construction management training projects, undertaking mainly customer and internally driven project work.

The organization has a private ownership structure and operates within a medium competitive environment. Local competition is low in this sector as demand is substantially greater than supply. All competitors provide similar services. The predominant culture in the organization is innovative, entrepreneurial, and customer focused.

Project management has been a part of the organization since 2001 and there is a maturity of project management in this organization classified at 1.5 of 3 for this research. The most recent project management improvement implemented by this organization, in 2007, was new software for project communication. The implementation was put in place to improve the transparency of project information and allow project managers and project teams to respond creatively to customers' needs. The current project management implementation is thought to be well suited for the organization at this time. Project management is considered as a pillar of the company culture; project orientation and management of projects is customized to local culture and relies on world-wide best practice recommendations. Overall, the company prides itself with a high level of customer satisfaction and a significant "fit" perceived between project management practices, company strategy, and customer focus. A respected view of project management exists within this organization.

The perceived value trend for the organization is positive demonstrating definite tangible and definite intangible benefits.

Case 33 experienced value benefits:

Tangible	*Intangible*
• Revenue Increases	• Attainment of Strategic Objectives
• Customer Retention	• New Product/Service Streams
	• More Effective Human Resources
	• Improved Corporate Culture

	Organization:		Attributes:
	Name: 34		Region: Europe
	Entity: Organization Wide		Country: UK
			Industry: Education

DESCRIPTION:

Based in the UK and operating nationally and internationally this organization carries out work in the education sector. This case considered strategic change projects, undertaking mainly internally driven project work; however, the organization as a whole does also undertake customer-driven projects.

The organization operates within a highly competitive environment. Competition in this sector is also complex, based on a number of factors such as price, resource, quality, and reputation. The predominant culture in this organization is innovative, customer, and stakeholder focused.

Project management has been a part of the organization since the 1990s and there is a maturity of project management in this organization classified at 1.5 of 3 for this research. The most recent project management improvement implemented by this organization, in 2006, was to implement best-practice project management procedures known as PRINCE2. The implementation was put in place to facilitate formal control, visibility, and promotion of a series of interlinked projects. The current project management implementation is thought to be only partly appropriate for this organization at this time; customer satisfaction and alignment of project business cases with the organization's strategy is appropriate. However, a combative view of project management exists within the organization.

The perceived value trend for the organization is neutral demonstrating no tangible but moderate intangible benefits.

Case 34 experienced value benefits:

Tangible	*Intangible*
	• Attainment of Strategic Objectives
	• Improved Overall Management
	• Improved Corporate Culture

Organization:		Attributes:
Name:	35	Region: Asia
Entity:	Whole	Country: CHINA
	Organization	Industry: Construction

DESCRIPTION:

Based in China and operating from Beijing nationally this organization carries out work in the construction sector. The whole organization is responsible for construction projects, undertaking mainly customer-driven project work.

The organization has a state ownership structure and operates within a highly competitive environment. It is in the top 20 of China's largest construction organizations. Competition in this sector is fierce, in a well-regulated environment, and it expects decreasing business margins. The predominant culture in the organization is customer and investor focused.

Project management has been a part of the organization since the mid 1990s and there is a maturity of project management in this organization classified at 3 of 3 for this research. This organization employs a heavy project management implementation. The most recent project management improvement implemented by the organization, in 2006, was a lessons learned case book publication and human resource quality and safety initiative. The implementation was put in place originally to comply with government regulations and most recently to improve employee and organization project management capability. The current project management implementation is thought to be well suited for the organization at this time; its capability matches its customer, subcontractor, and supplier expectations. A respected view of project management exists within the organization.

The perceived value trend for the organization is strongly positive demonstrating no tangible and definite intangible benefits.

Case 35 experienced value benefits:

Tangible	*Intangible*
	• **Improved Competitiveness**
	• **Improved Quality of Life**
	• **More Effective Human Resources**
	• **Improved Reputation**
	• **Improved Overall Management**
	• **Improved Corporate Culture**
	• **Improved Regulatory Compliance**

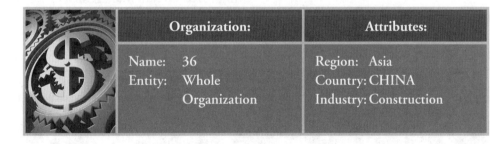

Organization:		Attributes:
Name: 36		Region: Asia
Entity: Whole		Country: CHINA
Organization		Industry: Construction

DESCRIPTION:

Based in China and operating from Beijing regionally this organization carries out work in the construction sector. The whole organization is responsible for design projects, undertaking mainly customer-driven project work.

The organization has a state ownership structure and operates within a very highly competitive environment, and is ready to accept lower profit margins for projects as necessary. The predominant culture in this organization is investor focused.

Project management has been a part of the organization since 2001 and there is a maturity of project management in this organization classified at 2.5 of 3 for this research. This organization has a light project management implementation. The most recent project management improvement implemented by this organization, from 2002 to 2005, was to compile a full set of project management standards/processes/templates for ISO certification. The implementation was put in place to establish and standardize the organization's management system and provide training for new employees. The current project management implementation is thought to be partly appropriate for the organization at this time. Employees perceive it to have increased administration and reduced opportunities for creativity. There is a need to follow the governmental regulations and common practices in the industry rather than the organization's desires. A cooperative view of project management does however exist within the organization.

The perceived value trend for the organization is neutral demonstrating no tangible and definite intangible benefits.

Case 36 experienced value benefits:

Tangible	*Intangible*
	• **Improved Competitiveness**
	• **Attainment of Strategic Objectives**
	• **More Effective Human Resources**
	• **Improved Reputation**
	• **Improved Overall Management**

Organization:		Attributes:
Name:	39	Region: Asia
Entity:	Department	Country: CHINA
	of Project	Industry: Construction
	Management	

DESCRIPTION:

Based in China and operating from Shanghai this organization carries out work in the construction sector. The Department of Project Management is responsible for the organization's projects, undertaking mainly customer-driven project work.

The organization has a widely held ownership structure and operates within a moderately competitive environment. The organization is one of the largest construction organizations in China and has won many awards. The predominant culture in this organization is excellence seeking through study, dedication, honesty, and cooperation. The organization operates a project-based structure.

Project management has been a part of this organization since the 1950s and there is a maturity of project management in this organization classified at 2 of 3 for this research. The most recent project management improvement implemented by this organization, in 2000, was program management and portfolio management. The implementation was put in place to link project management with the enterprise development strategy. The current project management implementation is thought to be well suited for this organization at this time: formal project management process and procedures are rigorously followed; scope of delivery is clearly defined; the success criteria for projects are clearly defined; project participants always know how to make the project manager aware of problems; all of the project team members are sufficiently informed about their role in project teams; and all important aspects of project (schedule, budget, resources) are monitored and controlled. A respected view of project management exists within the organization.

The perceived value trend for this organization is positive demonstrating no tangible but definite intangible benefits.

Case 39 experienced value benefits:

Tangible	*Intangible*
	• **More Effective Human Resources**
	• **Improved Reputation**
	• **Improved Overall Management**

Organization:		Attributes:
Name: 42		Region: Australia
Entity: Human Services		Country: AUSTRALIA
		Industry: Government

DESCRIPTION:

Based in Australia and operating from Queensland this organization carries out work in the government sector. The human services department is responsible for human services projects, undertaking all types of project work (internal, product, and customers).

The organization has a state ownership structure and operates within a low competitive environment. This organization has no real competitors due to its sector; however, project staff works alongside other government departments and non-government organizations in meeting stakeholder needs. The predominant culture in this organization is customer and stakeholder focused.

Project management has been a part of this organization since 2003. There is a low maturity of project management in this organization, which is classified at 1.5 of 3 for this research. This organization had a complex chaotic project environment with low employee satisfaction about project management. In a human services organization where outcomes are often intangible, project management provides the organization with an accountable methodology and approach. The most recent project management improvement implemented by this organization, in 2007, was a program portfolio office. The implementation was put in place to progress the organization's project management approach in a period of extended change by consistent project management deployment, especially in response to increasing complexity and increased levels of risk. The office provides a community of best practice and support intended to set up a performance culture within the emerging project management capability. The current project management implementation is thought to be partly appropriate for the organization at this time; providing the department with the ability to report to government with evidence to support its need to provide initiatives and the capacity to provide information for regular audits against service standards. A dismissive to cooperative view of project management exists within the organization.

The perceived value trend for this organization is positive demonstrating no tangible but definite intangible benefits.

Case 42 experienced value benefits:

Tangible	*Intangible*
	• **Attainment of Strategic Objectives**
	• **Greater Social Good**
	• **Improved Reputation**
	• **Improved Overall Management**
	• **Improved Corporate Culture**

Organization:		Attributes:
Name: 43 Entity: Department of Roads		Region: Australia Country: AUSTRALIA Industry: Government

DESCRIPTION:

Based in Australia and operating from Queensland regionally this organization carries out work in the government sector. The Department of Roads is responsible for public sector projects, undertaking all types of project work.

The organization has a state ownership structure and operates within a medium competitive environment. Although competition for projects is low there is a high level of competition with the private sector for resources (both staff and materials) for this organization. The predominant culture in this organization is innovative, customer, and stakeholder focused.

Project management has been a part of the organization since 1990 and there is a maturity of project management in the organization classified at 2 of 3 for this research. The most recent project management improvement implemented by the organization, in 2007, was a Project Manager Management Unit. The implementation was put in place to provide support for use and understanding of the project management framework. The current project management implementation is thought to be well suited for the organization at this time. Project management is central to the organization's existence; however, only partial implementation currently exists. A cooperative view of project management exists within the organization.

The perceived value trend for the organization is neutral (it is early in its most recent implementation) demonstrating no tangible but definite intangible benefits.

Case 43 experienced value benefits:

Tangible	*Intangible*
	• **Improved Competitiveness**
	• **Attainment of Strategic Objectives**
	• **More Effective Human Resources**
	• **Improved Corporate Culture**

Organization:		Attributes:
Name:	44	Region: Australia
Entity:	Subset of the Department of Housing	Country: AUSTRALIA
		Industry: Government

DESCRIPTION:

Based in Australia and operating from Ashfield in New South Wales this organization carries out work in the government sector. The subset of the department of housing is responsible for public sector projects, undertaking all type of project work.

The organization has a state ownership structure and operates within a medium competitive environment. The organization, although an internal agency with no direct competition, has been tested for competitiveness by outsourcing its work to external organizations—it compares favorably. The predominant culture in the organization is customer focused.

Project management has been a part of the organization since 1990 and there is a maturity of project management in the organization classified at 2.5 of 3 for this research. The most recent project management improvement implemented by the organization, in 2007, was an integrated project management tool. The implementation was put in place to increase capability and process consistency by implementing a single point of access for project managers, by replacing multiple systems the tangible benefit of all projects can be managed consistently across the organization. The current project management implementation is thought to be well suited for the organization at this time; every project has a consistent, clearly defined process, and is quality assured resulting in increased project efficiency and professionalism. As a result, high-end project managers manage multiple projects and are operating in a mature project organization where utilization is managed across all projects. A cooperative view of project management exists within the organization.

The perceived value trend for the organization is strongly positive demonstrating no tangible but considerable intangible benefits.

Case 44 experienced value benefits:

Tangible	*Intangible*
	• Improved Competitiveness
	• Attainment of Strategic Objectives
	• Greater Social Good
	• More Effective Human Resources
	• Improved Reputation
	• Improved Overall Management
	• Improved Corporate Culture

Organization:		Attributes:
Name:	45	Region: Australia
Entity:	Project Service Branch of the Office of Public Works and Services	Country: AUSTRALIA Industry: Government

DESCRIPTION:

Based in Australia and operating from Sydney in New South Wales this organization carries out work in the government sector. The project service branch is responsible for public sector projects, undertaking all types of project work.

The organization has a state ownership structure and operates within a highly competitive environment. Recent changes have required the organization to compete for projects with the private sector. There is an increasing level of competition. The predominant culture in this organization is competitive and customer focused.

Project management has been a part of the organization since 1990 and there is a maturity of project management in the organization classified at 2.5 of 3 for this research. The most recent project management improvement implemented by the organization, was a SAP-based project management system. It is a single integrated project management tool that manages costs, risk management, and scope management. The implementation was put in place as a more holistic approach to a management tool. The current project management implementation is thought to be well suited for the organization at this time. The organization is accredited to offer a project management consulting service, and has become measurably more efficient (a 2005 benchmarking exercise involving comparative organizations indicated it to be highly successful in its project management capability). The organization has ongoing improvement; the Project Support Centre performs regular state wide audits of compliance with project management procedures and develops responses to any gaps in compliance, regularly updating procedures. A cooperative view of project management exists within the organization.

The perceived value trend for the organization is positive demonstrating few tangible but considerable intangible benefits.

Case 45 experienced value benefits:

Tangible	*Intangible*
• Cost Savings	• Attainment of Strategic Objectives
	• More Effective Human Resources
	• Improved Reputation
	• Improved Corporate Culture

Organization:		Attributes:	
Name:	46	Region:	North America
Entity:	IT Consulting Group	Country:	CANADA
		Industry:	Telecommunications

Description:

Based in Canada this organization carries out work in the telecommunication sector worldwide. It is responsible for IT projects, undertaking all types of project work.

The organization has a crown corporation ownership structure and operates within a highly competitive environment. There is no predominant culture in the organization as the organization has grown rapidly through mergers and acquisitions over the last 10 years and no consistent culture has emerged.

Project management has been a part of the organization since the 1990s and there is maturity of project management in the organization classified at 1.5 of 3 for this research. The most recent project management improvement implemented by this organization, in 2005, was the implementation of a PMO. The implementation was put in place to enable the organization to achieve ISO 9000 registration. The current project management implementation is thought to be well suited for this organization at this time; however, there has been substantial resistance to it from existing project managers. Turnover rates in the group are more than 50%. An ambiguous view of project management exists within this organization, senior managers are very pleased but project managers are not.

The perceived value trend for the organization is neutral even though the organization is demonstrating tangible and intangible benefits.

Case 46 experienced value benefits:

Tangible	*Intangible*
• Cost Savings	• Attainment of Strategic Objectives
• Revenue Increases	• Improved Reputation
• Reduced Write-offs and rework	• Improved Overall Management
	• New Product/Service Streams
	• Improved Regulatory Compliance

Organization:		Attributes:	
Name:	47	Region:	Europe
Entity:	Business Unit for a Stand-Alone Project	Country:	UK
		Industry:	Defense, Aerospace

DESCRIPTION:

Based in the UK and operating multinationally this organization carries out work in the defense/aerospace sector. The stand-alone project business unit is responsible for engineering projects, undertaking mainly customer and product-driven project work.

The organization has a widely held ownership structure. The organization works in a global industry providing service to governments worldwide. The predominant culture in the organization is customer and stakeholder focused.

Project management has been a part of this sub-organization since 1996 and there is a low maturity of project management in the organization classified at 1.5 of 3 for this research. The most recent project management improvement implemented by this organization, in 2003/2004, was Earned Value Reporting. The implementation was put in place to increase client perception of project control and management. The current project management implementation is thought to be suited for the organization at this time. The organization is happy with what they have in place; however, there does not appear to be a FIT between what the parent organization and the case study organization management tells us about the practice of project management in this case and the actual observed practice and attitudes toward project management. A cooperative but dismissive view of project management exists within this case organization.

The perceived value trend for this case organization is negative although the case management sees it demonstrating considerable tangible and moderate intangible benefits.

Case 47 experienced value benefits:

Tangible	*Intangible*
• Revenue Increases	• Improved Reputation
• Customer Retention	
• Increased Customer Share	
• Greater Market Share	
• Reduced Write-offs and Rework	

Organization:		Attributes:	
Name:	48	Region:	Europe
Entity:	IT Department	Country:	DENMARK
		Industry:	Manufacturing / Engineering

DESCRIPTION:

Based in Denmark and operating worldwide this organization carries out work in the manufacturing and engineering sector. The IT Department is responsible for IT projects, undertaking mainly internally driven project work.

This organization has a narrowly held ownership structure and operates within a medium competitive environment. The IT Department of this organization is one of the largest IT houses in Denmark and operates with a good reputation in a highly competitive market. The predominant culture in the organization is customer focused.

Project management has been a part of this organization since 1996 and there is a maturity of project management in the organization classified at 2.5 of 3 for this research. The most recent project management improvement implemented by the organization, in 2007, was a four-month mandatory personal leadership development program for all project managers. The implementation was put in place to ensure project managers accessed suitable personal development to avoid burnout. The current project management implementation is thought to be well suited for the organization at this time. The organization is shaking the "PM is for IT only" feel. A combative to respected view of project management exists within the organization.

The perceived value trend for the organization is positive demonstrating no tangible but definite intangible benefits.

Case 48 experienced value benefits:

Tangible	*Intangible*
	• **More Effective Human Resources**
	• **Improved Reputation**

Organization:		Attributes:
Name:	49	Region: North America
Entity:	Information	Country: CANADA
	Technology	Industry: Energy
	Department	

DESCRIPTION:

Based in Canada and operating regionally this organization carries out work in the energy production sector. The IT Department is responsible for IT projects, undertaking mainly internally driven-project work.

The organization has a municipal ownership structure and operates within a competitive environment. The organization has grown rapidly in recent years and now operates across North America. The non-regulated operations are open to competition, and are sensitive to costs and profitability, while costs for the regulated side are defined based upon what they are able to justify to the regulator in their rate case. The predominant culture in the organization is conservative, socially conscious, and stakeholder focused.

Project management has been a part of the organization since 1997 and there is a low maturity of project management in the organization classified at 1.5 of 3 for this research. The most recent project management improvement implemented by the organization, in 2005, was a Project Delivery Centre. The implementation was put in place to improve creditability on delivery; manage project costs effectively; and re-centralize IT services with efficiency gains. The organization continues to depend on externally sourced project managers and provides little to no training of support. The current project management implementation is thought to be only partly appropriate for the organization at this time: it allows executive monitoring and support of projects; project performance is strong and process alignment around core deliverables present. A cooperative view of project management exists within this organization.

The perceived value trend for the organization is neutral demonstrating moderate tangible and moderate intangible benefits. The neutral trend recognizes the organization's dependence on externally sourced project managers in a very competitive market.

Case 49 experienced value benefits:

Tangible	*Intangible*
• Cost Savings	• Improved Reputation
	• Improved Corporate Culture
	• Improved Regulatory Compliance

Organization:		Attributes:
Name: 51		Region: North America
Entity: IT Group		Country: USA
		Industry: Financial

DESCRIPTION:

Based in the USA and operating from New Jersey this organization carries out work in the financial sector. The IT Group is responsible for IT projects, undertaking mainly internally product-driven project work.

The organization has a private ownership structure and operates within a moderately competitive environment. The organization has attained some market saturation and market domination in its primary markets. Its growth now focuses on different markets. The predominant culture in the organization is innovation and customer and stakeholder focused.

Project management has been part of the organization since 1998. There is a maturity of project management in the organization classified at 1.5 of 3 for this research. The most recent project management improvement implemented by the organization, in 2003, was the TOC - Critical Chain software package CCPulse interfacing with Microsoft Project. The implementation was put in place to increase product competitiveness, improve accountability, resource utilization, and gain greater customer satisfaction. The current project management implementation is thought to be well suited for the organization at this time. A respected view of project management exists within the organization.

The perceived value trend for this organization is positive demonstrating moderate tangible and moderate intangible benefits.

Case 51 experienced value benefits:

Tangible	*Intangible*
• Cost Savings	• More Effective Human Resources
• Reduced Write-offs and Rework	

Organization:		Attributes:
Name:	52	Region: Europe
Entity:	Supply Operations & Engineering	Country: DENMARK
		Industry: Pharmaceutical

DESCRIPTION:

Based in Denmark and operating from Copenhagen internationally this organization carries out work in the pharmaceutical sector. The Supply Operations & Engineering Department is responsible for production and logistics projects, undertaking mainly product-driven project work.

The organization has a widely held ownership structure and operates within a moderately competitive environment. The organization is facing a major competitive challenge that will impact them in the next four to six years. The predominant culture in this organization is strongly professional with some silos of knowledge.

Project management has been a part of the organization since the 1990s and there is a maturity of project management in the organization classified at 1.5 of 3 for this research. The most recent project management improvement implemented by the organization, in 2007, was development of the project management method. The implementation was put in place to strengthen interaction between a larger number of projects with higher complexity. The current project management implementation is thought to be well suited for the organization at this time. A respected view of project management exists within the organization.

The perceived value trend for the organization is neutral demonstrating no tangible but definite intangible benefits.

Case 52 experienced value benefits:

Tangible	*Intangible*
	• **Attainment of Strategic Objectives**
	• **More Effective Human Resources**
	• **Improved Corporate Culture**

Organization:		Attributes:	
Name: 53		Region: Europe	
Entity: IT Department		Country: SWEDEN	
		Industry: Transport	

DESCRIPTION:

Based in Sweden and operating multinationally this organization carries out work in the transport sector. The IT Department is responsible for IT projects, undertaking mainly internal or product-driven project work.

The organization has a private ownership structure and operates within a competitive environment. The organization is one of the most successful players in its market with a steady stream of above-normal organic growth and profits. The predominant culture in the organization is open and helpful.

Project management has been a part of the organization since 1992 and there is a maturity of project management in the organization classified at 2 of 3 for this research. The most recent project management improvement implemented by the organization, in 2007, was an up-to-date management information system implementation. The implementation was put in place to improve communication. The current project management implementation is thought to be well suited for the organization at this time; project management visualization of methods and processes are in focus, a lot of trust is put in the models and processes. The organization's culture encourages continuous improvement efforts; however, this results in a high degree of administrative work. A cooperative view of project management exists within the organization.

The perceived value trend for this organization is positive demonstrating no tangible but moderate intangible benefits.

Case 53 experienced value benefits:

Tangible	*Intangible*
	• **Improved Reputation**
	• **Improved Overall Management**
	• **Improved Corporate Culture**

Organization:		Attributes:
Name: 54		Region: Europe
Entity: IT Division		Country: SWEDEN
		Industry: Energy

DESCRIPTION:

Based in Sweden and operating internationally this organization carries out work in the energy sector. The IT Division is responsible for IT projects.

The organization has a widely held ownership structure and operates within a competitive environment. The organization holds leading market positions in all its business areas. The predominant culture in the organization is one of strong identity and loyal workforce.

There is a low maturity of project management in the organization classified at 1.5

of 3 for this research. The most recent project management improvement implemented by the organization, in 2006, was a new key performance index developed for the project portfolio. The current project management implementation is thought to be well suited for the organization at this time. Projects are vital for its business and everyone agrees that project management is something that is very important for the organization. However, people have not agreed how this should be done. A cooperative view of project management exists within the organization.

The perceived value trend for the organization is positive demonstrating no tangible but moderate intangible benefits.

Case 54 experienced value benefits:

Tangible	*Intangible*
	• **Attainment of Strategic Objectives**
	• **More Effective Human Resources**

	Organization:	Attributes:
	Name: 55 Entity: PMO	Region: North America Country: USA Industry: Government Defense

DESCRIPTION:

Based in the USA and operating from New Jersey this organization carries out work in the government defense sector. The PMO is responsible for engineering projects, undertaking mainly customer and product-driven project work.

The organization has a state ownership structure and operates within a moderately competitive environment. The agency competes directly with and collaborates with private organizations in its sector. The predominant culture in the organization is customer focused.

Project management has been a part of the organization since the 1980s and there is a maturity of project management in this organization classified at 2.5 of 3 for this research. The organization applies project management to the largest of its projects. The most recent project management improvement implemented by the organization, in 2006, was CMMI software level 5. The implementation was put in place to increase organizational collaboration and decrease internal competition, gain greater customer satisfaction, and increase product competitiveness. The current project management implementation is thought to be partly appropriate for the organization at this time; the breakthrough projects need project management due to risks, and a better identification of customer needs if appropriate; however, a dismissive view of project management exists within the organization.

The perceived value trend for the organization is neutral demonstrating no tangible but considerable intangible benefits.

Case 55 experienced value benefits:

Tangible	*Intangible*
	• **Improved Competitiveness**
	• **Improved Reputation**
	• **Improved Overall Management**
	• **Improved Corporate Culture**

	Organization:		Attributes:
	Name:	56	Region: Asia
	Entity:	Department of Steel Ring Project; HR Department; R&D Department	Country: CHINA Industry: Manufacturing

DESCRIPTION:

Based in China and operating from Shanghai internationally this organization carries out work in the manufacturing sector. The organization undertakes mainly internally and customer-driven project work.

The organization has a partnership (dual owners) ownership structure and operates within a moderately competitive environment. The organization is highly aware of its international market and takes steps to remain relevant and competitive. The culture in the organization has a wide focus. The organization was the only one in the study who had tracked cost information over a sustainable period of time (10 years).

Project management has been a part of the organization since 1998 and there is a maturity of project management in the organization classified at 1.5 of 3 for this research. The most recent project management improvement implemented by the organization, in 2004/2005, was to promote the maturity of their project management work. The improvement was put in place to implement project management in a new work location primarily to manage cost, time, and quality. The current project management implementation is thought to be well suited for this organization at this time: projects are conducted within budget, on schedule and with good quality. A cooperative view of project management exists within this organization.

The perceived value trend for this organization is neutral demonstrating no tangible but moderate intangible benefits.

Case 56 experienced value benefits:

Tangible	*Intangible*
	• More Effective Human Resources
	• Improved Reputation
	• Improved Overall Management

Organization:		Attributes:	
Name:	57	Region:	Asia
Entity:	Whole Organization	Country:	CHINA
		Industry:	Real Estate

DESCRIPTION:

Based in China and operating from Shanghai this organization carries out work in the real estate sector. The project management department is responsible for projects across the whole organization, undertaking mainly internally driven project work.

The organization has a municipal ownership structure and operates within a moderately competitive environment. Although the organization is a large company in this market, it is aware of the high risks within a rapidly developing market. The predominant culture in the organization is creative and confident.

Project management has been a part of the organization since 1996 and there is a maturity of project management in this organization classified at 2 of 3 for this research. The most recent project management improvement implemented by the organization, from 2002 to 2003, were management procedures for use in uncertain environments. The implementation was put in place to improve ability of projects to finish on time, within budget, and with good quality under a high risk environment. The current project management implementation is thought to be well suited for the organization at this time. Projects can be finished on time, within budget, and in good quality and the successful management of projects leads directly to customer satisfaction for the organization. A respected view of project management exists within the organization.

The perceived value trend for the organization is neutral demonstrating moderate tangible and moderate intangible benefits.

Case 57 experienced value benefits:

Tangible	*Intangible*
• **Cost Savings**	• **Improved Overall Management**
• **Customer Retention**	

Organization:		Attributes:	
Name:	59	Region:	North America
Entity:	Whole Organization	Country:	CANADA
		Industry:	Government/ Research

DESCRIPTION:

Based in Canada and operating globally this organization carries out work in the government research sector. The whole organization is responsible for research projects, undertaking mainly product and customer-driven project work.

The organization has a state ownership structure and operates within a moderately competitive environment. Recently the organization has undergone a change of culture from a free floating research organization to a strategically oriented and publically accountable research institute. The organization operates in a competitive global market and competes for federal funding. The predominant culture in the organization is innovative.

Project management has been a part of the organization since 2002 and there is a low maturity of project management in the organization classified at 1.5 of 3 for this research. The most recent project management improvement implemented by the organization, in 2007, was the rollout of the portfolio management and project management system. The systems provide project management support function and consistent processes and templates. The implementation was put in place to provide for better portfolio management in response to more external clients. The current project management implementation is thought to be partly appropriate for the organization at this time. The organization is perceived as highly innovative and to some extent customer oriented (geared toward strategic receptor areas). Good stakeholder relations and constructive feedback on improving project management are considered important by employees; however, the administrative load of project management is unwelcome to research employees. A respected view of project management exists within the organization.

The perceived value trend for the organization is neutral demonstrating no tangible but moderate intangible benefits.

Case 59 experienced value benefits:

Tangible	*Intangible*
	• **Attainment of Strategic Objectives**
	• **More Effective Human Resources**
	• **Improved Overall Management**
	• **Improved Corporate Culture**

Organization:		Attributes:
Name:	61	Region: North America
Entity:	A Department	Country: USA
		Industry: Manufacturing

DESCRIPTION:

Based in the USA and operating from New Jersey this organization carries out work in the manufacturing sector. The department studied is responsible for R&D projects, undertaking mainly product-driven project work.

The organization has a partnership (dual owners) ownership structure and operates within a moderately competitive environment. The organization is a world leader in its sector. The four main competitors to the organization are also major customers.

The predominant culture in the organization is customer focused.

Project management has been a part of this organization since 1999. There is a low maturity of project management in the organization classified at 1 of 3 for this research. The most recent project management improvement implemented by the organization, in 2004, was a stage-gate process model for product development. The implementation was put in place to: improve triple constraint compliance; gain greater organizational integration, conflict resolution, and portfolio prioritization; and achieve greater satisfaction from external clients with improved financial returns and better alignment with business strategy. The current project management implementation is thought to be well suited for the organization at this time. By recognizing best practices, baselines, needs definition project performance by justification and planning can be improved. A cooperative view of project management exists within the organization.

The perceived value trend for the organization is positive demonstrating moderate tangible and moderate intangible benefits.

Case 61 experienced value benefits:

Tangible	*Intangible*
• Revenue Increases	• Attainment of Strategic Objectives
• Increased Customer Share	• Improved Overall Management
	• Improved Corporate Culture

Organization:		Attributes:	
Name:	62	Region:	North America
Entity:	Whole Organization	Country:	USA
		Industry:	Manufacturing

DESCRIPTION:

Based in the USA, operating from Silicon Valley, California and worldwide, this organization carries out work in the manufacturing sector. The organization is responsible for engineering projects, undertaking mainly product-driven project work.

The organization has a narrowly held ownership structure and operates within a moderately competitive environment. As a recent start-up, revenue generation has not fully kicked in for the organization; however, it does have a backlog of customer orders and is expected to become very competitive. The culture in the organization has a wide focus.

Project management has been a part of the organization since its outset and there is a maturity of project management in the organization classified at 1.5 of 3 for this research. The most recent project management improvement implemented by the organization, in 2007, was the implementation of project management practices from best practice. The implementation was put in place to: improve triple constraint adherence, accelerate problems solving, and focus on mission critical deliverables. The current project management implementation is thought to be partly appropriate for the organization at this time. A cooperative view of project management exists within the organization.

The perceived value trend for the organization is positive demonstrating no tangible but moderate intangible benefits.

Case 62 experienced value benefits:

Tangible	*Intangible*
	• **Attainment of Strategic Objectives**
	• **Improved Reputation**

Organization:	Attributes:
Name: 63	Region: North America
Entity: IT PMO	Country: CANADA
	Industry: Energy

DESCRIPTION:

Based in Canada and operating regionally across western Canada this organization carries out work in the energy sector. The IT PMO is responsible for IT projects, undertaking mainly internally driven project work.

The organization has an income trust ownership structure and operates within a medium competitive environment. The organization operates in a competitive environment of rapid growth and unpredictable demand. Operating many lines of business, competitors in one line can be customers in another line and partners in another line. Competition is friendly and collaborative yet intense and complex. The predominant culture in the organization is one of growth and entrepreneurship.

Project management has been a part of the organization since 1994 and there is a maturity of project management in the organization classified at 1.5 of 3 for this research. The most recent project management improvement implemented by the organization, in 2007/2008, was the creation of a formal project management methodology and an IT PMO. The implementation was put in place to prove the concept of and value of project management within IS and ultimately move the PMO out of IS and become an organizational shared service. Specifically, there is an aim to formalize project management structure and processes and as such improve project management competency within the organization. The current project management implementation is thought to be well suited for the organization at this time—the expenditure on project management is seen as essential and worth every penny. The implementation fits strategy and is formal but grounded in a project management framework. A cooperative to respected view of project management exists within the organization.

The perceived value trend for the organization is positive demonstrating some tangible and considerable intangible benefits.

Case 63 experienced value benefits:

Tangible	*Intangible*
• Revenue Increases	• Attainment of Strategic Objectives
• Reduced Write-offs and Rework	• More Effective Human Resources
	• Improved Overall Management
	• Improved Corporate Culture
	• Improved Regulatory Compliance

Organization:		Attributes:
Name: 64		Region: South America
Entity: State Secretaries		Country: BRAZIL
		Industry: Government

DESCRIPTION:

Based in Brazil and operating regionally this organization carries out work in the government sector. Several of the State Secretaries are responsible for projects, undertaking mainly internally driven project work.

The organization has a state ownership structure and operates within a moderately competitive environment. There is no external competition for the organization. The predominant culture in the organization is political and socially conscious.

Project management has been a part of the organization since 2006 and there is a maturity of project management in the organization classified at 1.5 of 3 for this research. The most recent project management improvement implemented by the organization, in 2007, was a centralized PMO. The implementation was put in place to increase throughput of the organization's actions. The current project management implementation is thought to be well suited for this organization at this time; the concept of the project has been embraced by the corporate entity that needs to integrate a large number of actions. A respected view of project management exists within the organization.

The perceived value trend for the organization is neutral demonstrating no tangible but moderate intangible benefits.

Case 64 experienced value benefits:

Tangible	*Intangible*
	• **Attainment of Strategic Objectives**
	• **Improved Overall Management**
	• **Improved Corporate Culture**
	• **Improved Regulatory Compliance**

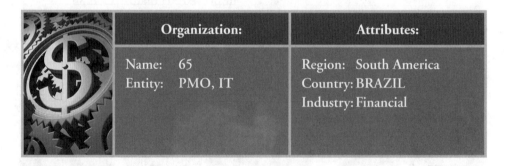

	Organization:	Attributes:
	Name: 65	Region: South America
	Entity: PMO, IT	Country: BRAZIL
		Industry: Financial

DESCRIPTION:

Based in Brazil and operating regionally this organization carries out work in the financial sector. The PMO is responsible for IT projects, undertaking mainly customer-driven project work.

This organization has a state ownership structure. There is no competition for the organization; it is government run to aid promotion for this region of Brazil. The predominant culture in the organization is socially conscious with good morale.

Project management has been a part of the organization since 2004 and there is a maturity of project management in the organization classified at 2 of 3 for this research. The most recent project management improvement implemented by the organization, in 2007, was a project management information system. The implementation was put in place by the strategic planning team to ensure projects are mapped with strategic planning. The current project management implementation is thought to be well suited for the organization at this time. The project management process adheres to corporate rigorous control standards; the project management practice has become a strong tool to obtain conformity with these standards. A cooperative view of project management exists within the organization.

The perceived value trend for the organization is positive demonstrating no tangible but moderate intangible benefits.

Case 65 experienced value benefits:

Tangible	*Intangible*
	• **Attainment of Strategic Objectives**
	• **More Effective Human Resources**
	• **Improved Overall Management**
	• **Improved Regulatory Compliance**

Organization:		Attributes:	
Name:	67	Region:	Middle East
Entity:	Whole Organization	Country:	UAE
		Industry:	Construction

DESCRIPTION:

Based in the UAE and operating locally in Dubai this organization carries out work in the construction sector. The whole organization is responsible for engineering projects, undertaking mainly customer-driven project work.

The organization has a partnership (dual owners) structure and operates within a medium competitive environment. The construction market in Dubai is growing so fast that there is enough buffer to support some inefficiency in the short term. The predominant culture in the organization is very cautious and customer and investor focused.

Project management has been a part of the organization since 2003 and there is a low maturity of project management in the organization classified at 1 of 3 for this research. The most recent project management improvement implemented by the organization, in 2003, was a formalization of processes and use of formal tools, procedures, and documents. The implementation was put in place to improve project profitability. The current project management implementation is thought to be well suited for the organization at this time, as the company is concerned with turning into a successful and profitable company. Any higher level project management would be costly and would not have ROI for the additional costs. A respected view of project management exists within the organization.

The perceived value trend for the organization is positive demonstrating definite tangible and definite intangible benefits.

Case 67 experienced value benefits:

Tangible	*Intangible*
• Revenue Increases	• Improved Reputation
	• Improved Overall Management
	• Improved Corporate Culture

	Organization:	Attributes:
	Name: 69 Entity: Whole Organization	Region: Middle East Country: UAE Industry: Construction Engineering

DESCRIPTION:

Based in the UAE and operating locally in Dubai this organization carries out work in the construction engineering sector. The whole organization is responsible for engineering projects, undertaking mainly customer-driven project work.

The organization has a partnership (dual owners) ownership structure and operates within a moderately competitive environment. Competition is intensifying in this national market. The predominant culture in the organization is very cautious and customer and investor focused.

Project management has been a part of the organization since 2006 and there is a low maturity of project management in the organization classified at 1 of 3 for this research. The most recent project management improvement implemented by the organization, in 2005, was introducing organizational chart for the company and a formalization of policy and procedure reflecting what is done. The implementation was put in place to improve efficiency in work methods and procedures and maximize profit. The current project management implementation is thought to be well suited for the organization at this time; it suits the number and complexity of projects the organization handles. A respected view of project management exists within the organization.

The perceived value trend for the organization is positive demonstrating definite tangible and definite intangible benefits.

Case 69 experienced value benefits:

Tangible	*Intangible*
• Revenue Increases	• Improved Reputation
	• Improved Overall Management
	• Improved Corporate Culture

Organization:		Attributes:	
Name:	70	Region:	Middle East
Entity:	Whole Organization	Country:	UAE
		Industry:	Construction

DESCRIPTION:

Based in the UAE and operating locally in Dubai this organization carries out work in the construction sector. The whole organization is responsible for engineering projects, undertaking mainly customer-driven project work.

The organization has a partnership (dual owners) ownership structure and operates within a moderately competitive environment. Competition is intensifying in the organization's market due to emerging companies. The predominant culture in the organization is very cautious with customer and investor focused.

Project management has been a part of the organization since 1990 and there is a low maturity of project management in the organization classified at 1 of 3 for this research. The most recent project management improvement implemented by the organization, in 2006, was the scheduling tool for the main work resource. The implementation was put in place to increase efficiency of resource usage; for this organization being efficient means maximization of profit. The current project management implementation is thought to be partly appropriate for the organization at this time. A respected view of project management exists within the organization.

The perceived value trend for the organization is neutral demonstrating moderate tangible and moderate intangible benefits.

Case 70 experienced value benefits:

Tangible	*Intangible*
• Revenue Increases	• Improved Reputation
	• Improved Overall Management
	• Improved Corporate Culture

	Organization:	Attributes:
	Name: 71 Entity: Business Electronics and Advanced Technology Division	Region: North America Country: USA Industry: Engineering

DESCRIPTION:

Based in the Pacific Northwest and operating internationally this organization carries out work in the engineering sector. The business electronics and advanced technology division is responsible for construction projects, undertaking mainly customer-driven project work.

The organization has a widely held ownership structure and operates within a moderately competitive environment. The organization maintains a 25% market share in an international market place. The predominant culture in the organization is widely focused and has high employee loyalty.

Project management has been a part of the organization for more than 20 years. There is a maturity of project management in the organization classified at 3 of 3 for this research. The most recent project management improvement implemented by the organization, in 2006-2008, was a revision and consolidation of best project management policies and procedures. The implementation was put in place primarily to consolidate the best policies and procedures from each business division into a single unified body of knowledge and practice. The current project management implementation is thought to be well suited for the organization at this time. Project management is the organization's business; doing it better means more success. A respected view of project management exists within the organization.

The perceived value trend for the organization is positive demonstrating definite tangible and definite intangible benefits.

Case 71 experienced value benefits:

Tangible	*Intangible*
• **Customer Retention**	• **Attainment of Strategic Objectives**
• **Increased Customer Share**	• **Staff Retention**
	• **Improved Overall Management**

Organization:		Attributes:
Name:	72	Region: Asia
Entity:	Head Office	Country: CHINA
	and the	Industry: Construction
	Projects Under	
	Construction	

DESCRIPTION:

Based in China and operating from the Sichuan province of southwest China this organization carries out work in the construction sector. The Head Office and the Projects Under Construction are responsible for energy generation and construction projects, undertaking mainly internally driven project work.

The organization has a state ownership structure and operates within a highly competitive environment. The large-scale nature of the projects contracted to the organization means it has little competitive pressure over the next 10-20 years.

Project management has been a part of the organization since 1998 and there is a maturity of project management in the organization classified at 2.5 of 3 for this research. The organization implemented project management because it was legally required to. The most recent project management improvement implemented by the organization, in 2006, was a set of guidelines for multi-project management; project management training, self learning, and PMP certification; and effective management research projects. The implementation was put in place to rise to the challenge of managing multi-giant projects. The current project management implementation is thought to be well suited for the organization at this time. The organization is project oriented. It has full set of management methods, processes, and templates for planning, controlling, and governing various aspects of a project throughout its whole life cycle, including, but not limited to, the established methods/templates for contractors' selection and materials procurement through competitive bidding. A respected view of project management exists within the organization.

The perceived value trend for this organization is positive demonstrating definite tangible and considerable intangible benefits.

Case 72 experienced value benefits:

Tangible	*Intangible*
• Revenue Increases	• Attainment of Strategic Objectives
• Customer Retention	• Greater Social Good
• Increased Customer Share	• More Effective Human Resources
	• Improved Reputation
	• Improved Overall Management
	• Improved Corporate Culture
	• Improved Regulatory Compliance

	Organization:	Attributes:
	Name: 73	Region: Asia
	Entity: Head Office	Country: CHINA
	and the	Industry: Construction
	Projects Under	
	Construction	

DESCRIPTION:

Based in China and operating from the Hubei province this organization carries out work in the construction sector. The Head Office and the Projects Under Construction are responsible for energy generation and construction projects, undertaking mainly internally driven project work.

The organization has a state ownership structure and operates within a moderately competitive environment. The large-scale nature of the projects contracted to this organization means it has little competitive pressure over the next 10-20 years. The predominant culture in the organization is customer focused.

Project management has been a part of the organization since 1993 and there is a maturity of project management in the organization classified at 2.5 of 3 for this research. The most recent project management improvements implemented by the organization, in 1993, were project management standards; a quality control system; and the development of a software system for project management. The implementation was put in place to improve project management systems and develop ownership of them. The current project management implementation is thought to be well suited for the organization at this time. The company has invested more than US$10 million to develop its information management system. The company owns the copyright of TGPMS and has already started to sell it to other users. A respected view of project management exists within the organization.

The perceived value trend for the organization is positive demonstrating definite tangible and considerable intangible benefits.

Case 73 experienced value benefits:

Tangible	*Intangible*
• Revenue Increases	• Attainment of Strategic Objectives
• Customer Retention	• Greater Social Good
• Increased Customer Share	• More Effective Human Resources
	• Improved Reputation
	• Improved Overall Management
	• Improved Corporate Culture
	• Improved Regulatory Compliance

Organization:		Attributes:
Name:	74	Region: Asia
Entity:	Head Office	Country: CHINA
	and the	Industry: Construction
	Projects Under	
	Construction	

DESCRIPTION:

Based in China and operating regionally from the Sichuan province this organization carries out work in the construction sector. The Head Office and the Projects Under Construction are responsible for energy generation projects, undertaking mainly internally driven project work.

The organization has a private ownership structure and operates within a highly competitive environment. As a new private company the organization has faced competition in obtaining authorization and approval for its projects. Despite a good reputation it faces fierce competition. The predominant culture in the organization is customer focused.

Project management has been a part of the organization since 2003 and there is a maturity of project management in the organization classified at 2 of 3 for this research. The most recent project management improvement implemented by the organization, in 2006, was process reengineering of its project management system and to compile a detailed project management manual covering structures, methods, and roles/responsibilities definition and buy and customize two project management software tools. The implementation was put in place to increase effectiveness and efficiency in management of multi-projects. The current project management implementation is thought to be well suited for the organization at this time. The serious use of the project management methods and tools has improved its work efficiency and helped to raise its profile as a well-organized and disciplined company. It has adopted project management concepts and methods showing that it has followed the relevant regulations about adopting project management methods. A respected view of project management exists within the organization.

The perceived value trend for the organization is positive demonstrating definite tangible and considerable intangible benefits.

Case 74 experienced value benefits:

Tangible	*Intangible*
• Revenue Increases	• Improved Competitiveness
• Customer Retention	• Attainment of Strategic Objectives
• Increased Customer Share	• More Effective Human Resources
• Reduced Write-offs and Rework	• Improved Reputation
	• Improved Overall Management
	• Improved Corporate Culture
	• Improved Regulatory Compliance

Organization:	Attributes:
Name: 75 Entity: IT PMO	Region: North America Country: CANADA Industry: Energy

DESCRIPTION:

Based in Canada and operating from Alberta across North America this organization carries out work in the energy sector. The IT PMO is responsible for IT projects, undertaking mainly internally driven project work.

The organization has a widely held ownership structure and operates within a moderately competitive environment. Parts of this organization's business are highly regulated. It operates in a competitive environment of rapid growth and unpredictable demand. With many lines of business, competitors in one line can be customers in another line, and partners in another line. Competition is friendly and collaborative yet intense and complex. The predominant culture in the organization is in transition with some silos of quite different culture.

Project management has been a part of the organization since 1999 and there is a maturity of project management in the organization classified at 2 of 3 for this research. The most recent project management improvement implemented by the organization, in 2006, was a redefinition of the PMO from a methodology/support PMO to a delivery PMO. The implementation was put in place to improve project performance and enforce adherence to procedures and processes and to create consistency as project results had slipped since their highest in 2005. The current project management implementation is thought to be partly appropriate for the organization at this time. The company clearly could not be successful without a project management capability. Project managers are, however, conflicted about the value that project management brings to the organization. Those who received the original training and who understand the purpose and methods are strongly supportive of the project management implementation than those who did not. Project results are getting worse as is project management consistency. A cooperative to dismissive view of project management exists within the organization.

The perceived value trend for the organization is strongly negative despite currently demonstrating definite tangible and definite intangible benefits based on previous investments in project management.

Case 75 experienced value benefits:

Tangible	*Intangible*
• Cost Savings	• Attainment of Strategic Objectives
• Revenue Increases	• Improved Quality of Life
	• More Effective Human Resources
	• Improved Reputation
	• Improved Regulatory Compliance

Organization:		Attributes:	
Name:	76	Region:	North America
Entity:	Whole Organization	Country:	CANADA
		Industry:	Consulting

DESCRIPTION:

Based in Canada and operating regionally from Calgary this organization carries out work in the consulting sector. The Whole Organization is responsible for IT projects, undertaking mainly customer-driven project work.

The organization has a private ownership structure and operates within a moderately competitive environment. Its main competitor is large (about three times larger) and focuses on volume rather than differentiation of service. The predominant culture in the organization is very people oriented, both customer and employee focused.

Project management has been a part of the organization since 1986 and there is a maturity of project management in the organization classified at 2 of 3 for this research. Projects generate 40% of income in the organization. The most recent project management improvement implemented by the organization, in 2006, was a project management framework (PMF) and associated templates using Excel and Word. More recently, it has moved to introducing program management, resource management, and adapting the PMF for smaller projects. The implementation was put in place to improve quality around scope, schedule, and budget; formalize a framework for project management stages and processes; transparency of project and project performance; consistency in client facing project management; improve transitioning to support services at the end of a project; improve project management capability reputation; and improve professionalism. The current project management implementation is thought to be well suited for the organization at this time. The PMF and the metrics are all aligned with and support the four elements of the organization's balanced scorecard. A respected view of project management exists within the organization.

The perceived value trend for the organization is strongly positive demonstrating considerable tangible and definite intangible benefits.

Case 76 experienced value benefits:

Tangible	*Intangible*
• Cost Savings	• Improved Competitiveness
• Revenue Increases	• Attainment of Strategic Objectives
• Customer Retention	• New Product/Service Streams
• Increased Customer Share	• More Effective Human Resources
• Greater Market Share	• Improved Reputation
• Reduced Write-offs and Rework	

Organization:	Attributes:
Name: 77 Entity:	Region: Asia Country: CHINA Industry: Telecommunications

DESCRIPTION:

The qualitative data for this case had not been received at the time of writing.

Organization:	Attributes:
Name: 78 Entity:	Region: Asia Country: CHINA Industry: Telecommunications

DESCRIPTION:

The qualitative data for this case had not been received at the time of writing.

Organization:	Attributes:
Name: 79 Entity:	Region: Asia Country: CHINA Industry: Petrochemical

DESCRIPTION:

The qualitative data for this case had not been received at the time of writing.

Organization:		Attributes:
Name: 81		Region: South America
Entity: PMO		Country: BRAZIL
		Industry: Consulting

DESCRIPTION:

Based in Brazil and operating regionally this organization carries out work in the consulting sector. The PMO is responsible for IT projects, undertaking mainly customer-driven project work.

The organization has a private ownership structure and operates within a highly competitive environment. The organization's competitors are very similar to this organization.

Project management has been a part of the organization since 2005 and there is a maturity of project management in the organization classified at 2 of 3 for this research. The most recent project management improvement implemented by the organization, in 2007, was the use of a new project management software tool, the PMIS module of Protheus ERP. The organization also revised and improved its methodology. The implementation was put in place to reduce project delivery costs and time and increase customer satisfaction. The current project management implementation is thought to be well suited for the organization at this time. Its ERP implementation is more efficient, reducing time, rework, and costs, which is a competitive strategy of this organization. A view of project management exists within the organization.

The perceived value trend for the organization is positive demonstrating moderate tangible and definite intangible benefits.

Case 81 experienced value benefits:

Tangible	*Intangible*
• Customer Retention	• Improved Competitiveness
• Reduced Write-offs and Rework	• More Effective Human Resources
	• Improved Overall Management

Organization:		Attributes:
Name: 82		Region: South America
Entity: Project Management and Procurement Department		Country: BRAZIL
		Industry: Engineering

DESCRIPTION:

Based in Brazil and operating regionally this organization carries out work in the engineering sector. The Project Management and Procurement Department is responsible for projects, undertaking mainly customer-driven project work.

The organization operates within a medium competitive environment. The organization is very competitive within this region and has two world leaders as its (main) customers.

Project management has been a part of the organization since 2007 and there is a low maturity of project management in the organization classified at 1.5 of 3 for this research. The most recent project management improvement implemented by the organization, in 2007, was the acquisition of a project management information system. The implementation was put in place to control project costs and time. The current project management implementation is thought to be partly appropriate for the organization at this time. Project management is understood as a tool for their day-to-day work and most activities are well support by its project management culture. This project management control practice has been facilitating and improving its project performance. However, project management has low integration with strategic planning or high management administration. A dismissive view of project management exists within the organization.

The perceived value trend for the organization is neutral demonstrating no tangible but moderate intangible benefits.

Case 82 experienced value benefits:

Tangible	*Intangible*
	• **Attainment of Strategic Objectives**
	• **Improved Overall Management**

Organization:	Attributes:
Name: 83 Entity: Global R&D	Region: Europe Country: UK Industry: Pharmaceutical

DESCRIPTION:

Based in the UK and operating worldwide this organization carries out work in the pharmaceutical sector. Global R&D is responsible for R&D projects, undertaking mainly product-driven project work.

The organization has a widely held ownership structure and operates within a highly competitive environment. The organization is a world leader and operates in an intensely regulated industry dominated by global corporations. The predominant culture in the organization is one of innovation and revenue generation.

Project management has been a part of the organization since at least 1988 and there is a maturity of project management in the organization classified at 1.5 of 3 for this research. The most recent project management improvement implemented by the organization, in 2005, was a central project management organization (PMC). The PMC was put in place to establish the central role of professional project management to the organization. The current project management implementation is thought to be well suited for the organization at this time; professionalization and planning are relevant to the business. A cooperative view of project management exists within the organization. However, the organization is going through more change and there is some question as to whether the project management implementation will continue to deliver value.

The perceived value trend for the organization is neutral demonstrating no tangible but definite intangible benefits.

Case 83 experienced value benefits:

Tangible	*Intangible*
	• **Improved Competitiveness**
	• **More Effective Human Resources**
	• **Improved Reputation**
	• **Improved Overall Management**

Organization:		Attributes:	
Name:	84	Region:	South America
Entity:	Engineering and Planning, IT	Country:	BRAZIL
		Industry:	Energy

DESCRIPTION:

Based in Brazil and operating regionally this organization carries out work in the energy sector. Engineering and Planning, IT is responsible for engineering projects, undertaking mainly customer-driven project work.

The organization has a privately held ownership structure and operates within a medium competitive environment. The organization has a state grant monopoly and no competitors.

Project management has been a part of the organization since 2006 and there is a maturity of project management in the organization classified at 1.5 of 3 for this research. The most recent project management improvement implemented by the organization, in 2007, was the unification of the technical and sales teams bringing about unification and shared management for technical areas. The implementation was put in place to improve cost effectiveness and efficient use of resources and increase investor and customer satisfaction. The current project management implementation is thought to be partly appropriate for the organization at this time. A general project management implementation would likely be beneficial to the organization but it is thought to be too costly to be suited the current business strategy. There is, however, strong alignment between the limited formalized project management implementation and the project managers' actions. A cooperative view of the limited project management structure exists within the organization.

The perceived value trend for the organization is neutral demonstrating few tangible but moderate intangible benefits.

Case 84 experienced value benefits:

Tangible	*Intangible*
• Cost Savings	• More Effective Human Resources

Organization:		Attributes:	
Name:	86	Region:	Europe
Entity:	System Development PMO	Country:	RUSSIA
		Industry:	Banking

DESCRIPTION:

Based in Russia and operating from Moscow nationally this organization carries out work in the banking sector. The System Development PMO is responsible for IT projects, undertaking mainly internally driven project work.

The organization has a state ownership structure. The organization is the main regulatory bank in this sector; it has no competitors.

Project management has been a part of the organization since 1993 and there is a low maturity of project management in the organization classified at 1.5 of 3 for this research. The most recent project management improvement implemented by the organization, in 2006, was the introduction of the PMO. The implementation was put in place to align internal organization with changes in the parent organization, change management, and business process reengineering. The current project management implementation is thought to be well suited for the organization at this time. A cooperative view of project management exists within the organization.

The perceived value trend for the organization is neutral demonstrating no tangible but moderate intangible benefits.

Case 86 experienced value benefits:

Tangible	*Intangible*
	• **Attainment of Strategic Objectives**
	• **Improved Overall Management**
	• **Improved Regulatory Compliance**

Organization:		Attributes:
Name:	87	Region: Europe
Entity:	Whole	Country: RUSSIA
	Organization	Industry: Construction

DESCRIPTION:

Based in Russia and operating from Moscow nationally this organization carries out work in the construction sector. The Whole Organization is responsible for construction projects, undertaking mainly customer- and internally driven project work.

The organization has a state ownership structure. The organization is a market leader and top national brand in Russia. The predominant culture in the organization is quality first ensuring adherence to legal and technical regulations.

Project management has been a part of the organization since the mid 1960s and there is a relatively high maturity of project management in the organization classified at 2.5 of 3 for this research. The most recent project management improvement implemented by the organization was two-fold: three new project management models to support subcontractors; and the integration and unification of the project management procedures of daughter companies with the parent company. The implementation was put in place to manage complex projects more efficiently with a better allocation of resources and multi-project management. The current project management implementation is thought to be well suited for the organization at this time. Project success directly influences profitability. A cooperative view of project management exists within the organization; project management is a core competency.

The perceived value trend for the organization is positive demonstrating moderate tangible and definite intangible benefits.

Case 87 experienced value benefits:

Tangible	*Intangible*
• Revenue Increases	• Attainment of Strategic Objectives
	• Improved Reputation
	• Improved Overall Management
	• Improved Regulatory Compliance

Organization:		Attributes:
Name: 88		Region: Europe
Entity: Commercial		Country: RUSSIA
Services		Industry: Food

DESCRIPTION:

Based in Russia and operating from Moscow internationally this organization carries out work in the food sector. Commercial Services is responsible for production projects, undertaking mainly internally driven project work.

The organization has a widely held ownership structure and operates within a competitive environment. The competition is very strong in the market; this organization holds 16.2% of the Russian market. Globalization is making business challenging for this organization.

Project management has been a part of the organization since 2003 and there is a low maturity of project management in the organization classified at 1 of 3 for this research. The most recent project management improvement implemented by the organization, in 2006, was a SAP implementation. The implementation was put in place to establish unified access and control procedures across organizational sites. The current project management implementation is thought to be partly appropriate for the organization at this time; however, many of the processes are not actually followed. A dismissive view of project management exists within the organization.

The perceived value trend for the organization is negative demonstrating no tangible and few intangible benefits.

Case 88 experienced value benefits:

Tangible	*Intangible*
	• **Improved Overall Management**

Organization:		Attributes:
Name:	89	Region: Europe
Entity:	Software Services	Country: RUSSIA
	Development and	Industry: IT
	Implementation	
	Group	

DESCRIPTION:

This organization is a subsidiary of one of the world's largest consulting organization. Based in Russia and operating across the central and eastern European region this organization carries out work in the IT sector. The software group is responsible for IT projects, undertaking mainly customer-driven project work.

The organization has a widely held ownership structure and operates within a competitive environment. The organization operates in the fast growing central and eastern European region against global competitors. The predominant culture in this organization is investor focused.

Project management has been a part of the organization since it was established; however, there is a relatively low maturity of project management in the organization classified at 1.5 of 3 for this research. The most recent project management improvement implemented by the organization was the introduction of an independent project management unit. The implementation was put in place to manage revenue streams, improve customer care, and better control projects with respect to time and budget. The current project management implementation is thought to be well suited for the organization at this time. An enthusiastically cooperative view of project management exists within the organization.

The perceived value trend for the organization is strongly positive demonstrating definite tangible and definite intangible benefits.

Case 89 experienced value benefits:

Tangible	*Intangible*
• Cost Savings	• Improved Competitiveness
• Revenue Increases	• Attainment of Strategic Objectives
• Customer Retention	• New Product/Service Streams
• Increased Customer Share	• More Effective Human Resources
	• Improved Overall Management

Organization:		Attributes:
Name: 90		Region: Europe
Entity: Whole		Country: RUSSIA
Organization		Industry: Mining

DESCRIPTION:

Based in the UK this organization carries out work in the mining sector in Russia. The whole organization is responsible for engineering and strategic projects, undertaking mainly product-driven project work.

The organization has a widely held ownership. It trades internationally. The predominant culture in the organization is economic.

Project management has been a part of the organization since 2000 and there is a maturity of project management in the organization classified at 2.5 of 3 for this research. The most recent project management improvement implemented by the organization, was a project communication strategy. The implementation was put in place to increase financial returns and improve performance. The current project management implementation is thought to be well suited for the organization at this time. Unifying project management is culturally problematic; nevertheless, a cooperative view of project management exists in the organization.

The perceived value trend for the organization is positive demonstrating no tangible but moderate intangible benefits.

Case 90 experienced value benefits:

Tangible	*Intangible*
	• **Attainment of Strategic Objectives**
	• **Staff Retention**
	• **Improved Overall Management**

Organization:		Attributes:
Name:	91	Region: Europe
Entity:	Business	Country: SERBIA
	Department of	Industry: Financial - Insurance
	the Larger Group	

DESCRIPTION:

Based in Serbia and operating multinationally in Eastern Europe this organization carries out work in the insurance sector. The business department of the larger group is responsible for projects, undertaking mainly product and internally driven project work.

The organization has a privately held ownership structure. The organization's market share is 15% and it is the third largest in its market place. Competition is fierce and unfair as major competitors can include state-owned insurance companies. There are 16 companies operating successfully in this market.

Project management has been a part of the organization since 2005 and there is a maturity of project management in the organization classified at 1 of 3 for this research. The most recent project management improvement implemented by the organization, in 2008, was a PMO. The implementation was put in place to bring a new product to market more quickly. The current project management implementation is thought to be partly appropriate for the organization at this time; committed employees are happy to pursue project management and embed it into the company culture. A dismissive to cooperative view of project management exists within the rest of the organization.

The perceived value trend for the organization is positive demonstrating some tangible and some intangible benefits.

Case 91 experienced value benefits:

Tangible	*Intangible*
• Cost Savings	• More Effective Human Resources
	• Improved Reputation
	• Improved Overall Management
	• Improved Corporate Culture

Organization:		Attributes:
Name: 92		Region: Europe
Entity: Research and Development		Country: UK
		Industry: Defense

DESCRIPTION:

Based in the UK and operating internationally this organization carries out highly specialized research work in the defense sector. The organization is responsible for engineering and R&D projects, undertaking mainly product, customer-driven project work.

The organization operates within a competitive environment. The predominant culture in the organization is driven by technical efficiency.

Project management has been a part of the parent organization since 1996 and there is a low maturity of project management in the organization classified at 2 of 3 for this research. The most recent project management improvement implemented by the organization, in 2006, was the training of all project managers in the parent company's developed project management models. The implementation was put in place to standardize project management across the organization as a result of a few large failures. The current project management implementation is thought to be well suited for the organization at this time. A positive view of project management exists within the organization.

The perceived value trend for the organization is positive demonstrating both tangible and intangible benefits.

Case 92 experienced value benefits:

Tangible	*Intangible*
• Customer Retention	• Attainment of Strategic Objectives
• Reduced Write-Offs and Rework	• More Effective Human Resources
	• Improved Reputation
	• Improved Overall Management
	• Improved Corporate Culture

Appendix B

References

Abrahamson, E. (1991). Managerial fads and fashions: The diffusion and rejection of innovations. *Academy of Management Review, 16*(3): 596-612.

Andrews, K. R. (1971). *The concept of corporate strategy.* Homewood, IL: Irwin.

Ansoff, H. I. (1965). *Corporate strategy: An analytical approach to business policy and expansion.* New York: McGraw-Hill Book Company.

Argyris, C., & Schön, D. (1978). *Organizational learning: A theory of action approach.* Reading, MA: Addison-Wesley.

Ashton, R. H. (2005). Intellectual capital and value creation: A review. *Journal of Accounting Literature,* 24.

Balkin, D. F., & Gomez-Mejia, L. R. (1990). Matching compensation and organizational strategies. *Journal of Organizational Behavior, 12,* 55-62.

Balkin, D. F., & Gomez-Mejia, L. R. (1987). Toward a contingency theory of compensation strategy. *Strategic Management Journal , 8*(4), 169-182.

Bani-Ali, A. S., & Anbari, F. T. (2004). Project management software acceptance and its impact on project success. *Proceedings of the International Research Network on Organizing by Projects* (IRNOP VI), Turku, Finland.

Bardhan, I. R., Krishnan, V. V., et al. (2007). Project performance and the enabling role of information technology: An exploratory study on the role of alignment. *Manufacturing & Service Operations Management, 9*(4), 579.

Barney, J. B. (1991). Firm resources and sustained competitive advantage. *Journal of Management, 17*(1), 99-120.

Bartlett, C. A., & Mahmood, T. (1996). Skandia AFS: Developing intellectual capacity globally. HBS case 9-396-412. Boston: Harvard Business School.

Barua , A., Lee ,C. H. S., & Whinston, T. A. (1996). The calculus of re-engineering. *Information Systems Research, 7*(4), 409.

Barua, A., & Mukhopadhyay, T. (2000). Information technology and business performance: Past, present and future? In M. Zmud, & R. Wed (Eds.), Framing the domains of IT research: Projecting the future through the past (pp. 65-84). M. Zmud and R. Wed. Cincinnati, OH: Pinnaflex Educational Resources.

Becker, H. S. (1958). Problems of inference and proof in participant observation. *American Sociological Review, 23*, 652-660.

Beer, M., Voelpel, S. C., Leibold, M., & Tekie, E. B. (2005). Strategic management as organizational learning: Developing fit and alignment through a disciplined process. *Long Range Planning, 38*(5), 445-465.

Beischel, M. E., & Smith, K. R. (1991). Linking the shop floor to the top floor. *Management Accounting, 73*(October), 25-29.

Bitektine, A. (2008). Prospective case study design: Qualitative method for deductive theory testing. *Organizational Research Methods, 11,* 160.

Bontis, N., Dragonetti, N. C., Jacobsen, K. & Roos, G. (1999). The knowledge toolbox: A review of the tools available to measure and manage intangible resources. *European Management Journal, 17*(4), 391-403.

Boulton, R. E. S., Libert, B. D., & Samek, S. M. (2000). *Cracking the value code: How successful businesses are creating wealth in the new economy.* New York: Harper Business.

Boyd, B. K., & Salamin, A. (2001). Strategic reward systems: A contingency model of pay system design. *Strategic Management Journal, 22*(8), 777-792.

Bridges, W. (1986). Managing organization transitions. *Organizational Dynamics, 15*(1), 24-33.

Brotheridge, C., & Power, J. (2007). Spending consulting dollars wisely: A guide for management teams. *Team Performance Management, 13*(1/2), 53-56.

Bruner, J. (1990). *Acts of meaning.* Cambridge, MA: Harvard University Press.

Bryde, D. J. (2003). Modeling project management performance. *The International Journal of Quality & Reliability Management, 20*(2/3), 228-244.

Bryman, A. (2007). Barriers to integrating quantitative and qualitative research. *Journal of Mixed Methods Research, 1,* 8-22.

Burkett, H. (2005a). ROI on a shoe-string: Strategies for resources-constrained environments. *Industrial & Commercial Training, 37*(1), 10.

Burkett H. (2005b). ROI on a shoe-string: Strategies for resources-constrained environments. *Industrial & Commercial Training, 37*(2/3), 97.

Burney, L. L., & Matherly, M. (2007). Examining performance management from an integrated perspective. *Journal of Information Systems, 21*(2), 49.

Cabanis-Brewin, J. (2000). The elusive ROI. *PM Network*, April, 45-50.

Callon, M. (1990). Actor network theory—The market test. In J. Law, & J. Hassard (Eds.), Actor Network theory and After (pp. 181-195). Oxford, England: Blackwell.

Carmeli, A., & Tishler, A. (2004). The relationships between intangible and organizational elements and organizational performance. *Strategic Management Journal, 25*(13), 1257-1278.

Chakravarthy, B. S., & White, R. E. (2002). Strategy process: Forming, implementing and changing strategies. In Petigrew, A., Thomas, H., & Whittington, R. (Eds.), Handbook of strategy and management. London: Sage.

Chan, Y. E., & Huff, S. I. (1993). Strategic information systems alignment. *Business Quarterly, 98*(1), 1-5.

Chan, Y.E., Sabherwal, R. and Thatcher, J.B. (2006), Antecedents and outcomes of strategic IS alignment: an empirical investigation, IEEE Transactions on Engineering Management, Vol. 53 No. 1, pp. 27-47

Chatfield, C., & Collins, A. J. (1980). *Introduction to multivariate data analysis.* London: Chapman and Hall.

Checkland, P., & Holwell, S. (1998). Action research: It's nature and validity. *Systemic Practice and Action Research*, 11(1).

Child, J., & Mansfield, R. (1972). Technology size and organization structure. *Sociology 6*(September), 369-373.

Cicmil, S. (2000). Quality in project environments: A non-conventional agenda. *International Journal of Quality & Reliability Management, 17*(4/5), 554-570.

Cicmil, S., Williams, T., Thomas, J., & Hodgson, D. (2006). Rethinking project management: Researching the actuality of projects. *International Journal of Project Management, 24*, 675-686.

Cooke-Davies, T. J. (2002a). Establishing the link between project management practices and success. Proceedings of the PMI Research Conference 2002.

Cooke-Davies T. J. (2002b). The "real" success factors on projects. *International Journal of Project Management, 20*(3), 185-190.

Cooke-Davies, T. J., & Arzymanow, A. (2003). The maturity of project management in different industries: An investigation into variations between project management models. *International Journal of Project Management, 21*(6), 471.

Cooke-Davies,T., Cicmil, S., Crawford, L., & Richardson, K. (2007). We're not in Kansas anymore, Toto: Mapping the strange landscape of complexity theory, and its relationship to project management. *Project Management Journal , 38*(2), 50.

Craft, R. C., & Leake, C. (2002). The Pareto principle in organizational decision making. *Management Decision, 40*(7/8), 729.

Crawford, K., & Pennypacker, J. (2001). The value of project management: Proof at Last. PMI 32nd Annual Seminars & Symposium. Nashville, Tennessee.

Crawford, L. H., Hobbs, J. B., & Turner, J. R. (2006). Aligning capability with strategy: Categorizing projects to do the right projects and do them right. *Project Management Journal, 43*(2), 60-67.

Dai, C. X. (2002). The role of the project management office in achieving project success. Ph.D. Dissertation, The George Washington University, Washington, DC.

Dai C. X., & Wells, W. G. (2004). An exploration of project management office features and their relationship to project performance. *International Journal of Project Management, 22*(7), 523-532.

Damanpour, F. (1987). The adoption of technological, administrative, and ancillary innovations: impact of organizational factors. *Journal of Management, 13*(4), 675-688.

Damanpour, F. (1996). Organizational complexity and innovation: Developing and testing multiple contingency models. *Management Science, 42*(5), 693-716.

Damanpour, F., & Evan, W. M. (1984). Organizational innovation and performance: The problem of organizational lag. *Administrative Science Quarterly, 29*, 392-409.

Dawes, J. (2000). Market orientation and company profitability: Further evidence incorporating longitudinal data. *Australian Journal of Management, 25*(2), 173.

Denrell, J., Fang, C., & Winter, S. G.(2003). The economics of strategic opportunity. *Strategic Management Journal, 24*, 977-990.

Dvir, D., Lipovetsky, S., Shenhar, A., & Tishler, A. (1998). In search of project classification: A non universal approach to project success factors. *Research Policy, 27*(9), 915-972.

Easterby, M., & Danusia, M. (1999). Cross cultural collaborative research: Toward reflexivity. *Academy of Management Journal, 42*(1), 76.

Eccles, R. G. (1991). The performance measurement manifesto. *Harvard Business Review, 69*(Jan/Feb), 131-137.

Eccles, R. G., & Pyburn, P. J. (1992). Creating a comprehensive system to measure performance. *Management Accounting, 14*(October), 41-44.

Eccles, R. G., Herz, R. H., Keegan, E. M., & Philips, D. M. H. (2001). *The value reporting revolution: Moving beyond the earnings game.* New York: John Wiley and Sons.

Egan, C. (1995). *Creating organizational advantage.* Oxford: Butterworth-Heinemann.

Eisenhardt, K. M., & Graebner, M. E. (2007). Theory building from cases: Opportunities and challenges. *Academy of Management Journal, 50*(1). 25-32.

Eisenhardt, K., & Martin, J. (2000). Dynamic capabilities: What are they? *Strategic Management Journal, 21*, 1105-1121.

Eisenhardt, K. M. (1989). Building theories from case study research. *Academy of Management Review, 14*, 532-550.

Eriksson, H., & Hansson, J. (2003). The impact of TQM on financial performance. *Measuring Business Excellence, 7*(1), 36-50.

Escrig-Tena, A. B., & Bou-Llusar, J. C. (2005). A model for evaluating organizational competencies: An application in the context of a quality management initiative. *Decision Sciences, 36*(2), 221.

Everitt, B. S., & Dunn, G. (2001). *Applied multivariate data analysis.* London: Edward Arnold.

Fisher, J. (1992). Use of non-financial performance measures. *Journal of cost Management, 6*(Spring), 31-38.

Gephart, Robert P. (1988). *Ethnostatistics: Qualitative foundations for quantitative research.* Newbury Park, CA: Sage Publications.

Githens, G. (1998). Financial models, right questions, good decisions. *PM Network*, 29-32.

Glaser, B., & Strauss, A. (1967). *The discovery of grounded theory. Strategies for qualitative research.* Chicago: Aldine.

Glaser, B. (1992). *Basics of branded theory analysis.* Mill Valley, CA: Sociology Press.

Gomes, C. F., Yasin, M. M., & Lisboa, J. V. (2007). The dimensionality and utilization of performance measures in a manufacturing operational context. Organizational change implications. *Cross Cultural Management: An International Journal, 14*(4), 286-306.

Gordon, S. R., & Tarafdar, M. (2007). How do a company's information technology competences influence its ability to innovate? *Journal of Enterprise Information Management, 20*(3), 271.

Grant, R. M. (1991). The resource-base theory of competitive advantage: Implication for strategy formulation. *California Management Review*, (Spring), 15-21.

Gray, B., Matear, S., Boshoff, C. & Matheson, P. (1998). Developing a better measure of marketing orientation. *European Journal of marketing, 32*(9-10), 844-903.

Guha, S., Grover, V., Kettinger, W. J., & Teng, J. T. C (1997). Business process change and organizational performance: Exploring an antecedent model. *Journal of Management Information Systems, 14*(1), 119-154.

Guler, L., Guillen, M., & Macpherson, J. M. (2002). Global competition, institutions, and the diffusion of organizational practices: The international spread of ISO 9000 quality certificates. *Administrative Science Quarterly, 47*, 207-232.

Hackman, J. R., & Wageman, R. (1995). Total quality management: Empirical, conceptual and practical issues. *Administrative Sciences Quarterly, 40*(2), 309-342.

Hambrick, D. (2003). On the staying power of Miles and Snow's defenders, analyzers and prospectors. *Academy of Management Executive, 17*(4), 115-118.

Handy, C. (1993). *Understanding organizations, 4th ed.* Harmondworth, London: Penguin.

Hay, D., & Louri, H. (1995). An empirical note on the investment behavious of U.K. forms, 1960-1985. *Journal of Post Keynesian Economics, 17*(4), 579.

Henderson, J. C. & Venkatraman, N. (1993). Strategic alignment: Leveraging information technolog/ for transforming organizations. *IBM Systems Journal, 32*(1), 4-16.

Henri, J. F. (2004). Performance measurement and organizational effectiveness: Bridging the gap. *Managerial Finance, 30*(6), 93.

Hesketh, A., & Fleetwood, S. (2006). Beyond measuring the human resources –organizational performance link: Applying critical realist meta- theory. *Organization, 13*(5), 677-699.

Hillson, D. (2003). Assessing organisational project management capability. *Journal of Facilities Management, 2*(3), 298.

Hofstede, G. (2001). *Culture's consequences: Comparing values, behaviours, institutions, and organizations across nations.* Thousand Oaks, CA: Sage Publications.

Humphreys, W. (1992). *Introduction to software process improvement.* Pittsburgh: Software Engineering Institute, Carnegie Mellon University.

Ibbs, C. W. (2000). Measuring project management's value: New directions for quantifying PM/ROI. PMI Research Conference. Paris, France.

Ibbs, C. W., & Kwak, Y. H. (2000). Assessing project management maturity. *Project Management Journal, 31*(1), 32-43.

Ibbs, C. W., & Kwak, Y. H. (1997). *The benefits of project management: Financial and organizational rewards to corporations.* Sylva, NC: Project Management Institute.

Ibbs, C. W., & Reginato, J. M. (2002). *Quantifying the value of project management.* Newtown Square, PA: Project Management Institute.

Ibbs, C. W., Reginato, J. & Kwak, Y. H. (2004). Developing project management capability—Benchmarking, maturity, modeling, gap analyses, ROI studies. In P. W. G. Morris, & J. K. Pinto (Eds.), The Wiley Guide to Managing Projects. New York: John Wiley.

Ittner, C. D., & Larcker, D. F. (2003). Coming up short on nonfinancial performance measurement. *Harvard Business Review, 81*(11), 88-95.

Jachimowicz, V. A. (2003). Project management maturity model. *Project Management Journal, 34*(1), 55.

Jack, E.P., & Raturi, A. S. (2006). Lessons learned from methodological triangulation in management research. *Management Research News, 29*(6), 345-357.

Johnson, R. B., Onwuegbuzie, A. J., & Turner, L. A. (2007). Toward a definition of mired methods research. *Journal of Mixed Methods Research, 1,* 112-133.

Jugdev, K. (2002). Blueprint for value creation: Developing and sustaining a project management competitive advantage through the resource-based view. PMI Research Conference.

Jugdev, K. (2004). Through the looking glass: Examining theory development in project management with the resource-based view lens. *Project Management Journal, 35*(3), 15.

Jugdev, K., & Mathur, G. (2006). Project management elements as strategic assets: Preliminary findings. *Management Research News, 29*(10), 604-617.

Jugdev, K., & Thomas, J. (2002). Project management maturity models: The silver bullet of competitive advantage? *Project Management Journal, 33*(4), 4-14.

Jugdev, K., Mathur, G., & Fung, T. (2007). Project management assets and their relationship with the project management capabilities of the firm. *International Journal of Project Management, 25,* 560- 568.

Kaplan, R. S. (1983). Measuring manufacturing performance: A challenge for managerial account research. *The Accounting Review, 58*(October), 688-705.

Kaplan, R. S. (1984). The evolution of management accounting. *The Accounting Review, 59*(July), 390-418.

Kaplan, R. S. (2005). How the balanced scorecard complements the McKinsey 7-S model. *Strategy & Leadership, 33*(3), 41-6.

Kaplan, R. S., & Norton, D. P. (1996a). Using the balanced scorecard as a strategic management system. *Harvard Business Review, 74*(1), 75.

Kaplan, R. S., & Norton, D. P. (1996b). The balanced scorecard is more than just a new measurement system. *Harvard Business Review, 74*(3), S3.

Kaplan, R. S., & Norton, D. P. (2004). Measuring the strategic readiness of intangible assets. *Harvard Business Review, 82*(2), 52.

Kathuria, R., & Porth, S. J. (2003). Strategy implementation: Managing the organizational issues. In S. J. Porth (Ed.), *Strategic management: A cross functional approach.* Englewood Cliffs, NJ: Prentice Hall.

Katz, J. (1983). A theory of qualitative methodology. In R. M. Emerson (Ed.), *Contemporary field research.* Prospect Heights, IL: Waveland.

Kaufman, R., & Watkins, R. (1996). Cost-consequences analysis. *Human Resources Development Quarterly, 7*(1), 87.

Kearns, G. S., & Lederer, A. I. (2000). The effect of strategic alignment on the use of IS-based resources for competitive advantage. *Journal of Strategic Information Systems, 9*(4), 265-293.

Kearns, P. (2005). From return on investment to added value evaluation: The foundation for organizational learning. *Advances in Developing Human Resources, 7*(1), 135.

Keegan, D. P., Eiler, R. G., & Jones, C. R. (1989). Are your performances measures obsolete? *Management Accounting, 70*(June), 45-50.

Kimberly, J. R., & Evanisko, M. J. (1981). Organizational innovation: The influence of individual, organizational and contextual factors on hospital adoption of technological and administrative innovations. *Academy of Management Journal, 24*(4), 689-713.

Knutson, J. (1999). From making sense to making sense: Measuring project management ROI. *PM Network.*

Kohli, R. D., & Devaraj, S. (2003). Measuring information technology payoff: A meta-analysis of structural variables in firm-level empirical research. *Information Systems Research, 14*(2), 127–142.

Kohli, R., Sherer, S. A., & Baron, A. (2003). IT investment payoff in e-business environments: Research issues. *Information System Frontiers, 5*(3), 239.

Kwak, Y. H., & Ibbs, C. W. (2000). Calculating project management's return on investment. *Project Management Journal, 31*(2), 38-47.

Kwak, Y. H., & Ibbs, C. W. (2002). Project management process maturity model. *ASCE Journal of Management in Engineering, 18*(3), 150-155.

Lado, A. A., & Wilson, M. C. (1994). Human resource systems and sustained competitive advantage: A competency-based perspective. *Academy of Management Review, 19*(4), 699-727.

Lado, A. A., Boyd, N. G., & Wright P. (1992). A competency-based model of sustainable competitive advantage: Toward a conceptual integration. *Journal of Management, 18*(1), 77-91.

Latham, J. R. (2008). Building bridges between researchers and practitioners: A collaborative approach to research in performance excellence. *Quality Management Journal, 15*(1), 8-15.

Latour, B. (1987). *Science in action.* Cambridge, MA: Harvard University Press.

Latour, B. (1999). *Pandora's hope: Essays on the reality of science studies.* Cambridge, MA: Harvard University Press.

Lepak, D.P., Smith, K. G., & Taylor, M. S. (2007). Value creation and value capture: A multilevel perspective. *Academy of Management Review, 32*(1), 180-194.

Lev, B. (2001). *Intangibles: Management, measurement and reporting.* Washington, DC: The Brookings Institution.

Lewis, M. W., & Keleman, M. L. (2002). Multiparadigm inquiry: Exploring organizational pluralism and paradox. *Human Relations, 55*(2), 251-275.

Lian, Y.-S. (2006). The effect of fit between organizational life cycle and human resource management control on firm performance. *Journal of American Academy of Business, 8*(1), 192.

Lippman, S. A., & Rumelt, R. P. (2003). The payments perspective: Micro-foundations of resource analysis. *Strategic Management Journal, 24*, 903-927.

Lundin, R. A., & Söderholm, A. (1995). A theory of the temporary organization. *Scandinavian Journal of Management, 11* 437-455.

Mack, J.G. and Sutton, J.T. (1997) organizations performance as a dependent variable Organizational Science. 8 (6) pp. 698-706.

Marcus, M. L., & Soh, W. L. (1993). Banking on information technology: Converting IT spending into firm performance. In R. D. Banker, R. J. Kauffman, & M. A. Mahmood (Eds.), *Strategic information technology management: Perspectives on organizational growth and competitive advantage.* London: Idea Group Publishing.

Maskell, B. (1989). Performance measures for world class manufacturing. *Management Accounting*, May, 32-33.

McAdam, R., Leonard, D., Henderson, J., & Hazlett, S. (2006). A grounded theory research approach to building and testing TQM theory in operations management. *Omega (International Journal of Management Science)*, 36, 825-837.

McNair, C. J., Lynch, R. L., & Cross, K. F. (1990). Do financial and non-financial performance measures have to agree? *Management Accounting, 72*(November), 28-36.

Mele, C. (2007). The synergic relationship between TQM and marketing in creating customer value. *Managing Service Quality, 17*(3), 240.

Merriam, S. (1988). *Case study research in education*. New York: Jossey-Bass.

Miles, M. B., & Huberman, A. M. (1994). *Qualitative data analysis, 2nd ed.* Newbury Park, CA: Sage.

Miles, R. E., & Snow, C. C. (1978). *Organizational, strategy, structure and process*. New York: McGraw-Hill.

Miller, D. (1996). Configurations revisited. *Strategic Management Journal, 17,*(7), 505-512.

Mintzberg, H. (1979). *The structuring of organizations*. Englewood Cliffs, NJ: Prentice Hall.

Montemayor, E. F. (1996). Congruence between pay policy and competitive strategy in high-performing firms. *Journal of Management, 22*(6), 889-908.

Montes, F. J. L., Jover, A. V., & Molina Fernandez, L. M. (2003). Factors affecting the relationship between total quality management and organizational performance. *International Journal of Quality and Reliability Management, 20*(2),: 188.

Morris, P. W. G. (2001). Updating the project management bodies of knowledge. *Project Management Journal, 32*(3), 21.

Morris, P. W. G., & Jamieson, A. (2005). Moving from corporate strategy to project strategy. *Project Management Journal, 36*(4), 5.

Mottiwalla, I., &Fairfield–Sonn, J. (1998). Measuring the impact of expert systems. *Journal of Business and Economic Studies, 4*(2), 1.

Mullaly, M. (2006). Longitudinal analysis of project management maturity. *Project Management Journal, 37*(3), 62-74.

O'Connor, G. C., Rice, M. S., Peters, L., & Veryzer, R. W. (2003). Managing interdisciplinary, longitudinal research teams: Extending grounded theory-building methodizes. *Organization Science, 14*(4), 353-373.

Packendorff, J. (1995). Inquiring into the temporary organization: New directions for project management research. *Scandinavian Journal of Management, 11*(4), 319-333.

Pennypacker, J., &Grant, K. (2003). Project management maturity: An industry benchmark. *Project Management Journal, 34*(1), 4-11.

Peteraf, M. (1993). The cornerstones of competitive advantage: A resource-based view. *Strategic Management Journal, 14*(3), 179-191.

Peters, T., & Waterman, R. (1982). *In search of excellence: Lessons from America's best run companies.* New York: Harper & Row Publishers.

Pettigrew, A., & Whipp, R. (1993). *Managing change for competitive success.* Oxford: Blackwell.

Philips , J. J., Bothel, T. W., & Snead, G. L. (2002). *The project management scorecard: Measuring the success of project management solutions.* New York: Elsevier.

Phillips, J. J. (1998). Measuring the return on investment in organization development. *Organization Development Journal, 16*(4), 29.

Phillips, P. P., & Philips, J. J. (2004). ROI in the public sector: Myths and realities. *Public Personnel Management, 33*(2), 139.

Porter, M. E. (1980). *Competitive strategy.* New York: The Free Press.

Porter, M. E. (1996). What is strategy? *Harvard Business Review, 74*(6), 61-78.

Powell, T. C. (1995). Total quality management as competitive advantage: A review and empirical study. *Strategic Management Journal, 16*, 15-37.

Powell, T. C., & Dent-Micallef, A. (1997). Information technology as competitive advantage: The role of human, business, and technology resources. *Strategic Management Journal, 18*(5), 375-405.

Purcell, J. (1999). Best practice or best fit: Chimera or cul-de-sac. *Human Resource Management Journal, 9*(3), 26-41.

Rau, S. E. (2003). Making IT pay off—The quest for value. *ABA Banking Journal, 95*(6), 82.

Reed, M. (1985). *Redirections in organizational analysis.* London: Tavistock.

Reginato, J., & Ibbs, W. (2002). Project management as a core competency. PMI Research Conference. Seattle, Washington.

Reich, B. H. (2007). Managing knowledge and learning in IT projects: A conceptual framework and guidelines for practice. *Project Management Journal, 38*(2), 5.

Reichheld, F. R., & Sasser, W. E. (1990). Zero defections: Quality comes to services. *Harvard Business Review* (Sept/Oct), 105-111.

Roos, J., Roos, G., Dragonetti, N. C., & Edvinsson, L. (1998). Intellectual capital: Navigating in the new business landscape. New York: University Press.

Russ, R. (2001). Economic value added: Theory, evidence, a missing link. *Review of Business, 22*(1), 66-71.

Russ-Eft, D., & Preskill, H. (2005). In search of the Holy Grail: Return on investment evaluation in human resource development. *Advances in Developing Human Resources, 7*(1), 71-85.

Sapolsky, H. M. (1972). *The Polaris system development, bureaucratic and programmatic success in government.* Cambridge, MA: Harvard University Press.

Sawaya, N., & Trapanese, P. (2004). Measuring project management maturity. *SDM, 34*(1), 44.

Shenhar et al. (various teams; 1996, 1998, 2002)

Shenhar, A. J., & Dvir, D. (1996). Toward a typographical theory of project management. *Research Policy, 25*, 607-632.

Sherer, S. A., Kohli, R. & Baron, A. (2003). Complementary investment in change management and IT payoff. *Information System Frontiers, 5*(3), 321-333.

Siggelkow, N. (2007). Persuasion with cases. *Academy of Management Journal, 50*(1), 20-24.

Silvi, R., & Cuganesan, S. (2006). Investigating the management of knowledge for competitive advantage. *Journal of Intellectual Capital, 7*(3), 309-323.

Skulmoski, G. (2001). Project maturity and competence interface. *Cost Engineering, 43*(6), 11.

Smith, A. E. (2007). Leximancer (Version 2.25) [Computer Software]. St. Lucia, Brisbane, Australia: Leximancer Pty Ltd. (http://www.leximancer.com).

Smith, N. (1981). *Metaphors for evaluation.* Newbury Park, CA: Sage.

Smith, S., & Barker, J. (1999). Benefit-cost ratio: Selection tool or trap? *PM Network,* 23-26.

Soderlund, J. (2004). *On the evolution of project competence: Empirical regularities in four Swedish Firms.* IRNOP VI. Torku, Finland.

Solovy, A., & Chaiken, B. (2003). ROI under scrutiny: The radical redefinition of a core concept. *Frontiers of Health Services Management, 19*(3), 17.

Sonka, K. J., & Koeszegi, S. T. (2007). From words to numbers: How to transform qualitative data into meaningful quantitative results. *SBR, 59,* 29-57.

SPSS. (2001). *The SPSS two step cluster component: A scalable component enabling more efficient customer segmentation.* Technical Report retrieved from the internet July 31, 2008 http://www.spss.ch/upload/1122644952_The%20SPSS%20TwoStep%20Cluster%20Component.pdf

Sribannaboon, S., & Milosevic, D. (2006). A two-way influence between business strategy and project management. *International Journal of Project Management, 24*(6), 493-505.

Srivannaboon, S. (2006). Linking project management with business strategy. *Project Management Journal, 37*(5), 88-96.

Starbuck, W. H. (1982). Congealing oil: Inventing ideologies to justify acting ideologies out. *Journal of Management Studies,* 19(1), 3.

Strauss, A., & Corbin, J. (1998). *Basics of Qualitative Research. Techniques and Procedures for Developing Grounded Theory.* 2nd Edition. Thousand Oaks, CA: Sage Publishers.

Strauss, A. L. (1987). *Qualitative analysis for social scientists*. New York: Cambridge University Press.

Thomas, J., & Mullaly, M. (2005). What's the benefit? Challenges in demonstrating the value of project management. PMI North American Global Congress. Toronto, Ontario.

Thomas, J., Delisle, C., Jugdev, K., & Buckle, P. (2002). Selling project management to senior executives. Newtown Square, PA: Project Management Institute.

Thomas, J. L., & Mullaly M. E. (2007). Understanding the value of project management: First steps on an international investigation in search of value. *Project Management Journal, 38*(3), 74-90.

Thomas, J. L., & Buckle-Henning, P. (2007). Dancing in the white spaces: Exploring gendered assumptions in successful project managers' discourse about their work. *International Journal of Project Management, 25*(6), 552.

Thomas, J. L. (2000). Making sense of project management: Contingency and sensemaking in transitory organizations. Ph.D., University of Alberta, Canada.

Treacy, M., & Wiersema, F. (1995). *The discipline of market leaders*. Reading, MA: Perseus Books.

Trompenaars, A., & Hampden-Turner, C. (1997). Riding the waves of culture. New York: McGraw Hill Professional.

Tsai, W. (2002). Social structure of competition within a multiunit organization: Coordination, competition, and intraorganizational knowledge sharing. *Organization Science, 13*(2), 179.

Truss, C., & Gratton, L. (1994). Strategic human resource management: A conceptual approach. *International Journal of Human Resource Management, 5*(3), 663-686.

Tuttle, T., & Romankowski, J. (1985). Assessing performance and productivity in white collar organizations. *National Productivity Review*, 211-224.

Tyson, S. (1997). Human resource strategy: A process for managing the contribution of HRM to organizational performance. *International Journal of Human Resource Management, 8*(3), 277-290.

Venkatraman, N. (1989). The concept of 'fit' in strategy research: Toward verbal and statistical correspondence. *Academy of Management Review, 14*(3), 423-444.

Venkatraman, N., & Camillus, J. C. (1984). Exploring the concept of 'fit' in strategic management. *Academy of Management Review, 9*(4), 513-525.

Voelpel, S. C., Leibold, M., Eckhoff, R. A., & Davenport, T. H. (2006). The tyranny of the balanced scorecard in the innovation economy. *Journal of Intellectual Capital, 7*(1), 43-60.

Voetsch, R. J., Cioffi, D. F., & Anbari, F. T. (2004). Project risk management practices and their association with reported project success. Proceedings of the International Research Network on Organizing by Projects (IRNOP VI), Turku, Finland.

Vokurka, R. J., Lummus, R. R., & Krumwiede, D. (2007). Improving manufacturing flexibility: The enduring value of JIT and TQM. *S.A.M. Advanced Management Journal, 72*(1), 14.

Walker, O. C., & Ruekert, R. W. (1987). Marketing`s Role in Implementation of Business Strategies: A Critical Review and Conceptual Framework. *Journal of Marketing, 51*(July), 15-33.

Webber, S., Simsarian, T., & Torti, M. T. (2004). Project managers doubling as client account executives. *Academy of Management Executive, 18*(1).

Weber, R. P. (1990). *Basic content analysis* (2nd edition). Newbury Park, CA: Sage Publishers.

Wernerfelt, B. (1984). A resource-based view of the firm. *Strategic Management Journal, 12,* 75-94.

Westerveld, E. (2003). Project excellence model: Linking success criteria and success factors. *International Journal of Project Management, 21,* 411-418.

Westphal, J. D., Gulati, R., & Shortell, S. M. (1997). Customization or conformity? An institutional and network perspective on the content and consequences of TQM adoption. *Administrative Science Quarterly, 42,* 366-394.

Westphal, J. D., Gulati, R., & Shortell, S. M. (1996). The institutionalization of total quality management: The emergence of normative TQM adoption and the consequences for organizational legitimacy and performance. *Academy of Management Proceedings,* 249-253.

Wheelwright, S. C., & Clark, K. B. (1992). Creating project plans to focus product development. *Harvard Business Review, 70*(2), 67-83.

Winter, M., Smith, C., Morris, P. W. G., & Cicmil, S. (2006). Directions for future research in project management: The main findings of a UK government funded research network. *International Journal of Project Management, 24,* 638-649.

Wisner, J. D., & Fawcet, S. E. (1991). Linking firm strategy to operating decisions through performance measurement. *Production and Inventory Management Journal, 32*(3), 5-11.

Wittkowski, K. M., Lee, E., Nussbaum, R., Chamian, F. N., & Krueger, J. G. (2004). *Statistics in medicine, 23,* 1579-1592.

Woodside, A. G., & Wilson, E. S. (2003). Case study research methods for theory building. *Journal of Business and Industrial Marketing, 18*(6/7), 493-508.

Yin, R. K. (1994). *Case study research.* Thousand Oaks, CA: Sage Publishers.

Zbaracki, M. (1998). Rhetoric and reality of total quality management. *Administrative Sciences Quarterly, 43*(3), 602-636.

Zhang, M. J. (2007). Assessing the performance impacts of information systems from the resource based perspective: An empirical test of the indirect effect of IS. *Journal of Business Strategies, 24*(2), 141.

Znaniecki, F. (1934). *The method of sociology.* New York: Farrar & Rinehart.

Appendix C
Research Team

A research project of this scale and magnitude is not possible without the commitment, dedication, and hard work of a large number of people. Over the past four years, we have been blessed to work with a strong and capable team that has dedicated significant amounts of time and effort to this project.

The participants in each of the key events in this project are listed below. Behind them are a host of others who have provided advice, support, and assistance. We are grateful to each and every one of them for helping to make this project possible. Thank you.

As well, our sincere thanks go to the Project Management Institute for the commitment and courage in funding this project, and to the case study organizations that agreed to participate and make this research project possible.

PROPOSAL TEAM

The following team members contributed to the development of the original proposal:

- Dr. Frank Anbari, The George Washington University

- Dr. Ben Arbaugh, University of Wisconsin, Oshkosh

- Dr. Tim Brady, University of Brighton

- Dr. Walid Belassi, Athabasca University

- Dr. Christophe Bredillet, ESC Lille

- Dr. Peter Checkland, Emeritus, Lancaster University

- Dr. Svetlana Cicmil, University of the West of England

- Dr. Terry Cooke-Davies, Human Systems

- Dr. Lynn Crawford, Bond University

- Dr. Fathi Elloumi, Athabasca University

- Dr. Young Hoon Kwak, The George Washington University

- Dr. Harvey Maylor, Cranfield University

- Dr. Thomas Mengel, University of New Brunswick

- Mr. Mark Mullaly, Interthink Consulting Incorporated

- Dr. Janice Thomas, Athabasca University

- Dr. Terry Williams, University of Southampton

- Dr. Mark Winter, University of Manchester

WORKSHOP ONE

The following team members were participants in the first workshop in Broadway, United Kingdom:

- Dr. Frank Anbari, The George Washington University

- Dr. Erling Andersen, BI Norwegian School of Management

- Dr. Walid Belassi, Athabasca University

- Dr. Tim Brady, University of Brighton

- Dr. Christopher Bredillet, ESC Lille

- Dr. Peter Checkland, Emeritus, Lancaster University

- Dr. Ping Chen, Tsinghua University

- Dr. Svetlana Cicmil, University of the West of England

- Dr. Lynn Crawford, Bond University

- Dr. Terry Cooke-Davies, Human Systems

- Dr. Fathi Elloumi, Athabasca University

- Dr. Patrick Fong, Hong Kong Polytechnic University

- Dr. Zhai Li, Fudan University

- Dr. Harvey Maylor, Cranfield University

- Dr. Thomas Mengel, University of New Brunswick

- Mr. Mark Mullaly, Interthink Consulting Incorporated

- Dr. Shi Qian, Tongji University

- Dr. Maria Romanova, IBM Russia

- Dr. Jonas Soderlund, Linkoping University

- Dr. Janice Thomas, Athabasca University

- Dr. Rodney Turner, ESC Lille

- Dr. Terry Williams, University of Southampton

- Dr. Mark Winter, University of Manchester

- Dr. Zhai Li, Fudan University

- Dr. Khim Teck Yeo, Nanyang Technological University

- Dr. Harry Stefanou, Project Management Institute

- Dr. Edwin Andrews, Project Management Institute

- Ms. Janice Janzen, Interthink Consulting Incorporated

WORKSHOP TWO

The following team members were participants in the second workshop in Montreal, Canada:

- Dr. Frank Anbari, The George Washington University

- Dr. Erling Andersen, BI Norwegian School of Management

- Dr. Tim Brady, University of Brighton

- Dr. Christopher Bredillet, ESC Lille

- Dr. Peter Checkland, Emeritus, Lancaster University

- Dr. Ping Chen, Tsinghua University

- Dr. Svetlana Cicmil, University of the West of England

- Dr. Lynn Crawford, Bond University

- Dr. Terry Cooke-Davies, Human Systems

- Dr. Fathi Elloumi, Athabasca University

- Dr. Pernille Eskerod, University of Southern Denmark

- Dr. Patrick Fong, Hong Kong Polytechnic University

- Dr. Merlyn Foo, Athabasca University

- Dr. Stella George, Athabasca University

- Dr. Zhai Li, Fudan University

- Dr. Harvey Maylor, Cranfield University

- Dr. Thomas Mengel, University of New Brunswick

- Dr. Qiang Maoshan, Tsinghua University

- Mr. Mark Mullaly, Interthink Consulting Incorporated

- Dr. Shi Qian, Tongji University

- Dr. Maria Romanova, IBM Russia

- Dr. Jonas Soderlund, Linkoping University

- Dr. Janice Thomas, Athabasca University

- Dr. Rodney Turner, ESC Lille

- Dr. Vaidotas Viliunas, Vytautus Magnus University

- Dr. Terry Williams, University of Southampton

- Dr. Mark Winter, University of Manchester

- Dr. Xue Yan, Beijing University

- Dr. Khim Teck Yeo, Nanyang Technological University

- Dr. Harry Stefanou, Project Management Institute

- Dr. Edwin Andrews, Project Management Institute

- Ms. Marguerite LeBlanc, Interthink Consulting Incorporated

WORKSHOP THREE

The following team members were participants in the third workshop in Esbjerg, Denmark:

- Dr. Frank Anbari, The George Washington University

- Dr. Walid Belassi, Athabasca University

- Dr. Ping Chen, Tsinghua University

- Dr. Svetlana Cicmil, University of the West of England

- Dr. Terry Cooke-Davies, Human Systems

- Dr. Lynn Crawford, Bond University

- Dr. Zoran Djordjevic, Yu Build

- Dr. Pernille Eskerod, University of Southern Denmark

- Dr. Stella George, Athabasca University

- Mr. Nils Gerdes, Linkoping University

- Dr. Thomas Lechler, Stevens Institute of Technology

- Dr. Zhai Li, Fudan University

- Dr. Thomas Mengel, University of New Brunswick

- Mr. Mark Mullaly, Interthink Consulting Incorporated

- Dr. Shi Qian, Tongji University

- Ms. Eva Riis, University of Southern Denmark

- Dr. Maria Romanova, IBM Russia

- Dr. Jonas Soderlund, Linkoping University

- Dr. Janice Thomas, Athabasca University

- Ms. Anne Live Vaagaasar, BI Norwegian School of Management

- Dr. Vaidotas Viliunas, Vytautus Magnus University

- Ms. Jia Ning Wang, Tsinghua University

- Dr. Terry Williams, University of Southampton

- Dr. Khim Teck Yeo, Nanyang Technological University

- Dr. Sasa Zivanovic, European Centre for Peace and Development

- Dr. Edwin Andrews, Project Management Institute

- Ms. Marguerite LeBlanc, Interthink Consulting Incorporated

WORKSHOP FOUR

The following team members were participants in the fourth workshop in Lake Louise, Canada:

- Mr. Marcos Santos Abreu, PM21 Project Solutions

- Dr. Walid Belassi, Athabasca University

- Dr. Ping Chen, Tsinghua University

- Dr. Svetlana Cicmil, University of the West of England

- Mr. Martin Cohen, Stevens Institute of Technology

- Dr. Terry Cooke-Davies, Human Systems

- Ms. Lisa Danquah, University of Southampton

- Dr. Zoran Djordjevic, Yu Build

- Dr. Pernille Eskerod, University of Southern Denmark

- Dr. Merlyn Foo, Athabasca University

- Dr. Stella George, Athabasca University

- Ms. Jane Helm, Human Systems

- Dr. Mimi Hurt

- Dr. Zhai Li, Fudan University

- Dr. Thomas Mengel, University of New Brunswick

- Mr. Mark Mullaly, Interthink Consulting Incorporated

- Dr. Shi Qian, Tongji University

- Ms. Eva Riis, University of Southern Denmark

- Ms. Kathy Sahadath, Hydro One

- Dr. Janice Thomas, Athabasca University

- Dr. Rodney Turner, ESC Lille

- Ms. Anne Live Vaagaasar, BI Norwegian School of Management

- Dr. Terry Williams, University of Southampton

- Dr. Sasa Zivanovic, European Centre for Peace and Development

- Dr. Edwin Andrews, Project Management Institute

- Ms. Dianne Ingram, Interthink Consulting Incorporated

CASE STUDY TEAM LEADS

The following team members led case study teams of between one and six case studies. Many of them worked with additional team members to complete the case studies:

- Canada

  o Dr. Mimi Hurt

  o Dr. Thomas Mengel, University of New Brunswick

  o Mr. Mark Mullaly, Interthink Consulting Incorporated

  o Dr. Janice Thomas, Athabasca University

- United States

  o Dr. Thomas Lechler, Stevens Institute of Technology

- Brazil

  o Mr. Marcos Santos Abreu, PM21 Project Solutions

- United Kingdom

  o Dr. Tim Brady, University of Brighton

  o Dr. Svetlana Cicmil, University of the West of England

  o Dr. Terry Cooke-Davies, Human Systems

  o Dr. Harvey Maylor, Cranfield University

  o Dr. Janice Thomas, Athabasca University

- Germany

  o Dr. Thomas Mengel, University of New Brunswick

- Serbia

  o Dr. Svetlana Cicmil, University of the West of England

- Denmark

  o Dr. Pernille Eskerod, University of Southern Denmark

- Norway

  o Dr. Erling Andersen, BI Norwegian School of Management

- Lithuania

  o Dr. Vaidotas Viliunas, Vytautus Magnus University

- Sweden

  o Dr. Jonas Soderlund, Linkoping University

- Russia

  o Dr. Maria Romanova, IBM Russia

- United Arab Emirates

    o Dr. Walid Belassi, Athabasca University

- China

    o Dr. Ping Chen, Tsinghua University

    o Dr. Shi Qian, Tongji University

    o Dr. Xue Yan, Beijing University

    o Dr. Zhai Li, Fudan University

- Australia

    o Dr. Lynn Crawford, Bond University

ANALYSIS TEAM

The following team members formed the analysis team that conducted the cross-case analysis of the full data set in preparation for this monograph:

Qualitative Team

- Dr. Svetlana Cicmil, University of the West of England

- Dr. Ping Chen, Tsinghua University

- Dr. Pernille Eskerod, University of Southern Denmark

- Dr. Zhai Li, Fudan University

- Dr. Thomas Mengel, University of New Brunswick

- Mr. Mark Mullaly, Interthink Consulting Incorporated

- Dr. Janice Thomas, Athabasca University

Quantitative Team

- Dr. Terry Williams, University of Southampton

- Ms. Lisa Danquah, University of Southampton

- Dr. Merlyn Foo, Athabasca University

- Dr. Thomas Lechler, Stevens Institute of Technology

- Dr. J.W. (Mac) McDonald, University of Southampton

- Mr. Mark Mullaly, Interthink Consulting Incorporated

- Dr. Janice Thomas, Athabasca University